32.00

MINORITIES
A CHANGING ROLE
IN AMERICAN SOCIETY

MINORITIES
A CHANGING ROLE
IN AMERICAN SOCIETY

Mei Ling Rein

INFORMATION PLUS REFERENCE SERIES
Formerly published by Information Plus, Wylie, Texas

Detroit
New York
San Francisco
London
Boston
Woodbridge, CT

MINORITIES: A CHANGING ROLE IN AMERICAN SOCIETY

Mei Ling Rein, *Author*

The Gale Group Staff:

Editorial: John F. McCoy, *Project Manager and Series Editor*; Michael T. Reade, *Series Associate Editor*; Jason M. Everett, *Series Assistant Editor*; Rita Runchock, *Managing Editor*; Luann Brennan, *Editor*; Thomas Carson, *Editor*; Andrew Claps, *Editor*; Kathleen Droste, *Editor*; Nancy Matuszak, *Editor*; Christy Wood, *Associate Editor*; Ryan McNeill, *Assistant Editor*; Jeffrey Telford, *Assistant Editor*

Image and Multimedia Content: Barbara J. Yarrow, *Manager, Imaging and Multimedia Content*; Robyn Young, *Project Manager, Imaging and Multimedia Content*; Dean Dauphinais, *Senior Editor, Imaging and Multimedia Content*; Kelly A. Quin, *Editor, Imaging and Multimedia Content*; Leitha Etheridge-Sims, Mary K. Grimes, and David G. Oblender, *Image Catalogers*; Pamela A. Reed, *Imaging Coordinator*; Randy Bassett, *Imaging Supervisor*; Robert Duncan, *Senior Imaging Specialist*; Dan Newell, *Imaging Specialist*; Christine O'Bryan, *Graphic Specialist*

Indexing: Jennifer Dye, *Indexing Specialist*; Lynne Maday, *Indexing Specialist*

Permissions: Maria Franklin, *Permissions Manager*; Margaret Chamberlain, *Permissions Specialist*; Julie Juengling, *Permissions Specialist*

Product Design: Michelle DiMercurio, *Senior Art Director*; Mike Logusz, *Graphic Artist*; Kenn Zorn, *Product Design Manager*

Production: Mary Beth Trimper, *Composition Manager*; Gary Leach, *Typesetting Specialist*; NeKita McKee, *Buyer*; Dorothy Maki, *Manufacturing Manager*

ISBN 0-7876-5103-6 (set)
ISBN 0-7876-5143-5 (this volume)
ISSN 1532-1185 (this volume)
Printed in the United States of America
10 9 8 7 6 5 4 3 2 1

TABLE OF CONTENTS

CHAPTER 1

Hispanic, Black, Asian, and Native American populations make up a growing percentage of our nation. These groups are discussed in terms of their origin, fertility, geographic distribution and other aspects concerning population.

CHAPTER 2

Regardless of their composition, families are generally considered one of the cornerstones of society. However, the role and makeup of families, particularly minority families, have been undergone great change in the late twentieth century. This chapter focuses on the status of America's minority families.

CHAPTER 3

Minorities and ethnic groups have always been an important part of the American labor force. This chapter discusses labor participation, unemployment, and work force projections for minority groups.

CHAPTER 4

Minorities are more likely to work in certain professions than in others. This chapter examines the different types of occupations held by minorities. Minority owned businesses are also discussed.

CHAPTER 5

Racial and ethnic backgrounds play a big role in the economic status of Americans. Within this chapter income and poverty is examined by social and economic characteristics. Access to technology, a key economic health indicator, is also explored with regard to race and ethnicity.

CHAPTER 6

In general, persons belonging to minority groups are not as healthy and die at a younger age than those of the White majority. This chapter discusses the health problems that are particularly common among certain minorities, as well as drug abuse among minority populations.

CHAPTER 7

As the minority population grows, enrollment in kindergarten through college grows as well. This chapter explores the educational attainment and performance of minority groups.

CHAPTER 8

Crime is an important issue to all Americans, but especially for minorities. Minorities are more likely than Whites to be the victims of crime. The volume of crime allegedly perpetrated by some minority groups as well as their representation in prisons and jails is disproportionately large, compared to their percentage of the general population. This chapter examines minority crime statistics.

CHAPTER 9

The political participation of minority groups plays a critical role in correcting imbalances in how American society treats them. The number of minority voters, voter turnout, minorities elected to public office, and the issue of redistricting are explored here.

CHAPTER 10

Americans of all racial and ethnic backgrounds are concerned about discrimination, affirmative action, civil rights legislation, and the progress that has been made by minorities. Nevertheless, polls reveal a persistent and notable difference between the opinions of minorities and the White majority.

PREFACE

Minorities: A Changing Role in American Society is the latest volume in the ever-growing *Information Plus Reference Series*. Previously published by the Information Plus company of Wylie, Texas, the *Information Plus Reference Series* (and its companion set, the *Information Plus Compact Series*) became a Gale Group product when Gale and Information Plus merged in early 2000. Those of you familiar with the series as published by Information Plus will notice a few changes from the 1999 edition. Gale has adopted a new layout and style that we hope you will find easy to use. Other improvements include greatly expanded indexes in each book, and more descriptive tables of contents.

While some changes have been made to the design, the purpose of the *Information Plus Reference Series* remains the same. Each volume of the series presents the latest facts on a topic of pressing concern in modern American life. These topics include today's most controversial and most studied social issues: abortion, capital punishment, care for the elderly, crime, health care, the environment, immigration, minorities, social welfare, women, youth, and many more. Although written especially for the high school and undergraduate student, this series is an excellent resource for anyone in need of factual information on current affairs.

By presenting the facts, it is Gale's intention to provide its readers with everything they need to reach an informed opinion on current issues. To that end, there is a particular emphasis in this series on the presentation of scientific studies, surveys, and statistics. This data is generally presented in the form of tables, charts, and other graphics placed within the text of each book. Every graphic is directly referred to and carefully explained in the text. The source of each graphic is presented within the graphic itself. The data used in these graphics is drawn from the most reputable and reliable sources, in particular from the various branches of the U.S. government and from major independent polling organizations. Every effort was made to secure the most recent information available. The reader should bear in mind that many major studies take years to conduct, and that additional years often pass before the data from these studies is made available to the public. Therefore, in many cases the most recent information available in 2000 dated from 1997 or 1998. Older statistics are sometimes presented as well, if they are of particular interest and no more-recent information exists.

Although statistics are a major focus of the *Information Plus Reference Series* they are by no means its only content. Each book also presents the widely held positions and important ideas that shape how the book's subject is discussed in the United States. These positions are explained in detail and, where possible, in the words of those who support them. Some of the other material to be found in these books includes: historical background; descriptions of major events related to the subject; relevant laws and court cases; and examples of how these issues play out in American life. Some books also feature primary documents, or have pro and con debate sections giving the words and opinions of prominent Americans on both sides of a controversial topic. All material is presented in an even-handed and unbiased manner; the reader will never be encouraged to accept one view of an issue over another.

HOW TO USE THIS BOOK

Race and ethnicity are amongst the most divisive factors in all of American history. Many people, from all racial and ethnic backgrounds, have struggled, sometimes at great peril to themselves, to make the United States equal for all people. Nevertheless, it is an undeniable fact that Blacks, Hispanics, Native Americans, Asian Americans, and other minority groups have a very different experience living in the United States than do Whites. The book reports on and examines the differences between major minority groups and White Americans across the economic, political, and social spectrums of the United States.

Minorities: A Changing Role in American Society consists of ten chapters and three appendices. Each chapter is devoted to a particular aspect or state of minorities in the United States. For a summary of the information covered in each chapter, please see the synopses provided in the Table of Contents at the front of the book. Chapters generally begin with an overview of the basic facts and background information on the chapter's topic, then proceed to examine sub-topics of particular interest. For example, Chapter 7: Minorities and Education begins with a look at the overall number of minority students in the United States. The chapter then examines the typical educational attainment of members of America's largest minority groups, and how their level of education affects their earnings. Next, it turns to the issue of how minorities typicaly score on standardized tests. It then discusses the drop out rate for minorities. Minorities in college comes next, and a discussion of school desegregation rounds out the chapter. Readers can find their way through any chapter by looking for the section and sub-section headings, which are clearly set off from the text. Or, they can refer to the book's extensive index, if they already know what they are looking for.

Statistical Information

The tables and figures featured throughout *Minorities: A Changing Role in American Society* will be of particular use to the reader in learning about this issue. These tables and figures represent an extensive collection of the most recent and important statistics on minorities. For example, the number of different minority peoples living in the United States and in specific regions of the United States, their average earnings as compared to Whites, the rates at which they are arrested for and are the victims of various crimes, the health problems that disproportionately afflict certain minority groups, and much more. Gale believes that making this information available to the reader is the most important way in which we fulfill the goal of this book: To help readers understand the issues and contro-

versies surrounding minorities in the United States, and reach their own conclusions about them.

Each table or figure has a unique identifier appearing above it, for ease of identification and reference. Titles for the tables and figures explain their purpose. At the end of each table or figure, the original source of the data is provided. The reader can also find the source information for all of the tables and figures gathered together in the Acknowledgments section.

In order to help readers understand these often complicated statistics, all tables and figures are explained in the text. References in the text direct the reader to the relevant statistics. Furthermore, the contents of all tables and figures are fully indexed. Please see the opening section of the index at the back of this volume for a description of how to find tables and figures within it.

In addition to the main body text and images, *Minorities: A Changing Role in American Society* has three appendices. The first appendix is the Important Names and Addresses directory. Here the reader will find contact information for organizations that study the fate of minorities in the United States, or play a prominent role in shaping opinions and policies on minority issues. The second appendix is the Resources section, which is provided to assist the reader in conducting his or her own research. In this section, the author and editors of *Minorities: A Changing Role in American Society* describe some of the sources that were most useful during the compilation of this book. The final appendix is this book's index. It has been greatly expanded from previous editions, and should make it even easier to find specific topics in this book.

COMMENTS AND SUGGESTIONS

The editor of the *Information Plus Reference Series* welcomes your feedback on *Minorities: A Changing Role in American Society.* Please direct all correspondence to:

Editor
Information Plus Reference Series
27500 Drake Rd.
Farmington Hills, MI, 48331-3535

ACKNOWLEDGMENTS

Photographs and illustrations appearing in **Information Plus-Minorities**, were received from the following sources:

The Gallup Poll Monthly, tables 10.1, 10.2, 10.12, 10.13, 10.14, July 1996. Gallup Organization. Reproduced by permission.

The Gallup Poll Monthly, tables 10.3, 10.4, November 1999. Gallup Organization. Reproduced by permission.

The Gallup Poll Monthly, table 10.5, August, 1996. Gallup Organization. Reproduced by permission.

Table 7.16, 1998, From **Trends in average (mean) SAT mathematics and verbal scores, by race/ethnicity: 1991-1996.** National Science Foundation. Reproduced by permission.

Table 9.7, 1999, National Conference of Black Mayors, Inc. Reproduced by permission.

YOUTHviews, table 10.6, Vol. 4, No. 5, January 1997. The George H. Gallup International Institute. Reproduced by permission.

Tables 10.7, 10.8, 1999, The Gallup Organization. Reproduced by permission.

Figure 10.1, National Opinion Research Center at the University of Chicago. Reproduced by permission.

Figures 10.2, 10.3, 10.4, 1997, New York Times/CBS News Poll. Reproduced by permission.

CHAPTER 1

DEMOGRAPHY

MINORITIES ARE A GROWING PERCENTAGE OF THE NATION

The U.S. Bureau of the Census has estimated that, as of March 1, 2000, there were 274,337,000 people in the United States. (See Table 1.1.) More than 1 out of every 4 Americans (29.4 percent) was a member of a minority racial or ethnic group. Although women are a majority of the nation's population (140.2 million versus 134.1 million men on March 1, 2000), women are often considered a "minority" in social issues. Women are treated in this particular publication, however, only as they apply to racial or ethnic minority. Estimates of future population predict that by 2020, 1 out of 3 Americans will be a minority, and by 2050, the minority population will increase to 50 percent. (See Table 1.2.)

RACIAL/ETHNIC ORIGIN CLASSIFICATIONS

In 1977 the Office of Management and Budget (OMB) issued the *Race and Ethnic Standards for Federal Statistics and Administrative Reporting*, a policy directive that established four racial and two ethnicity categories. The racial categories were White, Black, American Indian/Alaska Native, and Asian/Pacific Islander. The ethnicity categories were Hispanic origin and Not of Hispanic origin. (People of Hispanic origin may be of any race.)

In the past, for decennial (occurring every 10 years) censuses, the Census Bureau divided the American population into the four racial categories identified by the OMB, adding the category Some Other Race. The U.S. government uses these race/ethnic origin data to make decisions, among other things, about funding and laws. For example, federal programs use the race information to promote support programs for the elderly and equal employment opportunity, while states use the data to ensure compliance with redistricting requirements.

As ethnic identity has become more complex due to immigration and interracial marriages and births, a growing number of people have objected to categories based on race. It is no longer unusual to find people who have backgrounds that include two or more races. According to the National Center for Health Statistics, the number of interracial births (where the races of both mother and father are known) increased 200 percent between 1978 and 1992, and babies of mixed race increased from 2 percent of all births in 1978 to 5 percent in 1995.

In 1994 the Census Bureau conducted hearings to consider adding new choices to the categories that had been used in the 1990 census. The bureau found that Arab Americans were unhappy with their official designation of "White, non-European." This group includes persons from the Middle East, Turkey, and North Africa. Many native Hawaiians wanted to be recategorized from Pacific Islander to Native American, reflecting historical accuracy and giving them access to greater minority benefits.

Some Hispanics wanted the Census Bureau to identify them as a race and not of an ethnic origin, and to replace the term "Hispanic" with "Latino." They claimed "Hispanic" recalls the colonization of Latin America by Spain and Portugal and has become as offensive as the term "Negro" for American Blacks. When Hispanics were surveyed, however, the results showed they preferred to be identified by their families' country of origin, such as Puerto Rican, Colombian, or Cuban, or even just American.

About 1 in 3 Black Americans wanted the Census Bureau to adopt the term "African American." Blacks from the Caribbean, however, preferred to be labeled by their families' country of origin, such as Jamaican or Haitian American. Africans who are not American also find the term inaccurate. Although "African American" is sometimes used in spoken English, it is not used as often

TABLE 1.1

Resident Population Estimates of the United States by Sex, Race, and Hispanic Origin, April 1, 1990–July 1, 1999
(Numbers in thousands. Consistent with the 1990 population estimates base.)

	Mar. 1, 2000	July 1, 1999	July 1, 1998	July 1, 1997	July 1, 1996	July 1, 1995
ALL RACES						
Population	274,337	272,691	270,248	267,784	265,229	262,803
(Percent of total)	100.0	100.0	100.0	100.0	100.0	100.0
Median age (years)	35.7	35.5	35.2	34.9	34.7	34.3
Mean age (years)	36.5	36.4	36.2	36.1	35.9	35.8
Male population	134,111	133,277	132,030	130,783	129,504	128,294
Female population	140,226	139,414	138,218	137,001	135,724	134,510
WHITE						
Population	225,704	224,611	222,980	221,333	219,636	218,023
(Percent of total)	82.3	82.4	82.5	82.7	82.8	83.0
Median age (years)	36.8	36.6	36.3	36.0	35.7	35.4
Mean age (years)	37.4	37.3	37.1	37.0	36.9	36.7
Male population	110,906	110,336	109,480	108,624	107,749	106,920
Female population	114,799	114,275	113,500	112,710	111,888	111,104
BLACK						
Population	35,164	34,862	34,427	33,989	33,537	33,116
(Percent of total)	12.8	12.8	12.7	12.7	12.6	12.6
Median age (years)	30.3	30.1	29.9	29.7	29.5	29.2
Mean age (years)	32.2	32.1	31.9	31.7	31.5	31.3
Male population	16,706	16,557	16,342	16,127	15,907	15,706
Female population	18,458	18,305	18,085	17,863	17,630	17,411
AMERICAN INDIAN, ESKIMO, AND ALEUT						
Population	2,422	2,397	2,361	2,326	2,290	2,256
(Percent of total)	0.9	0.9	0.9	0.9	0.9	0.9
Median age (years)	27.7	27.6	27.4	27.2	27.0	26.8
Mean age (years)	30.5	30.4	30.2	30.0	29.8	29.5
Male population	1,199	1,187	1,169	1,152	1,134	1,117
Female population	1,223	1,211	1,192	1,174	1,156	1,138
ASIAN AND PACIFIC ISLANDER						
Population	11,047	10,820	10,479	10,135	9,765	9,408
(Percent of total)	4.0	4.0	3.9	3.8	3.7	3.6
Median age (years)	31.9	31.7	31.4	31.2	30.9	30.7
Mean age (years)	32.8	32.6	32.4	32.2	32.0	31.8
Male population	5,301	5,196	5,039	4,881	4,714	4,551
Female population	5,746	5,624	5,441	5,254	5,051	4,857
HISPANIC ORIGIN (of any race)						
Population	32,077	31,337	30,252	29,182	28,099	27,107
(Percent of total)	11.7	11.5	11.2	10.9	10.6	10.3
Median age (years)	26.6	26.5	26.4	26.3	26.2	26.1
Mean age (years)	29.0	28.8	28.7	28.5	28.4	28.3
Male population	16,121	15,761	15,233	14,716	14,193	13,713
Female population	15,955	15,576	15,018	14,466	13,906	13,394
WHITE, NOT HISPANIC						
Population	196,465	196,049	195,414	194,746	194,037	193,328
(Percent of total)	71.6	71.9	72.3	72.7	73.2	73.6
Median age (years)	38.3	38.1	37.7	37.4	37.0	36.6
Mean age (years)	38.6	38.5	38.3	38.1	38.0	37.8
Male population	96,202	95,962	95,590	95,207	94,810	94,418
Female population	100,263	100,087	99,824	99,539	99,228	98,909

in the written language because it is too long. Lack of agreement and the length of the term had been significant factors in preventing its adoption by the government.

Census 2000

In October 1997 the OMB announced the revised standards for collecting and tabulating federal information on race and ethnicity. The OMB expected all surveys to comply with these standards by January 1, 2003.

Conforming to the OMB revised standards, Census 2000 categorized the races into White, Black/African American, American Indian/Alaska Native, Native Hawaiian/Other Pacific Islander, and Asian. The Census Bureau added a sixth category—Some Other Race. In addition, the bureau included two ethnicity categories—Hispanic/Latino and Not Hispanic/Not Latino. Hispanics and Latinos could report one or more races.

The American Indian/Alaska Native category (which replaced the American Indian, Eskimo, or Aleut categories of the 1990 census) had a write-in space for tribal affiliation. The Asian category further listed six specific Asian groups, while Pacific Islanders (following the Native Hawaiian category) could choose from three specific groups. Persons who chose Other Asian, Other

TABLE 1.1

Resident Population Estimates of the United States by Sex, Race, and Hispanic Origin, April 1, 1990–July 1, 1999 [CONTINUED]

(Numbers in thousands. Consistent with the 1990 population estimates base.)

	July 1, 1994	July 1, 1993	July 1, 1992	July 1, 1991	July 1, 1990	Apr. 1, 1990
ALL RACES						
Population	260,327	257,783	255,030	252,153	249,464	248,791
(Percent of total)	100.0	100.0	100.0	100.0	100.0	100.0
Median age (years)	34.1	33.7	33.4	33.1	32.8	32.8
Mean age (years)	35.7	35.6	35.4	35.3	35.2	35.2
Male population	127,049	125,788	124,424	122,956	121,626	121,284
Female population	133,278	131,995	130,606	129,197	127,838	127,507
WHITE						
Population	216,379	214,691	212,874	210,975	209,196	208,741
(Percent of total)	83.1	83.3	83.5	83.7	83.9	83.9
Median age (years)	35.0	34.7	34.4	34.1	33.8	33.7
Mean age (years)	36.6	36.5	36.4	36.2	36.1	36.1
Male population	106,067	105,208	104,287	103,297	102,399	102,163
Female population	110,312	109,483	108,586	107,678	106,796	106,578
BLACK						
Population	32,672	32,195	31,683	31,137	30,629	30,517
(Percent of total)	12.6	12.5	12.4	12.3	12.3	12.3
Median age (years)	29.0	28.7	28.4	28.2	27.9	27.9
Mean age (years)	31.1	31.0	30.9	30.8	30.7	30.7
Male population	15,491	15,262	15,014	14,738	14,495	14,439
Female population	17,181	16,933	16,669	16,399	16,134	16,078
AMERICAN INDIAN, ESKIMO, AND ALEUT						
Population	2,222	2,187	2,149	2,112	2,075	2,067
(Percent of total)	0.9	0.8	0.8	0.8	0.8	0.8
Median age (years)	26.7	26.5	26.4	26.2	26.0	26.0
Mean age (years)	29.3	29.1	28.9	28.7	28.5	28.5
Male population	1,101	1,084	1,065	1,047	1,029	1,025
Female population	1,121	1,103	1,084	1,065	1,046	1,042
ASIAN AND PACIFIC ISLANDER						
Population	9,054	8,710	8,324	7,929	7,564	7,467
(Percent of total)	3.5	3.4	3.3	3.1	3.0	3.0
Median age (years)	30.4	30.2	29.9	29.7	29.5	29.4
Mean age (years)	31.6	31.4	31.2	31.0	30.8	30.8
Male population	4,390	4,234	4,057	3,874	3,703	3,657
Female population	4,664	4,476	4,267	4,055	3,861	3,810
HISPANIC ORIGIN (of any race)						
Population	26,160	25,222	24,283	23,391	22,571	22,379
(Percent of total)	10.0	9.8	9.5	9.3	9.0	9.0
Median age (years)	26.0	25.8	25.7	25.6	25.4	25.3
Mean age (years)	28.2	28.1	28.0	27.9	27.8	27.8
Male population	13,248	12,793	12,337	11,901	11,497	11,402
Female population	12,912	12,430	11,945	11,490	11,074	10,977
WHITE, NOT HISPANIC						
Population	192,538	191,697	190,726	189,634	188,596	188,315
(Percent of total)	74.0	74.4	74.8	75.2	75.6	75.7
Median age (years)	36.3	35.9	35.5	35.2	34.8	34.8
Mean age (years)	37.6	37.5	37.3	37.2	37.0	37.0
Male population	93,985	93,539	93,028	92,433	91,901	91,751
Female population	98,552	98,158	97,698	97,201	96,694	96,564

SOURCE: *Resident Population Estimates of the United States by Sex, Race, and Hispanic Origin: April 1, 1990 to July 1, 1999, with Short-Term Projection to March 1, 2000.* U.S. Bureau of the Census: Washington, D.C., April 11, 2000

Pacific Islander, or Some Other Race were provided with a write-in area. The Hispanic-origin question had a write-in space for subgroups other than the major groups of Mexican, Cuban, and Puerto Rican.

HISPANICS

"Hispanic" is a broad term used to describe a varied group of individuals who trace their cultural heritage to Spain or to Spanish-speaking countries in Latin America. The term can also refer to persons whose Spanish ances-

tors were residents of the southwestern region of the United States that was formerly under Spanish or Mexican control.

Americans of Hispanic origin are the second-largest minority group in the United States. Their population in the United States is growing rapidly. In 1950 Hispanics were less than 3 percent of the population. By 1980 they represented 6.4 percent of the population (14.6 million). In 1990 there were about 22.5 million Hispanics, representing 9.1 percent of the total U.S. population—one out

TABLE 1.2

Percent Distribution of the Population by Race and Hispanic Origin, 1990–2050
[As of July 1. Resident population]

Year	Total	Race				Hispanic origin[3]	Not of Hispanic origin			
		White	Black	American Indian[1]	Asian[2]		White	Black	American Indian[1]	Asian[2]
ESTIMATE										
1990	100.0	83.9	12.3	0.8	3.0	9.0	75.6	11.8	0.7	2.8
PROJECTIONS										
Middle Series										
1995	100.0	83.0	12.6	0.9	3.6	10.2	73.6	12.0	0.7	3.3
2000	100.0	82.1	12.9	0.9	4.1	11.4	71.8	12.2	0.7	3.9
2005	100.0	81.3	13.2	0.9	4.6	12.6	69.9	12.4	0.8	4.4
2010	100.0	80.5	13.5	0.9	5.1	13.8	68.0	12.6	0.8	4.8
2020	100.0	79.0	14.0	1.0	6.1	16.3	64.3	12.9	0.8	5.7
2030	100.0	77.6	14.4	1.0	7.0	18.9	60.5	13.1	0.8	6.6
2040	100.0	76.1	14.9	1.1	7.9	21.7	56.7	13.3	0.9	7.5
2050	100.0	74.8	15.4	1.1	8.7	24.5	52.8	13.6	0.9	8.2
Lowest Series										
2050	100.0	75.7	15.7	1.2	7.4	22.0	55.8	14.2	1.0	7.0
Highest Series										
2050	100.0	73.5	15.8	1.0	9.7	25.7	50.5	13.8	0.8	9.2

[1]American Indian represents American Indian, Eskimo, and Aleut.

[2]Asian represents Asian and Pacific Islander.

[3]Persons of Hispanic origin may be of any race. The information on the total and Hispanic population shown in this report was collected in the 50 States and the District of Columbia and, therefore, does not include residents of Puerto Rico.

SOURCE: *Population Projections of the United States by Age, Sex, Race, and Hispanic Origin: 1995–2050.* U.S. Bureau of the Census: Washington, D.C., 1996

TABLE 1.3

Population by Race and Hispanic Origin, 1990–2050
[In thousands. As of July 1. Resident population]

Year	Total	Race				Hispanic origin[3]	Not of Hispanic origin			
		White	Black	American Indian[1]	Asian[2]		White	Black	American Indian[1]	Asian[2]
ESTIMATE										
1990	249,402	209,180	30,599	2,073	7,550	22,549	188,601	29,374	1,802	7,076
PROJECTIONS										
Middle Series										
1995	262,820	218,078	33,144	2,241	9,357	26,936	193,566	31,598	1,931	8,788
2000	274,634	225,532	35,454	2,402	11,245	31,366	197,061	33,568	2,054	10,584
2005	285,981	232,463	37,734	2,572	13,212	36,057	199,802	35,485	2,183	12,454
2010	297,716	239,588	40,109	2,754	15,265	41,139	202,390	37,466	2,320	14,402
2020	322,742	254,887	45,075	3,129	19,651	52,652	207,393	41,538	2,601	18,557
2030	346,899	269,046	50,001	3,515	24,337	65,570	209,998	45,448	2,891	22,993
2040	369,980	281,720	55,094	3,932	29,235	80,164	209,621	49,379	3,203	27,614
2050	393,931	294,615	60,592	4,371	34,352	96,508	207,901	53,555	3,534	32,432
Lowest Series										
2050	282,524	213,782	44,477	3,383	20,882	62,230	157,701	40,118	2,793	19,683
Highest Series										
2050	518,903	381,505	81,815	5,384	50,199	133,106	262,140	71,863	4,295	47,498

[1]American Indian represents American Indian, Eskimo, and Aleut.

[2]Asian represents Asian and Pacific Islander.

[3]Persons of Hispanic origin may be of any race. The information on the total and Hispanic population shown in this report was collected in the 50 States and the District of Columbia and, therefore, does not include residents of Puerto Rico.

SOURCE: *Population Projections of the United States by Age, Sex, Race, and Hispanic Origin: 1995–2050.* U.S. Bureau of the Census: Washington, D.C., 1996

TABLE 1.4

Percent of Total Population Growth by Race and Hispanic Origin, 1990–2050
[Middle series. As of July 1. Resident population]

Year	Total	Race				Hispanic origin[3]	Not of Hispanic origin			
		White	Black	American Indian[1]	Asian[2]		White	Black	American Indian[1]	Asian[2]
PROJECTIONS										
1990 to 1995	100.0	66.3	19.0	1.3	13.5	32.7	37.0	16.6	1.0	12.8
1995 to 2000	100.0	63.1	19.6	1.4	16.0	37.5	29.6	16.7	1.0	15.2
2000 to 2005	100.0	61.1	20.1	1.5	17.3	41.3	24.2	16.9	1.1	16.5
2005 to 2010	100.0	60.7	20.2	1.5	17.5	43.3	22.0	16.9	1.2	16.6
2010 to 2020	100.0	61.1	19.8	1.5	17.5	46.0	20.0	16.3	1.1	16.6
2020 to 2030	100.0	58.6	20.4	1.6	19.4	53.5	10.8	16.2	1.2	18.4
2030 to 2040	100.0	54.9	22.1	1.8	21.2	63.2[4]	(X)	17.0[4]	1.4[4]	20.0[4]
2040 to 2050	100.0	53.8	23.0	1.8	21.4	68.2[4]	(X)	17.4[4]	1.4[4]	20.1[4]

[1]American Indian represents American Indian, Eskimo, and Aleut.

[2]Asian represents Asian and Pacific Islander.

[3]Persons of Hispanic origin may be of any race. The information on the total and Hispanic population shown in this report was collected in the 50 States and the District of Columbia and, therefore, does not include residents of Puerto Rico.

[4]Percentages do not add to 100 percent because of the declining size of the White, not Hispanic population.

X Not applicable.

SOURCE: *Population Projections of the United States by Age, Sex, Race, and Hispanic Origin: 1995–2050*. U.S. Bureau of the Census: Washington, D.C., 1996

of every 11 persons was Hispanic. In March 2000 Hispanics accounted for 11.7 percent of the population (32 million). (See Table 1.1.) When the Census Bureau predicts future population growth, it makes low, middle, and high projections. The middle projections indicate that the Hispanic population could increase to 52.7 million by 2020 (16.3 percent of the nation's total population), and 96.5 million by 2050 (24.5 percent of the U.S. population). (See Table 1.3.)

The Census Bureau predicted that by 2005, Hispanics will replace Black Americans as the largest minority group in the United States. Hispanic growth could contribute 43.5 percent of the nation's total growth between 2000 and 2020, and well over half the growth (61.6 percent) between 2020 and 2050. (See Table 1.4.)

Immigration and high birth rates are the major reasons for the large growth of the Hispanic population. As a result of the Immigration Reform and Control Act of 1986 (PL 99-603), by 1992 about 2.6 million Mexicans were granted legal status in the United States. In 1997 the Immigration and Naturalization Service estimated that, as of October 1996, approximately 5 million (with a range of 4.6 to 5.4 million) illegal aliens lived in the United States, with the majority (2.7 million) coming from Mexico. The Census Bureau counts all persons in the United States regardless of legal status, although illegal aliens are certainly a group that is undercounted.

Hispanic Origins

Hispanic Americans trace their origins to a number of countries. Of the 31.5 million Hispanics in the United States in 1999, 65.4 percent (20.6 million) persons were of Mexican heritage. Fourteen percent (4.5 million) were of Central and South American origin, and 10 percent (3 million) were of Puerto Rican heritage. Another 7 percent (2 million) had origins in the Caribbean and other countries, while 4 percent (1.4 million) were of Cuban descent. The differences in origin can often mean significant variations in where Hispanics live, their education, income, and living conditions.

Fertility

The fertility rate refers to the number of live births per 1,000 women ages 15 to 44 in a specified group. The Bureau of the Census, in *Fertility of American Women: June 1995 (Update)* (Washington, DC, 1997), reported an estimated fertility rate of 79.6 births per 1,000 Hispanic women ages 15 to 44, compared to a fertility rate of 59.1 births per 1,000 non-Hispanic women. (See Table 1.5.) In 1995 Hispanic women had lower rates of childlessness (34 percent) than women in the general population (43.6 percent). Hispanic women in the prime childbearing years (15 to 44 years old) had an average of 1.5 children each, compared to an average of 1.2 children among the general population in the same age group.

A Younger Population

In March 2000 the median (half are older, half are younger) age of Hispanics was 26.6 years, considerably lower than the median age of the non-Hispanic White population of 38.3 years, indicating a great concentration of younger people. (See Table 1.1.) A 1998 population survey conducted by the Census Bureau found that over

TABLE 1.5

Women 15 to 44 Years Old Who Have Had a Birth in the Last Year per 1,000 Women, by Selected Characteristics, June 1995

[Numbers in thousands]

Characteristic	Women, 15 to 44 Years Old			Women, 15 to 29 Years Old			Women, 30 to 44 Years Old		
		Women who had a birth in the last year, per 1,000 women			Women who had a birth in the last year, per 1,000 women			Women who had a birth in the last year, per 1,000 women	
	Number of women	Total births	First births	Number of women	Total births	First births	Number of women	Total births	First births
Total	60,225	61.4	23.2	27,742	81.2	38.1	32,483	44.4	10.4
Race									
White	48,603	59.2	22.6	22,001	82.3	36.5	26,602	44.0	11.4
Black	8,617	70.6	26.4	4,276	106.1	49.6	4,342	31.2	3.7
Asian and Pacific Islander	1,579	58.9	22.8	720	68.5	16.9	59.2	27.8	
Hispanic									
Hispanic	6,632	79.6	25.0	3,511	124.8	40.6	3,120	62.4	7.5
Not Hispanic	53,593	59.1	22.9	24,230	81.2	37.8	29,363	41.0	10.7

SOURCE: Amara Bachu. *Fertility of American Women: 1995 (Update)*. U.S. Bureau of the Census: Washington, D.C., 1997

one-third (35.5 percent) of all Hispanics were less than 18 years old, compared to 23.8 percent of the non-Hispanic White population. Slightly over 5 percent of Hispanics were 65 years and over, compared to 14 percent of non-Hispanic Whites. Among Hispanic subgroups, over one-third (38.6 percent) of Mexican-origin persons and over one-fifth (21.2 percent) of people of Cuban heritage were under 18 years old.

Geographic Distribution

The majority of Hispanic Americans live in the southwest United States. As of July 1998, 10.1 million of California's residents were Hispanic. Another 5.9 million Hispanics resided in Texas. Together, these two states were home to more than half of the Hispanics in the United States. The other five states with at least 1 million Hispanics were New York (2.6 million), Florida (2.2 million), Illinois (1.2 million), New Jersey (1 million), and Arizona (1 million).

In 1998 Hispanics made up the highest percentage of state population in the five contiguous (located next to each other) southwestern states of New Mexico (40 percent), California (31 percent), Texas (30 percent), Arizona (22 percent), and Colorado (15 percent). These five states also had the highest percentages of Hispanic residents in 1980. In other parts of the country, the two states with the highest proportion of Hispanics were Nevada (16 percent) and Florida (15 percent).

Mexican Americans

The majority of Hispanic Americans are descendants of the Spanish and Mexicans who lived in the West and Southwest when those regions were first Spanish and later Mexican territory. Their forebears were absorbed into the United States when Texas revolted, broke away from Mexico, became a republic, and then finally joined

the United States during the 1840s. The Mexican-American War (1846–48) added California, the Southwest (New Mexico, Utah, Colorado, and Arizona), and the Rio Grande boundary to the United States with the signing of the Treaty of Guadalupe-Hidalgo in 1848. As a result, Hispanics living in those areas became Americans.

The Mexican-origin population, which more than doubled in the last two decades of the twentieth century, continues to grow. Hispanic Americans of Mexican origin numbered 20.6 million in 1999 and remain largely concentrated in the Southwest. The large percentages of Hispanics in New Mexico, California, Texas, Arizona, and Colorado are nearly all of Mexican origin.

In 1999, of the nearly 81 percent of Hispanics who lived in metropolitan areas, those with Mexican origins accounted for 89.6 percent of these urban residents. Residents with Mexican origins were also more likely than other Hispanics to live in nonmetropolitan areas. In 1999, 10.3 percent of Hispanics with Mexican origins lived in nonmetropolitan areas, compared to Hispanics whose origins were Puerto Rican, 3.9 percent; Cuban, 1.5 percent; and Central and South American, 2.1 percent.

Puerto Rican Americans

The situation of Puerto Rican Americans is unique in American society. Ceded to the United States by the terms of the Treaty of Paris in 1898, which ended the Spanish-American War, the Caribbean island of Puerto Rico, formerly a Spanish colony, became a U.S. commonwealth. In 1917 the Revised Organic Act (the Jones Act) granted the island a bill of rights and its own legislature. It also conferred U.S. citizenship to all Puerto Ricans.

Following World War II an industrialization program was launched in Puerto Rico. While the program benefited many, it sharply reduced the number of agricultural jobs, driving many rural residents to the cities. Combined with a high birth rate, this led to unemployment, overcrowding, and poverty. More recently, industries have moved away in search of cheaper labor, further compounding the economic problems. As a result, between 1940 and 1970, approximately 750,000 Puerto Ricans emigrated to the U.S. mainland. In 1940 fewer than 70,000 Puerto Ricans lived in the continental United States; in 1999, 3 million called the United States home. In recent years, however, some Puerto Ricans have returned to Puerto Rico from the mainland.

Most of the first Puerto Ricans who arrived in the United States settled in New York City in the Manhattan neighborhood of East Harlem, which came to be known as El Barrio (the neighborhood). Eventually, Puerto Rican migrants moved out into other boroughs of the city and into New Jersey. Today, sizable settlements of Puerto Ricans are located in Philadelphia, Boston, Cleveland, Los Angeles, and Miami, with the largest total concentrations remaining in the Northeast. The Puerto Rican population is more likely than the Mexican-origin population to live in the largest metropolitan areas. In 1997, New York, New Jersey, Illinois, Florida, and California each had over 100,000 residents with Puerto Rican origins.

Cuban Americans

Cuban Americans are the third-largest group of Hispanic Americans, and numbered 1.4 million (4 percent of U.S. Hispanics) in 1999. Fleeing from Cuba during the early 1960s after the Batista regime was overthrown by Fidel Castro, many Cubans settled in Miami, Florida, and surrounding Dade County. Most of these political refugees were older, middle class, and educated. Many fled to be able to maintain a capitalist way of life, and many succeeded in achieving economic prosperity in the United States. While language differences caused initial difficulties, most Cubans adapted well and are economically the most successful of the Hispanic ethnic groups. Unlike Americans of Mexican and Puerto Rican backgrounds, who began migrating throughout the country over the past decade, the Cuban population has generally remained concentrated in Florida, although large numbers also live in New Jersey, New York, and California.

In 1980 Castro ousted 125,000 persons from Cuba in what became known as the Mariel Boatlift, named after the town in Cuba from which they sailed. Because most of these new immigrants were from less wealthy and less educated backgrounds than their predecessors, and some were actually criminals or people who were mentally ill, many had difficulty fitting into the existing Cuban communities in the United States. Also, unlike the Cubans who came before them, they had spent 20 years living under a communist form of government very different from the government they encountered in the United States.

In 1993 and 1994 more than 29,000 Cubans tried to enter the United States after fleeing a severe economic crisis in their own country. Most attempted the trip by boats and rafts, but were intercepted by the U.S. Coast Guard and taken back to Cuba, where they were detained at a U.S. air force base on Guantanamo Bay. By January 1996 most detainees had been allowed to enter the United States, and the detention camps were closed.

BLACK OR AFRICAN AMERICANS

Black Americans, some of whom prefer the term "African Americans," trace their ancestry back to the Negroid race in Africa. The first Africans arrived in what was to become the United States in 1619. After that, their numbers increased rapidly to fill the vast need for labor in the new land. The first slaves were brought into this country via the West Indies, but as demand increased, they were soon brought directly to the English colonies in North America. Most were delivered to the South and worked on plantations, where they supplied cheap labor.

The vast majority of Blacks in the United States continued to be kept as slaves until the Civil War (1860–65). In 1862 President Abraham Lincoln issued the Emancipation Proclamation, freeing slaves in the Confederate states, which were then rebelling against the Union. In 1865 the Thirteenth Amendment to the U.S. Constitution abolished slavery throughout the United States. In 1868 the Fourteenth Amendment afforded the freed slaves equal protection under the law, while the Fifteenth Amendment of 1870 granted them the right to vote. The present population of Black Americans includes not only those descended from former slaves, but also those who have since migrated from Africa, the West Indies, and Central and South America.

Between 1981 and 1990 according to the Bureau of the Census, the Black population increased from 27.1 million to 30.6 million, making Black Americans 12.3 percent of the U.S. population in 1990, up from 11.7 percent in 1980. As of March 2000 the Black population of 35.1 million comprised 12.8 percent of the nation's population. (See Table 1.1.) This proportion of Blacks was the largest since 1880, when Blacks, recently freed from slavery, made up 13.1 percent of the population.

Geographic Distribution

Few Blacks voluntarily migrated from the southern farms and plantations in the first decades after the abolition of slavery. As a result, at the beginning of the twentieth century, 90 percent of U.S. Blacks still lived in the South. When World War I, however, interrupted the flow of immigrant labor from Europe, large numbers of Blacks migrated from the rural South to northern industrial cities. Compared to the oppressive system of segregation in the South, economic and social conditions were better

TABLE 1.6

Population by Region, Sex, and Race and Hispanic Origin, March 1999
(Numbers in thousands.)

Total Population					Race and Hispanic Origin[1]					
	Total		Black		Non-Hispanic, White		Other			
	Number	Percent	Number	Percent	Number	Percent	Number	Percent		
Total										
Total	271,743	100.0	35,070	100.0	193,074	100.0	43,599	100.0		
Northeast[2]	51,876	19.1	6,565	18.7	38,957	20.2	6,355	14.6		
Midwest[3]	63,295	23.3	6,467	18.4	52,925	27.4	3,902	9.0		
South[4]	94,887	34.9	19,131	54.6	62,885	32.6	12,871	29.5		
West[5]	61,684	22.7	2,908	8.3	38,306	19.8	20,471	47.0		
Male										
Total	132,764	100.0	16,360	100.0	94,705	100.0	21,699	100.0		
Northeast[2]	24,920	18.8	2,971	18.2	18,877	19.9	3,072	14.2		
Midwest[3]	31,173	23.5	2,998	18.3	26,119	27.6	2,056	9.5		
South[4]	46,105	34.7	8,946	54.7	30,781	32.5	6,378	29.4		
West[5]	30,566	23.0	1,444	8.8	18,929	20.0	10,193	47.0		
Female										
Total	138,979	100.0	18,711	100.0	98,368	100.0	21,900	100.0		
Northeast[2]	26,956	19.4	3,593	19.2	20,080	20.4	3,283	15.0		
Midwest[3]	32,122	23.1	3,469	18.5	26,807	27.3	1,846	8.4		
South[4]	48,783	35.1	10,185	54.4	32,104	32.6	6,493	29.6		
West[5]	31,118	22.4	1,463	7.8	19,377	19.7	10,278	46.9		

[1]Hispanic refers to people whose origin are Mexican, Puerto Rican, Cuban, South or Central American, or other Spanish, regardless of race.

[2]The Northeast region includes Connecticut, Maine, Massachusetts, New Hampshire, New Jersey, New York, Pennsylvania, Rhode Island, and Vermont.

[3]The Midwest region includes Illinois, Indiana, Iowa, Kansas, Michigan, Minnesota, Missouri, Nebraska, North Dakota, Ohio, South Dakota, and Wisconsin.

[4]The South region includes Alabama, Arkansas, Delaware, District of Columbia, Florida, Georgia, Kentucky, Louisiana, Maryland, Mississippi, North Carolina, Oklahoma, South Carolina, Tennessee, Texas, Virginia, and West Virginia.

[5]The West region includes Alaska, Arizona, California, Colorado, Hawaii, Idaho, Montana, Nevada, New Mexico, Oregon, Utah, Washington, and Wyoming.

SOURCE: U.S. Bureau of the Census, Population Division, Racial Statistics Branch: Washington, D.C., 2000

in the North for many African Americans, encouraging a continuous flow of migrants. During each decade between 1910 and 1970 at least 300,000 Blacks left the South; in the three decades between 1940 and 1970, more than 1 million left. The Black migrations following World War I and World War II are among the largest voluntary internal migrations in history.

Most Blacks moved to the Northeast and Midwest, although after 1940, significant numbers moved West. In 1999, 18.7 percent of Blacks lived in the Northeast, 18.4 percent in the Midwest, and 8.3 percent in the West, about the same proportions as in 1992 and in 1970. (See Table 1.6.) The traditional migration from the South to the North dwindled dramatically in the 1970s. In fact between 1975 and 1990, due largely to the favorable economic conditions developing in booming Sunbelt cities, more Blacks moved to the South than to any other region. In 1999, 19.1 million Blacks lived in the South—54.6 percent of the Black population. (See Table 1.6.)

Median Age and Fertility

In 1980 the median age for Blacks was 24.8 years. Two decades later, in 2000, the median age reached 30.3 years. The Black population remained younger, compared to the median age of 36.8 years for Whites in 2000. (See

Table 1.1.) As of March 1999, one-third (32.8 percent) of Blacks were under age 18, compared to about one-quarter (23.7 percent) of non-Hispanic Whites under 18 years.

In 1995 Black women had a fertility rate of 70.6 births per 1,000 women ages 15 to 44, more than that of White women (59.2), but less than the rate for Hispanic women (79.6). (See Table 1.5.) Black women tended to have their children earlier and were far less likely to be childless between ages 25 and 34 (24.9 percent) than White women (36.3 percent). As a result, the trend in birth rates was reversed for older women. The birth rate for White women ages 30 to 44 having their first baby (11.4 per 1,000 women) was three times that for Black women in the same age group (3.7 per 1,000 women). (See Table 1.5.)

ASIAN AMERICANS

The Asian/Pacific Islander (API) American population more than doubled between 1981 and 2000, from 4.2 million to 11 million. (See Table 1.1.) Their proportion of the U.S. population doubled in the 1980s, from 1.5 percent to 3 percent, and grew to 4 percent by 2000. Between 1980 and 1990 the API population grew by at least 40 percent. California's API population rose more than ninefold, from 1.3 million in 1980 to 12.1 million in 1998. In 1998 in Hawaii, APIs accounted for the majority—63.4 percent of the state's population.

Sharp Rise in Immigration

The incredible growth of the Asian American population during the 1980s continued a trend that began in the 1960s, when the population rose by more than 55 percent, and during the 1970s, when the API population increased 141 percent. Although the rapid growth based on immigration slowed in the 1990s (the political situation that originally fueled the flow of immigration was resolved—see below), the growth is expected to continue for a number of reasons.

First, the large number of Asian Americans currently in the United States will make it possible for more relatives to enter under the family reunification provisions of the present immigration laws. Second, changes made in 1990 to the immigration laws increased the total number of immigrants allowed to enter the United States, permitting entry to more Asians. Third, preference for admission is given to immigrants who have work skills needed by American businesses. Typically, many Asian immigrants come with the highly developed skills sought by business and industry.

Between 1980 and 1991 almost half (46.2 percent) of all immigrants admitted to the United States arrived from Asia. Asian and Pacific Islander immigration during the 1980s can be divided into two "streams." The first stream came from Asian countries that already had large populations in the United States (such as China, Korea, and the Philippines). These immigrants, many of whom were highly educated, came primarily for family reunification and through employment provisions of the immigration laws.

The second stream consisted primarily of immigrants and refugees from the war-torn countries of Southeast Asia (Vietnam, Laos, and Cambodia). They were admitted under U.S. policies that supported admitting political refugees after the Vietnam War, as well as those escaping unstable economic and political conditions in neighboring countries. Between 1975 and 1994 more than 1.2 million refugees arrived in the United States from Southeast Asia and China. Vietnam, Cambodia, and Laos accounted for less than 10 percent of the Asian population in the United States in 1980. By the early 1990s they made up 39 percent of Asian immigrants.

China and the Philippines were the leading Asian countries of origin for U.S. immigrants between 1981 and 1996, with 20 percent each. Vietnam had the second-highest percentage (17 percent) of immigrants moving to the United States, followed by India (12 percent), and Korea (11 percent). Other Asian immigrants comprised 19 percent of newcomers from that part of the world.

The Immigration and Naturalization Service reported that in 1998, China (5.6 percent), India (5.6 percent), and the Philippines (5.2 percent) were the top three Asian countries of origin for U.S. immigrants. Nearly 3 percent of Asian immigrants came from Vietnam, and 2.2 percent arrived from Korea.

Geographic Distribution

In 1999, 53.1 percent of the Asian/Pacific Islander population lived in the western region of the United States, compared to only 19.8 percent of non-Hispanic Whites and 26 percent of other racial and ethnic groups. In 1998 most (81 percent) APIs were heavily concentrated in five states—Hawaii (63.4 percent), California (12.1 percent), Washington (5.8 percent), New Jersey (5.6 percent), and New York (5.5 percent).

In 1999 nearly all those of Asian origin lived in metropolitan areas. APIs (96.4 percent) were more likely than non-Hispanic Whites (77.5 percent) to reside in metropolitan areas. Nearly half (44.6 percent) of APIs lived in central cities of metropolitan areas, while only 21.7 percent of non-Hispanic Whites did. On the other hand, only 3.7 percent of the Asian-origin population resided in rural areas, compared to 22.5 percent of the non-Hispanic White population.

Median Age and Fertility

The median age of the Asian-origin population in the United States was 31.9 years in March 2000. It was higher than that of Hispanics (26.6 years), but lower than that of Whites (36.8 years). (See Table 1.1.) Nearly 3 out of 10 (29 percent) Asians/Pacific Islanders were under 18 years of age, and 7 percent were 65 years or over. In comparison, non-Hispanic Whites under age 18 comprised 24 percent of their population, while 14 percent were age 65 and older.

Early Asian American immigrants tended to marry later and have fewer children than the rest of the population. As greater numbers of less-educated, more-rural Asians came to the United States, the Asian fertility rate increased. In 1995 Asian/Pacific Islander women had a fertility rate of 58.9 births per 1,000 women 15 to 44 years old, similar to that of the White rate of 59.2 births per 1,000 women. (See Table 1.5.)

Asian Origins

In 1990 most APIs were of Chinese (22.6 percent) or Filipino (19.3 percent) origins. (See Table 1.7.) The 1990 census also counted 821,692 Other Asians and Pacific Islanders, a 347 percent increase over 1980. The Pacific Islander group includes Hawaiians, Samoans, Tongans, Tahitians, Fijians, and Guamanians. Hawaiians made up 57.8 percent of the Pacific Islander population; Samoans, 17.2 percent; and Guamanians, 13.5 percent. (See Figure 1.1.) Pacific Islanders had a young median age of 25 years.

TABLE 1.7

Our Growing Asian and Pacific Islander Population

	Population			Percent change	
	1970	1980	1990	1970-80	1980-90
Total	1,356,638	3,726,440	7,273,662	174.7	95.2
Chinese	431,583	812,178	1,645,472	88.2	102.6
Filipino	336,731	781,894	1,406,770	132.2	79.9
Japanese	588,324	716,331	847,562	21.8	18.3
Asian Indian	(NA)	387,223	815,447	(NA)	110.6
Korean	69,510	357,393	798,849	414.2	123.5
Vietnamese	(NA)	245,025	614,547	(NA)	150.8
Hawaiian	(NA)	172,346	211,014	(NA)	22.4
Samoan	(NA)	39,520	62,964	(NA)	59.3
Guamanian	(NA)	30,695	49,345	(NA)	60.8
Other Asian and Pacific Islander	(NA)	183,835	821,692	(NA)	347.0

NA Not available from 1970 and 1980 tabulations.

Note: The 1970 total for the Asian and Pacific Islander population is not comparable with the 1980 and 1990 totals. The 1970 data reflect only those Asian and Pacific Islander groups shown separately in the race item. The 1980 sample count and the 1990 100-percent tabulation are comparable because they include a count for Asian and Pacific Islander groups not listed separately in the race item. The 1970 data on the Korean population excluded the State of Alaska.

SOURCE: *The Nation's Asian and Pacific Islander Population–1994.* Statistical Brief, SB/95-24. U.S. Bureau of the Census: Washington, D.C., 1995

FIGURE 1.1

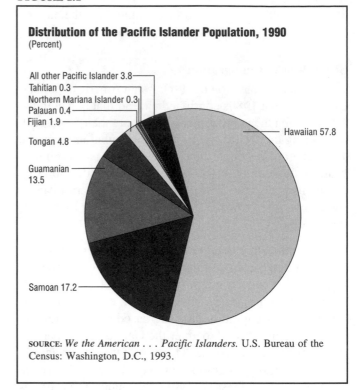

Distribution of the Pacific Islander Population, 1990
(Percent)

All other Pacific Islander 3.8
Tahitian 0.3
Northern Mariana Islander 0.3
Palauan 0.4
Fijian 1.9
Tongan 4.8
Guamanian 13.5
Samoan 17.2
Hawaiian 57.8

SOURCE: *We the American . . . Pacific Islanders.* U.S. Bureau of the Census: Washington, D.C., 1993.

NATIVE AMERICANS

Most experts agree that the people known as American Indians, Eskimos, and Aleuts arrived in North America from northeast Asia at least 30,000 years ago during the last of the Ice Age glaciations (coverings of large areas of Earth with ice). At that time, the two continents were connected by a land bridge over what is currently called the Bering Strait. Recent studies indicate that they may have actually come over many tens of thousands of years earlier.

Migrants, who settled on the northern coast of Alaska and the Yukon River Valley, which were free of ice barriers, became known as Eskimos and Aleuts. Those who ventured farther south followed the eastern slope of the Rocky Mountains and continued along the mountainous spine of North America into Central and South America. There, they moved east throughout the central plains and eastern highlands of both continents and were later erroneously named Indians by exploring Spaniards. The misnomer is attributed to Christopher Columbus, who, upon landing in the Bahamas in 1492, thought he had reached the islands off the eastern region of Asia, called the Indies. He, therefore, greeted the inhabitants as "Indians." Today, most descendants of the original settlers prefer to be called Native Americans.

Native Americans have always been associated with having a close relationship with the earth. Some have been farmers, while others have specialized in hunting and fishing. Regardless of their way of life, the arrival of White men from Europe eventually ended the life Native

Americans had known for thousands of years. Devastating wars, the annihilation of the buffalo, loss of land fit for cultivation, and terrible diseases led to the elimination of most of their race. Most Native Americans now live in poverty on federally administered reservations.

Since the American Indian, Eskimo, and Aleut population is so small, most statistics are available only when the decennial census is taken. In 1990 the Native American, Eskimo, and Aleut population made up less than 1 percent of the U.S. population. The 1990 census counted 1,959,234 Native Americans—1,878,285 were American Indians, 57,152 were Eskimos, and 23,797 were Aleuts. The only tribes with more than 100,000 persons were the Cherokee, Navajo, Chippewa, and Sioux. (See Figure 1.2.)

Although the number of Native Americans grew 16 percent between 1990 and 1999 (compared to 9.7 percent growth for the nation's population), their population remained at .9 percent (2.4 million) as of March 2000. (See Table 1.1.) The middle-series projections by the Census Bureau show the Native American population growing to 1.1 percent of the nation's population by the year 2050. (See Table 1.2.) The largest increases are anticipated to take place in New Mexico, Oklahoma, and California.

Geographic Distribution

The Bureau of Indian Affairs (BIA) estimated that more than 950,000 Native Americans and Alaska Natives (NAs/ANs) live on, or adjacent to, federal Indian reservations. The United States administers 312 Indian reserva-

FIGURE 1.2

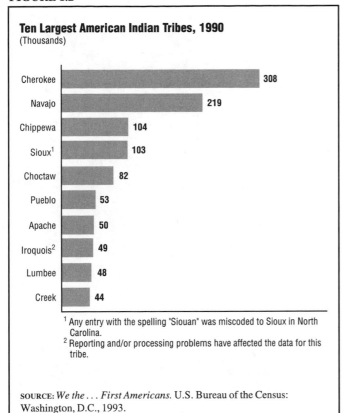

Ten Largest American Indian Tribes, 1990
(Thousands)

Tribe	
Cherokee	308
Navajo	219
Chippewa	104
Sioux[1]	103
Choctaw	82
Pueblo	53
Apache	50
Iroquois[2]	49
Lumbee	48
Creek	44

[1] Any entry with the spelling "Siouan" was miscoded to Sioux in North Carolina.
[2] Reporting and/or processing problems have affected the data for this tribe.

SOURCE: *We the... First Americans.* U.S. Bureau of the Census: Washington, D.C., 1993.

FIGURE 1.3

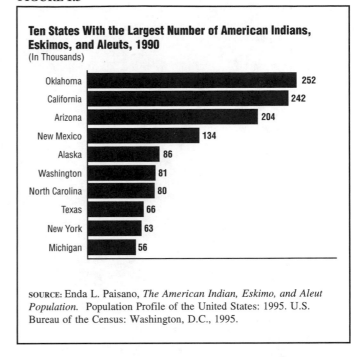

Ten States With the Largest Number of American Indians, Eskimos, and Aleuts, 1990
(In Thousands)

State	
Oklahoma	252
California	242
Arizona	204
New Mexico	134
Alaska	86
Washington	81
North Carolina	80
Texas	66
New York	63
Michigan	56

SOURCE: Enda L. Paisano, *The American Indian, Eskimo, and Aleut Population.* Population Profile of the United States: 1995. U.S. Bureau of the Census: Washington, D.C., 1995.

TABLE 1.8

Ten Largest American Indian Reservations, 1990
[American Indian population in thousands]

Navajo, AZ-NM-UT*	143.4
Pine Ridge, NE-SD*	11.2
Fort Apache, AZ	9.8
Gila River, AZ	9.1
Papago, AZ	8.5
Rosebud, SD*	8.0
San Carlos, AZ	7.1
Zuni Pueblo, AZ-NM	7.1
Hopi, AZ*	7.1
Blackfeet. MT	7.0

*Includes trust lands.

SOURCE: *1990 Census Profile: Race and Hispanic Origin.* U.S. Bureau of the Census: Washington, D.C., 1993.

Because such a large proportion of Native Americans live on, or near, reservations, their population is more concentrated than the total U.S. population. In 1990 the majority of the Native American population lived in six states. More than 3 in 5 (65 percent) resided in the 10 states with the largest NA/AN populations. Oklahoma had the largest population of American Indians in 1990 (252,000), followed by California, Arizona, and New Mexico. (See Figure 1.3.)

In 1998 nearly half of the nation's NAs/ANs lived in western states. The five states with the largest NA/AN populations were California (309,000), Oklahoma (263,000), Arizona (256,000), New Mexico (163,000), and Washington (103,000). Between 1990 and 1998, Arizona added more NAs/ANs to its population than any other state. In 1998 Alaska, at 16 percent, had the largest proportion of NAs/ANs, followed by New Mexico (9 percent), and South Dakota and Oklahoma (8 percent each).

Median Age and Birth Rate

In March 2000 the NA/AN population had a median age of 27.7 years, 8 years younger than the U.S. median age of 35.7. (See Table 1.1.) In 1995 the fertility rate of Native Americans and Alaska Natives was 69.1 live births per 1,000 women ages 15 to 44, somewhat higher than the U.S. fertility rate for all races, 65.6 births per 1,000 women.

tions, the largest of which is the Navajo Reservation of more than 16 million acres in Arizona, New Mexico, and Utah. Table 1.8 lists the locations and population of the 10-largest American Indian reservations. As of December 30, 1998, the BIA recognized 556 tribal entities as eligible for federal funding and services.

CHAPTER 2

MARITAL STATUS, FAMILY, AND LIVING ARRANGEMENTS

Regardless of their composition, families are generally considered one of the cornerstones of society. For many years, particularly when the United States was primarily an agricultural society, extended families—multiple generations living in the same household—were considered normal. As the culture became more urban and mobile, nuclear families—two parents and their children—became, for many, the American ideal.

Shifts in economics, employment, moral values, and social condition, however, have led to an increasing number of single men and women living alone, co-habitations without marriage, and single-parent families. A growing number of children, especially minorities, are being raised by only one parent or by neither parent. Housing has become more difficult to afford, and homelessness among families is growing. The role and the makeup of families, particularly minority families, have been undergoing change.

MARITAL STATUS

In 1998, 118 million Americans were married (whether or not they lived with their spouses), up from 95 million in 1970 and 104.6 in 1980. The proportion of married people 18 years and over, however, decreased in that period from 72 percent in 1970 and 65.5 percent in 1980. In 1998 the Census Bureau (which counted married couples age 15 years and over instead of age 18 and over as it did in previous years) reported their proportion at 56.4 percent. The number of married Blacks decreased from 64 percent in 1970 and 51 percent in 1980 to 38.6 percent in 1998. Likewise, the proportion of married Whites and Hispanics (73 percent and 72 percent, respectively, in 1970, and 67 percent and 66 percent, respectively, in 1980) declined in 1998 to 58.8 percent and 54.6 percent, respectively. (See Table 2.1.)

Never Married

Racial differences among never-married people are significant. Among those over age 15, Blacks are far more likely than Whites or Hispanics to have never married. In 1998, 43.5 percent of Blacks had never been married, compared to 34.7 percent of Hispanics and 25.4 percent of Whites. (See Table 2.1.)

The proportions of men and women in their twenties and thirties who have never married have grown substantially for all races over the past three decades. Between 1970 and 1998 the proportion of never-married Black women ages 20 to 24 nearly doubled from 43.5 percent to 85.1 percent. The proportion that remained never-married at ages 25 to 29 more than tripled from 19 percent to 59.4 percent, while the proportion of those who were never-married at 30 to 34 years more than quadrupled from 11 percent in 1970 to 47.2 percent in 1998. Although the proportion of young White women who never married also rose quite sharply, only 17 percent had never been married by ages 30 to 34 years, compared to 47.2 percent of same-age Black women and 19.5 percent of same-age Hispanic women. (See Table 2.1.)

While many young White women may postpone marriage primarily to pursue educational and career opportunities, Black women, many of whom may be following similar paths, are more likely to be frustrated by the lack of available marriage partners. There are fewer Black men than Black women, a shortage that is compounded by the disproportionate number of Black men who are in prison, unemployed, or underemployed; drug and alcohol abusers; and victims of homicide. The increase in never-married Hispanic women may indicate that some may have reasons similar to Black women for having never married. Also, a growing number of Hispanic women are abandoning or postponing the traditional female role of marriage and family for education and careers. In addi-

TABLE 2.1

Marital Status of Persons 15 Years and Over, by Age, Sex, Race, Hispanic Origin, Metropolitan Residence, and Region, March 1998

[Numbers in thousands.]

Subject	Total, 15 years and over	15 to 17 years	18 and 19 years	20 to 24 years	25 to 29 years	30 to 34 years	35 to 39 years	40 to 44 years	45 to 54 years	55 to 64 years	65 to 74 years	75 to 84 years	85 years and over	Total, 18 years and over	Total, 65 years and over
UNITED STATES															
All Races															
Both sexes	**209,291**	**11,879**	**7,587**	**17,613**	**18,996**	**20,358**	**22,691**	**21,771**	**34,057**	**22,255**	**17,874**	**11,281**	**2,928**	**197,412**	**32,082**
Never married	58,303	11,742	7,270	13,538	8,511	5,158	4,069	2,771	2,744	1,110	753	485	151	46,561	1,389
Married,spouse present	110,619	57	241	3,313	8,818	12,449	14,573	14,608	23,564	15,613	11,328	5,386	668	110,562	17,382
Married,spouse absent	7,346	51	61	390	699	939	1,170	1,041	1,445	793	423	241	91	7,294	755
Separated	4,922	40	32	244	473	627	901	798	996	504	218	72	16	4,882	306
Other	2,424	11	29	146	227	313	268	243	449	289	205	169	75	2,413	449
Widowed	13,599	5	–	17	45	74	182	216	847	1,801	3,862	4,640	1,910	13,594	10,412
Divorced	19,424	24	15	355	923	1,737	2,697	3,135	5,457	2,937	1,508	529	107	19,400	2,144
Percent	100.0	100.0	100.0	100.0	100.0	100.0	100.0	100.0	100.0	100.0	100.0	100.0	100.0	100.0	100.0
Never married	27.9	98.8	95.8	76.9	44.8	25.3	17.9	12.7	8.1	5.0	4.2	4.3	5.2	23.6	4.3
Married,spouse present	52.9	.5	3.2	18.8	46.4	61.2	64.2	67.1	69.2	70.2	63.4	47.7	22.8	56.0	54.2
Married,spouse absent	3.5	.4	.8	2.2	3.7	4.6	5.2	4.8	4.2	3.6	2.4	2.1	3.1	3.7	2.4
Separated	2.4	.3	.4	1.4	2.5	3.1	4.0	3.7	2.9	2.3	1.2	.6	.6	2.5	1.0
Other	1.2	.1	.4	.8	1.2	1.5	1.2	1.1	1.3	1.3	1.1	1.5	2.6	1.2	1.4
Widowed	6.5	–	–	.1	.2	.4	.8	1.0	2.5	8.1	21.6	41.1	65.2	6.9	32.5
Divorced	9.3	.2	.2	2.0	4.9	8.5	11.9	14.4	16.0	13.2	8.4	4.7	3.7	9.8	6.7
Male	**101,123**	**6,114**	**3,807**	**8,826**	**9,450**	**10,076**	**11,299**	**10,756**	**16,598**	**10,673**	**7,992**	**4,527**	**1,006**	**95,009**	**13,524**
Never married	31,591	6,072	3,706	7,360	4,822	2,939	2,444	1,676	1,481	572	328	145	45	25,518	518
Married,spouse present	55,310	6	61	1,179	3,915	5,925	7,056	7,174	12,015	8,158	6,147	3,216	458	55,303	9,821
Married,spouse absent	3,323	24	30	153	304	420	542	459	650	401	184	111	44	3,298	339
Separated	2,018	21	20	79	166	229	382	350	406	225	91	38	10	1,996	139
Other	1,305	3	11	75	138	191	160	109	244	176	93	73	34	1,302	200
Widowed	2,569	3	–	–	10	20	44	50	150	275	707	888	423	2,567	2,017
Divorced	8,331	9	10	133	398	773	1,213	1,397	2,303	1,266	626	166	36	8,322	828
Percent	100.0	100.0	100.0	100.0	100.0	100.0	100.0	100.0	100.0	100.0	100.0	100.0	100.0	100.0	100.0
Never married	31.2	99.3	97.3	83.4	51.0	29.2	21.6	15.6	8.9	5.4	4.1	3.2	4.5	26.9	3.8
Married,spouse present	54.7	.1	1.6	13.4	41.4	58.8	62.4	66.7	72.4	76.4	76.9	71.0	45.6	58.2	72.6
Married,spouse absent	3.3	.4	.8	1.7	3.2	4.2	4.8	4.3	3.9	3.8	2.3	2.5	4.3	3.5	2.5
Separated	2.0	.3	.5	.9	1.8	2.3	3.4	3.3	2.4	2.1	1.1	.8	1.0	2.1	1.0
Other	1.3	.1	.3	.8	1.5	1.9	1.4	1.0	1.5	1.6	1.2	1.6	3.4	1.4	1.5
Widowed	2.5	–	–	–	.1	.2	.4	.5	.9	2.6	8.8	19.6	42.0	2.7	14.9
Divorced	8.2	.1	.3	1.5	4.2	7.7	10.7	13.0	13.9	11.9	7.8	3.7	3.6	8.8	6.1
Female	**108,168**	**5,765**	**3,780**	**8,788**	**9,546**	**10,282**	**11,392**	**11,015**	**17,459**	**11,582**	**9,882**	**6,754**	**1,923**	**102,403**	**18,558**
Never married	26,713	5,670	3,565	6,178	3,689	2,219	1,626	1,095	1,263	538	425	340	106	21,043	871
Married,spouse present	55,310	51	180	2,135	4,903	6,525	7,517	7,434	11,550	7,455	5,181	2,170	210	55,259	7,561
Married,spouse absent	4,023	27	31	237	395	519	628	582	795	392	239	130	48	3,996	417
Separated	2,904	19	12	165	307	397	520	448	590	279	126	34	7	2,885	167
Other	1,119	8	18	71	89	122	108	134	205	114	112	96	41	1,111	249
Widowed	11,029	2	–	17	35	55	138	166	697	1,526	3,155	3,752	1,487	11,027	8,394
Divorced	11,093	15	5	222	525	964	1,484	1,738	3,154	1,671	882	362	71	11,078	1,316
Percent	100.0	100.0	100.0	100.0	100.0	100.0	100.0	100.0	100.0	100.0	100.0	100.0	100.0	100.0	100.0
Never married	24.7	98.4	94.3	70.3	38.6	21.6	14.3	9.9	7.2	4.6	4.3	5.0	5.5	20.5	4.7
Married,spouse present	51.1	.9	4.8	24.3	51.4	63.5	66.0	67.5	66.2	64.4	52.4	32.1	10.9	54.0	40.7

TABLE 2.1

Marital Status of Persons 15 Years and Over, by Age, Sex, Race, Hispanic Origin, Metropolitan Residence, and Region, March 1998 [CONTINUED]

[Numbers in thousands.]

Subject	Total, 15 years and over	15 to 17 years	18 and 19 years	20 to 24 years	25 to 29 years	30 to 34 years	35 to 39 years	40 to 44 years	45 to 54 years	55 to 64 years	65 to 74 years	75 to 84 years	85 years and over	Total, 18 years and over	Total, 65 years and over
UNITED STATES															
All Races—Female															
Married, spouse absent	3.7	.5	.8	2.7	4.1	5.1	5.5	5.3	4.6	3.4	2.4	1.9	2.5	3.9	2.2
Separated	2.7	.3	.3	1.9	3.2	3.9	4.6	4.1	3.4	2.4	1.3	.5	.3	2.8	.9
Other	1.0	.1	.5	.8	.9	1.2	.9	1.2	1.2	1.0	1.1	1.4	2.1	1.1	1.3
Widowed	10.2	–	–	.2	.4	.5	1.2	1.5	4.0	13.2	31.9	55.6	77.4	10.8	45.2
Divorced	10.3	.3	.1	2.5	5.5	9.4	13.0	15.8	18.1	14.4	8.9	5.4	3.7	10.8	7.1
White															
Both sexes	174,708	9,371	6,091	14,168	15,298	16,481	18,697	18,039	28,871	19,140	15,760	10,211	2,582	165,337	28,553
Never married	44,389	9,257	5,814	10,549	6,288	3,616	2,818	1,921	2,095	838	636	419	138	35,132	1,193
Married, spouse present	97,415	47	221	2,937	7,637	10,705	12,706	12,609	20,631	13,972	10,350	4,995	605	97,368	15,950
Married, spouse absent	5,294	44	47	333	529	663	811	749	1,037	513	300	193	77	5,250	570
Separated	3,527	32	25	215	348	463	635	570	698	316	151	60	14	3,494	225
Other	1,768	11	22	119	180	200	175	179	339	196	149	133	62	1,756	345
Widowed	11,457	5	–	12	41	59	132	153	630	1,394	3,212	4,148	1,672	11,452	9,032
Divorced	16,153	19	9	337	803	1,439	2,231	2,606	4,478	2,422	1,262	456	91	16,134	1,809
Percent	100.0	100.0	100.0	100.0	100.0	100.0	100.0	100.0	100.0	100.0	100.0	100.0	100.0	100.0	100.0
Never married	25.4	98.8	95.5	74.5	41.1	21.9	15.1	10.7	7.3	4.4	4.0	4.1	5.3	21.2	4.2
Married, spouse present	55.8	.5	3.6	20.7	49.9	65.0	68.0	69.9	71.5	73.0	65.7	48.9	23.4	58.9	55.9
Married, spouse absent	3.0	.5	.6	2.4	3.5	4.0	4.3	4.2	3.6	2.7	1.9	1.9	3.0	3.2	2.0
Separated	2.0	.3	.4	1.5	2.3	2.8	3.4	3.2	2.4	1.7	1.0	.6	.5	2.1	.8
Other	1.0	.1	.4	.8	1.2	1.2	.9	1.0	1.2	1.0	.9	1.3	2.4	1.1	1.2
Widowed	6.6	.1	–	.1	.3	.4	.7	.8	2.2	7.3	20.4	40.6	64.7	6.9	31.6
Divorced	9.2	.2	.1	2.4	5.2	8.7	11.9	14.4	15.5	12.7	8.0	4.5	3.5	9.8	6.3
Male	85,219	4,835	3,110	7,212	7,743	8,249	9,434	9,030	14,284	9,258	7,109	4,103	851	80,385	12,063
Never married	24,775	4,805	3,027	5,887	3,697	2,214	1,807	1,238	1,199	451	285	129	37	19,970	450
Married, spouse present	48,775	4	60	1,056	3,433	5,086	6,146	6,207	10,520	7,296	5,585	2,970	412	48,771	8,968
Married, spouse absent	2,524	17	19	137	255	293	405	351	515	263	145	90	34	2,508	269
Separated	1,533	14	16	72	137	172	296	260	307	143	76	33	7	1,519	117
Other	991	3	4	66	118	121	109	90	208	120	69	57	26	988	152
Widowed	2,106	3	–	–	10	16	36	41	110	189	587	775	340	2,103	1,701
Divorced	7,038	6	4	131	348	639	1,041	1,194	1,940	1,060	507	138	29	7,032	675
Percent	100.0	100.0	100.0	100.0	100.0	100.0	100.0	100.0	100.0	100.0	100.0	100.0	100.0	100.0	100.0
Never married	29.1	99.4	97.3	81.6	47.7	26.8	19.1	13.7	8.4	4.9	4.0	3.1	4.3	24.8	3.7
Married, spouse present	57.2	.1	1.9	14.6	44.3	61.7	65.1	68.7	73.6	78.8	78.6	72.4	48.4	60.7	74.3
Married, spouse absent	3.0	.3	.6	1.9	3.3	3.6	4.3	3.9	3.6	2.8	2.0	2.2	3.9	3.1	2.2
Separated	1.8	.3	.5	1.0	1.8	2.1	3.1	2.9	2.1	1.5	1.1	.8	.9	1.9	1.0
Other	1.2	.1	.1	.9	1.5	1.5	1.2	1.0	1.5	1.3	1.0	1.4	3.1	1.2	1.3
Widowed	2.5	.1	–	–	.1	.2	.4	.5	.8	2.0	8.3	18.9	39.9	2.6	14.1
Divorced	8.3	.1	.1	1.8	4.5	7.7	11.0	13.2	13.6	11.4	7.1	3.4	3.4	8.7	5.6
Female	89,489	4,537	2,980	6,956	7,554	8,231	9,263	9,009	14,587	9,882	8,651	6,108	1,731	84,953	16,490
Never married	19,614	4,452	2,787	4,662	2,591	1,402	1,011	684	895	387	351	290	101	15,162	742
Married, spouse present	48,640	43	161	1,881	4,204	5,619	6,560	6,402	10,111	6,677	4,765	2,025	193	48,597	6,982

TABLE 2.1

Marital Status of Persons 15 Years and Over, by Age, Sex, Race, Hispanic Origin, Metropolitan Residence, and Region, March 1998 [CONTINUED]

[Numbers in thousands.]

Subject	Total, 15 years and over	15 to 17 years	18 and 19 years	20 to 24 years	25 to 29 years	30 to 34 years	35 to 39 years	40 to 44 years	45 to 54 years	55 to 64 years	65 to 74 years	75 to 84 years	85 years and over	Total, 18 years and over	Total, 65 years and over
UNITED STATES															
White — Female															
Married, spouse absent	2,770	27	28	196	274	369	406	398	522	250	155	102	43	2,743	301
Separated	1,994	19	9	143	211	290	340	309	391	174	75	26	7	1,975	108
Other	776	8	18	53	63	79	66	89	131	76	80	76	36	768	193
Widowed	9,351	2	–	12	30	42	96	112	520	1,206	2,625	3,373	1,332	9,349	7,330
Divorced	9,115	13	5	206	455	800	1,189	1,412	2,539	1,362	755	318	62	9,102	1,135
Percent	100.0	100.0	100.0	100.0	100.0	100.0	100.0	100.0	100.0	100.0	100.0	100.0	100.0	100.0	100.0
Never married	21.9	98.1	93.5	67.0	34.3	17.0	10.9	7.6	6.1	3.9	4.1	4.7	5.9	17.8	4.5
Married, spouse present	54.4	.9	5.4	27.0	55.7	68.3	70.8	71.1	69.3	67.6	55.1	33.1	11.1	57.2	42.3
Married, spouse absent	3.1	.6	.9	2.8	3.6	4.5	4.4	4.4	3.6	2.5	1.8	1.7	2.5	3.2	1.8
Separated	2.2	.4	.3	2.0	2.8	3.5	3.7	3.4	2.7	1.8	.9	.4	.4	2.3	.7
Other	.9	.2	.6	.8	.8	1.0	.7	1.0	.9	.8	.9	1.2	2.1	.9	1.2
Widowed	10.4	–	–	.2	.4	.5	1.0	1.2	3.6	12.2	30.3	55.2	77.0	11.0	44.5
Divorced	10.2	.3	.2	3.0	6.0	9.7	12.8	15.7	17.4	13.8	8.7	5.2	3.6	10.7	6.9
Black															
Both sexes	**24,998**	**1,907**	**1,151**	**2,563**	**2,603**	**2,697**	**2,851**	**2,648**	**3,663**	**2,224**	**1,613**	**789**	**289**	**23,091**	**2,691**
Never married	10,880	1,891	1,122	2,261	1,605	1,224	1,049	756	561	240	99	61	10	8,989	171
Married, spouse present	8,051	7	12	249	773	1,016	1,115	1,166	1,762	986	680	246	40	8,044	966
Married, spouse absent	1,607	8	12	37	133	209	289	228	338	234	83	29	6	1,599	119
Separated	1,214	8	7	19	109	140	234	181	271	171	63	8	2	1,207	74
Other	392	–	5	18	24	69	55	47	67	63	20	21	4	392	45
Widowed	1,752	–	–	2	2	14	40	53	161	334	540	391	216	1,752	1,147
Divorced	2,708	2	6	14	90	233	359	445	841	429	210	62	16	2,706	289
Percent	100.0	100.0	100.0	100.0	100.0	100.0	100.0	100.0	100.0	100.0	100.0	100.0	100.0	100.0	100.0
Never married	43.5	99.1	97.4	88.2	61.7	45.4	36.8	28.6	15.3	10.8	6.1	7.8	3.6	38.9	6.3
Married, spouse present	32.2	.4	1.0	9.7	29.7	37.7	39.1	44.0	48.1	44.4	42.2	31.1	13.9	34.8	35.9
Married, spouse absent	6.4	.4	1.0	1.4	5.1	7.8	10.1	8.6	9.2	10.5	5.2	3.7	2.2	6.9	4.4
Separated	4.9	.4	.6	.7	4.2	5.2	8.2	6.8	7.4	7.7	3.9	1.0	.8	5.2	2.7
Other	1.6	–	.4	.7	.9	2.6	1.9	1.8	1.8	2.8	1.2	2.6	1.4	1.7	1.7
Widowed	7.0	–	–	.1	.1	.5	1.4	2.0	4.4	15.0	33.5	49.5	74.7	7.6	42.6
Divorced	10.8	.1	.5	.5	3.5	8.6	12.6	16.8	23.0	19.3	13.0	7.9	5.6	11.7	10.7
Male	**11,283**	**986**	**536**	**1,183**	**1,177**	**1,212**	**1,306**	**1,211**	**1,636**	**968**	**657**	**295**	**116**	**10,297**	**1,068**
Never married	5,191	976	520	1,087	758	523	519	391	254	104	36	16	7	4,214	58
Married, spouse present	4,086	2	1	82	354	497	573	560	927	520	396	148	27	4,084	570
Married, spouse absent	589	8	9	14	31	77	98	79	118	120	24	9	4	581	37
Separated	407	8	4	7	25	37	68	66	92	79	15	5	2	400	22
Other	182	–	5	7	6	40	30	13	25	41	9	4	2	182	15
Widowed	382	–	–	–	–	3	3	9	34	71	97	95	71	382	264
Divorced	1,035	–	6	–	35	112	114	172	304	154	106	26	7	1,035	139
Percent	100.0	100.0	100.0	100.0	100.0	100.0	100.0	100.0	100.0	100.0	100.0	100.0	100.0	100.0	100.0
Never married	46.0	99.0	97.0	91.9	64.4	43.2	39.7	32.3	15.5	10.8	5.4	5.5	5.7	40.9	5.5
Married, spouse present	36.2	.2	.2	7.0	30.0	41.0	43.9	46.2	56.7	53.7	60.2	50.1	23.2	39.7	53.4

TABLE 2.1

Marital Status of Persons 15 Years and Over, by Age, Sex, Race, Hispanic Origin, Metropolitan Residence, and Region, March 1998 [CONTINUED]

[Numbers in thousands.]

Subject	Total, 15 years and over	15 to 17 years	18 and 19 years	20 to 24 years	25 to 29 years	30 to 34 years	35 to 39 years	40 to 44 years	45 to 54 years	55 to 64 years	65 to 74 years	75 to 84 years	85 years and over	Total, 18 years and over	Total, 65 years and over
UNITED STATES															
Black—Male															
Married, spouse absent	5.2	.8	1.6	1.2	2.7	6.3	7.5	6.5	7.2	12.4	3.6	3.1	3.5	5.6	3.5
Separated	3.6	.8	.7	.6	2.1	3.1	5.2	5.4	5.6	8.1	2.2	1.6	2.0	3.9	2.0
Other	1.6	—	.9	.6	.5	3.3	2.3	1.1	1.6	4.2	1.4	1.5	1.4	1.8	1.4
Widowed	3.4	—	—	—	—	.3	.2	.7	2.1	7.3	14.7	32.3	61.9	3.7	24.7
Divorced	9.2	—	1.2	—	2.9	9.3	8.7	14.2	18.6	15.9	16.1	9.0	5.7	10.1	13.0
Female	13,715	921	615	1,380	1,425	1,485	1,545	1,437	2,028	1,255	956	494	174	12,794	1,623
Never married	5,689	914	602	1,174	847	701	530	365	308	136	63	45	4	4,775	112
Married, spouse present	3,965	5	11	166	419	519	541	606	836	466	284	98	13	3,960	395
Married, spouse absent	1,018	—	—	23	102	133	191	149	220	114	20	20	2	1,018	82
Separated	807	—	3	12	84	103	166	115	179	93	49	4	—	807	52
Other	211	—	3	12	18	29	26	34	41	22	11	16	2	211	29
Widowed	1,370	—	—	2	2	11	37	44	127	263	444	296	145	1,370	884
Divorced	1,673	2	—	14	55	121	245	273	537	275	105	36	10	1,671	150
Percent	100.0	100.0	100.0	100.0	100.0	100.0	100.0	100.0	100.0	100.0	100.0	100.0	100.0	100.0	100.0
Never married	41.5	99.3	97.8	85.1	59.4	47.2	34.3	25.4	15.2	10.8	6.6	9.2	2.1	37.3	6.9
Married, spouse present	28.9	.5	1.7	12.1	29.4	35.0	35.0	42.2	41.2	37.1	29.7	19.8	7.7	31.0	24.3
Married, spouse absent	7.4	—	.5	1.7	7.1	8.9	12.4	10.4	10.9	9.1	6.2	4.0	1.4	8.0	5.0
Separated	5.9	—	.5	.9	5.9	7.0	10.7	8.0	8.8	7.4	5.1	.7	—	6.3	3.2
Other	1.5	—	—	.8	1.3	2.0	1.7	2.4	2.0	1.7	1.1	3.3	1.4	1.6	1.8
Widowed	10.0	—	—	.2	.1	.7	2.4	3.1	6.2	21.0	46.4	59.8	83.2	10.7	54.4
Divorced	12.2	.2	—	1.0	3.9	8.1	15.9	19.0	26.5	21.9	11.0	7.2	5.5	13.1	9.2
Hispanic[1]															
Both sexes	21,430	1,595	1,127	2,663	2,795	2,693	2,505	2,101	2,700	1,633	1,015	480	123	19,835	1,617
Never married	7,442	1,559	1,027	1,845	1,170	637	512	220	270	119	58	15	9	5,883	83
Married, spouse present	10,221	21	82	648	1,377	1,650	1,508	1,386	1,711	1,036	563	214	26	10,200	802
Married, spouse absent	1,485	8	17	136	166	218	208	196	278	159	65	26	8	1,477	99
Separated	883	7	6	75	77	127	141	126	161	99	46	13	4	876	64
Other	603	1	11	61	88	91	67	70	117	60	19	12	4	601	35
Widowed	749	2	—	5	9	12	23	20	83	109	218	190	78	747	486
Divorced	1,533	4	2	29	74	176	254	279	357	211	110	36	1	1,528	148
Percent	100.0	100.0	100.0	100.0	100.0	100.0	100.0	100.0	100.0	100.0	100.0	100.0	100.0	100.0	100.0
Never married	34.7	97.8	91.1	69.3	41.8	23.6	20.4	10.5	10.0	7.3	5.8	3.2	7.4	29.7	5.1
Married, spouse present	47.7	1.3	7.2	24.3	49.3	61.3	60.2	66.0	63.4	63.4	55.4	44.5	21.4	51.4	49.6
Married, spouse absent	6.9	.5	1.5	5.1	5.9	8.1	8.3	9.3	10.3	9.7	6.4	5.3	6.7	7.4	6.1
Separated	4.1	.4	.5	2.8	2.8	4.7	5.6	6.0	6.0	6.0	4.6	2.8	3.1	4.4	3.9
Other	2.8	.1	1.0	2.3	3.2	3.4	2.7	3.3	4.3	3.7	1.9	2.5	3.6	3.0	2.2
Widowed	3.5	.1	—	.2	.3	.4	.9	.9	3.1	6.7	21.5	39.5	63.3	3.8	30.0
Divorced	7.2	.3	.1	1.1	2.6	6.5	10.1	13.3	13.2	12.9	10.9	7.5	1.2	7.7	9.1
Male	10,944	862	573	1,455	1,510	1,408	1,339	1,025	1,322	768	429	199	53	10,082	681
Never married	4,370	857	546	1,112	747	386	358	130	159	44	23	4	3	3,513	31
Married, spouse present	5,051	—	21	266	635	830	744	686	863	550	304	131	20	5,051	456

TABLE 2.1

Marital Status of Persons 15 Years and Over, by Age, Sex, Race, Hispanic Origin, Metropolitan Residence, and Region, March 1998 [CONTINUED]

[Numbers in thousands.]

Subject	Total, 15 years and over	15 to 17 years	18 and 19 years	20 to 24 years	25 to 29 years	30 to 34 years	35 to 39 years	40 to 44 years	45 to 54 years	55 to 64 years	65 to 74 years	75 to 84 years	85 years and over	Total, 18 years and over	Total, 65 years and over
UNITED STATES															
Hispanic¹—Male															
Married, spouse absent	746	2	5	71	98	113	110	82	140	79	27	12	5	743	45
Separated	333	2	2	28	32	42	62	42	55	39	18	9	2	331	29
Other	413	–	3	43	67	71	48	40	85	40	10	3	3	413	16
Widowed	131	–	–	–	–	–	–	2	7	18	37	36	22	131	95
Divorced	647	3	–	6	29	79	120	126	154	77	37	15	1	644	53
Percent	100.0	100.0	100.0	100.0	100.0	100.0	100.0	100.0	100.0	100.0	100.0	100.0	(B)	100.0	100.0
Never married	39.9	99.3	95.4	76.4	49.4	27.4	26.8	12.7	12.0	5.7	5.4	2.1	(B)	34.8	4.5
Married, spouse present	46.1	–	3.7	18.3	42.1	58.9	55.5	66.9	65.2	71.6	71.0	65.9	(B)	50.1	67.0
Married, spouse absent	6.8	.3	.9	4.9	6.5	8.0	8.2	7.9	10.6	10.3	6.4	6.3	(B)	7.4	6.7
Separated	3.0	.3	.3	1.9	2.1	3.0	4.7	4.1	4.1	5.1	4.1	4.6	(B)	3.3	4.3
Other	3.8	–	.6	2.9	4.4	5.0	3.6	3.9	.5	5.2	2.3	1.7	(B)	4.1	2.4
Widowed	1.2	–	–	–	.1	–	.6	.2	.5	2.3	8.5	18.3	(B)	1.3	14.0
Divorced	5.9	.4	–	.4	1.9	5.6	8.9	12.3	11.7	10.1	8.6	7.5	(B)	6.4	7.8
Female	10,485	732	555	1,209	1,285	1,284	1,166	1,075	1,377	865	586	281	70	9,753	937
Never married	3,072	703	480	733	423	250	154	91	111	75	35	11	6	2,370	52
Married, spouse present	5,171	21	60	382	742	820	764	700	849	486	258	82	6	5,149	346
Married, spouse absent	740	6	13	65	68	105	98	114	138	79	38	13	3	734	54
Separated	550	4	4	47	46	85	78	85	106	59	29	4	2	545	34
Other	190	1	8	18	22	20	20	30	32	20	9	9	1	189	19
Widowed	617	2	–	5	7	12	16	17	76	91	182	153	55	616	390
Divorced	885	1	2	23	45	97	134	153	203	133	73	21	–	884	94
Percent	100.0	100.0	100.0	100.0	100.0	100.0	100.0	100.0	100.0	100.0	100.0	100.0	(B)	100.0	100.0
Never married	29.3	95.9	86.6	60.7	32.9	19.5	13.2	8.4	8.1	8.7	6.0	3.9	(B)	24.3	5.5
Married, spouse present	49.3	2.9	10.9	31.6	57.7	63.8	65.5	65.1	61.6	56.2	44.0	29.4	(B)	52.8	37.0
Married, spouse absent	7.1	.8	2.3	5.4	5.3	8.2	8.4	10.6	10.0	9.2	6.5	4.6	(B)	7.5	5.7
Separated	5.2	.6	.8	3.9	3.6	6.6	6.7	7.9	7.7	6.9	4.9	1.5	(B)	5.6	3.7
Other	1.8	.2	1.5	.8	1.7	1.6	1.7	2.8	2.3	2.3	1.6	3.1	(B)	1.9	2.1
Widowed	5.9	.3	–	.4	.6	.9	1.4	1.6	5.5	10.6	31.0	54.6	(B)	6.3	41.7
Divorced	8.4	.1	.3	1.9	3.5	7.5	11.5	14.2	14.7	15.4	12.5	7.5	(B)	9.1	10.1
White, not Hispanic															
Both sexes	154,205	7,837	5,027	11,631	12,607	13,905	16,318	16,028	26,298	17,560	14,789	9,743	2,463	146,368	26,995
Never married	37,348	7,755	4,846	8,810	5,174	3,025	2,341	1,716	1,838	725	582	406	130	29,593	1,119
Married, spouse present	87,524	26	143	2,307	6,300	9,099	11,259	11,269	18,987	12,965	9,806	4,784	578	87,498	15,169
Married, spouse absent	3,886	36	31	199	373	462	611	563	778	357	238	170	68	3,850	477
Separated	2,693	26	19	140	278	350	502	449	548	219	106	46	10	2,667	162
Other	1,193	10	12	59	95	112	109	114	230	138	133	124	58	1,183	315
Widowed	10,733	3	–	7	31	47	110	134	552	1,288	3,004	3,961	1,596	10,730	8,561
Divorced	14,714	18	7	308	729	1,272	1,997	2,346	4,143	2,225	1,158	422	90	14,696	1,669
Percent	100.0	100.0	100.0	100.0	100.0	100.0	100.0	100.0	100.0	100.0	100.0	100.0	100.0	100.0	100.0
Never married	24.2	99.0	96.4	75.7	41.0	21.8	14.3	10.7	7.0	4.1	3.9	4.2	5.3	20.2	4.1
Married, spouse present	56.8	.3	2.9	19.8	50.0	65.4	69.0	70.3	72.2	73.8	66.3	49.1	23.5	59.8	56.2

TABLE 2.1

Marital Status of Persons 15 Years and Over, by Age, Sex, Race, Hispanic Origin, Metropolitan Residence, and Region, March 1998 [CONTINUED]

[Numbers in thousands.]

Subject	Total, 15 years and over	15 to 17 years	18 and 19 years	20 to 24 years	25 to 29 years	30 to 34 years	35 to 39 years	40 to 44 years	45 to 54 years	55 to 64 years	65 to 74 years	75 to 84 years	85 years and over	Total, 18 years and over	Total, 65 years and over
UNITED STATES															
White, not Hispanic[1]															
Both sexes															
Married, spouse absent	2.5	.5	.6	1.7	3.0	3.3	3.7	3.5	3.0	2.0	1.6	1.7	2.8	2.6	1.8
Separated	1.7	.3	.4	1.2	2.2	2.5	3.1	2.8	2.1	1.2	.7	.5	.4	1.8	.6
Other	.8	.1	.2	.5	.8	.8	.7	.7	.9	.8	.9	1.3	2.4	.8	1.2
Widowed	7.0	–	–	.1	.2	.3	.7	.8	2.1	7.3	20.3	40.6	64.8	7.3	31.7
Divorced	9.5	.2	.1	2.6	5.8	9.2	12.2	14.6	15.8	12.7	7.8	4.3	3.6	10.0	6.2
Male	**74,703**	**4,009**	**2,568**	**5,824**	**6,275**	**6,890**	**8,156**	**8,049**	**13,009**	**8,519**	**6,698**	**3,907**	**798**	**70,694**	**11,403**
Never married	20,606	3,982	2,510	4,830	2,973	1,848	1,468	1,116	1,048	411	261	125	33	16,623	420
Married, spouse present	43,877	4	39	801	2,810	4,278	5,429	5,546	9,681	6,766	5,291	2,841	392	43,873	8,523
Married, spouse absent	1,807	14	16	68	164	188	298	272	378	183	120	78	28	1,792	226
Separated	1,222	11	14	44	113	137	236	220	255	103	58	24	5	1,210	88
Other	585	3	2	24	51	50	62	52	123	80	62	53	23	582	138
Widowed	1,977	3	–	–	9	16	28	38	103	171	552	738	317	1,974	1,608
Divorced	6,437	6	4	126	319	560	932	1,076	1,799	988	474	125	28	6,431	627
Percent	100.0	100.0	100.0	100.0	100.0	100.0	100.0	100.0	100.0	100.0	100.0	100.0	100.0	100.0	100.0
Never married	27.6	99.3	97.7	82.9	47.4	26.8	18.0	13.9	8.1	4.8	3.9	3.2	4.2	23.5	3.7
Married, spouse present	58.7	.1	1.5	13.7	44.8	62.1	66.6	68.9	74.4	79.4	79.0	72.7	49.1	62.1	74.7
Married, spouse absent	2.4	.4	.6	1.2	2.6	2.7	3.7	3.4	2.9	2.2	1.8	2.0	3.5	2.5	2.0
Separated	1.6	.3	.6	.7	1.8	2.0	2.9	2.7	2.0	1.2	.9	.6	.6	1.7	.8
Other	.8	.1	.1	.4	.8	.7	.8	.6	.9	.9	.9	1.4	2.9	.8	1.2
Widowed	2.6	.1	–	–	.1	.2	.3	.5	.8	2.0	8.2	18.9	39.7	2.8	14.1
Divorced	8.6	.1	.1	2.2	5.1	8.1	11.4	13.4	13.8	11.6	7.1	3.2	3.5	9.1	5.5
Female	**79,502**	**3,828**	**2,459**	**5,807**	**6,332**	**7,015**	**8,162**	**7,979**	**13,289**	**9,040**	**8,091**	**5,836**	**1,664**	**75,674**	**15,592**
Never married	16,743	3,773	2,336	3,980	2,201	1,178	873	599	790	314	321	281	97	12,970	699
Married spouse present	43,647	21	104	1,506	3,490	4,821	5,830	5,722	9,306	6,199	4,515	1,944	187	43,625	6,646
Married spouse absent	2,079	21	15	131	209	274	313	291	400	174	119	93	40	2,058	251
Separated	1,471	14	5	96	165	213	266	229	293	116	48	22	5	1,457	75
Other	608	7	10	35	43	61	47	62	107	58	71	71	35	601	177
Widowed	8,756	–	–	7	23	30	81	96	449	1,116	2,452	3,222	1,279	8,756	6,953
Divorced	8,277	12	3	182	410	712	1,064	1,270	2,344	1,237	683	297	62	8,265	1,042
Percent	100.0	100.0	100.0	100.0	100.0	100.0	100.0	100.0	100.0	100.0	100.0	100.0	100.0	100.0	100.0
Never married	21.1	98.6	95.0	68.5	34.8	16.8	10.7	7.5	5.9	3.5	4.0	4.8	5.8	17.1	4.5
Married, spouse present	54.9	.6	4.2	25.9	55.1	68.7	71.4	71.7	70.0	68.6	55.8	33.3	11.2	57.6	42.6
Married, spouse absent	2.6	.6	.6	2.3	3.3	3.9	3.8	3.6	3.0	1.9	1.5	1.6	2.4	2.7	1.6
Separated	1.9	.4	.2	1.7	2.6	3.0	3.3	2.9	2.2	1.3	.6	.4	.3	1.9	.5
Other	.8	.2	.4	.6	.7	.9	.6	.8	.8	.6	.9	1.2	2.1	.8	1.1
Widowed	11.0	–	–	.1	.4	.4	1.0	1.2	3.4	12.4	30.3	55.2	76.8	11.6	44.6
Divorced	10.4	.3	.1	3.1	6.5	10.2	13.0	15.9	17.6	13.7	8.4	5.1	3.7	10.9	6.7

1 May be of any race.

SOURCE: *Marital Status and Living Arrangements: March 1998 (Update)*. U.S. Bureau of the Census, Population Division, Fertility and Family Statistics Branch: Washington D.C.,1999

TABLE 2.2

Interracial Married Couples, 1960–1998

(Numbers in thousands. Includes all interracial married couples with at least one spouse of White or Black race)

| | Interracial married couples | | | Black/White | | | |
Year	Total married couples	Total	Total	Black husband White wife	White husband Black wife	White Other race*	Black Other race*
Current Population Survey (CPS)							
1998	55,305	1,348	330	210	120	975	43
1997	54,666	1,264	311	201	110	896	57
1996	54,664	1,260	337	220	117	884	39
1995	54,937	1,392	328	206	122	988	76
1994	54,251	1,283	296	196	100	909	78
1993	54,199	1,195	242	182	60	920	33
1992	53,512	1,161	246	163	83	883	32
1991	53,227	994	231	156	75	720	43
1990	53,256	964	211	150	61	720	33
1989	52,924	953	219	155	64	703	31
1988	52,613	956	218	149	69	703	35
1987	52,286	799	177	121	56	581	41
1986	51,704	827	181	136	45	613	33
1985	51,114	792	164	117	47	599	29
1984	50,864	762	175	111	64	564	23
1983	50,665	719	164	118	46	522	33
1982	50,294	697	155	108	47	515	27
1981	49,896	639	132	104	28	484	23
1980	49,714	651	167	122	45	450	34
Decennial Census							
1990	51,718	1,461	213	159	54	1,173	75
1980	49,514	953	121	94	27	785	47
1970	44,598	310	65	41	24	233	12
1960	40,491	149	51	25	26	90	7

NA Not available.

*"Other race," is any race other than White or Black, such as American Indian, Japanese, Chinese, etc.

SOURCE: *Marital Status and Living Arrangements: March 1998 (Update)* and earlier reports. Current Population Reports, Series P20-514. U.S. Bureau of the Census: Washington, D.C.

tion, much of society no longer condemns unmarried relationships and single parenthood.

In 1970, 9.2 percent of both Black men and White men and 11 percent of Hispanic men ages 30 to 34 years were never married. By 1998, however, the Black rate had increased nearly fivefold to 43.2 percent, compared to a nearly threefold increase to 26.8 percent for White men and 27.4 percent for Hispanic men. (See Table 2.1.) Unemployment, drug and alcohol abuse, and a growing rate of imprisonment have made it particularly difficult for Black men to marry.

Interracial Marriage

The vast majority (at least 94 percent) of marriages in this country are between partners of the same race—Whites marry Whites and Blacks marry Blacks, etc. In 1998 there were 330,000 Black/White married couples, accounting for 24.5 percent of interracial couples, but comprising only .6 percent of all marriages. Nonetheless, this was twice the 167,000 Black/White marriages counted in the 1980 census. In 1998 Black men were nearly twice as likely to have married a White spouse (220,000 marriages) than Black women were to have married a White spouse (120,000 marriages), creating a further decline in the number of Black men available for Black women to marry. (See Table 2.2.)

Altogether, in 1998 there were 1.3 million interracial couples in which there was either a White or Black spouse (who may be married to a spouse of any race or Hispanic origin). In addition, there were 975,000 couples in which the spouses were White and "other race" (a race other than White or Black, including Native American and Asian). Another 43,000 couples were composed of spouses who were Black and "other race." (See Table 2.2.)

MIXED-RACE CHILDREN. Not surprisingly, as mixed-race marriage increases, so does the number of births of mixed-racial parentage. Figure 2.1 shows the number of mixed-race babies born in 1978 and in 1992 (the data are from the National Center for Health Statistics [NCHS]). Between 1978 and 1992, the number of biracial births increased 200 percent, to 133,200, while the number of all births increased 22 percent. In 1992 babies of mixed race made up almost 4 percent of all births, up from 2 percent in 1978. (See Table 2.3.) In 1995, 152,130 biracial children were born—5 percent of all births.

Although the overall numbers are still small, the proportional increase in Black/White births has been large. Between 1978 and 1992 the number of identified births, in which one parent was Black and the other White, increased 161 percent to 55,890. During that time, births in which both parents were Black rose about 27 percent. In 1995, according to the NCHS, there were 66,799 children born to Black and White couples. (See Table 2.3.) The data are approximate because on an increasing number of birth certificates, when the race of the mother is listed as Black, the race of the father is not indicated.

The second-largest group of mixed-race births was to Asian and White parents, doubling from almost 22,000 in 1978 to 42,033 in 1992. (See Figure 2.1.) In 1995 there were 47,068 births to Asian/White parents. (See Table 2.3.) A striking increase was among babies born to Japanese-origin

FIGURE 2.1

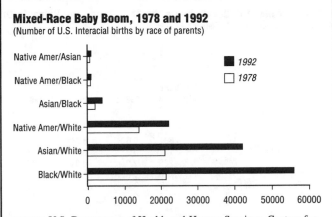

Mixed-Race Baby Boom, 1978 and 1992
(Number of U.S. Interacial births by race of parents)

SOURCE: U.S. Department of Health and Human Services, Centers for Disease Control and Prevention, National Center for Health Statistics

TABLE 2.3

Table of Mother's Race by Father's Race

MRACE FRACE
Frequency
Percent
Row Pct
Col Pct

	White 01	Black 02	American Indian 03	Chinese 04	Japanese 05	Hawaiian 06	Filipino 07	Other Asian Or PI 98	missing/ unknown 99	Total
01 White	2,697,430	51,836	12,611	1,693	1,961	1,292	4,109	8,696	319,257	3,098,885
	69.17	1.33	0.32	0.04	0.05	0.03	0.11	0.22	8.19	79.47
	87.05	1.67	0.41	0.05	0.06	0.04	0.13	0.28	10.30	
	98.00	13.14	47.79	6.78	28.20	26.78	18.46	11.46	53.99	
02 Black	14,963	337,661	474	56	44	51	183	523	249,184	603,139
	0.38	8.66	0.01	0.00	0.00	0.00	0.00	0.01	6.39	15.47
	2.48	55.98	0.08	0.01	0.01	0.01	0.03	0.09	41.31	
	0.54	85.61	1.80	0.22	0.63	1.06	0.82	0.69	42.14	
03 American Indian	11,444	1,234	12,796	20	36	89	98	232	11,329	37,278
	0.29	0.03	0.33	0.00	0.00	0.00	0.00	0.01	0.29	0.96
	30.70	3.31	34.33	0.05	0.10	0.24	0.26	0.62	30.39	
	0.42	0.31	48.49	0.08	0.52	1.84	0.44	0.31	1.92	
04 Chinese	3,145	138	27	21,722	295	87	175	1,000	791	27,380
	0.08	0.00	0.00	0.56	0.01	0.00	0.00	0.03	0.02	0.70
	11.49	0.50	0.10	79.34	1.08	0.32	0.64	3.65	2.89	
	0.11	0.03	0.10	86.97	4.24	1.80	0.79	1.32	0.13	
05 Japanese	3,317	289	44	332	3,763	397	269	210	280	8,901
	0.09	0.01	0.00	0.01	0.10	0.01	0.01	0.01	0.01	0.23
	37.27	3.25	0.49	3.73	42.28	4.46	3.02	2.36	3.15	
	0.12	0.07	0.17	1.33	54.11	8.23	1.21	0.28	0.05	
06 Hawaiian	1,165	214	92	63	318	2,131	544	341	919	5,787
	0.03	0.01	0.00	0.00	0.01	0.05	0.01	0.01	0.02	0.15
	20.13	3.70	1.59	1.09	5.50	36.82	9.40	5.89	15.88	
	0.04	0.05	0.35	0.25	4.57	44.17	2.44	0.45	0.16	
07 Filipino	9,116	1,381	163	259	316	592	16,486	755	1,483	30,551
	0.23	0.04	0.00	0.01	0.01	0.02	0.42	0.02	0.04	0.78
	29.84	4.52	0.53	0.85	1.03	1.94	53.96	2.47	4.85	
	0.33	0.35	0.62	1.04	4.54	12.27	74.07	.00	0.25	
98 Other Asian or Pacific Islander	11,974	1,655	181	831	221	185	394	64,113	8,114	87,668
	0.31	0.04	0.00	0.02	0.01	0.00	0.01	1.64	0.21	2.25
	13.66	1.89	0.21	0.95	0.25	0.21	0.45	73.13	9.26	
	0.44	0.42	0.69	3.33	3.18	3.83	1.77	84.50	1.37	
Total	2,752,554	394,408	26,388	24,976	6,954	4,824	22,258	75,870	591,357	3,899,589
	70.59	10.11	0.68	0.64	0.18	0.12	0.57	1.95	15.16	100.00

MRACE = mother's race   1 = White   6 = Hawaiian
FRACE = father's race   2 = Black   7 = Filipino
            3 = American Indian   98 = Other Asian or Pacific Islander
            4 = Chinese   99 = missing/unknown
            5 = Japanese

SOURCE: U.S. Department of Health and Human Services, Centers for Disease Control and Prevention, National Center for Health Statistics: Rockville, Md., 1998

TABLE 2.4

Births for Women Under 20 Years, by Age, Race, and Hispanic Origin of Mother, United States, 1998
[Rates per 1,000 women in specified group]

Age and race and Hispanic origin of mother	Number of births, 1998	Birth rates									Percent change in rates, 1991–98
		1998	1997	1996	1995	1994	1993	1992	1991	1990	
10–14 years											
Total	**9,462**	**1.0**	**1.1**	**1.2**	**1.3**	**1.4**	**1.4**	**1.4**	**1.4**	**1.4**	**−28.6**
White, total	4,801	0.6	0.7	0.8	0.8	0.8	0.8	0.8	0.8	0.7	−25.0
Non-Hispanic white	2,132	0.3	0.4	0.4	0.4	0.5	0.5	0.5	0.5	0.5	−40.0
Black	4,289	2.9	3.3	3.6	4.2	4.6	4.6	4.7	4.8	4.9	−39.6
American Indian[1]	197	1.6	1.7	1.7	1.8	1.9	1.4	1.6	1.6	1.6	0.0
Asian or Pacific Islander	175	0.4	0.5	0.6	0.7	0.7	0.6	0.7	0.8	0.7	−50.0
Hispanic[2]	2,716	2.1	2.3	2.6	2.7	2.7	2.7	2.6	2.4	2.4	−12.5
15–19 years											
Total	**484,895**	**51.1**	**52.3**	**54.4**	**56.8**	**58.9**	**59.6**	**60.7**	**62.1**	**59.9**	**−17.7**
White, total	340,694	45.4	46.3	48.1	50.1	51.1	51.1	51.8	52.8	50.8	−14.0
Non-Hispanic white	219,169	35.2	36.0	37.6	39.3	40.4	40.7	41.7	43.4	42.5	−18.9
Black	126,937	85.4	88.2	91.4	96.1	104.5	108.6	112.4	115.5	112.8	−26.1
American Indian[1]	8,201	72.1	71.8	73.9	78.0	80.8	83.1	84.4	85.0	81.1	−15.2
Asian or Pacific Islander	9,063	23.1	23.7	24.6	26.1	27.1	27.0	26.6	27.4	26.4	−15.7
Hispanic[2]	121,388	93.6	97.4	101.8	106.7	107.7	106.8	107.1	106.7	100.3	−12.3
15–17 years											
Total	**173,231**	**30.4**	**32.1**	**33.8**	**36.0**	**37.6**	**37.8**	**37.8**	**38.7**	**37.5**	**−21.4**
White, total	116,623	25.9	27.1	28.4	30.0	30.7	30.3	30.1	30.7	29.5	−15.6
Non-Hispanic white	68,619	18.4	19.4	20.6	22.0	22.8	22.7	22.7	23.6	23.2	−22.0
Black	50,103	56.8	60.8	64.7	69.7	76.3	79.8	81.3	84.1	82.3	−32.5
American Indian[1]	3,167	44.4	45.3	46.4	47.8	51.3	53.7	53.8	52.7	48.5	−15.7
Asian or Pacific Islander	3,338	13.8	14.3	14.9	15.4	16.1	16.0	15.2	16.1	16.0	−14.3
Hispanic[2]	48,234	62.3	66.3	69.0	72.9	74.0	71.7	71.4	70.6	65.9	−11.8
18–19 years											
Total	**311,664**	**82.0**	**83.6**	**86.0**	**89.1**	**91.5**	**92.1**	**94.5**	**94.4**	**88.6**	**−13.1**
White, total	224,071	74.6	75.9	78.4	81.2	82.1	82.1	83.8	83.5	78.0	−10.7
Non-Hispanic white	150,550	60.6	61.9	63.7	66.1	67.4	67.7	69.8	70.5	66.6	−14.0
Black	76,834	126.9	130.1	132.5	137.1	148.3	151.9	157.9	158.6	152.9	−20.0
American Indian[1]	5,034	118.4	117.6	122.3	130.7	130.3	130.7	132.6	134.3	129.3	−11.8
Asian or Pacific Islander	5,725	38.3	39.3	40.4	43.4	44.1	43.3	43.1	43.1	40.2	−11.1
Hispanic[2]	73,154	140.1	144.3	151.1	157.9	158.0	159.1	159.7	158.5	147.7	−11.6

[1]Includes births to Aleuts and Eskimos.
[2]Includes all persons of Hispanic origin of any race.

SOURCE: National Vital Statistics Reports, vol. 48, no. 6, April 2000

and White parents. According to the NCHS, there were 40 percent more Japanese-White mixed births reported in 1995 than births where both parents were of Japanese origin.

This trend poses complicated problems for tracking data on racial differences in the United States. How do children of mixed-race parents label their own race on official documents and for the census? (See Chapter 1 for information concerning new categories for the 2000 census.) How well do current racial categories serve the increasingly multicultural society in the United States? What are the implications for continuing group identity for groups where mixed births are outpacing births of same-race parentage?

In 1990 the NCHS changed the basis for tabulating birth data from the race of the child to the race of the mother. In the past, children with one minority parent were assigned to the race of that parent. The NCHS changed the policy for several reasons. First, birth data contain many questions associated with mothers—marital status, education, prenatal care, and method of delivery. Second, the incidence of interracial parentage is continuing to increase. Finally, the proportion of births with the race of the father not stated is growing.

Divorced

The Bureau of the Census reported in *Marital Status and Living Arrangements: March 1998 (Update)* (Washington, DC, December 1998) that, in 1998, 19.4 million (9.3 percent) of all adults who had ever been married, were divorced. This is not the proportion of all adults who had ever been divorced, but the proportion of adults who were divorced at the time of the survey. Because men are considerably more likely than women to remarry following divorce, there are significantly higher proportions of divorced women than men. A somewhat larger proportion of Blacks (10.8 percent) than Whites (9.2 percent) and Hispanics (7.2 percent) were divorced. (See Table 2.1.) Divorce for all groups was up sharply from 1970, when 4.4 percent of Blacks, 3.1 percent of Whites, and 3.9 percent of Hispanics were divorced.

The Census Bureau also reported that 9.2 percent of Black males and 12.2 percent of Black females age 15 years and over were divorced, while 8.3 percent of White males and 10.2 percent of White females were also divorced. Among those of Hispanic origin, 5.9 percent of men and 8.4 percent of women were divorced. (See Table 2.1.)

Widowhood

In 1998, 10 percent of Black women and 3.4 percent of Black men age 15 years and over were widowed, compared to 5.9 percent of Hispanic women and 1.2 percent of Hispanic men. The comparable rates for White women and White men were 10.4 and 2.5 percent, respectively. (See Table 2.1.)

TEENAGE PREGNANCY

Over the generations, a major change in American attitudes has removed much of the social stigma from unwed teenage motherhood. Unmarried women of all ages are having children openly and with a regularity that was unheard of just a couple of generations ago. Many women do not feel the need to marry just because they are pregnant.

Many possible reasons are offered for the high rates of teen motherhood, especially in the Black community. Among them are lack of access to birth control, lack of education, or little hope for the future, including absence of educational goals. Some young women hope that the baby will provide love they feel is lacking in their lives or give them independence from parents. For others, having babies is simply the result of incorrectly believing that even though they did not use birth control, pregnancy could not happen to them.

According to the National Center for Health Statistics (NCHS; *National Vital Statistics Reports,* vol. 48, no. 6, April 24, 2000), in 1998 the birth rate for Black teenagers ages 15 to 17, 56.8 births per 1,000 Black women, was more than twice the White rate, 25.9 per 1,000 White women. Hispanics in the same age group had the highest birth rate at 62.3 per 1,000 women. Asians/Pacific Islanders (APIs) had the lowest rate of 13.8 births per 1,000 API women, while American Indians had a birth rate of 44.4 births per 1,000 American Indian women. At 18 to 19 years of age, Hispanic females (140.1 births per 1,000 women) and Black females (126.9 per 1,000 women) were almost twice as likely to have a baby as White women (74.6 per 1,000). API teens (38.3 per 1,000 women) in the same age group had the lowest birth rates. American Indians (118.4 per 1,000) generally had higher birth rates than White teens, but lower birth rates than their Black counterparts. Note also that birth rates for these specified groups have been dropping since 1990. (See Table 2.4.)

MINORITY FAMILY STRUCTURE

Black Families

The Bureau of the Census defines a family as two or more persons living together who are related by birth, marriage, or adoption. A household, on the other hand, may be family or non-family, and is simply all persons who occupy a housing unit. Among family households, the proportion of married-couple families has declined for both Blacks and Whites. In 1970, 89 percent of White families were married-couple families, compared to 80.8 percent in 1998. In 1970, 68 percent of Black families were married-couple families; 28 years later, the rate had dropped to 46.6 percent. (See Table 2.5.)

The proportion of family households headed by females, no husband present, has grown for both Blacks and Whites, from 28 percent in 1970 to 46.7 percent in 1998 for Blacks, and from 9 percent to 14 percent for Whites. (See Table 2.5.) Single mothers are frequently poorer and less educated than mothers in married-couple families.

Hispanic Families

In 1998 Hispanic families made up 9.8 percent of all family households in the United States. Among Hispanic families, 69 percent were married-couple families, and females with no spouse present headed 23.2 percent of family households. (See Table 2.5.) There were significant differences among Hispanic subgroups. In 1998 Cuban Americans (80.7 percent) and Mexican Americans (72 percent) had the highest proportion of married-couple families, while Puerto Ricans had the highest proportion of families maintained by women with no husband present (37.7 percent). (See Table 5.4 in Chapter 5.)

Asian and Pacific Islander Families

As with all other American families, the proportion of married families among Asian/Pacific Islander (API) families has dropped—from 82 percent in 1990 to 81.7 percent in 1998. (See Table 5.5 in Chapter 5.) In 1998, among the 2.4 million Asian American family households (about 3 percent of all American family households), the proportion of married-couple family households was higher than that for any other minority race or ethnicity.

In addition, females with no spouse present headed only 11.7 percent of API families in 1998, far less than for Blacks (46.7 percent) and Hispanics (23.2 percent). API male

TABLE 2.5

Households, by type, Age of Members, age, Region of Residence, Race, and Hispanic Origin of Housholder, March 1998
[Numbers in thousands except for averages and medians.]

Characteristic	Total	Under 20 years	20 to 24 years	25 to 29 years	30 to 34 years	35 to 39 years	40 to 44 years	45 to 54 years	55 to 64 years	65 to 74 years	75 to 84 years	85 years and over	Median age
UNITED STATES-ALL RACES													
Households by Type													
All households	102,528	705	4,730	8,463	10,570	11,838	12,105	19,547	13,072	11,272	8,090	2,135	46.3
Family households	70,880	405	2,614	5,734	7,905	9,252	9,620	14,694	9,387	6,989	3,707	575	45.0
Married-couple family	54,317	86	1,287	3,967	5,919	6,941	7,239	11,734	7,936	5,841	3,003	365	46.4
Other family, male householder	3,911	167	384	462	404	493	562	700	352	210	139	37	40.4
Other family, female householder	12,652	152	943	1,305	1,582	1,818	1,819	2,260	1,099	938	565	173	41.4
Nonfamily households	31,648	301	2,116	2,729	2,665	2,587	2,485	4,853	3,685	4,283	4,384	1,560	50.8
Male householder	14,133	153	1,183	1,642	1,683	1,615	1,593	2,432	1,348	1,203	924	356	42.5
Female householder	17,516	147	933	1,088	982	971	892	2,421	2,337	3,080	3,460	1,204	60.8
Age of Household Members													
All members	268,984	1,967	11,424	22,997	32,547	38,990	39,111	54,679	29,511	21,634	13,123	3,001	(X)
Under 18 years	71,669	576	2,809	7,611	13,656	17,013	14,572	11,684	2,415	986	312	36	(X)
18 to 64 years	165,233	1,383	8,580	15,323	18,721	21,730	24,194	42,274	25,917	5,055	1,664	392	(X)
65 years and over	32,082	8	35	62	170	248	345	721	1,179	15,593	11,147	2,573	(X)
Households with members:													
Under 18 years	38,160	347	1,840	4,166	6,577	8,160	7,592	7,121	1,559	585	193	19	38.8
18 to 64 years	85,841	685	4,730	8,463	10,570	11,838	12,105	19,547	13,072	3,481	1,090	259	42.7
65 years and over	23,924	6	34	53	139	195	296	611	1,092	11,272	8,090	2,135	73.4
Average per household:	2.62	2.79	2.42	2.72	3.08	3.29	3.23	2.80	2.26	1.92	1.62	1.41	(X)
Under 18 years	.70	.82	.59	.90	1.29	1.44	1.20	.60	.18	.09	.04	.02	(X)
18 to 64 years	1.61	1.96	1.81	1.81	1.77	1.84	2.00	2.16	1.98	.45	.21	.18	(X)
65 years and over	.31	.01	.01	.01	.02	.02	.03	.04	.09	1.38	1.38	1.21	(X)
Size of Household													
Households	102,528	705	4,730	8,463	10,570	11,838	12,105	19,547	13,072	11,272	8,090	2,135	46.3
One person	26,327	139	1,112	1,687	1,992	2,023	2,031	4,120	3,301	4,098	4,301	1,524	55.2
Two persons	32,965	199	1,707	2,726	2,212	1,955	2,329	5,965	6,499	5,667	3,214	494	54.1
Three persons	17,331	167	1,122	1,793	2,205	2,210	2,399	4,122	1,891	944	403	77	42.4
Four persons	15,358	111	523	1,415	2,409	3,278	3,114	3,213	855	331	79	30	39.9
Five persons	7,048	57	190	586	1,143	1,619	1,509	1,438	310	143	44	9	39.8
Six persons	2,232	24	52	157	422	481	482	417	126	47	23	2	39.8
Seven or more persons	1,267	8	25	101	187	274	240	272	91	42	27	–	40.8
Total persons	268,984	1,967	11,424	22,997	32,547	38,990	39,111	54,679	29,511	21,634	13,123	3,001	(X)
Persons per household	2.62	2.79	2.42	2.72	3.08	3.29	3.23	2.80	2.26	1.92	1.62	1.41	(X)
UNITED STATES-WHITE													
Households by Type													
All households	86,106	530	3,712	6,891	8,453	9,699	10,062	16,400	11,163	9,917	7,371	1,908	47.1
Family households	59,511	289	1,981	4,641	6,324	7,557	8,046	12,454	8,145	6,222	3,356	495	45.7
Married-couple family	48,066	83	1,138	3,480	5,077	6,067	6,315	10,324	7,125	5,338	2,793	325	46.7
Other family, male householder	3,137	111	326	382	301	382	468	579	272	174	113	29	40.7
Other family, female householder	8,308	95	517	778	947	1,108	1,263	1,551	748	710	450	141	42.8
Nonfamily households	26,596	241	1,731	2,250	2,129	2,142	2,016	3,945	3,018	3,695	4,015	1,413	51.9
Male householder	11,725	133	979	1,365	1,339	1,340	1,326	1,992	1,081	1,035	831	304	42.7
Female householder	14,871	109	752	886	789	802	690	1,953	1,937	2,660	3,184	1,110	62.6

householders with no spouse present accounted for 6.6 percent of all API families, similar to their Black counterparts (6.7 percent) but lower than Hispanic male householders with no spouse present (7.8 percent). (See Table 5.5 in Chapter 5 for API data.) In comparison, White males with no spouse present headed only 5.3 percent of White families.

LIVING ARRANGEMENTS OF CHILDREN

Changes in the marital circumstances of adults naturally affect the living arrangements of children. High divorce rates, an increased delay in first marriages, and more out-of-wedlock births have resulted in fewer children living with two parents. In 1998, 68 percent of children under age 18 were living with two parents (not necessarily both natural parents), compared to 77 percent in 1980 and 85 percent in 1970. (See Table 2.6.) The largest proportions of single-parent children were those living either with a divorced mother (34.3 percent) or a mother who had never been married (40.3 percent). (See Table 2.7.) Minority children have been particularly affected by these changes.

TABLE 2.5

Households, by type, Age of Members, age, Region of Residence, Race, and Hispanic Origin of Housholder, March 1998 [CONTINUED]

[Numbers in thousands except for averages and medians.]

Characteristic	Total	Under 20 years	20 to 24 years	25 to 29 years	30 to 34 years	35 to 39 years	40 to 44 years	45 to 54 years	55 to 64 years	65 to 74 years	75 to 84 years	85 years and over	Median age
							Age of householder						
Age of Household Members													
All members	222,421	1,405	8,940	18,545	26,020	31,928	32,573	45,662	24,472	18,630	11,640	2,606	(X)
Under 18 years	56,698	398	1,929	5,803	10,675	13,873	12,195	9,405	1,624	618	161	18	(X)
18 to 64 years	137,159	1,000	6,984	12,690	15,232	17,892	20,132	35,674	21,851	4,123	1,282	300	(X)
65 years and over	28,563	7	27	52	113	163	246	584	997	13,889	10,197	2,288	(X)
Households with members:													
Under 18 years	30,636	255	1,321	3,277	5,267	6,662	6,375	5,795	1,153	396	125	10	38.9
18 to 64 years	70,959	512	3,712	6,891	8,453	9,699	10,062	16,400	11,163	2,982	875	210	43.1
65 years and over	21,128	5	25	42	95	126	208	491	939	9,917	7,371	1,908	73.7
Average per household:	2.58	2.65	2.41	2.69	3.08	3.29	3.24	2.78	2.19	1.88	1.58	1.37	(X)
Under 18 years	.66	.75	.52	.84	1.26	1.43	1.21	.57	.15	.06	.02	.01	(X)
18 to 64 years	1.59	1.89	1.88	1.84	1.80	1.84	2.00	2.18	1.96	.42	.17	.16	(X)
65 years and over	.33	.01	.01	.01	.01	.02	.02	.04	.09	1.40	1.38	1.20	(X)
Size of Household													
Households	86,106	530	3,712	6,891	8,453	9,699	10,062	16,400	11,163	9,917	7,371	1,908	47.1
One person	21,998	113	860	1,356	1,525	1,649	1,643	3,280	2,717	3,527	3,945	1,385	57.1
Two persons	28,817	159	1,377	2,291	1,788	1,587	1,924	5,208	5,862	5,212	2,980	431	55.1
Three persons	14,215	133	861	1,465	1,774	1,751	1,968	3,542	1,546	775	334	65	42.9
Four persons	12,654	67	406	1,137	1,981	2,744	2,646	2,670	668	252	64	21	40.0
Five persons	5,801	40	157	450	939	1,366	1,297	1,186	237	98	26	5	39.8
Six persons	1,738	13	38	123	316	409	389	319	87	30	14	2	39.6
Seven or more persons	883	5	14	71	129	194	195	196	47	23	8	–	40.7
Total persons	222,421	1,405	8,940	18,545	26,020	31,928	32,573	45,662	24,472	18,630	11,640	2,606	(X)
Persons per household	2.58	2.65	2.41	2.69	3.08	3.29	3.24	2.78	2.19	1.88	1.58	1.37	(X)
UNITED STATES-BLACK													
Households by Type													
All households	12,474	134	801	1,200	1,552	1,608	1,489	2,371	1,441	1,123	562	193	43.2
Family households	8,408	92	538	896	1,158	1,258	1,095	1,594	862	607	246	63	41.2
Married-couple family	3,921	1	110	348	510	538	528	884	485	369	126	23	44.3
Other family, male householder	562	43	48	51	61	66	74	103	62	24	20	9	40.8
Other family, female householder	3,926	49	380	498	587	654	492	607	314	214	100	32	38.4
Nonfamily households	4,066	42	263	304	394	350	394	778	579	516	316	130	48.4
Male householder	1,876	9	139	172	246	210	232	375	215	147	87	44	43.5
Female householder	2,190	33	124	132	148	140	162	403	365	369	229	86	53.9
Age of Household Members													
All members	34,271	430	1,989	3,468	4,715	5,142	4,427	6,430	3,739	2,466	1,124	342	(X)
Under 18 years	11,313	140	796	1,535	2,307	2,361	1,514	1,548	627	339	128	18	(X)
18 to 64 years	20,275	291	1,187	1,925	2,375	2,759	2,867	4,803	2,970	725	288	87	(X)
65 years and over	2,684	–	6	8	34	22	46	80	142	1,402	707	237	(X)
Households with members:													
Under 18 years	5,777	71	474	779	997	1,142	832	926	318	172	55	9	37.5
18 to 64 years	11,191	132	801	1,200	1,552	1,608	1,489	2,371	1,441	395	157	44	41.0
65 years and over	2,169	–	7	9	27	21	42	72	114	1,123	562	193	72.0
Average per household:	2.75	3.21	2.48	2.89	3.04	3.20	2.97	2.71	2.59	2.20	2.00	1.77	(X)
Under 18 years	.91	1.04	.99	1.28	1.49	1.47	1.02	.65	.44	.30	.23	.09	(X)
18 to 64 years	1.63	2.16	1.48	1.60	1.53	1.72	1.93	2.03	2.06	.65	.51	.45	(X)
65 years and over	.22	–	.01	.01	.02	.01	.03	.03	.10	1.25	1.26	1.23	(X)

Black Children

In 1998, two in five (36.2 percent) Black children under 18 years old lived with both parents, while 54.8 percent lived with one parent, 93.2 percent of whom lived with their mothers only. In 1970 the proportions of Black children who lived with one parent (31.8 percent) or two parents (58.5 percent) were virtually the reverse of their living arrangements in 1998. (See Table 2.8.) In 1998, according to the Census Bureau, 58.3 percent of all Black children living with only one parent lived with a never-married mother. (See Table 2.7.) In 1960 only 10 percent of Black children living with only one parent lived with one who had never married.

Hispanic Children

In 1998 almost two-thirds (63.6 percent) of Hispanic children under age 18 were living with both parents, compared to 76.5 percent of White children. (See Tables 2.9

TABLE 2.5

Households, by type, Age of Members, age, Region of Residence, Race, and Hispanic Origin of Housholder, March 1998 [CONTINUED]

[Numbers in thousands except for averages and medians.]

Characteristic	Total	Under 20 years	20 to 24 years	25 to 29 years	30 to 34 years	35 to 39 years	40 to 44 years	45 to 54 years	55 to 64 years	65 to 74 years	75 to 84 years	85 years and over	Median age
Size of Household													
Households	12,474	134	801	1,200	1,552	1,608	1,489	2,371	1,441	1,123	562	193	43.2
One person	3,576	17	185	220	360	299	334	721	511	501	305	123	49.7
Two persons	3,120	31	248	314	290	285	317	607	467	348	165	46	46.2
Three persons	2,338	29	216	274	299	346	335	406	225	146	51	11	40.1
Four persons	1,930	33	102	225	320	395	295	350	126	65	10	9	38.6
Five persons	916	12	26	118	166	185	133	174	52	35	10	4	38.7
Six persons	340	8	13	29	81	38	53	64	32	17	5	–	40.2
Seven or more persons	253	4	11	19	37	60	22	48	27	10	15	–	39.7
Total persons	34,271	430	1,989	3,468	4,715	5,142	4,427	6,430	3,739	2,466	1,124	342	(X)
Persons per household	2.75	3.21	2.48	2.89	3.04	3.20	2.97	2.71	2.59	2.20	2.00	1.77	(X)
UNITES STATES-HISPANIC[1]													
Households by Type													
All households	8,590	129	650	1,026	1,276	1,198	1,119	1,386	889	566	292	58	40.1
Family households	6,961	103	523	858	1,086	1,029	973	1,166	676	372	154	21	39.4
Married-couple family	4,804	29	271	578	767	729	698	812	507	282	120	10	40.
Other family, male householder	545	37	110	95	69	59	55	70	33	12	4	2	32.2
Other family, female householder	1,612	37	143	186	249	241	220	284	135	78	30	9	39.0
Nonfamily households	1,630	26	127	168	191	169	146	220	213	193	139	37	44.6
Male householder	875	14	83	113	136	121	100	125	76	62	31	13	38.8
Female householder	754	12	44	55	55	48	45	95	137	131	108	24	56.6
Age of Household Members													
All members	30,409	401	2,182	3,780	4,972	4,885	4,510	5,051	2,544	1,393	589	103	(X)
Under 18 years	10,971	165	760	1,546	2,360	2,324	1,885	1,389	361	156	19	6	(X)
18 to 64 years	17,822	235	1,414	2,214	2,574	2,502	2,568	3,570	2,085	477	157	25	(X)
65 years and over	1,617	1	8	21	38	59	57	92	98	760	413	71	(X)
Households with members:													
Under 18 years	5,010	91	409	686	988	934	846	734	219	85	14	5	36.8
18 to 64 years	8,002	124	650	1,026	1,276	1,198	1,119	1,386	889	248	70	15	38.9
65 years and over	1,205	1	7	12	26	44	42	67	92	566	292	58	69.9
Average per household:	3.54	3.10	3.35	3.68	3.90	4.08	4.03	3.64	2.86	2.46	2.01	(B)	(X)
Under 18 years	1.28	1.27	1.17	1.51	1.85	1.94	1.69	1.00	.41	.28	.06	(B)	(X)
18 to 64 years	2.07	1.82	2.17	2.16	2.02	2.09	2.30	2.58	2.35	.84	.54	(B)	(X)
65 years and over	.19	.01	.01	.02	.03	.05	.05	.07	.11	1.34	1.41	(B)	(X)
Size of Household													
Households	8,590	129	650	1,026	1,276	1,198	1,119	1,386	889	566	292	58	40.1
One person	1,240	15	63	109	123	122	108	169	180	182	135	34	49.1
Two persons	1,838	28	152	213	174	152	146	321	318	213	108	14	46.7
Three persons	1,728	37	202	225	259	211	203	295	181	81	27	8	38.3
Four persons	1,763	26	135	270	323	290	291	265	104	48	12	–	37.2
Five persons	1,199	13	64	129	255	238	218	185	66	25	4	2	37.9
Six persons	463	7	19	43	95	107	88	71	19	10	3	–	38.1
Seven or more persons	358	3	15	38	48	77	65	81	21	7	3	–	39.9
Total persons	30,409	401	2,182	3,780	4,972	4,885	4,510	5,051	2,544	1,393	589	103	(X)
Persons per household	3.54	3.10	3.35	3.68	3.90	4.08	4.03	3.64	2.86	2.46	2.01	(B)	(X)

[1]May be of any race.

SOURCE: U.S. Bureau of the Census, Population Division, Fertility & Family Statistics Branch: Washington, D.C., 1999

and 2.7.) Nearly one-third (31.3 percent) of Hispanic children were living in one-parent situations, considerably more than among Whites (23.5 percent), but well below the proportion for Blacks (54.8 percent). Nearly 37 percent of Hispanic children who lived in one-parent families lived with a never-married mother, and one-fourth (24.6 percent) lived with a mother whose spouse was absent. (See Tables 2.7, 2.8, and 2.9.)

Asian American Children

The Asian American family is typically close-knit and respectful of the authority of the older members of the family. Any deed that would disgrace the family, such as a child born to an unwed mother, is carefully avoided. As the younger generation becomes more assimilated into American culture, the unchallenged role of elders may not remain as strong, but overall, family tradition

TABLE 2.6

Living Arrangements of Children Under 18 years Old, 1960–1998

(Numbers in thousands. Excludes householders, subfamily reference persons, and their spouses. Also excludes inmates of institutions. Based on Current Population Survey (CPS) unless otherwise indicated)

Year	Total children under 18 yrs.	Two parents	Living with One parent			Other relatives	Non-relatives only
			Total	Mother only	Father only		
1998	71,377	48,642	19,777	16,634	3,143	2,126	833
1997	70,983	48,386	19,799	16,740	3,059	1,983	815
1996	70,908	48,224	19,752	16,993	2,759	2,137	795
1995	70,254	48,276	18,938	16,477	2,461	2,352	688
1994	69,508	48,084	18,591	16,334	2,257	2,150	684
1993	66,893	47,181	17,872	15,586	2,286	1,442	398
1992	65,965	46,638	17,578	15,396	2,182	1,334	415
1991	65,093	46,658	16,624	14,608	2,016	1,428	383
1990	64,137	46,503	15,867	13,874	1,993	1,421	346
1989	63,637	46,549	15,493	13,700	1,793	1,341	254
1988	63,179	45,942	15,329	13,521	1,808	1,516	392
1987	62,932	46,009	15,071	13,420	1,651	1,484	368
1986	62,763	46,384	14,759	13,180	1,579	1,348	272
1985	62,475	46,149	14,635	13,081	1,554	1,339	352
1984	62,139	46,555	14,024	12,646	1,378	1,227	333
1983*	62,281	46,632	14,006	12,739	1,267	1,349	294
1982*	62,407	46,797	13,701	12,512	1,189	1,557	352
1981	62,918	48,040	12,619	11,416	1,203	1,911	348
1980r	63,427	48,624	12,466	11,406	1,060	1,949	388
1980	61,744	47,286	12,162	11,131	1,031	1,912	384
1979	62,389	48,295	11,528	10,531	997	2,143	423
1978	63,206	49,132	11,710	10,725	985	1,941	423
1977	64,062	50,735	11,311	10,419	892	1,626	390
1976	65,129	52,101	11,121	10,310	811	1,500	407
1975	66,087	53,072	11,245	10,231	1,014	1,407	363
1974	67,047	54,561	10,489	9,647	842	1,532	465
1973	67,950	55,807	10,093	9,272	821	1,629	421
1972	68,811	57,201	9,634	8,838	796	1,593	383
1971	70,255	58,606	9,478	8,714	764	1,707	464
1970r	69,162	58,939	8,200	7,452	748	1,546	477
1970	70,213	59,694	8,438	7,678	760	1,599	482
1969	70,317	59,857	8,509	7,744	765	1,602	349
1968	70,326	60,030	8,332	7,556	776	1,660	304
1967	(NA)	(NA)	(NA)	(NA)	(NA)	(NA)	(NA)
1966	(NA)	(NA)	(NA)	(NA)	(NA)	(NA)	(NA)
1965	(NA)	(NA)	(NA)	(NA)	(NA)	(NA)	(NA)
1964	(NA)	(NA)	(NA)	(NA)	(NA)	(NA)	(NA)
1963	(NA)	(NA)	(NA)	(NA)	(NA)	(NA)	(NA)
1962	(NA)	(NA)	(NA)	(NA)	(NA)	(NA)	(NA)
1961	(NA)	(NA)	(NA)	(NA)	(NA)	(NA)	(NA)
1960 Census	63,727	55,877	5,829	5,105	724	1,601	420

NA Not available.

r Revised based on population from the decennial census for that year.

*Introduction of improved data collection and processing procedures that helped to identify parent-child subfamilies.

SOURCE: *Marital Status and Living Arrangements: March 1998 (Update)* and earlier reports. Current Population Reports, Series P20-514. U. S. Bureau of the Census: Washington, D.C.

and honor are still held in high regard. In 1998 most Asian American children under age 18 (83.7 percent) were living with both parents. About 12 percent lived with their mothers only, while 2.9 percent lived with their father only. Asian American women were also less likely to have children outside of marriage.

At a Disadvantage

Regardless of race or ethnicity, children who live with only one parent are likely to live in more economically disadvantaged circumstances than are children who live with two parents. Children living with one parent are more likely to have parents who are less educated, are unemployed, or have lower incomes. (See also Chapter 5.)

AID TO FAMILIES WITH DEPENDENT CHILDREN. Aid to Families with Dependent Children (AFDC) was established during the Great Depression of the 1930s as a cash program to help needy children. The program was designed primarily to aid children deprived of parental support or care because either a father or a mother was absent from the home, incapacitated, deceased, or unemployed.

TABLE 2.7

Living Arrangements of Children Under 18 years, by Marital Status and Race, March 1998

Numbers in thousands. Characteristics are shown for householder or reference person in married~couple situations.

Subject	Total, living with one or both parents	Living with both parents	Living with mother only					Living with father only				
				Marital status of mother					Marital status of father			
			Total	Divorced	Married, spouse absent	Widowed	Never married	Total	Divorced	Married, spouse absent	Widowed	Never married
ALL RACES Children under 18 years	68,418	48,642	16,634	5,704	3,558	671	6,700	3,143	1,397	578	123	1,046
WHITE Children under 18 years	54,319	41,547	10,210	4,525	2,345	490	2,850	2,562	1,230	488	99	745
BLACK Children under 18 years	10,392	4,137	5,830	992	1,037	157	3,644	424	118	56	20	230
HISPANIC[1] Children under 18 years	10,306	6,909	2,915	688	834	139	1,254	482	94	105	7	276

[1]May be of any race.

SOURCE: *Marital Status and Living Arrangements: March 1998 (Update)* and earlier reports. Current Population Reports, Series P20-514. U. S. Bureau of the Census: Washington, D.C.

In 1996, of the 4.5 million families receiving AFDC, 36 percent of the children had White caretakers; 37 percent Black caretakers; 21 percent Hispanic caretakers; 3 percent Asian caretakers; and just over 1 percent, Native American caretakers. The caretaker is usually a parent. (See Figure 2.2.)

In 1996 the Personal Responsibility and Work Opportunity Reconciliation Act (PL 104-193), also known as the welfare reform act, ended the AFDC program. The law created a federal block grant, the Temporary Assistance for Needy Families, leaving it to individual states to determine benefit-eligibility requirements and benefit levels.

HOME OWNERSHIP

In the first quarter of 2000, 70.7 percent of White householders owned their homes, higher than in the first quarter of 1995 (68.2 percent). In the first quarter of 2000, 47.4 percent of Black householders owned their homes, up from 41.2 percent in 1995. The 2000 home-ownership proportion for Hispanics (45.7 percent) was significantly higher than it had been in the first quarter of 1995 when it was at 41.8 percent. (See Table 2.10.)

Children's Housing

According to the Bureau of the Census, in *Marital Status and Living Arrangements: March 1998 (Update)* (Washington, DC, December 1998), 44.8 million children under 18 years of age lived in homes owned by their parents in 1998. An additional 23.7 million children lived in rental properties, 5.2 million of whom lived in public housing. Nearly two-thirds (64.5 percent) of those in public housing lived with their mothers only. Most White children (70.5 percent) lived in owned properties, while over half of Black children (59.5 percent) lived in rental housing. A little over 5 percent of all White children under 18 lived in public housing, compared to 18.6 percent of Black children. Hispanic children (55.7 percent) were as likely to live in rental properties as were Black children, while nearly 11.4 percent lived in public housing. (See Table 2.11.)

Over half (50.7 percent) of White children who lived in public housing lived with their mothers only, and of those, 41.5 percent lived with a never-married mother. Meanwhile, 87 percent of Black children in public housing lived alone with their mothers, and more than two-thirds (68.2 percent) of them were living with never-married mothers. Among Hispanic children, 57.4 percent in public housing lived with their mothers, and 45 percent of these had mothers who had never married. (See Table 2.11.)

HOUSING GRANDCHILDREN. Due to many factors, including the high cost of housing, drug addiction, and the inability of some parents to care for their children, many children are living with their grandparents. In 1998 the Census Bureau reported that 5.6 percent (nearly 4 million) of children under the age of 18 lived with their grandparents, nearly double the 3.2 percent in 1970. (See Table 2.12.) In 1998 Black children (12 percent) were much more likely to live with a grandparent than White (4.3 percent) or Hispanic (6.5 percent) children. (See Table 2.13.)

In 1998, of those children living with a grandparent, 50.3 percent of Blacks, 44.7 percent of Whites, and 49.5 percent of Hispanics had only one parent, their mother, present. A larger proportion of Black children (41.4 percent) than Whites (33 percent) or Hispanics (30.4 per-

TABLE 2.8

Living Arrangements of Black Children Under 18 Years Old, 1960–1998
(Numbers in thousands. Excludes householders, subfamily reference persons, and their spouses. Also excludes inmates of institutions. Based on Current Population Survey (CPS) unless otherwise indicated)

Year	Total children under 18 yrs.	Two parents	Total	Living with: One parent		Other relatives	Non-relatives only
				Mother only	Father only		
1998	11,414	4,137	6,254	5,830	424	843	172
1997	11,369	3,940	6,469	5,888	581	814	146
1996	11,434	3,816	6,560	6,056	504	883	175
1995	11,301	3,746	6,339	5,881	458	1,012	204
1994	11,177	3,722	6,384	5,967	417	898	173
1993	10,660	3,796	6,080	5,757	322	657	127
1992	10,427	3,714	5,934	5,607	327	625	154
1991	10,209	3,669	5,874	5,516	358	565	101
1990	10,018	3,781	5,484	5,132	353	655	98
1989	9,835	3,738	5,362	5,023	339	660	75
1988	9,699	3,739	5,247	4,959	288	627	86
1987	9,612	3,852	5,087	4,844	243	598	75
1986	9,532	3,869	5,058	4,827	231	542	63
1985	9,479	3,741	5,114	4,837	276	543	81
1984	9,375	3,845	4,978	4,705	273	468	84
1983*	9,377	3,818	5,024	4,789	234	482	53
1982*	9,377	3,978	4,614	4,422	192	711	74
1981	9,400	4,016	4,309	4,074	236	1,015	60
1980r	9,375	3,956	4,297	4,117	180	999	123
1980	9,290	3,917	4,252	4,070	183	998	123
1979	9,285	4,030	4,089	3,891	198	1,054	112
1978	9,394	4,094	4,173	3,978	195	970	157
1977	9,374	4,384	4,046	3,911	135	848	96
1976	9,461	4,688	3,936	3,791	145	742	95
1975	9,472	4,682	4,043	3,870	172	640	107
1974	9,526	4,831	3,774	3,602	171	773	148
1973	9,523	4,904	3,782	3,583	199	747	90
1972	9,583	5,201	3,385	3,207	178	870	127
1971	10,004	5,446	3,437	3,264	173	998	123
1970r	9,422	5,508	2,995	2,783	213	822	97
1970	9,910	5,804	3,139	2,919	221	862	105
1969	9,832	5,784	3,086	2,907	179	856	106
1968	9,714	5,702	3,052	2,842	210	861	99
1967	(NA)	(NA)	(NA)	(NA)	(NA)	(NA)	(NA)
1966	(NA)	(NA)	(NA)	(NA)	(NA)	(NA)	(NA)
1965	(NA)	(NA)	(NA)	(NA)	(NA)	(NA)	(NA)
1964	(NA)	(NA)	(NA)	(NA)	(NA)	(NA)	(NA)
1963	(NA)	(NA)	(NA)	(NA)	(NA)	(NA)	(NA)
1962	(NA)	(NA)	(NA)	(NA)	(NA)	(NA)	(NA)
1961	(NA)	(NA)	(NA)	(NA)	(NA)	(NA)	(NA)
1960 Census	8,650	5,795	1,897	1,723	173	826	132

NA Not available.

r Revised based on population from the decennial census for that year.

*Introduction of improved data collection and processing procedures that helped to identify parent-child subfamilies.

SOURCE: *Marital Status and Living Arrangements: March 1998 (Update)* and earlier reports. Current Population Reports, Series P20-514. U. S. Bureau of the Census: Washington, D.C.

cent) had neither parent present. Children in all categories were unlikely to have only a father present. (See Table 2.13.) The proportion of all children under 18 living with a grandparent with only their mother present rose from 36.9 percent in 1970 to 40 percent in 1980 to 49.5 percent in 1990. This percentage then dropped slightly to 47.2 percent in 1994 and then to 45.8 percent in 1998.

Affording a Home

For most Americans, owning one's home is the American dream. Unfortunately, for many Americans, especially minorities, being able to purchase a home can be a difficult task. The Bureau of the Census, in "Who Could Afford to Buy a House in 1995?" (Howard A. Savage, *Current Housing Reports,* Washington, DC, 1999), found that 19 percent of White married-couple renters could afford a modestly priced house in 1995, while 8 percent of Black married couples who rented could do so. Only 5 percent of Hispanic married couples who rented could afford a modestly priced house in 1995. (The Bureau of the Census defines a modestly priced house as one assessed so that 25 percent of all owner-occupied houses in the area are below this value and 75 percent are above.)

TABLE 2.9

Living Arrangements of Hispanic* Children Under 18 Years Old, 1970–1998

(Numbers in thousands. Excludes householders, subfamily reference persons, and their spouses. Also excludes inmates of institutions. Based on Current Population Survey (CPS) unless otherwise indicated)

Year	Total children under 18 yrs.	Two parents	Total	Living with: One parent		Other relatives	Non-relatives only
				Mother only	Father only		
1998	10,863	6,909	3,397	2,915	482	380	171
1997	10,526	6,748	3,260	2,819	441	377	140
1996	10,251	6,381	3,321	2,937	384	411	138
1995	9,843	6,191	3,215	2,798	417	318	120
1994	9,496	6,022	3,019	2,646	373	327	128
1993	7,776	5,017	2,472	2,176	296	229	58
1992	7,619	4,935	2,447	2,168	279	196	41
1991	7,462	4,944	2,222	1,983	239	230	66
1990	7,174	4,789	2,154	1,943	211	177	54
1989	6,973	4,673	2,129	1,940	189	142	29
1988	6,786	4,497	2,048	1,845	202	188	53
1987	6,647	4,355	2,027	1,843	184	199	66
1986	6,430	4,275	1,955	1,784	171	162	38
1985	6,057	4,110	1,746	1,612	134	159	42
1984	5,625	3,946	1,509	1,399	110	147	23
1983**	5,513	3,774	1,574	1,475	99	131	34
1982**	5,358	3,700	1,436	1,353	83	182	40
1981	5,267	3,703	1,341	1,212	129	198	25
1980r	5,459	4,116	1,152	1,069	83	183	8
1980	5,438	4,138	1,115	1,035	80	178	7
1979	(NA)	(NA)	(NA)	(NA)	(NA)	(NA)	(NA)
1978	(NA)	(NA)	(NA)	(NA)	(NA)	(NA)	(NA)
1977	(NA)	(NA)	(NA)	(NA)	(NA)	(NA)	(NA)
1976	(NA)	(NA)	(NA)	(NA)	(NA)	(NA)	(NA)
1975	(NA)	(NA)	(NA)	(NA)	(NA)	(NA)	(NA)
1974	(NA)	(NA)	(NA)	(NA)	(NA)	(NA)	(NA)
1973	(NA)	(NA)	(NA)	(NA)	(NA)	(NA)	(NA)
1972	(NA)	(NA)	(NA)	(NA)	(NA)	(NA)	(NA)
1971	(NA)	(NA)	(NA)	(NA)	(NA)	(NA)	(NA)
1970 Census	4,006	3,111	(NA)	(NA)	(NA)	(NA)	(NA)

Note: Data not available prior to 1970 census.

NA Not available.

r Revised based on population from the decennial census for that year.

*Persons of Hispanic origin may be of any race.

**Introduction of improved data collection and processing procedures that helped to identify parent-child subfamilies.

SOURCE: *Marital Status and Living Arrangements: March 1998 (Update)* and earlier reports. Current Population Reports, Series P20-514. U. S. Bureau of the Census: Washington, D.C.

For those who already owned homes in 1995, 78 percent of White families could have afforded to move to a modestly priced home in the area where they lived, compared to 53 percent of Black families and 52 percent of Hispanic families.

Policy makers see a need to improve home-ownership affordability for minorities. There are three policy alternatives that are often discussed as means of making home ownership more affordable:

• Lowering interest rates

• Requiring a lower down payment for home purchasers

• Providing a down-payment subsidy to home buyers

Lowering interest rates by as much as 3 percentage points would not have made a difference for either Black or Hispanic renters who could qualify for a mortgage on a modestly priced house in 1995. Requiring a 2.5 percent down payment would have increased by 1 percentage point the number of Black renters who could qualify for a mortgage on a modestly priced house. Not requiring a down payment would have increased that figure by 2 percentage points. If either scenario, however, were applied to Hispanic renters, no significant results could have been achieved. (See Table 2.14.)

To raise the percentage of Black renters who would have qualified for a mortgage in 1995 by a significant amount, a $2,500 down-payment subsidy would have had to be available. This would have increased the home-buying ability of Black renters by nearly 2 percentage points. A $5,000 subsidy would have raised the number by nearly 13 percentage points, a $7,500 subsidy by 19 percentage points, and a $10,000 subsidy by 22 percentage points. (See Table 2.14.)

FIGURE 2.2

AFDC Families by Race of Parent, 1995–1996

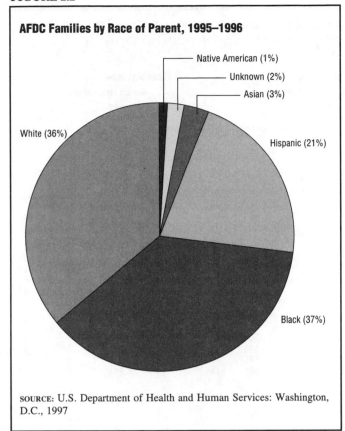

- Native American (1%)
- Unknown (2%)
- Asian (3%)
- White (36%)
- Hispanic (21%)
- Black (37%)

SOURCE: U.S. Department of Health and Human Services: Washington, D.C., 1997

For Hispanic renters, a $5,000 subsidy would have increased the number who would have qualified for a mortgage by 7 percentage points, a $7,500 subsidy by 12 percentage points, and a $10,000 subsidy by 16 percentage points. (See Table 2.14.)

TABLE 2.10

Homeownership Rates by Race and Ethnicity of Householder, 1996–2000

| Year/Quarter | Homeownership Rates[1] | | | | | |
	U.S. Total	White, total	White, non-Hispanic	Black, total	Other Race, total	Hispanic[2], total
2000						
First Quarter	67.1	70.7	73.4	47.4	53.6	45.7
1999						
Fourth Quarter	66.9	70.5	73.3	46.8	54.3	45.5
Third Quarter	67.0	70.7	73.5	46.6	54.5	45.5
Second Quarter	66.6	70.4	73.2	45.3	53.2	44.9
First Quarter	66.7	70.3	72.8	46.3	52.8	46.2
1998						
Fourth Quarter	66.4	70.1	72.6	45.9	52.7	45.7
Third Quarter	66.8	70.4	73.1	46.6	53.6	44.9
Second Quarter	66.0	69.7	72.5	44.7	53.5	43.9
First Quarter	65.9	69.6	72.1	45.2	52.3	44.4
1997						
Fourth Quarter	65.7	69.3	71.9	45.1	52.5	44.0
Third Quarter	66.0	69.5	72.3	45.3	53.1	43.0
Second Quarter	65.7	69.4	72.1	44.4	52.7	43.3
First Quarter	65.4	69.0	71.6	44.5	51.8	42.6
1996						
Fourth Quarter	65.4	69.1	71.8	44.4	51.4	42.3
Third Quarter	65.6	69.2	71.8	44.5	51.5	43.5
Second Quarter	65.4	69.2	71.7	43.7	50.0	43.9
First Quarter	65.1	68.7	71.4	43.8	50.9	41.4
1995						
Fourth Quarter	65.1	68.8	71.2	44.3	48.4	41.1
Third Quarter	65.0	69.0	71.1	43.0	46.5	42.5
Second Quarter	64.7	68.7	70.9	42.2	46.7	42.8
First Quarter	64.2	68.2	70.4	41.2	47.2	41.8

[1] Standard errors for quarterly homeownership rates by race and ethnicity of householder generally are 0.2 percent for White and White non-Hispanic householders, 0.5 percent for Black householders, 1.0 percent for Other Race householders, and 0.7 percent for Hispanic householders.

[2] Hispanics may be of any race.

Press Release, CBOO-61. U.S. Bureau of the Census: Washington, D.C., April 26, 2000

TABLE 2.11

Living Arrangements of Children Under 18 Years, by Marital Status and Selected Characteristics of Parent, March 1998

[Numbers in thousands. Characteristics are shown for householder or reference person in married-couple situations.]

Subject	Total, living with one or both parents	Living with both parents	Living with mother only					Living with father only				
				Marital status of mother					Marital status of father			
			Total	Divorced	Married, spouse absent	Widowed	Never married	Total	Divorced	Married, spouse absent	Widowed	Never married
All Races												
Children under 18 years	68,418	48,642	16,634	5,704	3,558	671	6,700	3,143	1,397	578	123	1,046
Tenure[1]:												
Owned	44,750	36,875	6,216	2,788	1,290	413	1,725	1,658	868	276	106	408
Rented	23,669	11,766	10,418	2,917	2,268	258	4,975	1,485	529	302	17	637
Public housing	5,192	1,659	3,349	779	697	42	1,831	184	59	35	4	86
Private housing	18,477	10,107	7,069	2,138	1,571	216	3,144	1,301	470	267	12	552
White												
Children under 18 years	54,319	41,547	10,210	4,525	2,345	490	2,850	2,562	1,230	488	99	745
Tenure[1]:												
Owned	38,292	32,401	4,503	2,387	952	315	848	1,388	796	215	86	290
Rented	16,028	9,146	5,707	2,138	1,392	175	2 001	1,175	434	273	13	455
Public housing	2,979	1,319	1,510	473	373	38	626	150	48	33	2	66
Private housing	13,049	7,827	4,197	1,666	1,019	137	1,376	1,025	386	240	11	389
Black												
Children under 18 years	10,392	4,137	5,830	992	1,037	157	3,644	424	118	56	20	230
Tenure[1]:												
Owned	4,211	2,534	1,502	335	280	82	804	175	48	30	16	81
Rented	6,181	1,603	4,329	657	757	75	2,840	250	71	26	4	149
Public housing	1,936	221	1,684	261	271	3	1,148	31	10	2	2	17
Private housing	4,245	1,382	2,644	396	486	72	1,691	219	61	24	2	132
Hispanic [2]												
Children under 18 years	10,306	6,909	2,915	688	834	139	1,254	482	94	105	7	276
Tenure[1]:												
Owned	4,564	3,672	733	222	213	52	247	159	47	30	6	77
Rented	5,742	3,237	2,182	466	622	87	1,008	323	47	75	1	200
Public housing	1,178	473	676	133	209	30	304	29	–	9	–	20
Private housing	4,564	2,764	1,506	333	412	57	703	294	47	65	1	180

[1]Refers to tenure of householder (who may or may not be the child's parent).
[2]May be of any race.

SOURCE: U.S. Bureau of the Census, Population Division, Fertility and Family Statistics Branch: Washington, D.C., 1999

TABLE 2.12

Grandchildren Living in the Home of their Grandparents, 1970–1998

(Numbers in thousands)

Year	Total children under 18	Grandchildren				
		Total	With parent(s) present			
			Both parents present	Mother only present	Father only present	Without parent(s) present
1998	71,377	3,989	503	1,827	241	1,417
1997	70,983	3,894	554	1,785	247	1,309
1996	70,908	4,060	467	1,943	220	1,431
1995	70,254	3,965	427	1,876	195	1,466
1994	69,508	3,735	436	1,764	175	1,359
1993	66,893	3,368	475	1,647	229	1,017
1992	65,965	3,253	502	1,740	144	867
1991	65,093	3,320	559	1,674	151	937
1990	64,137	3,155	467	1,563	191	935
1980 Census	63,369	2,306	310	922	86	988
1970 Census	69,276	2,214	363	817	78	957

SOURCE: *Marital Status and Living Arrangements: March 1998 (Update)* and earlier reports. Current Population Reports, Series P20-514. U.S. Bureau of the Census: Washington, D.C.

TABLE 2.13

Household Relationship and Presence of Parents for Persons Under 18 Years, by Age, Race, and Hispanic Origin, March 1998
[Numbers in thousands.]

Subject	Total, under 18 years[1]	In households	Living with both parents	Living with mother only	Living with father only	Living with neither parent
ALL RACES						
Both sexes	71,377					
Grandchild of householder		3,989	503	1,827	241	1,417
WHITE						
Both sexes	56,124					
Grandchild of householder		2,423	372	1,084	166	801
BLACK						
Both sexes	11,414					
Grandchild of householder		1,375	66	691	48	570
HISPANIC[2]						
Both sexes	10,863					
Grandchild of householder		701	94	347	47	213

[1]Excludes householders, subfamily reference persons, and their spouses.
[2]May be of any race.

SOURCE: U.S. Bureau of the Census, Population Division, Fertility and Family Statistics Branch: Washington, D.C., 1999

TABLE 2.14

Effects of Possible Policy Changes on the Affordability of a Modestly Priced House for Total, Black, and Hispanic Origin Renters, 1995

	Percentage who could afford to buy		
	Total	Black	Hispanic origin[1]
Current mortgage requirements [2]	10.2	3.4	2.6
Modified mortgage requirements			
Modified down payment			
2.5 percent down payment	11.3	4.4	2.9
No down payment	12.7	5.7	3.2
Modified interest rate			
Interest rate 1 percentage point lower	10.5	3.4	2.6
Interest rate 2 percentage points lower	10.8	3.4	2.7
Interest rate 3 percentage points lower	11.1	3.4	2.7
Modified cash assistance			
$1,000 down payment subsidy	11.0	4.2	2.9
$2,500 down payment subsidy	12.6	5.2	3.3
$5,000 down payment subsidy	21.2	16.1	9.9
$7,500 down payment subsidy	27.7	22.6	14.7
$10,000 down payment subsidy	31.9	25.5	18.6

[1]Hispanics may be of any race.

[2]Current mortgage requirements in 1995 were 5 percent down, a 8.67 percent interest rate for conventional mortgages, and no subsidy.

Note: Assumes conventional, fixed-rate, 30-year financing, with a 5-percent down payment.

SOURCE: Howard A. Savage, *Who Can Afford to Buy a House in 1995?* Current Housing Reports, H121/99-1. U.S. Bureau of the Census: Washington, D.C., August 1999

CHAPTER 3
LABOR FORCE PARTICIPATION

A HISTORICAL PERSPECTIVE OF MINORITIES IN THE LABOR FORCE

Minorities and ethnic groups have always been an important part of the American labor force. In many instances, groups were allowed, or even encouraged, to immigrate to the United States to fill specific labor needs. Perhaps the most obvious example is the involuntary immigration of Africans, who provided slave labor for southern plantations as early as the seventeenth century. Later, Asians and Hispanics were sought to mine resources, farm land, and build railroads.

Black Americans

Since 1619, with the arrival of the first slave ships to North American shores, Black Americans have been part of the labor force. While virtually all worked as unpaid slaves on southern plantations, a few were allowed to work for pay in order to purchase their freedom and that of their families, which often took many years. In addition to farm and house labor, some developed talents in masonry, music, or other skills and were hired out by their owners.

In 1890, less than 30 years after the Emancipation Proclamation (which freed the slaves in the Confederate states) and the Thirteenth Amendment (which outlawed slavery in the United States), approximately 3 million Blacks worked in the paid labor force. Between 1890 and 1930 this figure almost doubled to 5.5 million, a result not only of the growth in population, but also of the increase in the number of unskilled jobs that became available during and immediately following World War I. Job prospects were best in the North, and hundreds of thousands of Blacks left their rural southern homes, migrating north in search of unskilled work in factories and homes.

The Great Depression of the 1930s was very difficult for almost everyone, but Blacks were particularly hard hit. While the number of employed Whites increased by

4.5 million from 1930 to 1940, the number of Blacks in the labor force rose by only 170,000. During the 1940s arms production for World War II again attracted hundreds of thousands of Blacks to the North, bringing about a moderate increase in the number of Black workers. These migrations of Blacks from the South to the North following both World Wars were the largest movements of people within the United States and did much to influence recent American history.

Asian Americans

Between 1851 and 1880 about 229,000 Chinese immigrated to the United States, not only in search of newly found California gold, but also to work on the railroads, in the mines, in construction and manufacturing, and on the farms, mostly in the American West. Concern over increasing Chinese immigration, fueled by both racism and a fear that foreign workers would replace Americans and keep unskilled wages low, led to the passage of the Chinese Exclusion Act of 1882 (22 Stat 58), which stopped the flow of Chinese immigrants.

Eventually, Japanese laborers were brought in to replace Chinese workers. During the first decade of the twentieth century, almost 130,000 Japanese came to the rapidly expanding sugarcane plantations of Hawaii and the fruit and vegetable farms of California. Theodore Roosevelt and the Japanese government, however, in the "Gentleman's Agreement" of 1907, agreed to stop the flow of Japanese workers to the United States by withholding passports, thus cutting the flow to a trickle. The most recent wave of Asians came to the United States in the 1970s and 1980s, when more than a million Indochinese refugees were admitted following the Vietnam War.

Hispanic Americans

Many Hispanic Americans can trace their families back to when Mexico included what is today the Ameri-

TABLE 3.1

Employment Status of the Civilian Population by Race, Sex, Age, and Hispanic Origin
(Numbers in thousands)

Employment status, race, sex, age, and Hispanic origin	Not seasonally adjusted			Seasonally adjusted[1]					
	Apr. 1999	Mar. 2000	Apr. 2000	Apr. 1999	Dec. 1999	Jan. 2000	Feb. 2000	Mar. 2000	Apr. 2000
White									
Civilian noninstitutional population	172,730	173,983	174,092	172,730	173,821	173,812	173,886	173,983	174,092
Civilian labor force	115,633	117,451	117,281	116,344	117,008	117,716	117,821	117,832	117,988
Participation rate	66.9	67.5	67.4	67.4	67.3	67.7	67.8	67.7	67.8
Employed	111,439	113,006	113,458	111,886	112,951	113,704	113,634	113,630	113,915
Employment-population ratio	64.5	65.0	65.2	64.8	65.0	65.4	65.3	65.3	65.4
Unemployed	4,194	4,446	3,823	4,458	4,057	4,011	4,187	4,202	4,073
Unemployment rate	3.6	3.8	3.3	3.8	3.5	3.4	3.6	3.6	3.5
Men, 20 years and over									
Civilian labor force	59,548	60,123	59,958	59,651	59,889	60,179	60,387	60,282	60,048
Participation rate	77.1	77.2	76.9	77.2	77.0	77.3	77.6	77.4	77.0
Employed	57,758	58,131	58,327	57,834	58,221	58,487	58,631	58,541	58,386
Employment-population ratio	74.8	74.6	74.8	74.9	74.8	75.2	75.3	75.1	74.9
Unemployed	1,790	1,993	1,631	1,817	1,668	1,693	1,756	1,742	1,662
Unemployment rate	3.0	3.3	2.7	3.0	2.8	2.8	2.9	2.9	2.8
Women, 20 years and over									
Civilian labor force	49,486	50,622	50,532	49,674	50,011	50,404	50,335	50,448	50,726
Participation rate	59.8	60.7	60.6	60.0	60.1	60.5	60.4	60.5	60.8
Employed	47,862	48,966	49,101	47,885	48,486	48,857	48,792	48,820	49,150
Employment-population ratio	57.8	58.7	58.9	57.8	58.2	58.7	58.6	58.6	58.9
Unemployed	1,624	1,656	1,431	1,789	1,525	1,547	1,544	1,628	1,576
Unemployment rate	3.3	3.3	2.8	3.6	3.0	3.1	3.1	3.2	3.1
Both sexes, 16 to 19 years									
Civilian labor force	6,599	6,706	6,791	7,019	7,108	7,132	7,099	7,102	7,214
Participation rate	52.1	52.7	53.4	55.4	55.8	56.0	55.8	55.8	56.7
Employed	5,819	5,909	6,030	6,167	6,244	6,360	6,211	6,270	6,379
Employment-population ratio	45.9	46.5	47.4	48.7	49.0	50.0	48.8	49.3	50.2
Unemployed	780	797	761	852	864	772	888	832	835
Unemployment rate	11.8	11.9	11.2	12.1	12.2	10.8	12.5	11.7	11.6
Men	12.2	12.1	12.6	12.6	13.3	12.4	14.4	11.3	13.0
Women	11.4	11.7	9.7	11.6	10.9	9.1	10.4	12.1	10.0
Black									
Civilian noninstitutional population	24,765	25,105	25,135	24,765	25,051	25,047	25,076	25,105	25,135
Civilian labor force	16,159	16,466	16,504	16,288	16,513	16,622	16,785	16,572	16,636
Participation rate	65.2	65.6	65.7	65.8	65.9	66.4	66.9	66.0	66.2
Employed	14,979	15,231	15,412	15,011	15,204	15,254	15,471	15,356	15,444
Employment-population ratio	60.5	60.7	61.3	60.6	60.7	60.9	61.7	61.2	61.4
Unemployed	1,180	1,236	1,092	1,277	1,309	1,368	1,314	1,216	1,191
Unemployment rate	7.3	7.5	6.6	7.8	7.9	8.2	7.8	7.3	7.2
Men, 20 years and over									
Civilian labor force	7,092	7,252	7,324	7,118	7,273	7,386	7,441	7,300	7,351
Participation rate	71.7	72.2	72.8	72.0	72.6	73.7	74.2	72.6	73.0
Employed	6,661	6,762	6,858	6,670	6,766	6,839	6,910	6,830	6,864
Employment-population ratio	67.4	67.3	68.1	67.5	67.5	68.2	68.9	68.0	68.2
Unemployed	431	490	467	448	507	547	532	469	487
Unemployment rate	6.1	6.8	6.4	6.3	7.0	7.4	7.1	6.4	6.6
Women, 20 years and over									
Civilian labor force	8,222	8,333	8,293	8,223	8,260	8,315	8,344	8,314	8,291
Participation rate	66.3	66.2	65.8	66.3	65.8	66.3	66.4	66.1	65.8
Employed	7,681	7,815	7,830	7,657	7,706	7,715	7,805	7,808	7,807
Employment-population ratio	61.9	62.1	62.2	61.7	61.4	61.5	62.1	62.1	62.0
Unemployed	541	518	463	566	554	600	539	506	484
Unemployment rate	6.6	6.2	5.6	6.9	6.7	7.2	6.5	6.1	5.8
Both sexes, 16 to 19 years									
Civilian labor force	845	881	886	947	980	921	999	958	993
Participation rate	34.1	35.6	35.8	38.3	39.5	37.2	40.4	38.7	40.2
Employed	637	653	724	684	732	701	756	718	773
Employment-population ratio	25.7	26.4	29.3	27.6	29.5	28.3	30.6	29.0	31.3
Unemployed	208	228	162	263	248	220	243	240	220
Unemployment rate	24.6	25.9	18.3	27.8	25.3	23.9	24.3	25.1	22.2
Men	30.2	22.6	18.4	32.0	27.5	24.0	22.3	21.3	22.0
Women	19.7	29.3	18.2	23.8	23.0	23.8	26.6	28.9	22.4

See footnotes at end of table.

can Southwest. The ancestors of most Hispanic Americans, however, arrived after Mexico surrendered much of its territory following its defeat in the Mexican-American War of 1846–48. The U.S. policy toward Hispanic Ameri-

can workers (mainly from Mexico) has alternately encouraged and discouraged immigration, reflecting the nation's changing needs for labor. Prior to the start of the twentieth century, although there was little demand in the

TABLE 3.1
Employment Status of the Civilian Population by Race, Sex, Age, and Hispanic Origin [CONTINUED]

(Numbers in thousands)

Employment status, race, sex, age, and Hispanic origin	Not seasonally adjusted			Seasonally adjusted[1]					
	Apr. 1999	Mar. 2000	Apr. 2000	Apr. 1999	Dec. 1999	Jan. 2000	Feb. 2000	Mar. 2000	Apr. 2000
Hispanic Origin									
Civilian noninstitutional population	21,483	22,166	22,231	21,483	22,008	22,047	22,108	22,166	22,231
Civilian labor force	14,434	15,304	15,268	14,535	14,984	15,251	15,249	15,313	15,355
Participation rate	67.2	69.0	68.7	67.7	68.1	69.2	69.0	69.1	69.1
Employed	13,474	14,283	14,466	13,541	14,095	14,395	14,382	14,355	14,524
Employment-population ratio	62.7	64.4	65.1	63.0	64.0	65.3	65.1	64.8	65.3
Unemployed	960	1,021	802	994	889	856	868	958	831
Unemployment rate	6.7	6.7	5.3	6.8	5.9	5.6	5.7	6.3	5.4

[1] The population figures are not adjusted for seasonal variation; therefore, identical numbers appear in the unadjusted and seasonally adjusted columns.

NOTE: Detail for the above race and Hispanic-origin groups will not sum to totals because data for the "other races" group are not presented and Hispanics are included in both the white and black population groups. Beginning in January 2000, data reflect revised population controls used in the household survey.

SOURCE: BLS News, USDL 00-144, May 5, 2000

Southwest for Mexican labor, Mexicans moved back and forth across completely open borders to work in the mines, on ranches, and on the railroad.

As the Southwest began to develop, however, and Asian immigration slowed (see above), the demand for Mexican labor increased. Barely 1,000 Mexicans immigrated to the United States between 1891 and 1900. The need for Mexican labor, however, was so great that during World War I the Immigration and Naturalization Service exempted many Mexicans from meeting most immigration conditions, such as head taxes (paying a small amount to enter the country) and literacy requirements. Between 1921 and 1930, approximately 460,000 Mexicans came, primarily in search of work. While legal immigration rose, a large amount of illegal immigration also occurred. Some historians estimate that during the 1920s there were more illegal Mexican aliens than legal immigrants in the country.

During the Great Depression of the 1930s, when jobs became scarce, many Americans blamed the nation's unemployment on the illegal aliens. As a result, thousands of Mexicans, both legal immigrants and illegal aliens, were "repatriated" (sent home). During this time, the Mexican population in the United States fell by almost one-half.

When World War II began in Europe in 1939, the United States needed workers to help in its role of supplier to the Allies. When the lure of better-paying factory jobs brought many rural workers to the city, the nation looked to Mexico to fill the need for agricultural workers. The Bracero Program (1942–64) permitted entry of Mexican farm workers on a temporary contract basis with U.S. employers. While the program was considered an alternative to illegal immigration, it probably contributed to it since there were more workers who wanted to participate in the program than there were openings.

In the 1980s there was a surge of Mexican immigrants to the United States when the Mexican economy suffered a major downturn. Hispanics accounted for approximately one of every three legal immigrants to the United States during this period. In addition, experts estimate that about 1.3 million undocumented Hispanics also entered the country in search of jobs in the 1980s. Several hundred thousand also arrived from Central America, most notably from El Salvador and Guatemala, in order to escape bloody civil wars and repressive regimes. In 1986 the Immigration Control and Reform Act (PL 99-603) gave more than 2 million Mexicans legal status in the United States. In the 1990s Hispanics from Cuba, Central and South America, and Mexico continued to enter the United States, legally and illegally, in search of jobs.

LABOR FORCE PARTICIPATION

Participation in the labor force means that a person is either employed or actively seeking employment. Those who are not looking for work because they are "going to school" or "unable to work" are not considered part of the labor force. The labor force increases with long-term growth of the population. It responds to economic forces and social trends, and its size changes with the seasons.

Black Americans

Historically, Black workers have participated in the labor force in larger proportion than Whites, primarily because Black women were more likely to be working than their White counterparts. The increased entry of White women into the labor force over the past 40 years, however, has narrowed the gap between the two races. In 1960 White women had 36.5 percent participation, compared to 48.2 percent participation among Black and other minority women. By April 2000, 60.8 percent of all White women over age 20 were in the labor force, still somewhat less than the 65.8 percent participation of

TABLE 3.2

Employment Status of the Mexican, Puerto Rican, and Cuban Origin Population

(Numbers in thousands)

Employment status, sex, and age	Total Hispanic origin[1]		Mexican origin		Puerto Rican origin		Cuban origin	
	1998	1999	1998	1999	1998	1999	1998	1999
Total								
Civilian noninstitutional population	21,070	21,650	13,216	13,582	2,080	2,058	1,062	1,141
Civilian labor force	14,317	14,665	9,096	9,267	1,249	1,269	651	714
Percent of population	67.9	67.7	68.8	68.2	60.0	61.6	61.3	62.6
Employed	13,291	13,720	8,431	8,656	1,145	1,165	612	681
Agriculture	742	734	662	666	10	7	6	6
Nonagricultural industries	12,549	12,986	7,769	7,990	1,135	1,158	606	675
Unemployed	1,026	945	664	611	104	104	39	33
Unemployment rate	7.2	6.4	7.3	6.6	8.3	8.2	6.0	4.6
Not in labor force	6,753	6,985	4,121	4,315	832	789	411	427
Men, 16 years and over								
Civilian noninstitutional population	10,734	10,713	6,937	6,939	975	946	527	568
Civilian labor force	8,571	8,546	5,660	5,637	672	657	387	426
Percent of population	79.8	79.8	81.6	81.2	68.9	69.5	73.5	75.1
Employed	8,018	8,067	5,291	5,312	615	607	371	408
Agriculture	651	642	579	582	8	6	5	4
Nonagricultural industries	7,367	7,425	4,712	4,731	607	601	366	403
Unemployed	552	480	369	324	57	50	16	19
Unemployment rate	6.4	5.6	6.5	5.8	8.5	7.6	4.1	4.4
Not in labor force	2,164	2,167	1,276	1,302	303	289	140	142
Men, 20 years and over								
Civilian noninstitutional population	9,573	9,523	6,139	6,105	872	841	499	533
Civilian labor force	8,005	7,950	5,244	5,196	632	613	372	411
Percent of population	83.6	83.5	85.4	85.1	72.4	72.9	74.6	77.2
Employed	7,570	7,576	4,959	4,948	586	574	359	396
Agriculture	621	602	551	544	8	6	5	4
Nonagricultural industries	6,949	6,974	4,408	4,404	578	568	354	392
Unemployed	436	374	285	249	46	39	13	15
Unemployment rate	5.4	4.7	5.4	4.8	7.3	6.4	3.6	3.8
Not in labor force	1,568	1,573	895	909	241	228	127	121
Women, 16 years and over								
Civilian noninstitutional population	10,335	10,937	6,280	6,643	1,105	1,112	535	573
Civilian labor force	5,746	6,119	3,435	3,630	576	611	264	287
Percent of population	55.6	55.9	54.7	54.6	52.2	55.0	49.2	50.2
Employed	5,273	5,653	3,140	3,344	529	557	241	273
Agriculture	91	92	83	84	2	1	1	2
Nonagricultural industries	5,182	5,561	3,057	3,259	528	557	240	271
Unemployed	473	466	296	287	47	54	23	14
Unemployment rate	8.2	7.6	8.6	7.9	8.2	8.8	8.6	4.8
Not in labor force	4,589	4,819	2,844	3,013	529	500	272	285
Women, 20 years and over								
Civilian noninstitutional population	9,292	9,821	5,555	5,877	1,003	1,004	509	549
Civilian labor force	5,304	5,666	3,119	3,319	530	571	252	279
Percent of population	57.1	57.7	56.1	56.5	52.8	56.9	49.6	50.8
Employed	4,928	5,290	2,897	3,092	493	529	231	266
Agriculture	85	88	77	80	2	1	1	2
Nonagricultural industries	4,843	5,202	2,820	3,012	491	528	230	263
Unemployed	376	376	221	227	37	43	22	13
Unemployment rate	7.1	6.6	7.1	6.8	7.0	7.5	8.6	4.7
Not in labor force	3,988	4,155	2,436	2,558	473	432	257	270
Both sexes, 16 to 19 years								
Civilian noninstitutional population	2,204	2,307	1,523	1,600	205	213	54	59
Civilian labor force	1,007	1,049	733	752	87	84	26	24
Percent of population	45.7	45.5	48.1	47.0	42.5	39.3	48.1	39.9
Employed	793	854	575	617	66	62	22	20
Agriculture	36	45	34	42	1	–	–	–
Nonagricultural industries	757	809	541	574	65	61	22	20
Unemployed	214	196	158	135	21	22	4	4
Unemployment rate	21.3	18.6	21.5	18.0	24.1	26.3	(2)	(2)
Not in labor force	1,197	1,257	790	848	118	129	28	36

[1] Includes persons of Central or South American origin and of other Hispanic origin, not shown separately.
[2] Data not shown where base is less than 35,000.

NOTE: Beginning in January 1999, data reflect revised population controls used in the household survey.

SOURCE: *CPS Information.* U.S. Bureau of Labor Statistics, Office of Employment and Unemployment Statistics: Washington, D.C., February 8, 2000

TABLE 3.3

Employment Status of the Civilian Noninstitutional Population by Sex, Age, Race, and Hispanic Origin

(Numbers in thousands)

Employment status, sex, and age	Total 1998	Total 1999	White 1998	White 1999	Black 1998	Black 1999	Hispanic origin 1998	Hispanic origin 1999
Total								
Civilian noninstitutional population	205,220	207,753	171,478	173,085	24,373	24,855	21,070	21,650
Civilian labor force	137,673	139,368	115,415	116,509	15,982	16,365	14,317	14,665
Percent of population	67.1	67.1	67.3	67.3	65.6	65.8	67.9	67.7
Employed	131,463	133,488	110,931	112,235	14,556	15,056	13,291	13,720
Agriculture	3,378	3,281	3,160	3,083	138	117	742	734
Nonagricultural industries	128,085	130,207	107,770	109,152	14,417	14,939	12,549	12,986
Unemployed	6,210	5,880	4,484	4,273	1,426	1,309	1,026	945
Unemployment rate	4.5	4.2	3.9	3.7	8.9	8.0	7.2	6.4
Not in labor force	67,547	68,385	56,064	56,577	8,391	8,490	6,753	6,985
Men, 16 Years and Over								
Civilian noninstitutional population	98,758	99,722	83,352	83,930	10,927	11,143	10,734	10,713
Civilian labor force	73,959	74,512	63,034	63,413	7,542	7,652	8,571	8,546
Percent of population	74.9	74.7	75.6	75.6	69.0	68.7	79.8	79.8
Employed	70,693	71,446	60,604	61,139	6,871	7,027	8,018	8,067
Agriculture	2,553	2,432	2,376	2,273	118	99	651	642
Nonagricultural industries	68,140	69,014	58,228	58,866	6,752	6,928	7,367	7,425
Unemployed	3,266	3,066	2,431	2,274	671	626	552	480
Unemployment rate	4.4	4.1	3.9	3.6	8.9	8.2	6.4	5.6
Not in labor force	24,799	25,210	20,317	20,517	3,386	3,491	2,164	2,167
Men, 20 Years and Over								
Civilian noninstitutional population	90,790	91,555	76,966	77,432	9,727	9,926	9,573	9,523
Civilian labor force	69,715	70,194	59,421	59,747	7,053	7,182	8,005	7,950
Percent of population	76.8	76.7	77.2	77.2	72.5	72.4	83.6	83.5
Employed	67,135	67,761	57,500	57,934	6,530	6,702	7,570	7,576
Agriculture	2,350	2,244	2,182	2,094	112	96	621	602
Nonagricultural industries	64,785	65,517	55,319	55,839	6,418	6,606	6,949	6,974
Unemployed	2,580	2,433	1,920	1,813	524	480	436	374
Unemployment rate	3.7	3.5	3.2	3.0	7.4	6.7	5.4	4.7
Not in labor force	21,075	21,362	17,545	17,685	2,673	2,743	1,568	1,573
Women, 16 Years and Over								
Civilian noninstitutional population	106,462	108,031	88,126	89,156	13,446	13,711	10,335	10,937
Civilian labor force	63,714	64,855	52,380	53,096	8,441	8,713	5,746	6,119
Percent of population	59.8	60.0	59.4	59.6	62.8	63.5	55.6	55.9
Employed	60,771	62,042	50,327	51,096	7,685	8,029	5,273	5,653
Agriculture	825	849	784	810	20	18	91	92
Nonagricultural industries	59,945	61,193	49,543	50,286	7,665	8,011	5,182	5,561
Unemployed	2,944	2,814	2,053	1,999	756	684	473	466
Unemployment rate	4.6	4.3	3.9	3.8	9.0	7.8	8.2	7.6
Not in labor force	42,748	43,175	35,746	36,060	5,005	4,999	4,589	4,819
Women, 20 Years and Over								
Civilian noninstitutional population	98,786	100,158	82,073	82,953	12,203	12,451	9,292	9,821
Civilian labor force	59,702	60,840	49,029	49,714	7,912	8,224	5,304	5,666
Percent of population	60.4	60.7	59.7	59.9	64.8	66.1	57.1	57.7
Employed	57,278	58,555	47,342	48,098	7,290	7,663	4,928	5,290
Agriculture	768	803	729	765	19	17	85	88
Nonagricultural industries	56,510	57,752	46,612	47,333	7,272	7,646	4,843	5,202
Unemployed	2,424	2,285	1,688	1,616	622	561	376	376
Unemployment rate	4.1	3.8	3.4	3.3	7.9	6.8	7.1	6.6
Not in labor force	39,084	39,318	33,044	33,239	4,291	4,226	3,988	4,155
Both Sexes, 16 to 19 Years								
Civilian noninstitutional population	15,644	16,040	12,439	12,700	2,443	2,479	2,204	2,307
Civilian labor force	8,256	8,333	6,965	7,048	1,017	959	1,007	1,049
Percent of population	52.8	52.0	56.0	55.5	41.6	38.7	45.7	45.5
Employed	7,051	7,172	6,089	6,204	736	691	793	854
Agriculture	261	234	250	224	8	4	36	45
Nonagricultural industries	6,790	6,938	5,839	5,980	728	687	757	809
Unemployed	1,205	1,162	876	844	281	268	214	196
Unemployment rate	14.6	13.9	12.6	12.0	27.6	27.9	21.3	18.6
Not in labor force	7,388	7,706	5,475	5,652	1,427	1,520	1,197	1,257

NOTE: Detail for the above race and Hispanic-origin groups will not sum to totals because data for the "other races" group are not presented and Hispanics are included in both the white and black population groups.

Beginning in January 1999, data reflect revised population controls used in the household survey.

SOURCE: *CPS Information.* U.S. Bureau of Labor Statistics, Office of Employment and Unemployment Statistics: Washington, D.C., February 8, 2000

TABLE 3.4

Social and Economic Characteristics of the Asian and Pacific Islander Population, 1990 and 1998

As of March (6,679 represents 6,679,000). Excludes members of Armed Forces except those living off post or with their families on post. Data for 1990 are based on 1980 census population controls; 1998 data are based on 1990 census population controls. Based on Current Population Survey.

Characteristic	Number (1,000)		Percent distribution	
	1990	1998	1990	1998
Total persons	**6,679**	**10,492**	**100.0**	**100.0**
Under 5 years old	602	882	9.0	8.4
5 to 14 years old	1,112	1,727	16.6	16.4
15 to 44 years old	3,345	5,230	50.1	49.8
45 to 64 years old	1,155	1,950	17.3	18.5
65 years old and over	465	705	7.0	6.7
Educational Attainment				
Persons 25 years old and over	3,961	6,381	100.0	100.0
Elementary: 0 to 8 years	543	570	13.7	8.9
High school: 1 to 3 years	234	[1]397	5.9	[1]6.2
4 years	1,038	[2]1,466	26.2	[2]23.0
College: 1 to 3 years	568	[3]1,264	14.3	[3]19.8
4 years or more	1,578	[4]2,684	39.9	[4]42.1
Labor Force Status[5]				
Civilians 16 years old and over	4,849	7,689	100.0	100.0
Civilian labor force	3,216	5,263	66.3	68.5
Employed	3,079	5,023	63.5	65.3
Unemployed	136	240	2.8	3.1
Unemployment rate [6]	4.2	4.6	(X)	(X)
Not in labor force	1,634	2,425	33.7	31.5
Family Type				
Total families	1,531	2,381	100.0	100.0
Married couple	1,256	1,946	82.1	81.7
Female householder, no spouse present	188	278	12.3	11.7
Male householder, no spouse present	86	157	5.6	6.6
Family Income In Previous Year In Constant (1997) Dollars				
Total families	1,531	2,381	100.0	100.0
Less than $5,000	(NA)	69	(NA)	2.9
$5,000 to $9,999	(NA)	64	(NA)	2.7
$10,000 to $14,999	(NA)	126	(NA)	5.3
$15,000 to $24,999	(NA)	219	(NA)	9.2
$25,000 to $34,999	(NA)	233	(NA)	9.8
$35,000 to $49,999	(NA)	424	(NA)	17.8
$50,000 or more	(NA)	1,243	(NA)	52.2
Median income [7]	52,229	51,850	(X)	(X)
Poverty				
Families below poverty level [8]	182	244	11.9	10.2
Persons below poverty level [8]	938	1,468	14.1	14.0
Housing Tenure				
Total occupied units	1,988	3,125	100.0	100.0
Owner-occupied	977	1,650	49.1	52.8
Renter-occupied	982	1,438	49.4	46.0
No cash rent	30	37	1.5	1.2

NA Not available.   X Not applicable.

[1] Represents those who completed 9th to 12th grade but have no high school diploma.

[2] High school graduate.

[3] Some college or associate degree.

[4] Bachelor's or advanced degree.

[5] Data beginning 1994 not directly comparable with earlier years.

[6] Total unemployment as percent of civilian labor force.

SOURCE: *Statistical Abstract of the United States.* U.S. Bureau of the Census: Washington, D.C., 1999

FIGURE 3.1

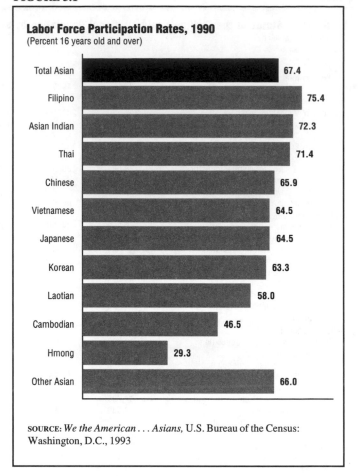

Labor Force Participation Rates, 1990
(Percent 16 years old and over)

Total Asian	67.4
Filipino	75.4
Asian Indian	72.3
Thai	71.4
Chinese	65.9
Vietnamese	64.5
Japanese	64.5
Korean	63.3
Laotian	58.0
Cambodian	46.5
Hmong	29.3
Other Asian	66.0

SOURCE: *We the American... Asians,* U.S. Bureau of the Census: Washington, D.C., 1993

past 50 years. In 1948, 87 percent of all Black males 20 years and older were employed or actively looking for work. By 1970 that share had fallen to 76.5 percent, and by April 2000 it had dropped to 73 percent. In comparison, 77 percent of all White males 20 years and older were in the labor force in April 2000. The overall participation rate for Blacks was 66.2 percent, compared with 67.8 percent among all Whites. (See Table 3.1.)

Hispanic Americans

The Bureau of Labor Statistics began maintaining annual employment data on Hispanics in 1973. In April 2000, overall, 69.1 percent of Hispanics participated in the labor force. (See Table 3.1.) At the end of the first quarter of 1999, Mexican Americans had the highest overall participation (68.2 percent), followed by Cuban Americans (62.6 percent), and Puerto Ricans (61.6 percent). (See Table 3.2.)

In 1999 among males 20 years and over, Hispanics had the greatest labor force participation at 83.5 percent, compared to 77.2 percent for White males and 72.4 percent for Black men. On the other hand, 57.7 percent of Hispanic females 20 years and older were in the labor force in 1999, compared to 59.9 percent of White females and 66.1 per-

Black women over age 20. (See Table 3.1, which gives monthly figures.)

On the other hand, the labor force participation rate of Black men 20 years and older has declined over the

cent of Black females. (See Table 3.3.) Although the proportion of Hispanic females in the labor force in 1999 was still lower than that of non-Hispanic women, it has increased since 1983, when fewer than half of Hispanic women (47 percent) were in the civilian labor force.

Asian Americans

In 1998 over two-thirds (68.5 percent) of Asians/Pacific Islanders (APIs) age 16 and over were in the civilian labor force. (See Table 3.4.) In 1999 a similar proportion (66 percent) of APIs were in the civilian labor force.

The U.S. government is just beginning to keep detailed statistics on the social conditions of APIs, so complete data are not as readily available as they are for Blacks and Hispanics. In 1990, among different Asian American populations, Filipinos had the highest labor force participation (75.4 percent), followed by Asian Indians (72.3 percent). The Hmong (29.3 percent) and Cambodians (46.5 percent) had the lowest level of labor force participation. Immigrants from Cambodia and Laos often have the least education and come from rural backgrounds that have not prepared them for life in the United States. (See Figure 3.1.)

Young adult APIs (ages 16–24) are the least likely minority group to be exclusively in the labor force, but are the most likely to be attending school only. In 1991 half (49 percent) of young adult Asian Americans were attending school, and an additional 19 percent were in school and working, while just 21 percent were working only. In contrast, four of 10 of young non-Hispanic Whites and Hispanics and 36 percent of young Blacks and Native Americans were working only. In 1998, seven in 10 non-Hispanic APIs ages 18 to 24 attended college, compared to half of non-Hispanic Whites.

At the opposite end of the age scale, APIs are somewhat less likely to retire from the labor force than their White counterparts. In 1990 more than three out of five (62 percent) APIs ages 55 to 64 were still in the workforce, compared to 57 percent of Whites. At age 65 and older, 16 percent of APIs were still in the labor force, compared to 12 percent of White Americans.

Older APIs tend to work longer because of the strong work ethic in Asian cultures and frequently because of economic need. Often they are employed in family businesses that do not offer early retirement packages. Depending on the time of their immigration and their work history, APIs age 65 and older may not be entitled to adequate Social Security benefits. Also, some may have immigrated under circumstances that prevented them from retaining any wealth they might have accumulated in their native lands.

FIGURE 3.2

SOURCE: *We the ... First Americans,* U.S. Bureau of the Census: Washington, D.C., 1993

Native Americans

Gathering accurate statistical data on the labor force participation rates of Native Americans/Alaska Natives is very difficult. They are often counted as "other" in Bureau of Labor Statistics and Census Bureau data, so specific information is hard to obtain. In addition, Native American data are updated only every 10 years during the national census. Based on the 1990 population count, the Census Bureau found that somewhat smaller percentages of the American Indian, Eskimo, and Aleut population were in the labor force than the total population. Compared to the rest of the population (74.4 percent participation), 69.4 percent of Native American males were in the labor force. The participation rate for Native American females increased from 48 percent in 1980 to 55.1 percent in 1990, only slightly less than the rate for all women at 56.8 percent. (See Figure 3.2.)

About 22 percent of Native Americans live on reservations and trust lands. In 1990 labor force participation varied among the different reservations from a high of 86.2 percent for the Zuni Pueblo of Arizona and New Mexico, to a low of 64.7 percent at Fort Apache, Arizona. (See Figure 3.3.)

UNEMPLOYMENT

The Bureau of Labor Statistics bases its unemployment data on the *Current Population Survey,* which samples about 60,000 households each month. To be classified as unemployed, a person must:

• Not have worked in the week specified for the survey

FIGURE 3.3

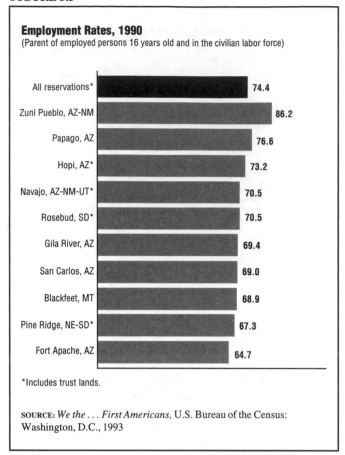

Employment Rates, 1990
(Parent of employed persons 16 years old and in the civilian labor force)

All reservations*	74.4
Zuni Pueblo, AZ-NM	86.2
Papago, AZ	76.6
Hopi, AZ*	73.2
Navajo, AZ-NM-UT*	70.5
Rosebud, SD*	70.5
Gila River, AZ	69.4
San Carlos, AZ	69.0
Blackfeet, MT	68.9
Pine Ridge, NE-SD*	67.3
Fort Apache, AZ	64.7

*Includes trust lands.

SOURCE: *We the . . . First Americans,* U.S. Bureau of the Census: Washington, D.C., 1993

• Have actively sought work sometime during the four weeks preceding the survey

• Be currently available to take a suitable job

In April 2000 approximately 6 million persons were unemployed in the United States. Minorities accounted for a large share of the unemployed—over 1 million were Black and 831,000 were Hispanic. (See Table 3.1.)

Black Americans

Although unemployment rates rise and fall with the strength of the economy, the unemployment rates for Blacks have run twice as high as for Whites for several decades. Blacks are more likely to remain unemployed for longer periods and account for nearly 30 percent of the long-term unemployed—those without work for at least 27 weeks.

In April 2000 the unemployment rate for Black men 20 years and over (6.6 percent) was more than double that of White men (2.8 percent) in the same age group. Black females age 20 and over (5.8 percent) had nearly twice the unemployment rate as White females (3.1 percent) 20 years and over. (See Table 3.1.)

Large numbers of Blacks are classified as discouraged workers—persons not in the labor force who want jobs but

have stopped looking because they do not think they can find them. Discouraged workers are not included among the unemployment figures. In some inner-city communities, the lure of "easy money" from drug dealing or other illegal activities attracts potential workers, causing unemployment figures to understate the number of Blacks without legitimate jobs. The unemployment figure also does not include those who are imprisoned (more than half of all inmates in state and federal prisons are Black).

HIGH UNEMPLOYMENT AMONG YOUNG BLACKS. In April 2000 the unemployment rate for Black teens ages 16 to 19 was 22.2 percent, down from 27.8 percent a year earlier, while the unemployment rate for White teens was about 11.6 percent in April 2000, down from 12.1 percent in 1999. (See Table 3.1.) Despite the downward trend of unemployment since mid-1992, Black teenagers continue to suffer the highest incidence of unemployment of all major groups. The unemployment rate among young Blacks who have not finished high school is particularly alarming since this higher unemployment rate among high school dropouts continues into adulthood. In May 2000 the unemployment rate of Blacks who were not enrolled in school and had no high school diploma was 34.4 percent, compared to an overall rate of 16 percent for the general population without a high school diploma. (See Table 3.5.)

Hispanic Americans

The unemployment rate for Hispanics over the age of 16 dropped significantly from 16.5 percent in 1983 to a low of 7.8 percent in 1989. The rate increased, however, to 11.9 percent in 1993. Hispanics were more likely to be unemployed than non-Hispanics in 1983 (10.6 percent), as well as in 1993 (7.1 percent). (See Figure 3.4.) The unemployment rate for Hispanics in April 2000 was 5.4 percent, down from 6.8 percent the previous year. (See Table 3.1.)

The Puerto Rican-origin population had the highest rate of unemployment in 1999 at 8.2 percent. Cuban Americans had the lowest rate of unemployment (4.6 percent), compared to 6.6 percent for Mexican Americans. (See Table 3.2.)

Asian Americans

Unemployment figures for Asian Americans are similar to those for non-Hispanic Whites. In 1990 the unemployment rate for Asians/Pacific Islanders was 5.3 percent, somewhat below the 6.3 percent figure for the U.S. population. The low rate of unemployment among Asian Americans can be attributed, in part, to their high educational attainment and their commitment to small family businesses. Japanese Americans had the lowest unemployment rate of any group, with a rate of 2.5 percent. Hmong Americans, many of whom are illiterate, had a very high unemployment rate of 17.9 percent. (See Table 3.6.)

TABLE 3.5

Employment Status of the Noninstitutional Population 16 to 24 Years of Age by School Enrollment, Educational Attainment, Sex, Race, and Hispanic Origin
(Numbers in thousands)

Enrollment status, educational attainment, race, and Hispanic origin	Civilian noninstitutional population	Total	Percent of population	May 2000 Civilian labor force						
				Employed			Unemployed			
				Total	Full time	Part time	Total	Looking for full-time work	Looking for part-time work	Percent of labor force
TOTAL NOT ENROLLED										
Total, 16 to 24 years	**16,518**	**13,628**	**82.5**	**12,353**	**10,525**	**1,828**	**1,275**	**1,121**	**154**	**9.4**
16 to 19 years	3,606	2,728	75.7	2,350	1,732	618	378	316	62	13.9
20 to 24 years	12,912	10,900	84.4	10,003	8,793	1,210	897	805	92	8.2
Less than a high school diploma	4,257	2,973	69.8	2,497	2,026	471	476	422	55	16.0
High school graduates, no college	6,904	5,821	84.3	5,281	4,500	782	539	479	61	9.3
Less than a bachelor's degree	3,822	3,401	89.0	3,206	2,701	505	195	163	32	5.7
College graduates	1,535	1,434	93.4	1,369	1,298	71	64	58	6	4.5
Men, 16 to 24 years	8,331	7,403	88.9	6,738	6,067	672	665	596	69	9.0
16 to 19 years	1,823	1,484	81.4	1,301	1,034	267	183	157	26	12.3
20 to 24 years	6,508	5,919	91.0	5,437	5,032	405	483	439	43	8.2
Less than a high school diploma	2,384	1,970	82.6	1,689	1,452	237	281	255	27	14.3
High school graduates, no college	3,582	3,216	89.8	2,943	2,700	243	273	254	19	8.5
Less than a bachelor's degree	1,759	1,629	92.6	1,550	1,372	177	79	61	18	4.9
College graduates	605	589	97.3	557	543	15	32	26	6	5.4
Women, 16 to 24 years	8,187	6,225	76.0	5,615	4,459	1,156	610	526	84	9.8
16 to 19 years	1,783	1,245	69.8	1,049	698	351	195	160	36	15.7
20 to 24 years	6,404	4,980	77.8	4,566	3,761	805	414	366	49	8.3
Less than a high school diploma	1,873	1,003	53.6	808	574	234	195	167	28	19.4
High school graduates, no college	3,321	2,605	78.4	2,339	1,800	539	266	225	42	10.2
Less than a bachelor's degree	2,063	1,772	85.9	1,656	1,329	327	116	101	15	6.5
College graduates	930	845	90.8	812	755	57	33	33	-	3.9
White										
Total, 16 to 24 years	**13,255**	**11,230**	**84.7**	**10,386**	**8,888**	**1,498**	**844**	**739**	**105**	**7.5**
16 to 19 years	2,899	2,310	79.7	2,013	1,505	509	297	251	47	12.9
20 to 24 years	10,357	8,919	86.1	8,373	7,383	989	546	488	58	6.1
Men	6,825	6,308	92.4	5,879	5,326	554	428	382	46	6.8
Women	6,430	4,922	76.5	4,506	3,562	944	415	356	59	8.4
Less than a high school diploma	3,397	2,496	73.5	2,164	1,763	400	332	295	37	13.3
High school graduates, no college	5,347	4,630	86.6	4,320	3,711	609	310	267	43	6.7
Less than a bachelor's degree	3,225	2,886	89.5	2,736	2,306	431	150	131	18	5.2
College graduates	1,287	1,217	94.6	1,166	1,108	58	51	45	6	4.2

TABLE 3.5

Employment Status of the Noninstitutional Population 16 to 24 Years of Age by School Enrollment, Educational Attainment, Sex, Race, and Hispanic Origin [CONTINUED]

(Numbers in thousands)

Enrollment status, educational attainment, race, and Hispanic origin	Civilian noninstitutional population		May 2000 Civilian labor force						
			Employed			Unemployed			
	Total	Percent of population	Total	Full time	Part time	Total	Looking for full-time work	Looking for part-time work	Percent of labor force
Black									
Total, 16 to 24 years	**2,615**	**72.7**	**1,520**	**1,261**	**259**	**382**	**344**	**39**	**20.1**
16 to 19 years	581	57.8	266	167	99	70	60	10	20.9
20 to 24 years	2,034	77.0	1,254	1,094	160	312	283	29	19.9
Men	1,211	70.5	641	542	99	213	192	21	24.9
Women	1,404	74.7	879	719	160	169	152	17	16.1
Less than a high school diploma	751	52.8	260	201	59	136	119	17	34.4
High school graduates, no college	1,309	76.9	796	646	150	212	197	14	21.0
Less than a bachelor's degree	448	88.2	363	322	41	32	25	7	8.1
College graduates	107	97.0	102	92	10	2	2	-	2.3
Hispanic origin									
Total, 16 to 24 years	**3,051**	**79.4**	**2,206**	**1,958**	**248**	**218**	**191**	**26**	**9.0**
16 to 19 years	798	75.8	529	450	79	76	67	9	12.6
20 to 24 years	2,253	80.7	1,677	1,508	169	141	124	17	7.8
Men	1,599	91.2	1,357	1,261	96	102	90	12	7.0
Women	1,452	66.4	849	697	152	115	101	14	12.0
Less than a high school diploma	1,577	74.8	1,048	911	138	131	114	17	11.1
High school graduates, no college	1,029	83.9	785	705	80	78	69	9	9.0
Less than a bachelor's degree	368	84.4	302	275	27	9	9	-	2.8
College graduates	77	91.4	70	67	3	-	-	-	(1)

[1]Data not shown where base is less than 75,000.

NOTE: In the summer months, the educational attainment levels of youth not enrolled in school are increased by the temporary movement of high school and college students into that group. Detail for the above race and Hispanic-origin groups will not sum to totals because data for the "other races" group are not presented and Hispanics are included in both the white and black population groups. Beginning in January 2000, data reflect revised population controls used in the household survey.

SOURCE: Labor Force Statistics, Monthly Tables from Employment and Earnings

FIGURE 3.4

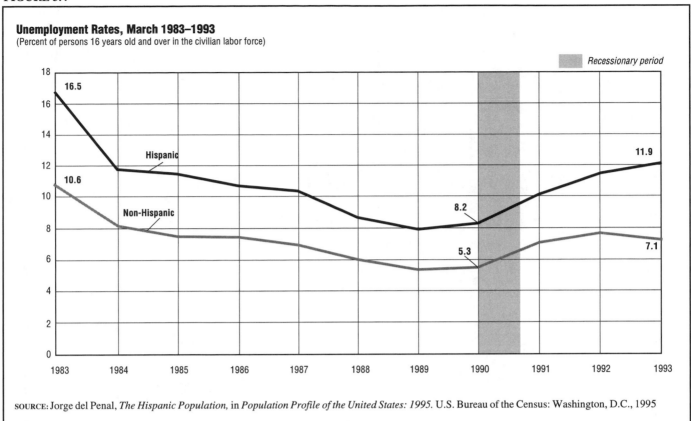

Unemployment Rates, March 1983–1993
(Percent of persons 16 years old and over in the civilian labor force)

SOURCE: Jorge del Penal, *The Hispanic Population*, in *Population Profile of the United States: 1995*. U.S. Bureau of the Census: Washington, D.C., 1995

Native Americans

It is as difficult to determine the unemployment rate for Native Americans as it is to determine the employment rate. Based on data from the Bureau of Indian Affairs (BIA), the proportion of those unemployed and seeking work ranges from 12 percent in Texas to 74 percent in South Dakota. It should be noted that the population served by the BIA in South Dakota is 58,000, compared to only 1,320 in Texas. Those served by the BIA usually live either on or adjacent to reservations, especially in South Dakota, and, in most cases, reservations do not generate jobs necessary to support American Indian families. This is a major reason that the leadership on American Indian reservations has been so quick to introduce or expand gambling on their reservations.

PROJECTIONS FOR THE YEAR 2008

The U.S. Bureau of Labor Statistics projected that more Hispanics than Blacks will enter the workforce between 1998 and 2008, making the two groups almost equal in size. The number of Blacks in the labor force will increase 19.5 percent. They will total more than 19.1 million workers and will represent 12.4 percent of the workforce. The participation rate among Hispanics is expected to grow 36.8 percent from 1998. They will number 19.6 million workers and are expected to make up 12.7 percent of the labor force in 2008, up from 10.4 percent in 1998. (See Table 3.7.) The growth of Hispanics in the workforce can be attributed to higher birth rates and increased immigration.

The proportion of "Asian and other" (which includes Asians, Pacific Islanders, American Indians, and Alaska Natives) in the labor force is expected to increase 40.3 percent between 1998 and 2008. Even growth of that proportion would still make this group only 5.7 percent of the labor force, up from 4.6 percent in 1998. (See Table 3.7.) As with most other minority groups, increases reflect continued high immigration and higher fertility rates.

The non-Hispanic White labor force is expected to grow more slowly than the overall labor force, causing the White proportion to decrease slightly from 73.9 percent in 1998 to 70.7 percent in 2008. (See Table 3.7.) The decrease is due to a relatively low immigration rate, projected lower birth rates, and declining participation by men, a reflection of the aging of the White male labor force.

TABLE 3.6

Selected Social and Economic Characteristics for the Asian Population, 1990

[Data for total persons, age, sex and type of family are based on l00-percent tabulations. Remaining data are based on sample tabulations]

Characteristics	United States	Asian and Pacific Islander	Asian Total	Chinese	Filipino	Japanese	Korean	Asian Indian	Vietnamese	Cambodian	Laotian	Hmong	Thai	Other
LABOR FORCE STATUS														
Persons 16 years old and over	191,829,271	5,403,615	5,167,530	1,309,042	1,078,817	724,683	579,867	576,157	423,121	85,500	87,683	40,649	71,907	190,104
Labor force	125,182,378	3,645,946	3,480,409	863,285	813,766	467,346	367,146	416,404	273,098	39,793	50,869	11,923	51,359	125,420
Percent in labor force	65.3	67.5	67.4	65.9	75.4	64.5	63.3	72.3	64.5	46.5	58.0	29.3	71.4	66.0
Civilian labor force	123,473,450	3,603,080	3,444,188	860,688	790,869	463,770	364,680	415,346	271,587	39,704	50,703	11,890	50,717	124,234
Percent unemployed	6.3	5.3	5.2	4.7	5.1	2.5	5.2	5.6	8.4	10.3	9.3	17.9	5.3	6.8
Females 16 years old and over	99,803,358	2,810,588	2,692,480	664,384	599,208	399,585	333,225	260,532	199,310	45,754	42,044	20,265	44,917	83,256
Labor force	56,672,949	1,688,145	1,614,323	393,077	433,262	221,857	185,078	152,718	111,282	17,080	20,799	4,039	30,268	44,863
Percent in labor force	56.8	60.1	60.0	59.2	72.3	55.5	55.5	58.6	55.8	37.3	49.5	19.9	67.4	53.9
Civilian labor force	56,487,249	1,684,082	1,610,906	392,696	431,564	221,299	184,719	152,621	111,170	17,080	20,786	4,039	30,201	44,731
Percent unemployed	6.2	5.5	5.5	5.0	4.7	2.7	6.1	7.6	8.9	9.9	9.3	19.0	6.2	7.7
OCCUPATION														
Employed persons 16 years old and over	115,681,202	3,411,586	3,264,268	819,932	750,613	452,005	345,655	391,949	248,881	35,623	46,010	9,756	48,028	115,816
Percent	100.0	100.0	100.0	100.0	100.0	100.0	100.0	100.0	100.0	100.0	100.0	100.0	100.0	100.0
Managerial and professional specialty	26.4	30.6	31.2	35.8	26.6	37.0	25.5	43.6	17.6	9.8	5.0	12.8	23.6	31.9
Technical, sales, and administrative support	31.7	33.2	33.3	31.2	36.7	34.4	37.1	33.2	29.5	23.3	15.2	18.9	26.5	33.6
Service	13.2	14.8	14.6	16.5	16.8	11.1	15.1	8.1	15.0	17.9	14.6	20.0	26.8	14.0
Farming, forestry, and fishing	2.5	1.2	1.1	0.4	1.5	2.7	0.7	0.6	1.4	1.7	1.5	2.3	0.7	0.8
Precision production, craft, and repair	11.3	8.0	7.8	5.6	7.4	7.8	8.9	5.2	15.7	17.2	19.8	13.9	7.5	7.3
Operators, fabricators, and laborers	14.9	12.1	11.9	10.6	11.0	6.9	12.8	9.4	20.9	30.0	43.9	32.1	15.0	12.4
WORKERS IN FAMILY IN 1989														
Families	65,049,428	1,577,820	1,506,724	389,818	293,229	208,165	163,149	192,836	118,309	28,185	28,592	14,374	16,710	53,357
Percent	100.0	100.0	100.0	100.0	100.0	100.0	100.0	100.0	100.0	100.0	100.0	100.0	100.0	100.0
No workers	13.0	8.3	8.3	7.9	4.1	8.7	7.6	2.8	13.6	38.1	26.7	49.9	5.0	7.7
1 worker	28.0	26.2	26.2	25.5	18.1	33.2	31.8	27.7	25.1	20.7	18.7	28.0	26.2	34.5
2 workers	45.6	45.7	45.7	47.6	48.2	42.9	44.8	51.8	40.0	27.7	35.7	15.4	53.3	43.4
3 or more workers	13.4	19.8	19.8	19.0	29.6	15.3	15.9	17.8	21.3	13.5	18.9	6.7	15.5	14.4
INCOME IN 1989														
Median household (dollars)	30,056	36,784	37,007	36,259	43,780	41,626	30,184	44,696	29,772	18,837	23,019	14,276	31,632	30,010
Median family (dollars)	35,225	(NA)	41,583	41,316	46,698	51,550	33,909	49,309	30,550	18,126	23,101	14,327	37,257	34,242
Per capita (dollars)	14,143	13,638	13,806	14,876	13,616	19,373	11,177	17,777	9,032	5,120	5,597	2,692	11,970	11,000
INCOME IN 1989 BELOW POVERTY LEVEL														
Families in poverty	6,487,515	182,507	171,816	43,184	15,267	7,131	24,037	13,964	28,131	11,872	9,207	8,885	1,806	8,332
Percent	10.0	11.6	11.4	11.1	5.2	3.4	14.7	7.2	23.8	42.1	32.2	61.8	10.8	15.6
Persons in poverty	31,742,864	997,196	938,930	225,777	89,081	59,127	106,822	74,972	149,567	62,312	50,580	59,530	11,178	49,984
Percent	13.1	14.1	14.0	14.0	6.4	7.0	13.7	9.7	25.7	42.6	34.7	63.6	12.5	18.2

NA Not available.

SOURCE: *We the American . . . Asians.* U.S. Bureau of the Census: Washington, D.C., 1993

TABLE 3.7

Civilian Labor Force 16 Years and Older by Sex, Age, Race, and Hispanic Origin, 1988, 1998, and Projected 2008
[Numbers in thousands]

Group	Level			Change		Percent change		Percent distribution		
	1988	1998	2008	1988-98	1998-2008	1988-98	1998-2008	1988	1998	2008
Total	121,669	137,673	154,576	16,004	16,903	13.2	12.3	100.0	100.0	100.0
Men	66,927	73,959	81,132	7,032	7,173	10.5	9.7	55.0	53.7	52.5
Women	54,742	63,714	73,444	8,972	9,729	16.4	15.3	45.0	46.3	47.5
Age 16 to 24	22,536	21,894	25,210	-642	3,316	-2.8	15.1	18.5	15.9	16.3
Age 25 to 54	84,041	98,718	104,133	14,677	5,415	17.5	5.5	69.1	71.7	67.4
Age 55 and older	15,092	17,062	25,233	1,970	8,171	13.1	47.9	12.4	12.4	16.3
White	104,756	115,415	126,665	10,659	11,251	10.2	9.7	86.1	83.8	81.9
Black	13,205	15,982	19,101	2,777	3,119	21.0	19.5	10.9	11.6	12.4
Asian and other[1]	3,708	6,278	8,809	2,570	2,531	69.3	40.3	3.0	4.6	5.7
Hispanic origin[2]	8,982	14,317	19,585	5,335	5,268	59.4	36.8	7.4	10.4	12.7
Other than Hispanic origin[2]	112,687	123,356	134,991	10,669	11,635	9.5	9.4	92.6	89.6	87.3
White non-Hispanic[2]	96,141	101,767	109,216	5,626	7,449	5.9	7.3	79.0	73.9	70.7

[1]The "Asian and other" group includes (1) Asians and Pacific Islanders and (2) American Indians and Alaska Natives.
 The historical data are derived by subtracting "black" from the "black and other" group; projections are made directly, not by subtraction.

[2]Data by Hispanic origin are not available before 1980.

SOURCE: *BLS Releases New 1998-2008 Employment Projections*, BLS News, USDL 99-339, U.S. Bureau of Labor Statistics: Washington, D.C., November 30, 1999

CHAPTER 4
OCCUPATIONS

BLACK AMERICANS AND JOBS

There were few noticeable changes in the occupational situations of Black Americans during the 1990s. Blacks are only two-thirds as likely as Whites to hold managerial and professional positions. In 1999 only 24.5 percent of all employed Black women and 18 percent of Black men were managers and professionals, compared to 33.4 percent of employed White women and 29.5 percent of White men. (See Table 4.1.)

Blacks are nearly twice as likely to work in service occupations. Any growth in professional employment has generally occurred in fields at the lower end of the earnings scale—particularly among social and recreational workers, engineering and science technicians, vocational and educational counselors, practical nurses, and health technologists. These were the same jobs held by large numbers of Black workers over a decade ago.

In 1999 Black workers were concentrated in three general occupational groupings: technical, sales, and administrative support (28.9 percent); service occupations (21.8 percent); and operators, fabricators, and laborers (18.9 percent)—primarily lower-wage occupations. Only 7.8 percent worked in precision production, craft, and repair—generally higher-wage technical occupations. (See Table 4.1.)

In 1999, in occupations involving technical, sales, and administrative support, 19.4 percent of Blacks were clinical laboratory technologists and technicians, and 18.4 percent were licensed practical nurses. Of Blacks working in personal service occupations, 25 percent were barbers and 30 percent were welfare service aides. In private household service occupations, 17.6 percent of Blacks worked as cleaners and servants. In cleaning and building service jobs, 46.4 percent were employed as maids and janitors. In protective service jobs, one-fourth (24.9 percent) of Blacks served as officers of correctional institutions. In the health service sector, Blacks made up 35.6 percent of nursing aides, orderlies, and attendants.

Within various job categories, Blacks tend to be in the lower-paying jobs. In 1999 for example, 11.4 percent of all Black managers were in personnel, training, and labor-relations positions. Within the health assessment and treatment occupations, 19.5 percent of Black professionals were dieticians, and 17.6 percent were respiratory therapists. The majority of Black women in managerial and professional occupations continue to be in the lower-paid fields of teaching, social work, and nursing.

In the fields of precision production, craft, and repair, 19.4 percent of Blacks were concrete and terrazzo finishers, and 15.7 percent were brick masons and stonemasons. Blacks made up 24 percent of taxicab drivers and chauffeurs and 24.5 percent of bus drivers.

At the other end of the occupational spectrum, Blacks were only 5.7 percent of all physicians, 7.5 percent of all mathematical and computer scientists, 4.6 percent of engineers, and 5 percent of lawyers. About 6 percent each of economists, college/university professors, and technical writers were Black. The proportion of Black Americans in managerial and professional jobs, however, increased from 16.5 percent in 1991 to 21.5 percent in 1999.

HISPANIC AMERICANS AND JOBS

Significant occupational differences exist among Hispanic subgroups. While, overall, Hispanics are slightly less likely than Blacks to hold professional and technical positions, a considerable proportion of Cuban Americans hold such jobs. As in all groups of women, a large proportion of Hispanic women work in clerical positions. Like Blacks, Hispanics, with the exception of the Cuban Americans who came to this country following the Cuban Revolution, are concentrated primarily in low-paying, low-skill jobs.

During the first quarter of 2000, Hispanics represented 12.7 percent of the total civilian labor force age 16 and over. (See Table 4.2.) One-quarter (21 percent) of Hispan-

TABLE 4.1

Employed Persons by Occupation, Race, and Sex
(Percent distribution)

Occupation and race	Total		Men		Women	
	1998	1999	1998	1999	1998	1999
TOTAL						
Total, 16 years and over (thousands)	131,463	133,488	70,693	71,446	60,771	62,042
Percent	100.0	100.0	100.0	100.0	100.0	100.0
Managerial and professional specialty	29.6	30.3	28.1	28.6	31.4	32.3
Executive, administrative, and managerial	14.5	14.7	15.0	15.0	13.9	14.2
Professional specialty	15.1	15.6	13.1	13.6	17.4	18.0
Technical, sales, and administrative support	29.3	29.2	19.5	19.7	40.7	40.0
Technicians and related support	3.2	3.3	2.8	2.9	3.8	3.6
Sales occupations	12.1	12.1	11.1	11.3	13.1	13.0
Administrative support, including clerical	14.0	13.8	5.6	5.5	23.8	23.4
Service occupations	13.6	13.4	10.2	9.9	17.5	17.4
Private household	6	.6	.1	.1	1.3	1.3
Protective service	1.8	1.8	2.8	2.8	.7	.7
Service, except private household and protective	11.1	11.0	7.3	7.1	15.4	15.4
Precision production, craft, and repair	11.0	10.9	18.7	18.6	2.0	2.1
Operators, fabricators, and laborers	13.9	13.6	19.5	19.3	7.4	7.0
Machine operators, assemblers, and inspectors	5.9	5.5	6.9	6.5	4.8	4.4
Transportation and material moving occupations	4.1	4.1	6.8	7.0	.9	.9
Handlers, equipment cleaners, helpers, and laborers	3.9	3.9	5.8	5.9	1.7	1.7
Farming, forestry, and fishing	2.7	2.6	4.0	3.8	1.1	1.1
White						
Total, 16 years and over (thousands)	110,931	112,235	60,604	61,139	50,327	51,096
Percent	100.0	100.0	100.0	100.0	100.0	100.0
Managerial and professional specialty	30.7	31.3	29.1	29.5	32.6	33.4
Executive, administrative, and managerial	15.2	15.4	15.8	15.9	14.6	14.7
Professional specialty	15.5	15.9	13.3	13.6	18.1	18.7
Technical, sales, and administrative support	29.3	29.2	19.5	19.7	41.1	40.6
Technicians and related support	3.2	3.2	2.7	2.9	3.8	3.6
Sales occupations	12.4	12.4	11.5	11.7	13.4	13.3
Administrative support, including clerical	13.7	13.5	5.2	5.1	24.0	23.6
Service occupations	12.4	12.2	9.2	8.9	16.3	16.2
Private household	6	.6	.1	(1)	1.3	1.3
Protective service	1.7	1.7	2.6	2.6	.6	.6
Service, except private household and protective	10.1	10.0	6.5	6.3	14.4	14.3
Precision production, craft, and repair	11.5	11.5	19.4	19.4	1.9	2.1
Operators, fabricators, and laborers	13.2	13.0	18.5	18.3	6.8	6.5
Machine operators, assemblers, and inspectors	5.5	5.2	6.6	6.2	4.3	4.0
Transportation and material moving occupations	3.9	4.0	6.5	6.6	.8	.8
Handlers, equipment cleaners, helpers, and laborers	3.7	3.8	5.4	5.5	1.6	1.7
Farming, forestry, and fishing	2.9	2.8	4.3	4.1	1.2	1.2
Black						
Total, 16 years and over (thousands)	14,556	15,056	6,871	7,027	7,685	8,029
Percent	100.0	100.0	100.0	100.0	100.0	100.0
Managerial and professional specialty	20.2	21.5	17.0	18.0	23.2	24.5
Executive, administrative, and managerial	9.4	9.9	8.6	8.5	10.1	11.1
Professional specialty	10.8	11.6	8.4	9.5	13.0	13.5
Technical, sales, and administrative support	29.3	28.9	18.3	18.4	39.1	38.2
Technicians and related support	3.0	3.1	2.5	2.7	3.5	3.5
Sales occupations	9.7	9.3	7.8	7.6	11.4	10.8
Administrative support, including clerical	16.5	16.5	8.0	8.1	24.2	23.9
Service occupations	21.6	21.8	17.8	17.4	25.0	25.6
Private household	8	.8	.1	.1	1.5	1.5
Protective service	3.2	3.2	4.8	4.9	1.7	1.8
Service, except private household and protective	17.6	17.7	12.9	12.4	21.9	22.4
Precision production, craft, and repair	8.0	7.8	14.6	14.3	2.0	2.1
Operators, fabricators, and laborers	19.7	18.9	30.1	29.8	10.4	9.4
Machine operators, assemblers, and inspectors	8.2	7.6	9.7	9.3	7.0	6.1
Transportation and material moving occupations	6.0	5.8	11.1	11.0	1.4	1.3
Handlers, equipment cleaners, helpers, and laborers	5.5	5.5	9.3	9.5	2.0	2.0
Farming, forestry, and fishing	1.2	1.1	2.2	2.2	.3	.2

[1] Less than 0.05 percent.

NOTE: Beginning in January 1999, data reflect revised population controls used in the household survey.

SOURCE: *Employment and Earnings, January 2000.* U.S. Bureau of Labor Statistics

TABLE 4.2

Employed Persons by Age, Sex, Race and Hispanic Origin
(In thousands)

Age and sex	Total		White		Black		Hispanic origin	
	1999	2000	1999	2000	1999	2000	1999	2000
Total, 16 years and over	131,759	133,935	110,926	112,580	14,752	15,143	13,436	14,253
16 to 19 years	6,624	6,773	5,730	5,846	645	655	799	852
16 to 17 years	2,483	2,532	2,173	2,196	215	224	198	262
18 to 19 years	4,141	4,240	3,557	3,649	430	431	602	591
20 to 24 years	12,501	12,911	10,431	10,76	1,464	1,581	1,832	1,942
25 years and over	112,634	114,251	94,765	95,969	12,642	12,907	10,804	11,458
25 to 54 years	95,717	96,744	79,839	80,548	11,289	11,439	9,727	10,340
55 years and over	16,917	17,507	14,926	15,421	1,353	1,468	1,077	1,118
Men, 16 years and over	70,206	71,302	60,103	60,902	6,874	7,079	7,893	8,322
16 to 19 years	3,308	3,457	2,878	2,974	297	339	446	484
16 to 17 years	1,236	1,309	1,090	1,114	98	126	95	148
18 to 19 years	2,073	2,149	1,788	1,860	199	213	351	335
20 to 24 years	6,496	6,760	5,563	5,743	625	721	1,090	1,185
25 years and over	60,402	61,084	51,662	52,185	5,952	6,020	6,357	6,654
25 to 54 years	51,057	51,446	43,331	43,586	5,333	5,339	5,716	5,993
55 years and over	9,345	9,638	8,331	8,598	619	681	641	661
Women, 16 years and over	61,552	62,633	50,822	51,678	7,877	8,063	5,543	5,930
16 to 19 years	3,316	3,315	2,852	2,872	348	316	353	369
16 to 17 years	1,248	1,223	1,083	1,083	117	98	103	113
18 to 19 years	2,068	2,092	1,768	1,789	231	218	251	255
20 to 24 years	6,004	6,150	4,868	5,022	839	860	742	758
25 years and over	52,232	53,167	43,103	43,784	6,690	6,887	4,447	4,804
25 to 54 years	44,660	45,299	36,508	36,962	5,956	6,100	4,011	4,347
55 years and over	7,572	7,869	6,595	6,822	735	787	436	457

NOTE: Beginning in January 2000, data reflect revised population controls used in the household survey.

SOURCE: *Employment and Earnings, January 2000.* U.S. Bureau of Labor Statistics

ics in the labor force were operators, fabricators, and laborers, and 14.4 percent worked in precision production, craft, and repair. Nearly 15 percent were in managerial and professional specialties.

In 1999 only 11.8 percent of Mexican-origin workers were in management and professional positions. They were more likely to be working as operators, fabricators, and laborers (23.6 percent) and act as technical, sales, and administrative support (21.9 percent). Workers of Puerto Rican-origin were the Hispanic group least likely to be in precision work (10.7 percent). Nearly one-third (31.4 percent) of Puerto Ricans and Cuban Americans (30.7 percent) worked in technical, sales, and administrative support, while 27.3 percent of Cuban-origin Hispanics held managerial and professional positions. (See Table 4.3.)

ASIAN AMERICANS AND JOBS

The higher educational attainment of many Asian Americans has resulted in a greater proportion working in higher-paying jobs than other minority groups. In 1998 over one-third of Asian/Pacific Islander (API) women (33.6 percent) and men (39.2 percent) were managers and professional specialists, compared to 28.1 percent of White women and 32.4 percent of White men. Over 12 percent of Black women and 11.1 percent of Black men worked in managerial and professional specialties, as did

10.4 percent of Hispanic women and 10.1 percent of Hispanic men. API men (9.3 percent) were more likely to be in service occupations than White men (6.2 percent), but less likely than Black men (17.8 percent) or Hispanic men (17.9 percent). API males were significantly less likely to be craft workers (6.6 percent) than White males (14.9 percent), Black males (10.2 percent), or Hispanic males (11.2 percent). (See Table 4.4.)

Some occupational differences exist between Pacific Islanders and Asians. In 1990 Pacific Islanders (18.1 percent) were little more than half as likely to be in managerial and professional occupations as those of Asian origin (30.6 percent). They were about equally likely, however, to be in technical, sales, and administrative support (32.1 percent and 33.2 percent, respectively). Pacific Islanders were also more often employed as service workers, precision production workers, and operators than were Asian Americans. (See Figure 4.1.)

AMERICAN INDIANS/ALASKA NATIVES AND JOBS

In 1998 the proportions of American Indians/Alaska Natives (AIs/ANs) in the managerial and professional areas were 18.2 percent for men and 16.1 percent for women. Even fewer AI/AN workers were technicians (6.2 percent men and 5.5 percent women). They were more likely to be employed in the lower-paying cate-

TABLE 4.3

Employed Mexican, Puerto Rican, and Cuban-Origin Workers by Sex, Occupation, Class of Worker and Full- or Part-Time Status
(Numbers in thousands)

Category	Total Hispanic origin[1]		Mexican origin		Puerto Rican origin		Cuban origin	
	1998	1999	1998	1999	1998	1999	1998	1999
Sex								
Total (all civilian workers)	13,291	13,720	8,431	8,656	1,145	1,165	612	681
Men	8,018	8,067	5,291	5,312	615	607	371	408
Women	5,273	5,653	3,140	3,344	529	557	241	273
Occupation								
Managerial and professional specialty	1,933	2,040	985	1,025	208	226	159	186
Executive, administrative, and managerial	1,028	1,097	536	557	103	118	89	101
Professional specialty	905	943	449	468	105	108	70	84
Technical, sales, and administrative support	3,186	3,286	1,845	1,896	365	366	210	209
Technicians and related support	283	279	156	163	30	25	28	22
Sales occupations	1,245	1,267	729	722	118	125	94	84
Administrative support, including clerical	1,657	1,740	961	1,011	217	216	88	102
Service occupations	2,670	2,716	1,653	1,697	217	217	85	90
Private household	262	244	130	130	6	4	3	2
Protective service	204	200	106	106	39	39	13	10
Service, except private household and protective	2,204	2,271	1,417	1,461	172	174	69	79
Precision production, craft, and repair	1,793	1,871	1,199	1,290	119	125	66	76
Mechanics and repairers	496	485	311	303	38	47	28	30
Construction trades	785	869	554	625	33	40	23	33
Other precision production, craft, and repair	512	517	334	361	48	38	15	13
Operators, fabricators, and laborers	2,917	3,014	2,047	2,043	223	217	85	114
Machine operators, assemblers, and inspectors	1,340	1,364	955	933	105	95	24	45
Transportation and material moving occupations	640	659	422	407	53	52	38	38
Handlers, equipment cleaners, helpers, and laborers	938	992	671	702	64	70	24	32
Construction laborers	193	233	149	185	9	7	3	3
Other handlers, equipment cleaners, helpers, and laborers	745	759	521	518	55	63	21	28
Farming, forestry, and fishing	792	793	703	706	13	14	7	6
Class of Worker								
Agriculture:								
Wage and salary workers	670	654	605	599	9	7	5	5
Self-employed workers	71	79	56	66	1	–	2	2
Unpaid family workers	2	1	1	1	–	–	–	–
Nonagricultural industries:								
Wage and salary workers	11,949	12,327	7,410	7,625	1,100	1,115	574	638
Government	1,355	1,426	833	894	180	181	60	82
Private industries	10,594	10,901	6,577	6,731	920	934	515	556
Private households	281	257	139	138	7	5	3	3
Other industries	10,312	10,644	6,438	6,593	913	929	511	553
Self-employed workers	590	651	351	361	34	42	31	37
Unpaid family workers	10	7	8	5	1	1	–	–
Full- or Part-Time Status								
Full-time workers	11,303	11,767	7,166	7,430	969	998	531	587
Part-time workers	1,988	1,953	1,265	1,226	176	166	81	94

[1] Includes persons of Central or South American origin and of other Hispanic origin, not shown separately.

NOTE: Beginning in January 1999, data reflect revised population controls used in the household survey.

SOURCE: *Employment and Earnings, January 2000.* U.S. Bureau of Labor Statistics

gories as service workers (10.5 percent males and 15.2 percent females), operators (20.7 percent men and 11 percent women), or sales personnel (10.1 percent men and 19.6 percent women). About 16 percent of AI/AN men were craftsmen, and 21.6 percent of AI/AN women were office and clerical workers. (See Table 4.4.)

MINORITIES AND GOVERNMENT EMPLOYMENT
At the Top Levels

White males hold approximately 90 percent of all top-grade positions in the federal government. Along with cabinet members, who are selected by the president, these high-level officials wield the power in federal gov-

ernment. This holds true for many agencies, including the Federal Bureau of Investigation (FBI), Immigration and Naturalization Service, and Customs Service.

A major contributor to this problem is time. It takes about 20 years to rise to the top of any organization. Twenty years ago, few women, Blacks, or Hispanics held any management positions in the federal government. Another factor is partiality. Many lower-level government employees believe that they have been cheated out of promotions because of gender or race and are filing bias complaints.

On May 17, 2000, the U.S. Equal Employment Opportunity Commission (EEOC) issued a new guid-

TABLE 4.4

Occupational Employment in Private Industry by Race/Ethnic Group/Sex and by Industry, United States, 1998

Race/Ethnic Group/Sex	Total Employment	Officials and Managers	Professionals	Technicians	Sales Workers	Office & Clerical Workers	Craft Workers	Operatives	Laborers	Service Workers
All Employers	100.0	10.5	15.7	6.1	11.8	14.4	8.3	14.4	7.7	11.0
Male	100.0	13.4	14.5	6.3	9.7	5.2	13.6	19.1	9.1	8.9
Female	100.0	7.3	17.0	5.9	14.3	24.9	2.2	9.2	5.9	13.4
White	100.0	12.6	17.8	6.5	12.2	14.3	9.0	13.3	5.9	8.4
Male	100.0	16.0	16.4	6.8	10.1	4.8	14.9	17.8	7.0	6.2
Female	100.0	8.7	19.4	6.2	14.6	25.4	2.2	8.0	4.6	11.0
Minority	100.0	5.0	10.0	5.1	10.9	14.8	6.3	17.5	12.5	18.0
Male	100.0	6.0	9.0	5.1	8.4	6.4	10.2	22.7	15.8	16.4
Female	100.0	4.0	10.9	5.1	13.5	23.5	2.2	12.1	9.1	19.5
Black	100.0	4.5	7.2	4.9	11.7	16.9	5.8	18.0	11.0	19.8
Male	100.0	5.5	5.6	4.4	9.3	7.0	10.2	25.2	15.1	17.8
Female	100.0	3.8	8.6	5.4	13.8	25.3	2.0	11.9	7.6	21.5
Hispanic	100.0	4.5	5.7	3.9	10.7	12.7	7.5	18.6	17.6	18.8
Male	100.0	5.1	5.0	4.1	8.0	5.4	11.2	22.9	20.4	17.9
Female	100.0	3.6	6.8	3.7	14.4	22.7	2.4	12.7	13.8	19.9
Asian/Pacific Islander	100.0	7.4	29.1	8.4	8.1	12.6	4.5	13.3	6.3	10.3
Male	100.0	9.4	29.8	9.6	6.9	7.1	6.6	14.7	6.7	9.3
Female	100.0	5.2	28.4	7.1	9.3	18.5	2.2	11.9	5.9	11.5
Amind/Alaskan Native	100.0	7.2	10.0	5.8	14.6	13.2	10.2	16.2	10.1	12.7
Male	100.0	8.6	9.6	6.2	10.1	5.8	16.2	20.7	12.3	10.5
Female	100.0	5.6	10.5	5.5	19.6	21.6	3.4	11.0	7.6	15.2

SOURCE: *Job Patterns for Minorities and Women in Private Industry: 1998.* U.S. Equal Employment Opportunity Commission: Washington, D.C., 1999

ance to facilitate the settlement of federal-sector discrimination complaints, including claims brought under Title VII of the Civil Rights Act of 1964 (PL 88-352), which prohibits employment discrimination based on race, color, religion, sex, and national origin. Under the administration of Chairwoman Ida L. Castro, the EEOC sought to reform its complaint process for federal employees. The new directive authorizes federal agencies to enter into settlement of bias claims, including monetary payment.

Law Enforcement

According to the U.S. Department of Justice, in *Federal Law Enforcement Officers, 1998* (Washington, DC, 2000), minorities made up 29.2 percent of all federal law enforcement officers in 1998. Hispanics accounted for 14.7 percent, and non-Hispanic Blacks made up 11.3 percent. Over 2 percent were Asians/Pacific Islanders, and 1.1 percent were American Indians. (See Figure 4.2.)

The Federal Protective Service, a part of the General Services Administration, is responsible for safeguarding federal buildings and property and the employees and visitors using them. In 1998 the Federal Protective Service had a 42.3 percent minority representation among personnel authorized to make arrests and carry firearms. The Immigration and Naturalization Service (INS) ranked second with 40.8 percent minorities. More than one-third (37.4 percent) of the officers of the Bureau of Prisons were from minority groups, as were 33.7 percent of the U.S. Customs Service. Other federal agencies with

FIGURE 4.1

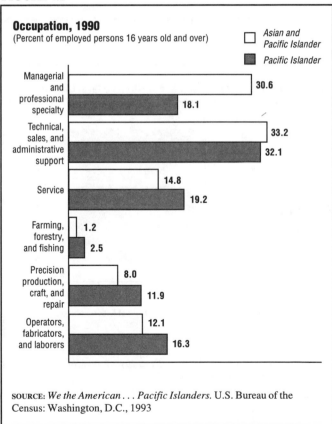

SOURCE: *We the American . . . Pacific Islanders.* U.S. Bureau of the Census: Washington, D.C., 1993

large percentages of minorities authorized to make arrests and carry firearms included the U.S. Postal Inspection Service (32.9 percent) and the U.S. Capitol Police (32.6 percent). (See Table 4.5.)

TABLE 4.5

Gender and Race or Ethnicity of Federal Officers with Arrest and Firearm Authority, Agencies Employing 500 or More Full-time Officers, June 1998

		Percent of full-time Federal officers with arrest and firearm authority							
			Gender				Race/ethnicity		
	Number of officers[a]	Total	Male	Female	White	American Indian	Black or African American	Asian or Pacific Islander	Hispanic or Latino of any race
Immigration and Naturalization	16,888	100%	88.3%	11.7%	59.2%	0.5%	5.3%	2.3%	32.0%
Federal Bureau of Prisons	12,751	100	87.9	12.1	62.6	1.4	23.4	0.9	11.7
Federal Bureau of Investigation	11,451	100	84.1	15.9	83.9	0.5	6.3	2.5	6.9
U.S. Customs Service	10,863	100	81.4	18.6	66.3	0.7	7.2	3.5	22.3
U.S. Secret Service	3,594	100%	91.4%	8.6%	79.7%	0.8%	12.9%	1.3%	5.3%
U.S. Postal Inspection Service	3,537	100	85.5	14.5	67.1	0.4	22.5	3.0	7.0
Internal Revenue Service	3,370	100	74.8	25.2	80.2	0.9	9.4	3.3	6.1
Drug Enforcement Administration	3,396	100	92.1	7.9	80.5	0.6	8.2	2.0	8.8
U.S. Marshals Service	2,755	100%	88.6%	11.4%	83.8%	0.7%	7.1%	1.9%	6.5%
National Park Service	2,207	100	86.8	13.2	86.4	1.3	6.5	2.4	3.4
Ranger Activities Division	1,534	100	85.0	15.0	90.0	1.9	3.1	2.2	2.8
U.S. Park Police	673	100	90.8	9.2	78.2	0.0	14.3	3.0	4.6
Bureau of Alcohol, Tobacco and Firearms	1,732	100	87.8	12.2	78.6	1.3	10.8	1.7	7.6
U.S. Capitol Police	1,055	100%	82.1%	17.9%	67.4%	0.4%	29.8%	0.8%	1.7%
GSA - Federal Protective Service	904	100	91.2	8.8	57.7	0.2	30.4	2.1	9.5
U.S. Fish and Wildlife Service	836	100	90.0	10.0	91.7	1.9	1.4	0.6	4.3
U.S. Forest Service	604	100	83.9	16.1	82.5	7.3	3.1	1.0	6.1

Note: Gender and race/ethnicity data for Drug Enforcement Administration are estimates based on Department of Justice data. Data on gender and race or ethnicity of officers were not provided by the Administrative Office of the U.S. Courts. Detail may not add to total because of rounding.

[a]Includes employees in U.S. Territories.

SOURCE: *Federal Law Enforcement Officers, 1998.* Bureau of Justice Statistics: Washington, D.C., 2000

FIGURE 4.2

Gender and Race or Ethnicity of Full-time Federal Officers with Arrest and Firearm Authority, June 1998

*Non-Hispanic

SOURCE: *Federal Law Enforcement Officers, 1998.* Bureau of Justice Statistics: Washington, D.C., 2000

---

centages of Hispanics. American Indians made up 7.3 percent of officers for the U.S. Forest Service, while Asians/Pacific Islanders comprised 3.5 percent of the Customs Service. (See Table 4.5.)

MINORITIES IN BUSINESS

Black-Owned Businesses

According to the Census Bureau, the number of Black-owned businesses increased 46 percent from 1987 (424,165) to 1992 (620,912). The latest survey, the 1992 *Survey of Minority-Owned Business Enterprises* (Washington, DC, 1996), reported that receipts from Black-owned businesses reached $32.2 billion, up significantly from $19.8 billion five years earlier. Service firms accounted for the greatest proportion of gross receipts ($11 billion, or 35 percent); followed by retail businesses ($7 billion); finance, insurance, and real estate ($3.8 billion); wholesale operations ($2.9 billion); and construction firms ($2.7 billion). (See Table 4.6.)

Of the 10 largest industry groups, service-industry firms accounted for 53.6 percent of all Black-owned firms. Within that same group, business services and personal services represented 47 percent of the firms. Retail trade accounted for 14 percent of all Black-owned businesses, followed by transportation and public utilities

The Federal Protective Service (30.4 percent), the U.S. Capitol Police (29.8 percent), the Bureau of Prisons (23.4 percent), and the U.S. Postal Inspection Service (22.5 percent) had high percentages of non-Hispanic Black officers. The INS (32 percent) and the U.S. Customs Service (22.3 percent) employed the highest per-

TABLE 4.6

Top Industry Receipt Leaders for Black-Owned Firms, 1992

Industry	Receipts (Millions dollars)
SERVICES	11,057
Health services	2,859
Business services	2,371
Personal services	1,469
Engineering, accounting, research management, and related services	1,353
Amusement and recreation services	665
RETAIL TRADE	6,968
Automotive dealers and gasoline service stations	2,384
Eating and drinking places	1,786
Miscellaneous retail	1,247
Food stores	978
Apparel and accessory stores	204
FINANCE, INSURANCE, AND REAL ESTATE	3,777
Depository institutions	(D)
Real estate	1,553
Insurance agents, brokers, and service	308
Holding and other investment offices	(D)
Security and commodity brokers	(D)
WHOLESALE TRADE	2,944
Wholesale trade-nondurable goods	1,837
Wholesale trade-durable goods	1,107
CONSTRUCTION	2,651
Special trade contractors	1,466
General building contractors	840
Subdividers and developers, n.e.c.	189
Heavy construction contractors	156

SOURCE: *Survey of Minority-Owned Business Enterprises: Black.* U.S. Bureau of the Census: Washington, D.C., 1996

FIGURE 4.3

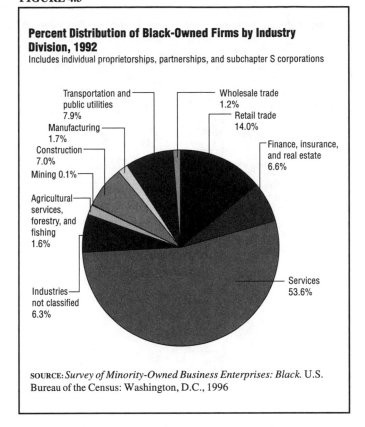

Percent Distribution of Black-Owned Firms by Industry Division, 1992
Includes individual proprietorships, partnerships, and subchapter S corporations

SOURCE: *Survey of Minority-Owned Business Enterprises: Black.* U.S. Bureau of the Census: Washington, D.C., 1996

TABLE 4.7

Comparison of Black-Owned Firms in 10 Largest Cities with Black-Owned Firms in State, 1992

City	Firms (number)	Receipts ($1,000)	State	Firms (number)	Receipts ($1,000)	Percent city to State Firms	Percent city to State Receipts
New York, NY	35,120	1,466,994	New York	51,312	2,267,600	68	65
Los Angeles, CA	15,371	2,628,903	California	68,968	5,478,365	22	48
Chicago, Il	15,328	1,087,267	Illinois	28,433	1,773,293	54	61
Houston, TX	13,592	537,490	Texas	50,008	2,339,221	27	23
District of Columbia	10,111	451,861	District of Columbia	(X)	(X)	09	(X)
Detroit, MI	9,275	486,092	Michigan	19,695	1,268,426	47	38
Baltimore, MD	7,542	233,164	Maryland	35,758	1,241,530	21	19
Philadelphia, PA	7,183	549,414	Pennsylvania	15,917	1,133,581	45	48
Dallas, TX	7,071	330,354	Texas	50,008	2,339,221	14	14
Atlanta, GA	5,762	280,701	Georgia	38,264	1,677,083	15	17

SOURCE: *Survey of Minority-Owned Business Enterprises: Black.* U.S. Bureau of the Census: Washington, D.C., 1996

(7.9 percent), construction (7 percent), and finance, insurance and real estate (6.6 percent). (See Figure 4.3.)

California had the largest number of Black-owned businesses, totaling 68,968, with gross receipts of $5.5 billion. New York was next with 51,312 firms earning nearly $2.3 billion. Texas had fewer Black-owned businesses (50,008) than New York, but had similar gross receipts.

Table 4.7 compares Black-owned firms in the 10 largest cities with Black-owned firms in their states. Figure 4.4 shows the average receipts for Black-owned businesses.

Hispanic-Owned Businesses

The number of Hispanic-owned firms increased 76 percent between 1987 and 1992, growing from 489,973

FIGURE 4.4

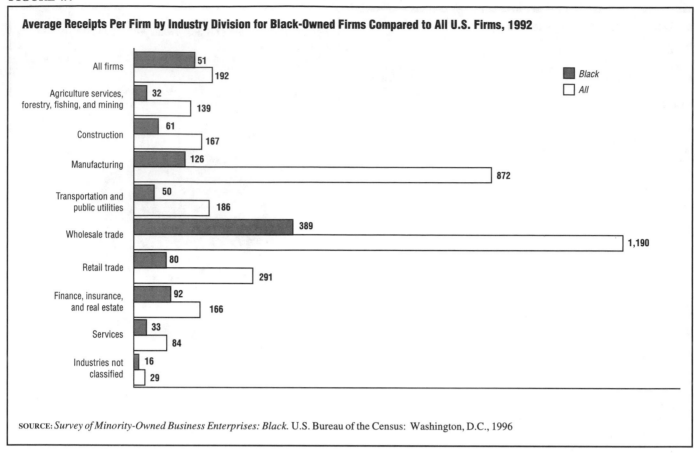

Average Receipts Per Firm by Industry Division for Black-Owned Firms Compared to All U.S. Firms, 1992

Legend: ■ Black □ All

- All firms: Black 51, All 192
- Agriculture services, forestry, fishing, and mining: Black 32, All 139
- Construction: Black 61, All 167
- Manufacturing: Black 126, All 872
- Transportation and public utilities: Black 50, All 186
- Wholesale trade: Black 389, All 1,190
- Retail trade: Black 80, All 291
- Finance, insurance, and real estate: Black 92, All 166
- Services: Black 33, All 84
- Industries not classified: Black 16, All 29

SOURCE: *Survey of Minority-Owned Business Enterprises: Black.* U.S. Bureau of the Census: Washington, D.C., 1996

FIGURE 4.5

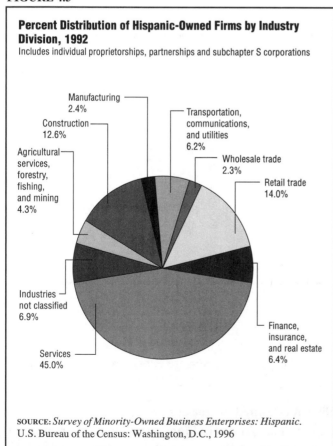

Percent Distribution of Hispanic-Owned Firms by Industry Division, 1992

Includes individual proprietorships, partnerships and subchapter S corporations

- Manufacturing 2.4%
- Construction 12.6%
- Agricultural services, forestry, fishing, and mining 4.3%
- Industries not classified 6.9%
- Services 45.0%
- Finance, insurance, and real estate 6.4%
- Retail trade 14.0%
- Wholesale trade 2.3%
- Transportation, communications, and utilities 6.2%

SOURCE: *Survey of Minority-Owned Business Enterprises: Hispanic.* U.S. Bureau of the Census: Washington, D.C., 1996

TABLE 4.8

Top Industry Receipt Leaders for Hispanic-Owned Firms, 1992

Industry	Receipts (million dollars)
RETAIL TRADE	17,731
Automotive dealers and gasoline service stations	5,475
Eating and drinking places	3,954
Food stores	
Miscellaneous retail	2,849
SERVICES	16,787
Health services	4,131
Business services	3,467
Engineering, accounting, research management, and related services	1,828
Personal services	1,758
Auto repair, services and parking	1,553
Legal services	1,286
WHOLESALE	12,489
Wholesale trade-nondurable goods	6,483
Wholesale trade-durable goods	6,006
CONSTRUCTION	8,212
Special trade contractors	4,626
General building contractors	2,205
Heavy construction	916
Subdividers and developers, n.e.c.	465

SOURCE: *Survey of Minority-Owned Business Enterprises: Hispanic.* U.S. Bureau of the Census: Washington, D.C., 1996

TABLE 4.9

Comparison of Hispanic-Owned Firms in 10 Largest Cities with Hispanic-Owned Firms in State, 1992

City	Firms (number)	Receipts ($1,000)	State	Firms (number)	Receipts ($1,000)	Percent city to State Firms	Percent city to State Receipts
Los Angeles, CA	47,673	2,874,019	California	249,717	19,552,637	19	15
New York, NY	34,495	3,082,038	NewYork	50,601	4,732,279	68	65
Houston, TX	22,657	1,893,943	Texas	155,909	11,796,301	15	16
Miami, FL	20,267	2,985,678	Florida	118,208	16,127,202	17	19
San Antonio, TX	17,081	1,495,414	Texas	155,909	11,796,301	11	13
El Paso, TX	11,714	919,709	Texas	155,909	11,796,301	8	8
Hialeah, FL	10,181	1,136,213	Florida	118,208	16,127,202	9	7
Chicago, IL	8,732	825,647	Illinois	18,368	1,950,685	48	42
San Diego, CA	8,232	664,054	California	249,717	19,552,637	3	3
Dallas, TX	7,742	1,172,496	Texas	155,909	11,796,301	5	10

source: *Survey of Minority-Owned Business Enterprises: Hispanic.* U.S. Bureau of the Census: Washington, D.C., 1996

to 862,605 firms. (At the same time, the number of all U.S. companies increased 26 percent, from 13.7 million to more than 17 million.) During this period, receipts for Hispanic-owned businesses more than doubled from $32.8 billion to $76.8 billion. (Receipts for all U.S. companies grew from $2 trillion to $3.3 trillion, a 67 percent increase.)

In 1992 most Hispanic-owned firms were concentrated in the service industries. These industries accounted for 45 percent of all Hispanic-owned businesses but for only 22 percent of gross receipts. The next largest proportion was in retail trade, with 14 percent of the firms and 23 percent of the receipts. (See Figure 4.5; see Table 4.8 for the largest Hispanic industry groups by receipts.)

About 15 percent of Hispanic-owned businesses surveyed in 1992 had paid employees. The number of firms of 100 or more employees rose from 129 in 1987 to 676 in 1992. The largest share of firms owned by Hispanics was in New Mexico, with 20.1 percent of all firms in that state. California had the largest number of Hispanic firms (249,717) and the highest receipts ($19.5 billion) of all the states. Texas had the second-largest number of Hispanic firms (155,909), with receipts of $11.8 billion. Table 4.9 compares the Hispanic-owned firms in the 10 largest cities and Hispanic-owned firms in their states.

In 1992 Hispanic-owned businesses comprised 5 percent of all firms in the United States and 2.3 percent of gross receipts. These businesses had average receipts of $94,000, compared to $192,000 for all U.S. firms. Hispanic firms with gross receipts of $1 million or more accounted for 51.7 percent of the total gross receipts but for only 1.2 percent of the total number of firms. Forty-seven percent of the firms had gross receipts of less than $10,000. Figure 4.6 shows the average receipts per firm by industry for Hispanic-owned firms.

TABLE 4.10

Asian-, Pacific Islander-, American Indian-, and Alaska Native-Owned Firms by Group, 1992

Group	1992 Firms (number)	1992 Receipts ($1,000,000)
Total	**705,672**	**104,100**
Asians and Pacific Islanders	603,439	96,048
Asian Indian	93,340	19,284
Chinese	153,096	30,189
Japanese	68,675	12,597
Korean	104,918	16,170
Vietnamese	59,674	4,313
Filipino	67,625	4,781
Hawaiian	11,587	1,058
Other Asian and Pacific Is.	44,524	7,656
American Indians and Alaska Natives	102,234	8,053
American Indian	95,003	7,415
Aleut	2,738	222
Eskimo	4,493	416

source: U.S. Bureau of the Census: Washington, D.C., 1996

American Indian and Asian American Businesses

The number of businesses owned by Asians/Pacific Islanders (APIs) increased 56 percent from 386,291 in 1987 to 603,439 in 1992. Receipts more than doubled from $36.5 billion to $96 billion.

American Indian- and Alaska Native-owned (AI/AN) businesses grew in number by 93 percent during the same six-year period, from 52,980 to 102,234. Receipts doubled from $3.7 billion to $8.1 billion. (See Table 4.10 for the number of firms and receipts for 1992.)

Receipts per firm owned by these groups averaged $165,000, compared to $193,000 for all U.S. companies. At the low end of the scale, 35 percent of these minority-owned firms (212,928) had receipts under $10,000. At the high end, 12,517 firms had sales of $1 million or more. Twenty-two percent (136,000) of AI/AN- and API-owned

FIGURE 4.6

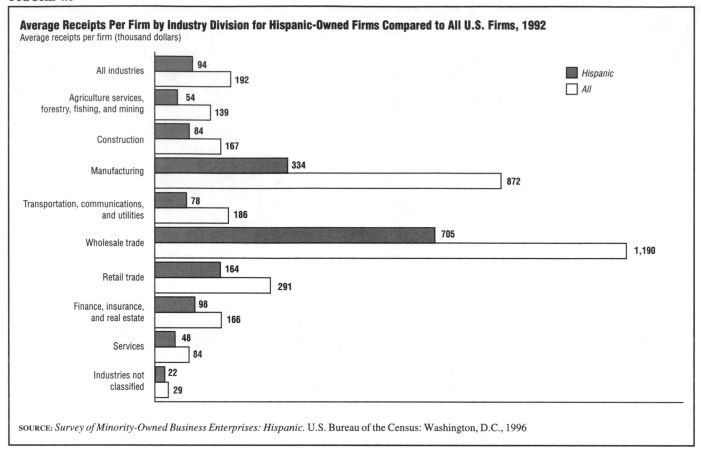

Average Receipts Per Firm by Industry Division for Hispanic-Owned Firms Compared to All U.S. Firms, 1992
Average receipts per firm (thousand dollars)

SOURCE: *Survey of Minority-Owned Business Enterprises: Hispanic.* U.S. Bureau of the Census: Washington, D.C., 1996

enterprises with paid employees were responsible for 81 percent of the gross receipts of these minority-owned firms. Of those, 705 had 100 or more employees and accounted for $17.9 billion in receipts.

As with Hispanic-owned businesses, service industries comprised most of the number of AI/AN businesses, but the retail industry accounted for most of the receipts. Service industries made up 45 percent of the businesses owned by AIs/ANs and APIs, but took in only 26 percent of gross receipts. While 22 percent of these firms were retail businesses, they earned 29 percent of the receipts.

Three populous states with many corporations—California, New York, and Texas—were home to 55 percent of the firms owned by APIs and AIs/ANs. Forty-nine percent of Hawaii's business firms and 44 percent of the receipts in that state were from these minority groups.

Minority Businesses Owned by Women

The report, "1996 Facts on Women-Owned Businesses: Trends among Minority Women-Owned Firms," prepared by the National Foundation for Women Business Owners and sponsored by IBM Corp., stated that large gains have been made since 1987 in the number of firms and employees and in sales revenues of businesses owned by Asian, Black, and Hispanic American women. Firms owned by minority women have seen their greatest growth in nontraditional sectors, including construction, wholesale trade, transportation, communications, and public utilities.

The report found that 13 percent of the nearly 8 million female-owned businesses in the United States were owned by minority women. As of 1996, 37 percent (405,200 female-owned firms) were held by Blacks. These firms employed 261,400 people and generated $24.7 billion in sales. Thirty-five percent (382,400) of women-owned minority firms were Hispanic-owned, and 28 percent (305,700) were owned by women of Asian, American Indian, or Alaska Native descent. (See Figure 4.7.)

Minority "Set-Asides"

Many levels of government, including the federal government, have "set-aside" programs that award a certain percentage of contracts to minority- and women-owned businesses. In 1989 the U.S. Supreme Court, in *City of Richmond v. Croson Co.* (488 U.S. 469), struck down a Richmond, Virginia, city ordinance that reserved 30 percent of city-financed construction contracts for minority-owned businesses. The Court ruled that the ordinance violated equal protection because there was no "specific" and "identified" evidence of past discrimination, "public or private," against the Richmond Minority Business Enterprise (MBE) in city contracting. The majority opinion, written by Justice Sandra Day O'Connor, also noted that the city had failed to "narrowly tailor" the remedy to accomplish any objective other than "outright racial balancing." The opinion further stated that it was a "completely unrealistic" assumption that a 30 percent assignment to MBEs in a particular trade would be a fair representation of the community.

Minority leaders and others nationwide attacked this decision as a dramatic setback for minority businesses. Only in recent years had they been able to take advantage of lucrative government contracts through "set-aside" programs. These programs developed because the cost of doing business with government agencies can be too expensive for small organizations with limited funds. Governments, especially the federal government, are often slow to pay their bills, so businesses frequently have to borrow money to bridge the gap between the delivery of goods and services that must be paid for and the time it takes the government to pay.

Acquiring government contracts can be very involved and confusing for businesses unfamiliar with the process. Also, minority businesses are often newer and smaller and have difficulty competing with older, larger businesses that know the process and can afford to make lower bids. Since the federal Government Services Administration (GSA) must now be self-sufficient, it began charging government contractors 1 percent of their contract, which will be used to support the GSA. As a result, the government is much more likely to grant contracts to larger contractors with larger customer bases who will contribute more to support the GSA.

ON THE OTHER HAND.... In 1989 the Department of Transportation awarded a contract for a federal highway project to a construction firm, which in turn subcontracted the job to a Disadvantaged Business Enterprise in compliance with the Subcontractor Compensation Clause. Adarand Constructors, a Colorado company whose owner is White, had submitted a low bid on part of the project, but did not get the project. Adarand subsequently sued the government, claiming the clause and the racial preference stemming from it violated the owner of Adarand's right to equal protection under the Fifth Amendment.

In 1995 the U.S. Supreme Court, in *Adarand Constructors, Inc. v. Peña, Secretary of Transportation* (515 U.S. 200), expressed doubt in the validity of the affirmative-action programs, based on the Surface Transportation and Uniform Relocation Assistance Act of 1987 (PL 100-17) that channeled $10 billion per year in construction contracts to women- and minority-owned businesses. The Court, citing the need for stricter and narrower standards in determining racial preferences when awarding contracts, remanded (returned) the case to the district court for review.

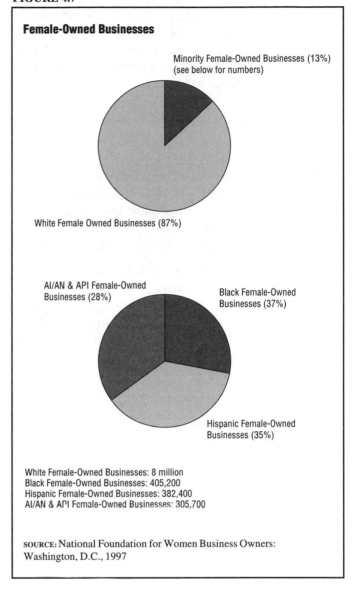

FIGURE 4.7

Female-Owned Businesses

Minority Female-Owned Businesses (13%)
(see below for numbers)

White Female Owned Businesses (87%)

AI/AN & API Female-Owned Businesses (28%)

Black Female-Owned Businesses (37%)

Hispanic Female-Owned Businesses (35%)

White Female-Owned Businesses: 8 million
Black Female-Owned Businesses: 405,200
Hispanic Female-Owned Businesses: 382,400
AI/AN & API Female-Owned Businesses: 305,700

SOURCE: National Foundation for Women Business Owners: Washington, D.C., 1997

In June 1997 the district court found for Adarand, ordering the Transportation Department to stop implementing the clause. The Transportation Department appealed the ruling. In the meantime, Adarand filed a second suit to challenge Colorado's certification practice regarding Disadvantaged Business Enterprises. Shortly after, Colorado changed its certification guidelines to simply require that applicants certify that they were socially disadvantaged due to racial, ethnic, or gender bias. Adarand, at the district court's advice, applied for the disadvantaged-business status and received it.

Learning of Adarand's new status, the Tenth Circuit Court of Appeals dismissed the government case as moot and annulled the district court's ruling favoring Adarand. Adarand appealed to the Supreme Court. On January 12, 2000, the Supreme Court, in *Adarand Constructors, Inc. v. Rodney Slater, Secretary of Transportation, et al.* (No. 99-295), reversed the appellate court's ruling, sending the case back for further proceedings. The Supreme Court reasoned that the Transportation Department, which had yet to approve Colorado's procedure for certifying Disadvantaged Business Enterprises, could not absolutely assure the Court that it would not revert back to its practice of racial preference.

INDIAN CASINOS—A MATTER OF SELF-RULE

The Indian Gaming Regulatory Act (PL 100-497, 1988) gives tribes "the exclusive right to regulate gaming on Indian lands if the gaming activity is not specifically prohibited by federal law and is conducted within a State which does not, as a matter of criminal law and public policy, prohibit such gaming activity." The law requires that only tribes, not individuals, can run gaming operations.

The National Indian Gaming Commission reported that, as of March 1999, 198 tribes in 24 states had permission to operate casinos. All in all, about 320 Indian gaming operations in these states brought in an estimated annual revenue of $8 billion (10 percent of the revenues made by nation's gaming industry).

These operations not only provide jobs, both to Indians and non-Indians, but also help to pay for social service programs, school tuition, and housing for tribe members. For example, a Sioux tribe near Morton, Minnesota, draws tens of thousands of customers weekly to its gambling operation. Proceeds are used to finance college costs of tribal members and to make "loans" to elderly members who want to purchase a new home or make home improvements. While recipients are asked to repay 10 percent of the loan, they are not required to do so.

Gambling casinos have provided a healthy income for reservations and people who have suffered some of the worst poverty in the country. The Mashantucket-Pequot Indians in Connecticut earned more than $800 million in profits in 1995. They planned to buy local land for future development. They were paying more than market value to acquire property, but once purchased and added to the federal trust land, the land became exempt from property taxes and local zoning laws. Some local residents were unhappy with the changes in their farmland and were angry that American Indians are not subject to the same laws as non-American Indians. The Pequots had two hotels, a monorail, a virtual-reality theater, a golf course, and a bingo and sporting events center, as well as a tribal community complex in the works.

CHAPTER 5
MONEY, INCOME, AND POVERTY STATUS

People are often defined, rightly or wrongly, by the amount of money they make or have. In turn, their income generally influences where they live, what they eat, how they dress, what they drive, and what schools their children attend. How much money and income a person has is usually determined by his or her occupation, which is often directly related to his or her education. Racial and ethnic backgrounds can play a big role in all these factors.

INCOME DIFFERENCES

In 1998 the median income (money income before taxes and not including the value of noncash benefits such as food stamps, Medicare, Medicaid, public housing, and employer-provided benefits) of American households for all races was $38,885. (A household consists of a person or persons who occupy the same housing unit. A household may have just one person [the householder who owns or rents the house]. It may also consist of related family members [family household] or unrelated persons [nonfamily household]). The median income of non-Hispanic White households ($42,439) was considerably higher than that of Hispanic ($28,330) and Black ($25,351) households, but less than the median income of Asian/Pacific Islander households ($46,637). (See Table 5.1.)

Married-Couple Households

In 1998, 76.6 percent of all families were married-couple families with a median (half make more, half make less) income of $54,180. The median income for White married-couple families was $54,736, while the income for Black married-couple families was $47,383. Hispanic married-couple families earned $34,816. (See Table 5.2.)

In 1998 married couples made up 80.7 percent of all White families, 68 percent of all Hispanic families, and 47 percent of all Black families. Although income for all

married-couple families was higher than for other types of households, the income of Black married-couple families was considerably higher than other types of Black families. The lower proportion of married-couple families among Blacks partially helps to explain the significant difference between their income ($47,383) and that of Black families in general ($29,404), which were far more likely than other groups to be headed by a woman without a husband present. (See Table 5.2.)

Female-Headed Households

Households headed by women with no husband present have considerably lower incomes than any other type of family household. In 1998 families with a female householder accounted for 17.9 percent of all families—14 percent of White families, 23.7 percent of Hispanic families, and 45 percent of Black families. The median income of all families with a female householder was $22,163—$25,175 for White families, $16,770 for Black families, and $16,532 for Hispanic families. (See Table 5.2.)

Per Capita Income

The per capita income is figured by dividing the total (aggregate or composite) national income by the total population. This means that if all the nation's earnings were divided equally among every man, woman, and child, each person would each receive this per capita amount. The per capita figure is often used to compare the wealth of countries or groups within countries. In 1998 the per capita income for non-Hispanic Whites was $22,952; Blacks, $12,957; Asians/Pacific Islanders, $18,709; and Hispanics, $11,434. (See Table 5.1.)

Table 5.3 shows the median income of White, Black, and Hispanic households by characteristics such as region, size and type of household, work experience, age, and number of earners—all factors that can directly affect a household's income. In 1998 the median income of

TABLE 5.1

Comparison of Summary Measures of Income by Selected Characteristics, 1989, 1997 and 1998

[Households and people as of March of the following year.]

Characteristics	Number (1,000)	1998 Median income Value (dollars)	1998 Median income 90-percent confidence interval (+/-) (dollars)	Median income in 1997 (in 1998 dollars) Value (dollars)	Median income in 1997 (in 1998 dollars) 90-percent confidence interval (+/-) (dollars)	Median income in 1989[r] (in 1998 dollars) Value (dollars)	Median income in 1989[r] (in 1998 dollars) 90-percent confidence interval (+/-) (dollars)	Percent change in real income 1997 to 1998 Percent change	Percent change in real income 1997 to 1998 90-percent confidence interval (+/-)	Percent change in real income 1989[r] to 1998 Percent change	Percent change in real income 1989[r] to 1998 90-percent confidence interval (+/-)
Households											
All households	**103,874**	**38,885**	**378**	**37,581**	**286**	**37,884**	**344**	***3.5**	**0.6**	***2.6**	**0.8**
Type of Household											
Family households	71,535	47,469	410	46,053	394	45,343	413	*3.1	0.6	*4.7	0.8
Married-couple families	54,770	54,276	530	52,486	388	50,702	458	*3.4	0.6	*7.0	0.9
Female householder, no husband present	12,789	24,393	655	23,399	657	22,662	603	*4.2	2.0	*7.6	2.5
Male householder, no wife present	3,976	39,414	1,633	37,205	1,201	39,717	1,607	*5.9	2.8	-0.8	3.5
Nonfamily households	32,339	23,441	467	22,043	347	22,568	363	*6.3	1.3	*3.9	1.6
Female householder	17,971	18,615	462	17,887	428	18,143	474	*4.1	1.8	2.6	2.2
Male householder	14,368	30,414	559	28,022	770	29,489	660	*8.5	1.8	*3.1	1.8
Race and Hispanic Origin of Householder											
All races[1]	103,874	38,885	378	37,581	286	37,884	344	*3.5	0.6	*2.6	0.8
White	87,212	40,912	336	39,579	413	39,852	320	*3.4	0.7	*2.7	0.7
Non-Hispanic White	78,577	42,439	401	41,209	354	40,792	331	*3.0	0.6	*4.0	0.8
Black	12,579	25,351	653	25,440	720	23,950	789	-0.3	1.9	*5.8	2.7
Asian and Pacific Islander	3,308	46,637	2,135	45,954	2,102	47,337	2,007	1.5	3.2	-1.5	3.7
Hispanic origin[2]	9,060	28,330	898	27,043	792	28,631	882	*4.8	1.8	-1.1	2.7
Age of Householder											
15 to 24 years	5,770	23,564	730	22,935	822	24,401	755	2.7	2.4	-3.4	2.6
25 to 34 years	18,819	40,069	696	38,769	755	39,041	603	*3.4	1.3	*2.6	1.5
35 to 44 years	23,968	48,451	730	47,081	637	49,310	675	*2.9	1.0	-1.7	1.2
45 to 54 years	20,158	54,148	877	52,683	727	54,575	893	*2.8	1.1	-0.8	1.4
55 to 64 years	13,571	43,167	989	42,000	763	40,569	878	*2.8	1.5	*6.4	2.0
65 years and over	21,589	21,729	395	21,084	406	20,719	381	*3.1	1.3	*4.9	1.6
Nativity of the Householder											
Native born	92,853	39,677	390	38,229	381	(NA)	(NA)	*3.8	0.7	(X)	(X)
Foreign born	11,021	32,963	1,230	31,806	802	(NA)	(NA)	3.6	2.3	(X)	(X)
Naturalized citizen	4,877	41,028	1,808	(NA)	(NA)	(NA)	(NA)	(X)	(X)	(X)	(X)
Not a citizen	6,143	28,278	1,199	27,379	971	(NA)	(NA)	3.3	2.8	(X)	(X)
Region											
Northeast	19,877	40,634	772	39,535	877	42,780	709	*2.8	1.5	*-5.0	1.5
Midwest	24,489	40,609	600	38,913	747	37,685	642	*4.4	1.3	*7.8	1.5
South	36,959	35,797	500	34,880	580	33,933	471	*2.6	1.1	*5.5	1.3
West	22,549	40,983	661	39,772	910	40,705	696	*3.0	1.4	0.7	1.4
Residence											
Inside metropolitan areas	83,441	40,983	352	39,994	448	40,776	346	*2.5	0.7	0.5	0.7
Inside central cities	32,144	33,151	638	32,039	456	(NA)	(NA)	*3.5	1.5	(X)	(X)
Outside central cities	51,297	46,402	512	45,364	568	(NA)	(NA)	*2.3	0.8	(X)	(X)
Outside metropolitan areas	20,433	32,022	630	30,525	690	29,393	636	*4.9	1.5	*8.9	1.9

TABLE 5.1

Comparison of Summary Measures of Income by Selected Characteristics, 1989, 1997 and 1998 [CONTINUED]

[Households and people as of March of the following year.]

Characteristics	Number (1,000)	1998 Median income		Median income in 1997 (in 1998 dollars)		Median income in 1989[r] (in 1998 dollars)		Percent change in real income 1997 to 1998		Percent change in real income 1989[r] to 1998	
		Value (dollars)	90-percent confidence interval (+/-) (dollars)	Value (dollars)	90-percent confidence interval (+/-) (dollars)	Value (dollars)	90-percent confidence interval (+/-) (dollars)	Percent change	90-percent confidence interval (+/-)	Percent change	90-percent confidence interval (+/-)
Earnings of Full-Time, Year-Round Workers											
Male	56,951	35,345	219	34,199	535	35,727	242	*3.4	0.9	*-1.1	0.6
Female	38,785	25,862	194	25,362	259	24,614	270	*2.0	0.7	*5.1	0.9
Per Capita Income											
All races[1]	271,743	20,120	199	19,541	202	18,280	132	*3.0	0.7	*10.1	0.8
White	223,294	21,394	237	20,743	239	19,385	147	*3.1	0.8	*10.4	0.8
Non-Hispanic White	193,074	22,952	268	22,246	271	(NA)	(NA)	*3.2	0.9	(X)	(X)
Black	35,070	12,957	322	12,543	346	11,406	253	*3.3	1.9	*13.6	2.1
Asian and Pacific Islander	10,897	18,709	1,094	18,510	1,128	(NA)	(NA)	1.1	4.4	(X)	(X)
Hispanic origin[2]	31,689	11,434	410	10,941	393	10,770	294	*4.5	2.3	*6.2	2.7

*Statistically significant change at the 90-percent confidence level.

[r]Revised to reflect the population distribution reported in the 1990 census.

[1]Data for American Indians, Eskimos, and Aleuts are not shown separately. Data for this population group are not tabulated from the CPS because of its small size.

[2]Hispanics may be of any race.

SOURCE: *Current Population Survey.* U.S. Bureau of the Census, March 1990, 1998, and 1999

TABLE 5.2

Median Income of Families by Selected Characteristics, Race, and Hispanic Origin of Householder, 1998, 1997, and 1996

[Families as of March of the following year. An asterisk (*) preceding percent change indicates statistically significant change at the 90-percent confidence level.]

Characteristic	1998 Median income			1997 Median income			1996 Median income			Percent change in real median income (1997-1998)
	Number (1,000)	Value (dollars)	Standard error (dollars)	Number (1,000)	Value (dollars)	Standard error (dollars)	Number (1,000)	Value (dollars)	Standard error (dollars)	
ALL RACES										
All families	71,551	46,737	241	70,884	44,568	267	70,241	42,300	209	*3.3
Type of Residence										
Inside metropolitan areas	56,993	49,407	308	56,350	47,315	280	55,930	45,117	277	*2.8
1 million or more	37,793	51,935	338	37,417	50,311	330	36,858	47,442	384	*1.6
Inside central cities	12,425	39,965	774	12,386	38,049	673	12,248	35,792	531	3.4
Outside central cities	25,368	58,104	524	25,030	55,809	443	24,610	52,577	417	*2.5
Under 1 million	19,200	44,768	513	18,934	42,917	459	19,071	41,395	371	*2.7
Inside central cities	7,188	41,099	641	7,206	39,276	758	7,287	37,633	736	3.0
Outside central cities	12,012	46,929	547	11,728	44,993	518	11,784	43,260	485	*2.7
Outside metropolitan areas	14,558	38,326	582	14,534	36,149	447	14,311	33,874	554	*4.4
Region										
Northeast	13,384	50,567	536	13,338	48,328	791	13,404	46,553	459	*.0
Midwest	16,875	49,552	543	16,594	46,734	501	16,457	44,957	485	*4.4
South	25,894	42,711	474	25,682	41,001	372	25,438	38,710	408	*2.6
West	15,398	46,819	496	15,270	45,590	537	14,943	42,569	519	1.1
Type of Family										
Married–couple families	54,778	54,180	321	54,321	51,591	231	53,604	49,707	305	*3.4
Wife in paid labor force	33,680	63,751	379	33,535	60,669	291	33,242	58,381	322	*3.5
Wife not in paid labor force	21,098	37,161	369	20,786	36,027	305	20,362	33,748	393	1.6
Male householder, no wife present	3,977	35,681	850	3,911	32,960	839	3,847	31,600	549	*6.6
Female householder, no husband present	12,796	22,163	325	12,652	21,023	308	12,790	19,911	306	*3.8
Age of Householder										
Under 65 years	60,053	50,259	239	59,614	47,825	315	59,107	45,517	248	*3.5
15 to 24 years	3,242	21,918	576	3,018	20,820	521	2,964	19,937	704	3.7
25 to 34 years	13,226	41,074	466	13,639	39,979	483	13,737	37,177	482	1.2
35 to 44 years	18,823	51,883	463	18,872	50,424	369	19,026	47,725	506	1.3
45 to 54 years	15,127	61,833	586	14,695	59,959	570	14,384	57,161	607	1.5
55 to 64 years	9,635	52,577	665	9,391	50,241	614	8,997	48,198	854	*3.0
65 years and over	11,498	31,568	394	11,270	30,660	386	11,133	28,983	356	1.4
65 to 74 years	7,051	34,719	594	6,989	33,372	495	7,120	31,366	496	2.4
75 years and over	4,447	27,717	454	4,282	26,611	463	4,013	25,510	463	2.6
Size of Family										
Two people	31,102	39,721	364	30,287	37,562	344	29,780	36,072	307	*4.1
Three people	16,227	48,933	547	16,231	46,783	463	16,239	44,108	450	*3.0
Four people	14,390	56,061	607	14,633	53,350	612	14,602	51,518	392	*3.5
Five people	6,573	54,357	893	6,555	51,101	640	6,326	48,058	925	*4.7
Six people	2,135	48,816	1,643	2,047	45,473	1,406	2,108	41,774	1,290	5.7
Seven people or more	1,124	45,254	1,773	1,130	42,001	1,838	1,186	40,339	1,665	6.1
Number of Earners										
No earners	9,692	20,689	297	9,835	19,731	274	9,947	18,088	274	*3.2
One earner	21,221	31,483	273	20,494	30,204	287	20,052	28,383	321	*2.6
Two earners or more	40,638	61,675	282	40,555	58,972	375	40,242	56,442	278	*3.0
Two earners	31,787	58,397	366	31,752	55,443	309	31,309	53,361	332	*3.7
Three earners	6,642	70,339	838	6,638	68,028	781	6,697	63,281	745	1.8
Four earners or more	2,209	88,031	1,851	2,165	85,978	1,503	2,236	79,371	1,370	0.8
WHITE										
All families	60,077	49,023	283	59,515	46,754	259	58,934	44,756	266	*3.2
Type of Residence										
Inside metropolitan areas	46,962	52,103	302	46,429	50,410	274	46,079	47,769	345	*1.8
1 million or more	30,374	55,930	418	30,060	53,572	462	29,624	50,977	343	*2.8
Inside central cities	8,120	46,290	815	8,147	43,444	990	8,024	40,743	643	*4.9
Outside central cities	22,253	59,387	531	21,913	57,063	496	21,600	54,027	480	*2.5
Under 1 million	16,588	46,640	488	16,369	44,819	491	16,455	43,316	442	*2.5
Inside central cities	5,683	44,059	857	5,717	42,206	872	5,699	41,713	708	2.8
Outside central cities	10,906	47,866	563	10,651	45,728	508	10,756	44,085	512	*3.1
Outside metropolitan areas	13,115	39,610	591	13,086	37,305	483	12,856	35,681	456	*4.6
Region										
Northeast	11,374	53,591	762	11,390	51,354	584	11,403	49,235	596	*2.8
Midwest	15,022	51,159	393	14,771	48,614	549	14,628	46,579	477	*3.6
South	20,540	46,239	477	20,358	43,915	494	20,184	41,955	362	*3.7
West	13,140	46,686	519	12,996	46,006	607	12,719	42,906	612	−0.1

TABLE 5.2

Median Income of Families by Selected Characteristics, Race, and Hispanic Origin of Householder, 1998, 1997, and 1996 [CONTINUED]

[Families as of March of the following year. An asterisk (*) preceding percent change indicates statistically significant change at the 90-percent confidence level.]

	1998			1997			1996			Percent change in real median income (1997-1998)
		Median income			Median income			Median income		
Characteristic	Number (1,000)	Value (dollars)	Standard error (dollars)	Number (1,000)	Value (dollars)	Standard error (dollars)	Number (1,000)	Value (dollars)	Standard error (dollars)	
Type of Family										
Married–couple families	48,461	54,736	335	48,070	52,098	247	47,650	50,190	257	*3.5
Wife in paid labor force	29,378	64,480	402	29,344	61,441	309	29,308	58,995	333	*3.3
Wife not in paid labor force	19,083	37,755	416	18,726	36,343	319	18,342	34,214	406	*2.3
Male householder, no wife present	3,087	37,798	1,099	3,137	34,802	950	2,944	32,439	962	*6.9
Female householder, no husband present	8,529	25,175	414	8,308	22,999	465	8,339	22,373	408	*7.8
Age of Householder										
Under 65 years	49,846	52,550	297	49,443	50,701	237	48,963	48,352	324	*2.1
15 to 24 years	2,504	24,283	637	2,270	22,431	809	2,204	22,419	825	*6.6
25 to 34 years	10,522	43,970	674	10,965	41,890	410	11,128	39,967	477	*3.4
35 to 44 years	15,619	54,682	584	15,603	52,753	549	15,686	50,741	398	*2.1
45 to 54 years	12,845	64,119	634	12,455	61,852	467	12,227	60,001	691	*2.1
55 to 64 years	8,356	54,476	771	8,149	51,598	550	7,718	50,419	672	*4.0
65 years and over	10,231	32,398	429	10,072	31,167	408	9,971	29,470	360	2.4
65 to 74 years	6,249	35,784	622	6,222	34,179	523	6,376	31,934	536	3.1
75 years and over	3,982	28,205	474	3,850	26,758	483	3,595	26,004	464	*3.8
Size of Family										
Two people	27,051	41,358	337	26,380	39,492	385	25,903	37,593	379	*3.1
Three people	13,235	51,331	432	13,312	50,149	523	13,316	47,239	536	0.8
Four people	11,952	58,834	702	12,078	56,022	583	12,100	53,816	647	*3.4
Five people	5,392	56,560	822	5,366	53,696	1,166	5,123	51,434	858	*3.7
Six people	1,655	52,421	1,732	1,598	48,079	1,679	1,663	43,377	1,774	*7.4
Seven people or more	792	51,196	2,509	782	45,816	2,539	828	45,416	2,149	10.0
Number of Earners										
No earners	8,152	22,672	310	8,367	21,516	293	8,198	20,311	323	*3.8
One earner	16,991	34,466	438	16,239	32,811	424	16,025	30,831	317	*3.4
Two earners or more	34,934	62,695	356	34,910	60,291	281	34,712	57,461	306	*2.4
Two earners	27,410	59,480	383	27,467	56,624	335	27,068	54,292	347	*3.4
Three earners	5,678	71,374	951	5,618	69,239	850	5,713	65,008	821	1.5
Four earners or more	1,846	91,307	1,627	1,824	87,747	1,532	1,931	80,110	1,485	2.5
BLACK										
All families	8,452	29,404	713	8,408	28,602	629	8,455	26,522	470	1.2
Type of Residence										
Inside metropolitan areas	7,314	30,159	687	7,242	29,737	667	7,279	28,468	846	−0.1
1 million or more	5,335	31,125	745	5,298	30,485	641	5,296	29,520	918	0.5
Inside central cities	3,414	26,265	926	3,350	26,210	994	3,343	24,882	883	−1.3
Outside central cities	1,921	41,571	1,774	1,949	38,703	1,639	1,953	37,572	1,225	5.8
Under 1 million	1,979	27,436	1,068	1,944	27,150	1,091	1,984	26,275	1,128	−0.5
Inside central cities	1,210	26,229	1,248	1,208	25,503	2,185	1,266	23,450	1,272	1.3
Outside central cities	769	29,677	2,007	736	30,982	2,082	718	31,135	1,322	−5.7
Outside metropolitan areas	1,138	25,981	1,361	1,166	24,619	1,448	1,176	18,990	1,152	3.9
Region										
Northeast	1,553	27,167	1,347	1,501	29,217	1,562	1,558	25,458	1,175	−8.4
Midwest	1,494	27,409	1,610	1,468	28,129	1,355	1,505	27,448	1,416	−4.1
South	4,723	29,512	863	4,721	27,734	814	4,707	25,552	605	4.8
West	682	37,036	3,051	717	33,604	1,898	686	36,571	2,411	8.5
Type of Family										
Married–couple families	3,979	47,383	1,165	3,921	45,372	755	3,851	41,963	965	2.8
Wife in paid labor force	2,852	55,579	984	2,716	51,702	748	2,636	50,805	1,002	*5.9
Wife not in paid labor force	1,127	27,927	1,056	1,205	28,757	1,499	1,216	27,594	1,173	−4.4
Male householder, no wife present	660	27,087	1,178	562	25,654	1,212	657	26,338	2,006	4.0
Female householder, no husband present	3,813	16,770	418	3,926	16,879	438	3,947	15,530	503	−2.2
Age of Householder										
Under 65 years	7,489	30,946	598	7,492	29,343	669	7,536	27,113	526	3.8
15 to 24 years	587	11,212	847	630	13,556	1,468	635	11,239	773	*−18.6
25 to 34 years	2,040	25,165	1,258	2,054	24,620	1,073	1,982	20,470	1,134	0.6
35 to 44 years	2,323	32,839	1,609	2,352	28,148	897	2,437	30,735	1,022	*14.9
45 to 54 years	1,642	45,785	2,139	1,594	41,903	1,817	1,584	40,009	1,749	7.6
55 to 64 years	898	34,749	1,792	862	36,415	2,133	897	33,703	2,088	−6.0
65 years and over	962	22,102	1,081	916	23,420	1,490	919	21,328	1,297	−7.1
65 to 74 years	605	22,419	1,539	607	23,767	2,039	604	23,885	1 734	−7.1
75 years and over	357	21,589	1,607	309	22,919	2,872	316	18,647	1 415	−7.2

TABLE 5.2

Median Income of Families by Selected Characteristics, Race, and Hispanic Origin of Householder, 1998, 1997, and 1996 [CONTINUED]

[Families as of March of the following year. An asterisk (*) preceding percent change indicates statistically significant change at the 90-percent confidence level.]

Characteristic	1998 Number (1,000)	1998 Median income Value (dollars)	1998 Median income Standard error (dollars)	1997 Number (1,000)	1997 Median income Value (dollars)	1997 Median income Standard error (dollars)	1996 Number (1,000)	1996 Median income Value (dollars)	1996 Median income Standard error (dollars)	Percent change in real median income (1997-1998)
Size of Family										
Two people	3,175	25,698	632	3,022	25,061	931	2,987	23,500	1,018	1.0
Three people	2,212	27,604	1,141	2,184	26,060	1,230	2,242	24,503	1,026	4.3
Four people	1,693	35,918	1,303	1,789	34,644	1,531	1,762	32,747	1,501	2.1
Five people	833	36,455	2,032	866	36,984	2,717	905	31,120	1,595	−2.9
Six people	318	31,754	3,264	317	31,197	1,128	313	30,871	2,031	0.2
Seven people or more	221	30,475	3,544	230	32,544	3,490	247	27,231	3,399	−7.8
Number of Earners										
No earners	1,271	9,422	446	1,202	9,012	468	1,402	7,776	447	3.0
One earner	3,348	20,524	441	3,396	19,597	486	3,222	19,066	462	3.1
Two earners or more	3,833	51,737	748	3,809	48,750	945	3,832	45,280	890	*4.5
Two earners	3,008	48,018	1,319	2,973	45,780	715	3,007	42,637	999	3.3
Three earners	613	58,438	2,417	676	57,701	1,835	676	51,457	1 844	−0.3
Four earners or more	211	74,299	4,764	160	75,641	5,576	149	70,325	9,334	−3.3
HISPANIC ORIGIN[1]										
All families	7,273	29,608	568	6,961	28,142	655	6,631	26,179	495	*3.6
Type of Residence										
Inside metropolitan areas	6,677	30,129	561	6,307	28,708	694	6,036	26,528	533	3.3
1 million or more	4,933	31,195	569	4,686	30,115	679	4,480	27,394	696	2.0
Inside central cities	2,481	26,750	660	2,394	24,567	853	2,309	22,951	742	*7.2
Outside central cities	2,452	36,410	888	2,292	36,718	1,051	2,171	33,092	1,158	−2.4
Under 1 million	1,744	26,177	822	1,621	25,244	1,085	1,556	23,547	1,247	2.1
Inside central cities	966	25,057	1,492	943	25,490	1,672	911	23,658	1 790	−3.2
Outside central cities	778	27,431	1,713	679	25,008	1,401	645	23,440	1,590	8.0
Outside metropolitan areas	596	25,120	1,714	654	24,130	2,144	595	22,423	2,229	2.5
Region										
Northeast	1,149	28,951	1,378	1,128	25,784	1,376	1,088	23,240	1,354	*10.6
Midwest	525	34,088	1,688	542	31,580	2,918	494	30,700	2,131	6.3
South	2,538	28,866	1,037	2,341	28,617	1,034	2,255	26,362	818	−0.7
West	3,061	29,471	904	2,950	28,014	1,046	2,794	26,252	790	3.6
Type of Family										
Married–couple families	4,945	34,816	745	4,804	33,914	902	4,520	31,930	611	1.1
Wife in paid labor force	2,726	45,188	980	2,650	42,280	893	2,536	40,956	778	*5.2
Wife not in paid labor force	2,219	24,939	716	2,153	23,749	724	1,984	22,769	675	3.4
Male householder, no wife present	600	29,227	1,357	545	25,543	1,780	494	25,875	1,249	*12.7
Female householder, no husband present	1,728	16,532	710	1,612	14,994	703	1,617	12,952	677	*8.6
Age of Householder										
Under 65 years	6,683	30,363	542	6,414	28,770	698	6,112	26,713	517	*3.9
15 to 24 years	659	19,738	1,106	626	17,900	1,079	545	15,695	973	8.6
25 to 34 years	2,008	27,587	831	1,944	26,291	756	1,905	25,645	727	3.3
35 to 44 years	2,128	32,299	1,050	2,002	31,431	959	1,925	27,877	1,052	1.2
45 to 54 years	1,194	39,277	1,876	1,166	34,592	1,983	1,074	33,390	2,083	*11.8
55 to 64 years	693	33,872	1,732	676	33,628	2,200	662	31,881	2,260	−0.8
65 years and over	591	21,935	1,353	547	22,677	1,482	519	21,068	1,257	−4.8
65 to 74 years	409	24,115	2,264	372	23,988	1,917	383	22,714	1,716	−1.0
75 years and over	181	20,420	1,888	174	20,419	2,108	136	18,228	2,083	−1.5
Size of Family										
Two people	1,889	24,671	1,042	1,748	23,593	1,228	1,731	21,466	730	3.0
Three people	1,686	27,854	977	1,669	26,210	1,110	1,571	25,275	1,106	4.6
Four people	1,715	32,230	1,193	1,678	31,462	1,175	1,555	29,962	1,126	0.9
Five people	1,192	32,960	1,674	1,108	31,175	1,142	931	29,926	1,256	4.1
Six people	479	32,604	1,940	445	30,233	2,199	488	26,460	1,535	6.2
Seven people or more	312	39,160	3,468	313	35,508	3,190	355	33,540	3,769	8.6
Number of Earners										
No earners	772	9,574	616	815	8,870	554	809	8,601	508	6.3
One earner	2,566	20,548	517	2,434	19,662	637	2,320	18,388	593	2.9
Two earners or more	3,936	42,679	847	3,712	41,153	629	3,502	39,354	880	2.1
Two earners	2,903	38,007	985	2,761	37,425	900	2,548	35,114	966	–
Three earners	733	49,408	2,167	669	47,549	1,635	694	48,292	2,232	2.3
Four earners or more	300	74,857	4,305	282	59,456	2,564	260	58,446	3,073	*24.0

[1]Hispanics may be of any race.

SOURCE: *Current Population Survey*. U.S. Bureau of the Census: Washington, D.C., March 1990, 1998, and 1999

White households was highest in the Northeast ($43,246) and lowest in the South ($38,489). White households located in larger metropolitan areas with populations of 1 million or more, but outside of central cities, earned $50,867, compared to $33,104 earned by those residing outside of metropolitan areas.

In 1998 the median income of Black households was highest in the West ($33,040) and lowest in the Northeast ($22,908). Black households in metropolitan areas of 1 million or more, but outside of central cities, earned more than one and one-half times ($35,646) as much as those outside of metropolitan areas ($21,123). (See Table 5.3.)

For Hispanic households, median income was highest in the Midwest ($32,365) and lowest in the Northeast ($26,009). As with Whites and Blacks, Hispanic households in larger metropolitan areas of 1 million or more people, but outside of central cities, earned more ($35,892) than households located outside of metropolitan areas ($24,537). (See Table 5.3.)

Earnings of Workers

The Bureau of the Census reported that, in 1998, among all full-time, year-round workers, Whites had the highest median income ($51,001), followed by Blacks ($39,565) and Hispanics ($37,152). (See Table 5.3.)

WOMEN STILL EARNING LESS. The bureau also reported that women earned considerably less than men in all races and groups. In 1996 White women working full-time, year-round had median earnings of $24,160. White men working full-time, year-round had median earnings of $32,966. Black women made $21,473, while Black men earned $26,404. Hispanic women earned $18,665, compared to Hispanic men's earnings of $21,056. Overall, in 1996, women made 74 cents for every dollar earned by men. Black and Hispanic women who worked full-time, year-round earned a greater percentage of their male counterparts' salaries (81 percent and 89 percent, respectively) than did White women (73 percent), highlighting the relatively low wages earned by Black and Hispanic men.

HISPANIC INCOME. In 1997 non-Hispanic White families earned a median income of $46,754, compared to $28,142 for Hispanic families. (See Table 5.2.) Among Hispanic subgroups in 1997, family incomes ranged from $23,729 for Puerto Ricans and $27,088 for Mexican Americans to $37,537 for Cuban-origin families, $30,030 for Hispanics of Central and South American descent, and $30,130 for other Hispanics. Over one-fifth of Puerto Rican families (22 percent) had incomes under $10,000, while only 9.6 percent of Cuban-origin families had incomes under $10,000. Over one-third (37.3 percent) of the Cuban-origin population had incomes over $50,000, compared to one-fifth (20.5 percent) of the Mexican-origin

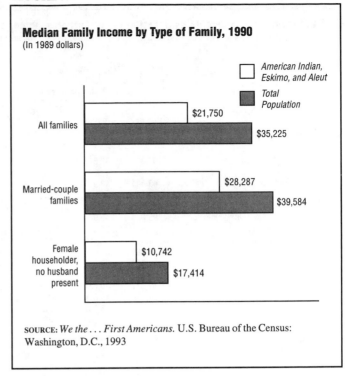

FIGURE 5.1

Median Family Income by Type of Family, 1990
(In 1989 dollars)

SOURCE: *We the . . . First Americans.* U.S. Bureau of the Census: Washington, D.C., 1993

population. Nearly one-third (31.5 percent) of all Puerto Rican families lived below the poverty level, as did 25.8 percent of Mexican American families. (See Table 5.4.)

NATIVE AMERICAN POPULATION. In 1990 the median Native American family income was $21,750, considerably below that of the nation as a whole ($35,225). For every $100 other families earned, Native American families earned $62. In 1990 nearly one-third of Native Americans (31 percent) had incomes below the poverty level, compared to a national rate of about 13 percent. Females with no husband present headed 27 percent of Native American households. The median income for female-headed families was $10,742, about 62 percent of the median for all families maintained by women without husbands. (See Figure 5.1.) This, in part, explains the high level of poverty among Native American families.

The Pine Ridge Reservation, located in Nebraska and South Dakota, is the home of the Oglala branch of the Sioux Indians. Pine Ridge has the highest poverty rate in the nation. The Census Bureau determined that 63 percent of the residents were poor in 1989, compared to the national poverty rate of 14 percent. The reservation had no transportation, very few shops or services, and the roads were unpaved. The infant mortality rate was three times the national average, while deaths from heart disease, pneumonia, influenza, and suicide were twice the national rate. Deaths from homicide were more than three times the national average; from adult diabetes, four times; and from alcoholism, 10 times the national average.

TABLE 5.3

Median Income of Households by Selected Characteristics, Race, and Hispanic Origin of Householder, 1998, 1997, and 1996

[Households as of March of the following year. An asterisk (*) preceding percent change indicates statistically significant change at the 90-percent confidence level.]

Characteristic	1998			1997			1996			Percent change in real median income (1997-1998)
		Median income			Median income			Median income		
	Number (1,000)	Value (dollars)	Standard error (dollars)	Number (1,000)	Value (dollars)	Standard error (dollars)	Number (1,000)	Value (dollars)	Standard error (dollars)	
ALL RACES										
All households	103,874	38,885	230	102,528	37,005	171	101,018	35,492	179	*,3.5
Type of Residence										
Inside metropolitan areas	83,441	40,983	214	82,122	39,381	268	80,950	37,640	245	*,2.5
1 million or more	55,541	43,431	372	54,667	41,502	254	53,760	39,815	327	*,3.0
Inside central cities	20,513	33,559	500	20,310	31,789	356	19,934	30,150	385	*,3.9
Outside central cities	35,028	49,940	394	34,357	47,981	476	33,825	45,526	365	*,2.5
Under 1 million	27,900	36,420	330	27,455	35,409	335	27,190	34,430	402	1.3
Inside central cities	11,631	32,488	535	11,597	31,168	425	11,413	30,659	405	2.6
Outside central cities	16,269	39,428	564	15,858	38,581	518	15,778	37,399	456	0.6
Outside metropolitan areas	20,433	32,022	383	20,406	30,057	413	20,068	28,089	395	*,4.9
Region										
Northeast	19,877	40,634	469	19,810	38,929	525	19,724	37,406	456	*,2.8
Midwest	24,489	40,609	365	24,236	38,316	447	23,972	36,579	365	*,4.4
South	36,959	35,797	304	36,578	34,345	347	35,693	32,422	288	*,2.6
West	22,549	40,983	402	21,905	39,162	545	21,629	37,125	387	*,3.0
Type of Household										
Family households	71,535	47,469	249	70,880	45,347	236	70,241	43,082	251	*,3.1
Married-couple families	54,770	54,276	322	54,317	51,681	232	53,604	49,858	290	*,3.4
Male householder, no wife present	3,976	39,414	993	3,911	36,634	719	3,847	35,658	909	*,5.9
Female householder, no husband present	12,789	24,393	398	12,652	23,040	393	12,790	21,564	326	*,4.2
Nonfamily households	32,339	23,441	284	31,648	21,705	208	30,777	20,973	205	*,6.3
Male householder	14,368	30,414	340	14,133	27,592	461	13,707	27,266	315	*,8.5
Living alone	10,966	26,021	334	11,010	23,871	425	10,442	24,050	401	*,7.3
Female householder	17,971	18,615	281	17,516	17,613	256	17,070	16,398	219	*,4.1
Living alone	15,640	16,406	236	15,317	15,530	245	14,961	14,626	183	*,4.0
Age of Householder										
Under 65 years	82,286	44,697	274	81,031	42,365	201	79,610	40,941	188	*,3.9
15 to 24 years	5,770	23,564	444	5,435	22,583	492	5,160	21,438	417	2.7
25 to 34 years	18,819	40,069	423	19,033	38,174	452	19,314	35,888	355	*,3.4
35 to 44 years	23,968	48,451	444	23,943	46,359	381	23,823	44,420	446	*,2.9
45 to 54 years	20,158	54,148	533	19,547	51,875	435	18,843	50,472	484	*,2.8
55 to 64 years	13,571	43,167	601	13,072	41,356	457	12,469	39,815	615	*,2.8
65 years and over	21,589	21,729	240	21,497	20,761	243	21,408	19,448	208	*,3.1
65 to 74 years	11,373	26,112	399	11,272	25,292	391	11,679	23,411	339	1.7
75 years and over	10,216	17,885	283	10,226	17,079	245	9,729	15,995	246	*,3.1
Size of Household										
One person	26,606	20,154	221	26,327	18,762	209	25,402	17,897	225	*,5.8
Two people	34,262	41,512	301	32,965	39,343	352	32,736	37,283	303	*,3.9
Three people	17,386	49,069	517	17,331	47,115	455	17,065	44,813	422	*,2.5
Four people	15,030	55,886	607	15,358	53,165	585	15,396	51,405	392	*,3.5
Five people	6,962	53,706	911	7,048	50,407	701	6,774	47,841	841	*,4.9
Six people	2,367	49,080	1,500	2,232	46,465	1,326	2,311	42,438	1,277	4.0
Seven people or more	1,261	46,646	1,675	1,267	42,343	1,688	1,334	40,337	1,458	*,8.5
Number of Earners										
No earners	21,263	14,442	147	21,280	14,142	152	21,228	13,320	143	0.6
One earner	36,216	31,162	182	35,150	29,780	259	34,026	27,895	237	*,3.0
Two earners or more	46,396	60,787	258	46,098	57,525	310	45,764	55,547	262	*,4.0
Two earners	36,501	57,388	319	36,188	54,192	340	35,753	52,416	276	*,4.3
Three earners	7,409	70,012	816	7,429	67,182	734	7,455	62,428	655	*,2.6
Four earners or more	2,485	86,676	1,640	2,480	84,816	1,324	2,556	78,504	1,349	0.6
Work Experience of Householder										
Total	**103,874**	**38,885**	**230**	**102,528**	**37,005**	**171**	**101,018**	**35,492**	**179**	***,3.5**
Worked	74,296	48,179	262	73,415	45,877	218	72,377	43,975	237	*,3.4
Worked full-time year-round	54,963	53,033	301	53,665	51,336	212	52,699	49,530	307	*,1.7
Did not work	29,578	19,093	193	29,113	18,143	194	28,641	16,730	171	*,3.6

TABLE 5.3

Median Income of Households by Selected Characteristics, Race, and Hispanic Origin of Householder, 1998, 1997, and 1996 [CONTINUED]

[Households as of March of the following year. An asterisk (*) preceding percent change indicates statistically significant change at the 90-percent confidence level.]

Characteristic	1998			1997			1996			Percent change in real median income (1997-1998)
		Median income			Median income			Median income		
	Number (1,000)	Value (dollars)	Standard error (dollars)	Number (1,000)	Value (dollars)	Standard error (dollars)	Number (1,000)	Value (dollars)	Standard error (dollars)	
WHITE										
All households	87,212	40,912	204	86,106	38,972	247	85,059	37,161	191	*,3.4
Type of Residence										
Inside metropolitan areas	68,821	43,491	330	67,800	41,576	232	67,006	40,113	238	*,3.0
1 million or more	44,738	46,831	334	44,096	44,581	409	43,436	42,207	286	*,3.4
Inside central cities	13,932	37,691	668	13,918	35,451	529	13,622	33,213	655	*,4.7
Outside central cities	30,806	50,867	370	30,179	49,290	502	29,813	46,460	389	1.6
Under 1 million	24,083	38,233	455	23,703	36,906	363	23,570	36,222	381	2.0
Inside central cities	9,338	35,290	572	9,258	33,113	646	9,095	32,943	653	*,4.9
Outside central cities	14,744	40,506	511	14,446	39,352	516	14,475	38,051	492	1.4
Outside metropolitan areas	18,392	33,104	520	18,307	31,110	428	18,053	29,536	405	*,4.8
Region										
Northeast	16,901	43,246	581	16,926	41,214	431	16,848	40,120	518	*,3.3
Midwest	21,659	42,218	423	21,465	40,040	414	21,254	38,057	473	*,3.8
South	29,305	38,489	414	28,948	36,681	340	28,382	35,214	365	*,3.3
West	19,347	41,122	437	18,767	39,479	579	18,575	37,281	439	*,2.6
Type of Household										
Family households	60,068	49,781	277	59,511	47,454	277	58,934	45,382	244	*,3.3
Married-couple families	48,456	54,845	329	48,066	52,199	248	47,650	50,302	250	*,3.5
Male householder, no wife present	3,086	41,384	889	3,137	38,511	1,141	2,944	36,938	887	*,5.8
Female householder, no husband present	8,526	27,542	434	8,308	25,670	422	8,339	24,375	407	*,5.6
Nonfamily households	27,144	24,582	310	26,596	22,380	247	26,125	21,536	222	*,8.2
Male,householder	11,995	31,659	366	11,725	30,009	459	11,481	28,520	486	*,3.9
Living alone	9,028	27,096	377	9,018	25,415	405	8,730	25,098	378	*,5.0
Female householder	15,150	19,239	286	14,871	17,997	273	14,644	16,765	227	*,5.3
Living alone	13,148	16,960	252	12,980	15,818	272	12,783	14,890	194	*,5.6
Age of Householder										
Under 65 years	67,958	47,303	238	66,910	45,210	241	65,877	43,353	253	*,3.0
15 to 24 years	4,587	25,108	502	4,242	24,423	620	4,040	22,606	523	1.2
25 to 34 years	15,062	42,131	406	15,344	40,477	347	15,661	38,283	435	*,2.5
35 to 44 years	19,793	51,091	410	19,761	49,695	520	19,642	47,046	389	1.2
45 to 54 years	16,939	56,704	509	16,400	54,879	622	15,936	52,750	575	1.7
55 to 64 years	11,577	45,803	696	11,163	43,053	788	10,598	42,027	583	*,4.8
65 years and over	19,254	22,442	263	19,196	21,374	255	19,182	19,977	230	*,3.4
65 to 74 years	9,998	27,385	435	9,917	26,363	415	10,366	24,169	355	2.3
75 years and over	9,257	18,205	294	9,279	17,410	257	8,816	16,402	246	3.0
Size of Household										
One person	22,176	20,845	237	21,998	19,288	219	21,513	18,426	235	*,6.4
Two people	29,897	43,218	451	28,817	40,954	296	28,534	39,039	393	*,3.9
Three people	14,217	51,462	441	14,215	50,269	483	14,042	47,529	541	0.8
Four people	12,476	58,580	676	12,654	55,819	556	12,739	53,704	649	*,3.3
Five people	5,699	56,169	772	5,801	52,493	916	5,459	51,102	842	*,5.4
Six people	1,848	52,721	1,579	1,738	48,974	1,668	1,831	44,782	1,906	6.0
Seven people or more	898	51,915	2,424	883	46,044	2,306	941	45,241	1,865	*,11.0
Number of Earners										
No earners	17,968	15,929	199	18,104	15,324	187	17,815	14,579	151	2.4
One earner	29,308	32,844	304	28,332	31,412	197	27,854	29,592	254	*,3.0
Two earners or more	39,936	61,747	284	39,670	58,947	380	39,391	56,521	288	*,3.1
Two earners	31,477	58,524	360	31,256	55,474	316	30,828	53,362	332	*,3.9
Three earners	6,380	70,882	912	6,306	68,363	799	6,356	63,919	827	2.1
Four earners or more	2,080	90,049	1,874	2,108	86,319	1,586	2,207	78,899	1,512	2.7
Work Experience of Householder										
Total	**87,212**	**40,912**	**204**	**86,106**	**38,972**	**247**	**85,059**	**37,161**	**191**	***,3.4**
Worked	62,385	50,360	232	61,469	47,973	297	61,132	45,813	231	*,3.4
Worked full-time, year-round	46,411	55,001	308	45,226	53,045	325	44,833	51,055	235	*,2.1
Did not work	24,827	20,463	235	24,637	19,342	201	23,927	18,003	206	*,4.2

TABLE 5.3

Median Income of Households by Selected Characteristics, Race, and Hispanic Origin of Householder, 1998, 1997, and 1996 [CONTINUED]

[Households as of March of the following year. An asterisk (*) preceding percent change indicates statistically significant change at the 90-percent confidence level.]

	1998			1997			1996			Percent change in real median income (1997-1998)
		Median income			Median income			Median income		
Characteristic	Number (1,000)	Value (dollars)	Standard error (dollars)	Number (1,000)	Value (dollars)	Standard error (dollars)	Number (1,000)	Value (dollars)	Standard error (dollars)	
BLACK										
All households	12,579	25,351	397	12,474	25,050	431	12,109	23,482	462	−0.3
Type of Residence										
Inside metropolitan areas	10,928	26,024	428	10,761	25,720	463	10,492	25,019	485	−0.4
1 million or more	8,001	26,828	551	7,884	26,967	529	7,739	25,693	537	−2.0
Inside central cities	5,274	22,717	706	5,157	23,156	703	4,999	21,573	605	−3.4
Outside central cities	2,726	35,646	1,348	2,727	34,949	1,261	2,740	34,448	1,072	0.4
Under 1 million	2,928	24,041	1,081	2,877	21,683	792	2,753	22,957	967	*,9.2
Inside central cities	1,832	22,386	1,061	1,876	19,901	913	1,825	19,941	1,118	*,10.8
Outside central cities	1,095	26,026	1,029	1,002	24,597	1,286	928	27,913	1,572	4.2
Outside metropolitan areas	1,651	21,123	1,076	1,713	20,184	1,735	1,617	16,903	1,013	3.0
Region										
Northeast	2,354	22,908	1,060	2,286	23,312	1,033	2,278	22,177	836	−3.2
Midwest	2,344	24,215	874	2,288	23,861	1,032	2,251	23,314	1,150	−0.1
South	6,817	25,420	528	6,814	25,074	555	6,519	23,277	647	−0.2
West	1,064	33,040	2,297	1,086	29,988	1,405	1,061	30,176	1,939	8.5
Type of Household										
Family households	8,444	30,636	574	8,408	29,915	570	8,455	27,496	631	0.8
Married-couple families	3,975	47,382	1,171	3,921	45,372	755	3,851	42,069	1,000	2.8
Male householder, no wife present	660	30,360	1,742	562	28,593	1,191	657	30,995	990	4.6
Female householder, no husband present	3,809	17,737	516	3,926	17,962	627	3,947	16,256	512	−2.8
Nonfamily households	4,135	16,071	646	4,066	17,073	559	3,654	15,454	661	*,−7.3
Male householder	1,827	20,673	912	1,876	19,459	864	1,669	20,525	960	4.6
Living alone	1,545	18,351	1,065	1,594	17,139	921	1,303	16,447	1,058	5.4
Female householder	2,308	13,608	592	2,190	15,341	722	1,985	12,434	654	*,−12.7
Living alone	2,087	12,397	540	1,982	13,738	837	1,823	11,529	559	*,−11.1
Age of Householder										
Under 65 years	10,703	27,764	611	10,595	27,238	455	10,291	25,699	410	0.4
15 to 24 years	866	13,630	1,611	935	15,056	1,284	871	13,246	918	−10.9
25 to 34 years	2,750	26,346	654	2,752	26,149	857	2,687	23,275	871	−0.8
35 to 44 years	3,110	31,297	835	3,096	27,710	769	3,095	29,859	939	*,11.2
45 to 54 years	2,444	35,472	1,123	2,371	33,761	1,766	2,210	33,878	1,738	3.5
55 to 64 years	1,532	25,200	1,243	1,441	27,350	1,936	1,428	23,449	1,227	−9.3
65 years and over	1,877	13,936	563	1,878	14,241	583	1,818	14,019	450	−3.6
65 to 74 years	1,084	14,560	764	1,123	16,287	965	1,085	15,944	837	*,−12.0
75 years and over	793	12,886	881	755	12,101	715	733	12,102	753	4.9
Size of Household										
One person	3,633	14,285	487	3,576	15,258	563	3,126	13,771	478	*,−7.8
Two people	3,339	26,506	638	3,120	26,870	775	3,196	24,844	944	−2.9
Three people	2,342	28,661	1,233	2,338	28,047	1,287	2,298	26,321	810	0.6
Four people	1,771	37,862	1,666	1,930	35,529	1,283	1,891	32,944	1,318	4.9
Five people	905	36,160	1,479	916	36,525	2,596	988	31,806	1,209	−2.5
Six people	348	31,752	2,325	340	32,050	2,871	333	30,931	1,875	−2.4
Seven people or more	242	31,420	1,756	253	30,799	3,558	277	27,318	2,842	0.5
Number of Earners										
No earners	2,759	8,084	214	2,660	8,172	249	2,800	7,612	220	−2.6
One earner	5,472	22,046	361	5,428	21,319	386	4,867	20,658	385	1.8
Two earners or more	4,348	50,668	704	4,386	47,602	776	4,442	45,129	841	*,4.8
Two earners	3,453	46,905	930	3,459	44,728	730	3,512	42,539	900	3.3
Three earners	657	58,713	2,611	755	57,599	1,698	745	51,894	1,837	0.4
Four earners or more	238	74,696	3,595	172	77,190	4,350	185	71,429	6,961	−4.7
Work Experience of Householder										
Total	**12,579**	**25,351**	**397**	**12,474**	**25,050**	**431**	**12,109**	**23,482**	**462**	**−0.3**
Worked	8,735	33,046	673	8,855	31,461	417	8,301	31,259	461	*,3.4
Worked full-time, year-round	6,221	39,565	810	6,141	36,928	541	5,742	36,939	593	*,5.5
Did not work	3,845	10,656	402	3,619	10,523	375	3,808	9,840	272	−0.3

TABLE 5.3

Median Income of Households by Selected Characteristics, Race, and Hispanic Origin of Householder, 1998, 1997, and 1996 [CONTINUED]

[Households as of March of the following year. An asterisk (*) preceding percent change indicates statistically significant change at the 90-percent confidence level.]

	1998 Median income			1997 Median income			1996 Median income			Percent change in real median income (1997-1998)
Characteristic	Number (1,000)	Value (dollars)	Standard error (dollars)	Number (1,000)	Value (dollars)	Standard error (dollars)	Number (1,000)	Value (dollars)	Standard error (dollars)	
HISPANIC ORIGIN[1]										
All households	9,060	28,330	545	8,590	26,628	474	8,225	24,906	482	*,4.8
Type of Residence										
Inside metropolitan areas	8,322	28,819	581	7,808	27,078	517	7,475	25,362	506	*,4.8
1 million or more	6,157	30,206	570	5,805	28,433	740	5,587	26,318	595	*,4.6
Inside central cities	3,258	25,655	638	3,099	23,398	789	2,995	21,903	591	*,8.0
Outside central cities	2,900	35,892	809	2,706	35,506	1,081	2,592	32,013	815	−0.5
Under 1 million	2,165	25,292	875	2,002	23,883	1,079	1,888	22,367	935	4.3
Inside central cities	1,241	23,543	1,521	1,180	23,262	1,551	1,126	21,823	1,107	−0.3
Outside central cities	924	26,748	1,318	822	24,408	1,273	762	23,334	1,447	7.9
Outside metropolitan areas	738	24,537	1,784	783	22,383	1,800	750	20,244	1,606	7.9
Region										
Northeast	1,526	26,009	1,244	1,468	24,023	1,435	1,424	20,859	1,041	6.6
Midwest	651	32,365	1,764	644	31,009	1,676	592	30,177	1,745	2.8
South	3,200	27,222	818	2,939	26,207	754	2,797	24,814	802	2.3
West	3,684	29,193	810	3,539	27,276	930	3,412	25,619	759	*,5.4
Type of Household										
Family households	7,270	30,812	505	6,961	29,253	638	6,631	27,152	541	*,3.7
Married-couple families	4,945	35,207	668	4,804	34,317	890	4,520	32,379	756	1.0
Male householder, no wife present	600	32,239	1,393	545	28,249	1,839	494	28,322	1,522	*,12.4
Female householder, no husband present	1,725	18,452	927	1,612	16,393	641	1,617	14,535	695	*,10.8
Nonfamily households	1,790	16,805	1,243	1,630	16,807	902	1,593	15,705	757	−1.5
Male householder	927	23,427	1,566	875	21,059	857	854	19,323	1,394	9.5
Living alone	644	18,358	1,975	623	16,524	930	575	14,506	1,240	9.4
Female householder	863	11,669	654	754	11,485	667	740	11,770	958	−
Living alone	685	9,812	529	617	9,666	605	621	9,746	619	−0.1
Age of Householder										
Under 65 years	8,096	30,131	507	7,674	28,315	644	7,329	26,368	489	*,4.8
15 to 24 years	908	21,739	1,156	780	19,341	1,021	687	17,200	858	*,10.7
25 to 34 years	2,423	28,980	854	2,303	27,519	879	2,263	26,444	705	3.7
35 to 44 years	2,412	32,488	1,029	2,316	31,148	900	2,229	27,781	974	2.7
45 to 54 years	1,447	37,026	1,383	1,386	32,074	1,290	1,296	30,709	1,641	*,13.7
55 to 64 years	906	28,765	1,720	889	27,648	2,325	854	26,294	1,956	2.4
65 years and over	964	14,729	802	916	14,168	868	895	14,006	1,045	2.4
65 to 74 years	632	16,542	1,167	566	15,885	1,271	611	16,104	1,035	2.5
75 years and over	332	12,246	935	350	11,015	1,261	284	11,337	934	9.5
Size of Household										
One person	1,329	12,584	676	1,240	12,222	777	1,195	11,894	632	1.4
Two people	1,972	26,522	917	1,838	26,390	961	1,815	22,258	803	−1.0
Three people	1,767	29,405	1,133	1,728	26,396	1,050	1,650	27,078	1,143	*,9.7
Four people	1,823	32,998	1,203	1,763	33,053	1,577	1,632	30,048	1,054	−1.7
Five people	1,264	33,714	1,677	1,199	31,586	1,247	995	30,356	1,152	5.1
Six people	544	33,797	1,699	463	30,185	2,045	538	27,510	1,953	10.2
Seven people or more	361	41,343	3,717	358	36,088	3,060	399	34,864	2,754	12.8
Number of Earners										
No earners	1,296	8,353	328	1,312	7,842	351	1,281	7,912	320	4.9
One earner	3,303	21,175	440	3,081	20,464	401	2,959	18,883	540	1.9
Two earners or more	4,461	42,941	771	4,197	41,081	590	3,984	39,231	864	*,2.9
Two earners	3,234	38,288	1,043	3,096	37,106	799	2,863	34,835	969	1.6
Three earners	842	48,156	1,743	759	47,569	1,604	787	47,044	1,735	−0.3
Four earners or more	386	71,630	2,486	342	58,360	2,270	334	58,055	2,792	*,20.9
Work Experience of Householder										
Total	**9,060**	**28,330**	**545**	**8,590**	**26,628**	**474**	**8,225**	**24,906**	**482**	***,4.8**
Worked	6,851	33,355	658	6,401	32,019	462	6,058	30,226	534	2.6
Worked full-time, year-round	4,922	37,152	647	4,592	36,701	629	4,228	35,038	765	−0.3
Did not work	2,209	13,618	569	2,189	11,893	442	2,167	11,737	438	* 12.8

[1]Hispanics may be of any race.

SOURCE: *Current Population Survey.* U.S. Bureau of the Census: Washington, D.C., March 1990, 1998, and 1999

TABLE 5.4

Social and Economic Characteristics of the Hispanic Population, 1998

[As of March, except labor force status, annual average (30,773 represents 30,773,000). Excludes members of the Armed Forces except those living off post or with their families on post. Based on Current Population Survey]

Characteristic	Number (1,000)						Percent distribution					
	His-panic, total	Mexi-can	Puerto Rican	Cuban	Central and South Ameri-can	Other His-panic	His-panic, total	Mexi-can	Puerto Rican	Cuban	Central and South Ameri-can	Other His-panic
Total persons	30,773	19,834	3,117	1,307	4,437	2,079	100.0	100.0	100.0	100.0	100.0	100.0
Under 5 years old	3,482	2,464	347	93	383	196	11.3	12.4	11.1	7.1	8.6	9.4
5 to 14 years old	5,862	4,106	569	141	665	382	19.0	20.7	18.2	10.8	15.0	18.4
15 to 44 years old	15,479	9,935	1,487	548	2,516	993	50.3	50.1	47.7	41.9	56.7	47.8
45 to 64 years old	4,333	2,475	516	270	702	370	14.1	12.5	16.6	20.7	15.8	17.8
65 years old and over	1,617	854	199	255	172	138	5.3	4.3	6.4	19.5	3.9	6.6
EDUCATIONAL ATTAINMENT												
Persons 25 years old and over	16,044	9,649	1,682	952	2,599	1,163	100.0	100.0	100.0	100.0	100.0	100.0
High school graduate or higher	8,901	4,657	1,074	645	1,686	840	55.5	48.3	63.8	67.8	64.9	72.2
Bachelor's degree or higher	1,768	719	201	211	452	186	11.0	7.5	11.9	22.2	17.4	16.0
LABOR FORCE STATUS												
Civilians 16 years old and over	21,070	13,216	2,080	1,062	3,215	1,497	100.0	100.0	100.0	100.0	100.0	100.0
Civilian labor force	14,317	9,096	1,249	651	2,343	978	67.9	68.8	60.0	61.3	72.9	65.3
Employed	13,291	8,431	1,145	612	2,201	902	63.1	63.8	55.0	57.6	68.5	60.3
Unemployed	1,026	664	104	39	143	76	4.9	5.0	5.0	3.7	4.4	5.1
Unemployment rate[2]	7.2	7.3	8.3	6.0	6.1	7.8	(X)	(X)	(X)	(X)	(X)	(X)
Male	6.4	6.5	8.5	4.1	5.4	7.2	(X)	(X)	(X)	(X)	(X)	(X)
Female	8.2	8.6	8.2	8.6	7.0	7.9	(X)	(X)	(X)	(X)	(X)	(X)
Not in labor force	6,753	4,121	832	411	872	517	32.1	31.2	40.0	38.7	27.1	34.5
FAMILY TYPE												
Total families	6,961	4,292	770	383	1,018	498	100.0	100.0	100.0	100.0	100.0	100.0
Married couple	4,804	3,093	415	309	688	298	69.0	72.1	53.9	80.8	67.6	59.8
Female householder, no spouse present	1,612	858	290	58	236	169	23.2	20.0	37.7	15.1	23.2	34.0
Male householder, no spouse present	545	341	65	16	93	31	7.8	7.9	8.4	4.1	9.2	6.2
FAMILY INCOME IN 1997												
Total families	6,961	4,292	770	383	1,018	498	100.0	100.0	100.0	100.0	100.0	100.0
Less than $5,000	352	219	52	8	45	27	5.1	5.1	6.8	2.2	4.4	5.5
$5,000 to $9,999	604	347	119	28	54	55	8.7	8.1	15.5	7.4	5.3	11.1
$10,000 to $14,999	759	500	81	44	89	44	10.9	11.7	10.5	11.5	8.8	8.9
$15,000 to $24,999	1,397	921	153	58	193	72	20.1	21.5	19.9	15.2	18.9	14.5
$25,000 to $34,999	1,066	688	92	44	164	77	15.3	16.0	11.9	11.5	16.1	15.6
$35,000 to $49,999	1,199	735	107	57	207	93	17.2	17.1	13.9	15.0	20.3	18.7
$50,000 or more	1,584	882	165	143	266	129	22.8	20.5	21.4	37.2	26.2	25.8
Median income (dol.)	28,141	27,088	23,729	37,537	32,030	30,130	(X)	(X)	(X)	(X)	(X)	(X)
Families below poverty level	1,721	1,106	243	60	188	124	24.7	25.8	31.5	15.6	18.4	25.0
Persons below poverty level	8,308	5,509	1,059	257	949	534	27.1	27.9	34.2	19.6	21.5	25.7
HOUSING TENURE												
Total occupied units	8,590	5,091	1,053	498	1,272	677	100.0	100.0	100.0	100.0	100.0	100.0
Owner-occupied	3,857	2,495	355	279	404	326	44.9	49.0	33.7	55.9	31.8	48.1
Renter-occupied[5]	4,733	2,597	698	220	868	351	55.1	51.0	66.3	44.1	68.2	51.9

X Not applicable.

[1] Total unemployment as percent of civilian labor force.

[2] Includes no cash rent.

SOURCE: *Statistical Abstract of the United States.* U.S. Bureau of the Census: Washington, D.C., 1999

ASIAN AMERICANS/PACIFIC ISLANDERS. The median income for Asian/Pacific Islander (API) families in 1998 was $51,850. Only 11 percent of API families had incomes of less than $15,000, and over half (52.2 percent) had family incomes of $50,000 or more. More than half (52.8 percent) of API families owned their own homes. Only 10.2 percent of API families lived below the poverty level. (See Table 5.5.)

POVERTY STATUS OF MINORITIES

Every year the Census Bureau establishes poverty thresholds that determine the distribution of different wel-

TABLE 5.5

Social and Economic Characteristics of the Asian and Pacific Islander Population, 1990 and 1998

[As of March. Excludes members of Armed Forces except those living off post or with their families on post. Data for 1990 are based on 1980 census population controls; 1996 data are based on 1990 census population controls]

CHARACTERISTIC	NUMBER (1,000)		PERCENT DISTRIBUTION	
	1990	1996	1990	1996
Total persons	**6,679**	**9,653**	**100.0**	**100.0**
Under 5 years old	602	867	9.0	9.0
5 to14 years old	1,112	1,565	16.6	16.2
15 to 44 years old	3,345	4,908	50.1	50.8
45 to 64 years old	1,155	1,692	17.3	17.5
65 years old and over	465	622	7.0	6.4
EDUCATIONAL ATTAINMENT				
Persons 25 years old and over	3,961	5,677	100.0	100.0
Elementary: 0 to 8 years	543	582	13.7	10.2
High school: 1 to 3 years	234	[1]370	5.9	[1]6.5
4 years	1,038	[2]1,233	26.2	[2]21.7
College: 1 to 3 years	568	[3]1,123	14.3	[3]19.8
4 years or more	1,578	[4]2,369	39.9	[4]41.7
LABOR FORCE STATUS[5]				
Civilians 16 years old and over	4,849	7,044	100.0	100.0
Civilian labor force	3,216	4,641	66.3	65.9
Employed	3,079	4,408	63.5	62.6
Unemployed	136	233	2.8	3.3
Unemployment rate[6]	4.2	5.0	(X)	(X)
Not in labor force	1,634	2,402	33.7	34.1
FAMILY TYPE				
Total families	**1,531**	**2,125**	**100.0**	**100.0**
Married couple	1,256	1,692	82.1	79.6
Female householder, no spouse present	188	260	12.3	12.2
Male householder, no spouse present	86	173	5.6	8.2
FAMILY INCOME IN PREVIOUS YEAR IN CONSTANT (1995) DOLLARS				
Total families	**1,531**	**2,125**	**100.0**	**100.0**
Less than $5,000	(NA)	59	(NA)	2.8
$5,000 to $9,999	(NA)	106	(NA)	5.0
$10,000 to $14,999	(NA)	131	(NA)	6.2
$15,000 to $24,999	(NA)	245	(NA)	11.6
$25,000 to $34,999	(NA)	224	(NA)	10.5
$35,000 to $49,999	(NA)	382	(NA)	18.0
$50,000 or more	(NA)	978	(NA)	46.0
Median income	49,593	46,356	(NA)	(NA)
Families below poverty level	182	264	11.9	12.4
Persons below poverty level	938	1,411	14.1	14.6
HOUSING TENURE				
Total occupied units	**1,988**	**2,777**	**100.0**	**100.0**
Owner-occupied	977	1,411	49.1	50.8
Renter-occupied	982	1,313	49.4	47.3
No cash rent	30	53	1.5	1.9

NA Not available.

X Not applicable.

[1]Represents those who completed ninth to twelfth grade, but have no high school diploma.

[2]High school graduate.

[3]Some college or associate degree.

[4]Bachelor's or advanced degree.

[5]Data beginning 1994 not directly comparable with earlier years.

[6]Total unemployment as percent of civilian labor force.

SOURCE: *Current Population Reports*, P20-459; and unpublished data. U.S. Bureau of the Census

fare benefits. A family of four was considered poor in 1998 if it had an income below the poverty threshold of $16,660. The average poverty threshold ranged from $7,818 for an elderly person 65 and over who lived alone, to $33,339 for a family with nine or more members. (See Table 5.6.)

The Bureau of the Census (*Poverty in the United States: 1998,* Washington, DC, 1999) reported that, in 1998, about 34.5 million persons—12.7 percent of the nation's population in the United States—were living below the official poverty level. The poverty rate in 1998

TABLE 5.6

Poverty Thresholds by Size of Family, 1998

[Numbers in thousands. Families and children as of March of the following year.]

Characteristic	One person			Two people			Three people	Four people	Five people	Six people	Seven people	Eight people	Nine or more people
	Total	Under 65	65 and over	Total	House-holder under 65	House-holder 65 and over							
TOTAL													
Number	42 539	31 975	10 564	31 102	21 637	9 465	16 227	14 390	6 573	2 135	691	268	166
Poverty threshold (dollars)	8 316	8 480	7 818	10 634	10 972	9 862	13 003	16 660	19 680	22 228	25 257	28 166	33 339
Families in poverty	8 478	6 328	2 150	2 505	1 973	532	1 592	1 417	945	428	167	73	59
People in poverty	8 478	6 328	2 150	5 116	4 001	1 115	4 813	5 724	4 778	2 550	1 199	592	598
NUMBER OF RELATED CHILDREN UNDER 18													
None:													
Number	42 539	31 975	10 564	27 168	17 770	9 398	5 234	1 533	280	53	12	–	4
Poverty threshold (dollars)	8 316	8 480	7 818	10 548	10 915	9 853	12 750	16 813	20 275	23 320	26 833	30 010	36 100
Families in poverty	8 478	6 328	2 150	1 358	858	501	163	32	4	–	–	–	–
People in poverty	8 478	6 328	2 150	2 824	1 777	1 048	533	145	27	–	–	–	–
One:													
Number	–	–	–	3 934	3 867	67	8 318	2 473	636	125	33	7	–
Poverty threshold (dollars)	–	–	–	11 234	11 235	11 193	13 120	17 088	20 570	23 413	27 000	30 275	36 275
Families in poverty	–	–	–	1 146	1 116	31	508	160	26	15	2	–	–
People in poverty	–	–	–	2 292	2 224	68	1 563	685	146	94	21	–	–
Two:													
Number	–	–	–	–	–	–	2 675	9 304	1 361	361	84	23	2
Poverty threshold (dollars)	–	–	–	–	–	–	13 133	16 530	19 940	22 930	26 423	29 730	35 793
Families in poverty	–	–	–	–	–	–	921	584	114	26	5	–	–
People In poverty	–	–	–	–	–	–	2 717	2 349	607	157	37	–	–
Three:													
Number	–	–	–	–	–	–	–	1 080	3 916	432	115	48	10
Poverty threshold (dollars)	–	–	–	–	–	–	–	16 588	19 453	22 468	26 020	29 253	35 388
Families in poverty	–	–	–	–	–	–	–	640	501	60	22	10	2
People in poverty	–	–	–	–	–	–	–	2 545	2 509	370	164	87	17
Four:													
Number	–	–	–	–	–	–	–	–	381	1 060	184	60	27
Poverty threshold (dollars)	–	–	–	–	–	–	–	–	19 155	21 780	25 270	28 575	34 723
Families in poverty	–	–	–	–	–	–	–	–	300	236	33	11	7
People in poverty	–	–	–	–	–	–	–	–	1 489	1 400	226	88	67
Five:													
Number	–	–	–	–	–	–	–	–	–	104	220	56	23
Poverty threshold (dollars)	–	–	–	–	–	–	–	–	–	21 373	24 395	27 715	33 808
Families in poverty	–	–	–	–	–	–	–	–	–	91	72	23	3
People in poverty	–	–	–	–	–	–	–	–	–	528	505	184	33
Six:													
Number	–	–	–	–	–	–	–	–	–	–	42	58	26
Poverty threshold (dollars)	–	–	–	–	–	–	–	–	–	–	23 435	26 820	32 980
Families in poverty	–	–	–	–	–	–	–	–	–	–	33	15	13
People in poverty	–	–	–	–	–	–	–	–	–	–	246	132	134
Seven:													
Number	–	–	–	–	–	–	–	–	–	–	–	16	49
Poverty threshold (dollars)	–	–	–	–	–	–	–	–	–	–	–	26 593	32 775
Families in poverty	–	–	–	–	–	–	–	–	–	–	–	14	18
People in poverty	–	–	–	–	–	–	–	–	–	–	–	102	176
Eight or more:													
Number	–	–	–	–	–	–	–	–	–	–	–	–	26
Poverty threshold (dollars)	–	–	–	–	–	–	–	–	–	–	–	–	31 513
Families in poverty	–	–	–	–	–	–	–	–	–	–	–	–	17
People in poverty	–	–	–	–	–	–	–	–	–	–	–	–	171

SOURCE: *Current Population Survey.* U.S. Bureau of the Census: Washington, D.C., Sept 1999

was lower than the peak of 15.2 percent reached in 1983 after the recession of the early 1980s. (See Figure 5.2 for 1959 to 1998 rates.) In 1998 the poverty rate among some minorities was significantly higher than the overall rate, with a Black poverty rate of 26.1 percent, and a Hispanic rate of 25.6 percent. The non-Hispanic White rate of 8.2 percent was considerably lower than the overall rate. (See Table 5.7.)

Although non-Hispanic Whites had a much lower poverty rate than other groups, they made up the biggest portion (45.8 percent) of poor persons in 1998. Blacks

FIGURE 5.2

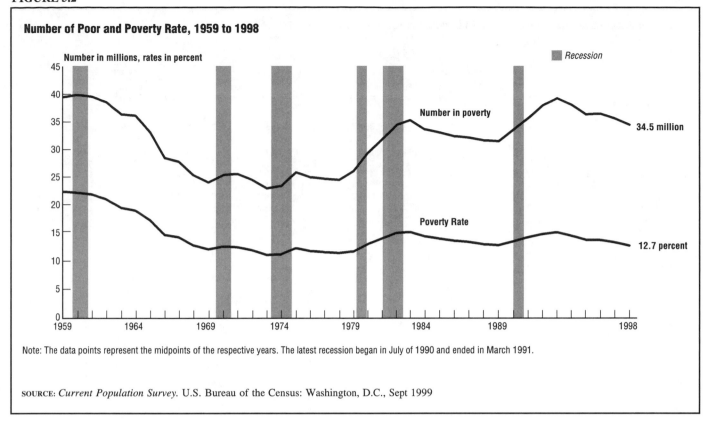

Number of Poor and Poverty Rate, 1959 to 1998

Number in millions, rates in percent

Recession

Number in poverty

34.5 million

Poverty Rate

12.7 percent

Note: The data points represent the midpoints of the respective years. The latest recession began in July of 1990 and ended in March 1991.

SOURCE: *Current Population Survey.* U.S. Bureau of the Census: Washington, D.C., Sept 1999

accounted for 26.4 percent of all persons below the poverty level. About 23 percent of all poor were Hispanics, who may be either White or Black. The remaining 4 percent were other races. Most of those in the "other" group were of Asian or Pacific Islander descent. (See Table 5.7.)

Poverty and Educational Attainment

Poverty rates decrease dramatically as the years of education increase. The overall poverty rate in 1997 was 24.1 percent for householders age 25 and older who had not completed high school, and 9.9 percent for those who had been graduated from high school but not attended college. The poverty rate was 6.6 percent for householders who had attended, but not completed college, and 2 percent for those who had been graduated from college. (See Table 5.8.)

In 1997 Blacks without a high school diploma (37.9 percent) were twice as likely as comparable Whites (21 percent) to be in poverty. Over one-third (35.1 percent) of Hispanics without a high school degree were in poverty. For those with a high school diploma, the percentage of families below the poverty level dropped to 22.8 percent for Blacks, 17.7 percent for Hispanics, and 7.8 percent for Whites. The percentages of all families living in poverty when the householder held a bachelor's degree were small—5.2 percent of Blacks, 7.8 percent of Hispanics, and 1.6 percent of Whites. (See Table 5.8.)

In 1998 Black men with bachelor's degrees ($35,792) earned less than White men with bachelor's degrees ($51,678), while the earnings of Black and Hispanic female college graduates were much more comparable ($29,091 versus $29,173, respectively). (See Table 5.9.)

CHILDREN LIVING IN POVERTY

Although there are various ways to define a poor household, the federal government's definition is having an income below the U.S. poverty threshold. (See Table 5.6, which shows poverty thresholds for 1998.)

In 1997 nearly one in every five (19.2 percent) children under the age of 18 lived in poverty. Although children in 1997 represented a quarter (25.9 percent) of the total U.S. population, they comprised nearly 40 percent of the poor population. About 15 percent of White children, compared to 36.8 percent of Black and 36.4 percent of Hispanic children, lived in poverty. (See Table 5.10.) In 1997 nearly 22 percent of related children under the age of six lived in poverty, while three in five (59 percent) living in families maintained by women with no spouse present were poor. This poverty rate is almost six times the rate for children under age six in married-couple families.

ELDERLY POOR

In the years prior to and including 1973, the poverty rate of the elderly (16.3 percent) exceeded that of chil-

TABLE 5.7

Persons and Families in Poverty by Selected Characteristics, 1989, 1997 and 1998

[Numbers in thousands.]

Characteristic	Below poverty, 1998				Below poverty, 1997				Below poverty, 1989[r]			
	Number	90-pct. C.I. (±)	Percent	90-pct. C.I. (±)	Number	90-pct. C.I. (±)	Percent	90-pct. C.I. (±)	Number	90-pct. C.I. (±)	Percent	90-pct. C.I. (±)
PEOPLE												
Total	**34,476**	**920**	**12.7**	**0.3**	**35,574**	**931**	**13.3**	**0.3**	**32,415**	**859**	**13.1**	**0.3**
Family Status												
In families	25,370	804	11.2	0.4	26,217	814	11.6	0.4	24,882	765	11.8	0.4
Householder	7,186	248	10.0	0.4	7,324	252	10.3	0.4	6,895	232	10.4	0.4
Related children under 18	12,845	479	18.3	0.7	13,422	485	19.2	0.7	12,541	454	19.4	0.7
Related children under 6	4,775	309	20.6	1.4	5,049	316	21.6	1.4	5,116	306	22.5	1.4
In unrelated subfamilies	628	66	48.8	6.0	670	67	46.5	5.5	727	67	54.6	6.1
Reference person	247	41	47.4	9.2	259	41	45.0	8.5	284	41	51.8	9.1
Children under 18	361	89	50.5	14.2	403	94	48.9	13.0	430	92	60.5	15.3
Unrelated individual	8,478	275	19.9	0.7	8,687	280	20.8	0.7	6,807	230	19.3	0.7
Male	3,465	161	17.0	0.8	3,447	161	17.4	0.9	2,577	132	15.8	0.8
Female	5,013	201	22.6	1.0	5,240	206	24.0	1.0	4,230	174	22.3	1.0
Race[2] and Hispanic Origin[3]												
White, total	23,454	776	10.5	0.3	24,396	790	11.0	0.4	21,294	712	10.2	0.3
White, not Hispanic	15,799	646	8.2	0.3	16,491	660	8.6	0.3	15,499	615	8.3	0.3
Black, total	9,091	434	26.1	1.2	9,116	434	26.5	1.3	9,525	423	30.8	1.4
Asian and Pacific Islander, total	1,360	181	12.5	1.7	1,468	186	14.0	1.8	1,032	155	14.2	2.1
Hispanic origin,[3] all races	8,070	411	25.6	1.3	8,308	413	27.1	1.3	6,086	357	26.3	1.5
Age												
Under 18 years	13,467	487	18.9	0.7	14,113	495	19.9	0.7	13,154	462	20.1	0.7
18 to 64 years	17,623	674	10.5	0.4	18,085	681	10.9	0.4	15,950	617	10.4	0.4
18 to 24 years	4,312	201	16.6	0.8	4,416	204	17.5	0.8	4,132	189	15.4	0.7
25 to 34 years	4,582	214	11.9	0.6	4,759	219	12.1	0.6	4,873	212	11.2	0.5
35 to 44 years	4,082	202	9.1	0.5	4,251	207	9.6	0.5	3,115	171	8.3	0.5
45 to 54 years	2,444	158	6.9	0.4	2,439	158	7.2	0.5	1,873	133	7.5	0.5
55 to 59 years	1,165	110	9.2	0.9	1,092	107	9.0	0.9	971	97	9.5	0.9
60 to 64 years	1,039	104	10.1	1.0	1,127	109	11.2	1.1	986	97	9.4	0.9
65 years and over	3,386	179	10.5	0.6	3,376	179	10.5	0.6	3,312	171	11.4	0.6
Nativity												
Native	29,707	860	12.1	0.4	30,336	869	12.5	0.4	NA	NA	NA	NA
Foreign-born	4,769	413	18.0	1.6	5,238	433	19.9	1.6	NA	NA	NA	NA
Naturalized citizen	1,087	199	11.0	2.0	1,111	201	11.4	2.1	NA	NA	NA	NA
Not a citizen	3,682	364	22.2	2.2	4,127	385	25.0	2.3	NA	NA	NA	NA
Region												
Northeast	6,357	385	12.3	0.8	6,474	388	12.6	0.8	5,213	336	10.2	0.7
Midwest	6,501	428	10.3	0.7	6,493	428	10.4	0.7	7,088	429	12.0	0.7
South	12,992	612	13.7	0.7	13,748	628	14.6	0.7	13,277	594	15.6	0.7
West	8,625	505	14.0	0.8	8,858	512	14.6	0.9	6,838	433	12.8	0.8
Residence												
Inside metropolitan areas	26,997	827	12.3	0.4	27,273	829	12.6	0.4	23,726	748	12.3	0.4
Inside central cities	14,921	630	18.5	0.8	15,018	632	18.8	0.8	14,151	589	18.5	0.8
Outside central cities	12,076	569	8.7	0.4	12,255	572	9.0	0.4	9,574	489	8.2	0.4
Outside metropolitan areas	7,479	554	14.4	1.1	8,301	582	15.9	1.1	8,690	571	15.9	1.1
FAMILIES												
Total	**7,186**	**248**	**10.0**	**0.4**	**7,324**	**252**	**10.3**	**0.4**	**6,895**	**232**	**10.4**	**0.4**
White, total	4,829	196	8.0	0.3	4,990	199	8.4	0.3	4,457	179	7.9	0.3
White, not Hispanic	3,264	156	6.1	0.3	3,357	160	6.3	0.3	3,287	151	6.4	0.3
Black, total	1,981	118	23.4	1.5	1,985	118	23.6	1.5	2,108	118	27.9	1.7
Asian and Pacific Islander, total	270	43	11.0	1.8	244	41	10.2	1.8	201	35	12.2	2.2
Hispanic origin,[3] all races	1,648	109	22.7	1.5	1,721	110	24.7	1.6	1,227	89	23.7	1.8
Type of Family												
Married-couple	2,879	146	5.3	0.3	2,821	145	5.2	0.3	2,965	143	5.7	0.3
White	2,400	132	5.0	0.3	2,312	130	4.8	0.3	2,347	125	5.0	0.3
White, not Hispanic	1,639	107	3.8	0.2	1,501	102	3.5	0.2	1,776	107	4.1	0.3
Black	290	44	7.3	1.1	312	46	8.0	1.2	444	53	11.7	1.4
Hispanic origin,[3] all races	775	72	15.7	1.5	836	76	17.4	1.6	592	61	16.4	1.8
Female householder, no husband present	3,831	171	29.9	1.5	3,995	176	31.6	1.5	3,575	158	32.6	1.6
White	2,123	123	24.9	1.6	2,305	130	27.7	1.7	1,886	112	25.8	1.7
White, not Hispanic	1,428	100	20.7	1.6	1,598	107	23.4	1.7	1,341	92	21.7	1.6
Black	1,557	105	40.8	3.1	1,563	105	39.8	3.0	1,553	100	46.7	3.4
Hispanic origin,[3] all races	756	72	43.7	4.7	767	72	47.6	5.1	576	59	48.0	5.7

See footnotes at end of table.

TABLE 5.7

Persons and Families in Poverty by Selected Characteristics, 1989, 1997 and 1998 [CONTINUED]

[Numbers in thousands]

Characteristic	Change 1997 to 1998[1]				Change 1989[r] to 1998[1]			
	Number	90-pct. C.I. (±)	Percent	90-pct. C.I. (±)	Number	90-pct. C.I. (±)	Percent	90-pct. C.I. (±)
PEOPLE								
Total	*-1,098	971	*-0.5	0.4	*2,060	1,258	-0.3	0.5
Family status								
In families	-847	849	*-0.5	0.4	488	1,109	*-0.6	0.5
Householder	-138	262	-0.3	0.4	291	341	-0.4	0.5
Related children under 18	*-577	505	*-0.9	0.8	304	660	*1.1	1.0
Related children under 6	-275	327	-1.0	1.5	-341	434	-1.9	2.0
In unrelated subfamilies	-42	69	2.2	6.0	*-99	94	-5.9	8.6
Reference person	-12	43	2.3	9.3	-36	58	-4.5	13.0
Children under 18	-42	95	1.6	14.3	-69	128	-10.0	20.9
Unrelated individual	-209	291	*-0.9	0.7	*1,671	359	0.7	1.0
Male	18	169	-0.4	0.9	*889	209	*1.2	1.2
Female	* -227	212	*-1.3	1.0	*782	265	0.3	1.4
Race[2] and Hispanic Origin[3]								
White, total	*-942	892	*-0.5	0.4	*2,160	1,053	0.3	0.5
White, not Hispanic	-692	745	*-0.4	0.4	301	892	-0.2	0.5
Black, total	-25	456	-0.4	1.3	-434	607	*-4.7	1.9
Asian and Pacific Islander, total	-108	192	-1.5	1.8	*327	237	-1.7	2.7
Hispanic origin[3], all races	-238	344	*-1.5	1.1	*1,984	544	-0.7	2.0
Age								
Under 18 years	*-647	515	*-1.0	0.7	312	671	*-1.2	1.0
18 to 64 years	-462	711	-0.4	0.4	*1,673	913	0.2	0.6
18 to 24 years	-104	212	*-0.9	0.8	181	276	*1.2	1.0
25 to 34 years	-177	227	-0.2	0.6	-292	301	0.7	0.7
35 to 44 years	-169	215	-0.4	0.5	*967	265	*0.8	0.6
45 to 54 years	5	165	-0.2	0.5	*571	206	-0.5	0.7
55 to 59 years	72	114	0.3	0.9	*194	146	-0.3	1.3
60 to 64 years	-88	112	*-1.1	1.1	52	143	0.6	1.4
65 years and over	10	188	-0.1	0.6	75	248	*-0.9	0.8
Nativity								
Native	-629	906	*-0.4	0.4	NA	NA	NA	NA
Foreign born	*-469	444	*-1.9	1.7	NA	NA	NA	NA
Naturalized citizen	-24	209	-0.4	2.1	NA	NA	NA	NA
Not a citizen	*-445	393	*-2.7	2.4	NA	NA	NA	NA
Region								
Northeast	-117	406	-0.4	0.8	*1,145	510	*2.0	1.0
Midwest	8	449	-0.1	0.7	-587	605	*-1.7	1.0
South	*-757	651	*-0.9	0.7	-285	854	*-1.9	1.0
West	-233	533	-0.6	0.9	*1,788	666	*1.2	1.2
Residence								
Inside metropolitan areas	-276	869	-0.3	0.4	*3,271	1,115	0.1	0.5
Inside central cities	-97	661	-0.3	0.8	770	862	–	1.1
Outside central cities	-179	599	-0.3	0.4	*2,501	750	0.5	0.6
Outside metropolitan areas	*-822	595	*-1.5	1.2	*-1,211	795	*-1.5	1.5
FAMILIES								
Total	**-138**	**285**	**-0.3**	**0.4**	**291**	**341**	**-0.4**	**0.5**
White, total	-162	234	-0.3	0.4	*371	265	0.1	0.5
White, not Hispanic	-93	188	-0.2	0.4	-23	217	-0.3	0.4
Black, total	-4	137	-0.2	1.7	-127	168	*-4.5	2.2
Asian and Pacific Islander, total	26	48	0.7	2.0	*69	54	-1.2	2.9
Hispanic origin[3], all races	-73	104	*-2.1	1.5	*421	140	-1.1	2.4

See footnotes at end of table.

dren (14.4 percent). Since then, however, the rate for children has increased, while the rate has decreased for the elderly. In 1998 the poverty rate for children under 18 years was 18.9 percent, while that for the elderly 65 and over was 10.5 percent. (See Table 5.7.)

The Census Bureau reported that, in 1997, poverty rates for minority elderly were much higher than those for White elderly. The rate for Black elderly persons (26 percent) and the rate for Hispanic elderly (23.8 percent) were more than two and one-half times the White rate (9 percent). Asians/Pacific Islanders 65 and over had a poverty rate of 12.3 percent.

GOVERNMENT PROGRAMS

The U.S. government offers various forms of assistance to the needy. These include means-tested (based on income) programs, such as Supplementary Security Income (SSI), General Assistance (all cash assistance

TABLE 5.7

Persons and Families in Poverty by Selected Characteristics, 1989, 1997 and 1998 [CONTINUED]

[Numbers in thousands.]

Characteristic	Change 1997 to 1998[1]				Change 1989[r] to 1998[1]			
	Number	90-pct. C.I. (±)	Percent	90-pct. C.I. (±)	Number	90-pct. C.I. (±)	Percent	90-pct. C.I. (±)
Type of Family								
Married-couple	58	166	0.1	0.3	−87	204	*−0.4	0.4
White	88	155	0.1	0.3	53	183	−0.1	0.4
White, not Hispanic	*138	125	*0.3	0.3	−137	153	*−0.4	0.4
Black	−22	51	−0.7	1.3	*−154	69	−4.5	1.8
Hispanic origin[3], all races	−61	71	*−1.7	1.5	*183	95	−0.7	2.3
Female householder, no husband present	−164	197	−1.6	1.7	*256	234	*−2.7	2.2
White	*−181	150	*−2.8	1.9	*238	166	−0.9	2.3
White, not Hispanic	*−170	122	*−2.7	1.9	86	137	−1.0	2.2
Black	−5	120	1.0	3.4	5	145	*−5.9	4.6
Hispanic origin,[3] all races	−11	69	−3.9	4.7	*179	94	−4.3	7.4

– Represents zero.

NA Not available.

[r] Revised, based on 1990 census population controls.

*Statistically significant at the 90-percent confidence level.

[1]As a result of rounding, some differences may appear to be slightly higher or lower than the difference of the reported rates.

[2]Data for American Indians, Eskimos, and Aleuts are not shown separately. Data for this population group should not be tablated from the CPS because of its small sample size.

[3]Hispanics may be of any race.

SOURCE: *Current Population Survey.* U.S. Bureau of the Census: Washington, D.C., Sept 1999

FIGURE 5.3

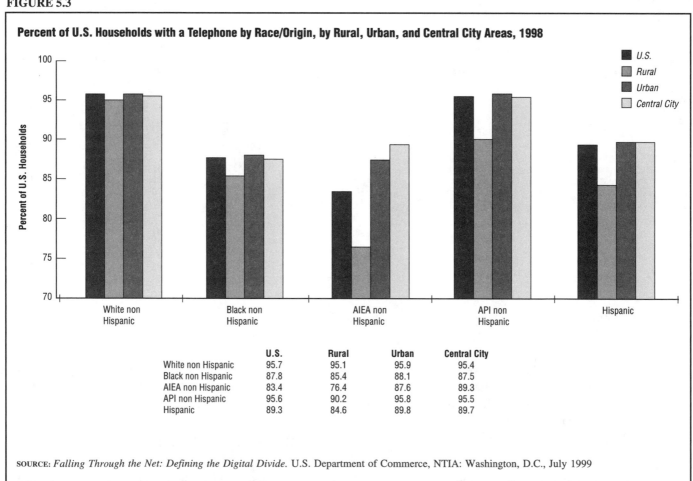

Percent of U.S. Households with a Telephone by Race/Origin, by Rural, Urban, and Central City Areas, 1998

	U.S.	Rural	Urban	Central City
White non Hispanic	95.7	95.1	95.9	95.4
Black non Hispanic	87.8	85.4	88.1	87.5
AIEA non Hispanic	83.4	76.4	87.6	89.3
API non Hispanic	95.6	90.2	95.8	95.5
Hispanic	89.3	84.6	89.8	89.7

SOURCE: *Falling Through the Net: Defining the Digital Divide.* U.S. Department of Commerce, NTIA: Washington, D.C., July 1999

TABLE 5.8

Families Below Poverty Level, by Selected Characteristics, 1997

Characteristic	Number below poverty level (1,000)				Percent below poverty level			
	All races[1]	White	Black	His-panic[2]	All races[1]	White	Black	His-panic[2]
Total	**7,324**	**4,990**	**1,985**	**1,721**	**10.3**	**8.4**	**23.6**	**24.7**
Age of householder:								
15 to 24 years old	897	580	299	213	31.0	26.5	49.6	35.8
25 to 34 years old	2,204	1,496	603	540	16.2	13.6	29.4	27.8
35 to 44 years old	1,982	1,323	557	522	10.5	8.5	23.7	26.1
45 to 54 years old	849	620	176	208	5.8	5.0	11.1	17.8
55 to 64 years old	658	485	138	121	7.0	6.0	16.0	17.9
65 years old and over	678	457	193	99	6.0	4.5	21.1	18.1
Education of householder:[3]								
No high school diploma	2,713	1,903	674	993	24.1	21.0	37.9	35.1
High school diploma, no college	2,179	1,454	636	285	9.9	7.8	22.8	17.7
Some college, less than Bachelor's degree	1,136	785	301	160	6.6	5.4	14.1	13.1
Bachelor's degree or more	344	240	55	53	2.0	1.6	5.2	7.8
Work experience of householder:								
Total[4]	**6,640**	**4,532**	**1,787**	**1,621**	**11.1**	**9.2**	**23.9**	**25.3**
Worked during year	3,864	2,677	1,011	940	7.5	6.2	16.4	17.9
Year-round, full-time	1,279	944	273	422	3.3	2.9	6.3	11.2
Not year-round, full-time	2,584	1,734	738	518	21.1	17.5	40.9	35.4
Did not work	2,776	1,855	776	681	34.3	29.0	58.8	58.4

[1] Includes other races not shown separately.
[2] Hispanic persons may be of any race.
[3] Householder 25 years old and over.
[4] Persons 16 years old and over.

SOURCE: *Statistical Abstract of the United States.* U.S. Bureau of the Census: Washington, D.C., 1999

TABLE 5.9

Earnings, by Highest Degree Earned, 1998

[For persons 18 years old and over with earnings. Persons as of March. Earnings for prior year. Based on Current Population Survey]

Characteristic	Total persons	Level of highest degree							
		Not a high school graduate	High school graduate only	Some college, no degree	Assoc ciate's	Bach-elor's	Master's	Profess-sional	Doctorate
Mean Earnings (dol.)									
All Persons[1]	29,514	16,124	22,895	24,804	29,872	40,478	51,183	95,148	77,445
Age:									
18 to 24 years old	11,264	7,737	12,001	9,813	15,931	19,444	23,007	14,045	4,158
25 to 34 years old	26,462	16,262	21,637	23,489	25,978	35,027	40,798	58,079	47,779
35 to 44 years old	34,081	18,532	26,235	30,353	32,429	45,298	53,594	103,418	77,982
45 to 54 years old	37,242	20,800	26,925	35,090	34,606	46,773	56,922	115,697	86,237
55 to 64 years old	35,924	21,096	26,202	26,392	32,063	45,129	53,547	145,699	79,931
65 years old and over	21,588	13,482	13,734	21,880	33,313	29,958	26,154	54,246	65,543
Sex:									
Male	36,556	19,575	28,307	31,268	36,392	50,056	63,220	109,206	87,426
Female	21,528	10,725	16,906	18,104	24,009	30,119	38,337	62,110	51.189
White	30,515	16,596	23,618	25,442	30,509	41,439	52,475	97,487	79,947
Male	37,933	20,071	29,298	32,294	37,362	51,678	65,421	110,977	89,110
Female	21,799	10,700	17,166	18,083	24,059	30,041	28,428	63,450	54,587
Black	21,909	13,185	18,980	22,105	25,527	32,062	40,610	51,004	(B)
Male	25,080	15,423	22,440	26,743	29,099	35,792	46,729	(B)	(B)
Female	19,161	10,607	15,789	18,346	23,416	29,091	37,425	(B)	(B)
Hispanic[2]	20,766	15,069	19,558	20,825	25,478	33,465	46,556	(B)	(B)
Male	23,520	17,447	22,253	24,807	29,627	37,963	54,790	(B)	(B)
Female	16,781	10,503	15,747	16,258	21,705	29,173	35,425	(B)	(B)

B Base figure too small to meet statistical standards for reliability of a derived figure. [1] Includes other races, not shown separately. [2] Persons of Hispanic origin may be of any race.

SOURCE: *Statistical Abstract of the United States.* U.S. Bureau of the Census: Washington, D.C., 1999

TABLE 5.10

Children Below Poverty Level, by Race and Hispanic Origin, 1960 to 1997

[Persons as of March of the following year. Covers only related children in families under 18 years old. Based on Current Population Survey]

Year	Number below poverty level (1,000)				Percent below poverty level			
	All races[1]	White	Black	Hispanic[2]	All races[1]	White	Black	Hispanic[2]
1960	17,288	11,229	(NA)	(NA)	26.5	20.0	(NA)	(NA)
1970	10,235	6,138	3,922	(NA)	14.9	10.5	41.5	(NA)
1980	11,114	6,817	3,906	1,718	17.9	13.4	42.1	33.0
1981	12,068	7,429	4,170	1,874	19.5	14.7	44.9	35.4
1982	13,139	8,282	4,388	2,117	21.3	16.5	47.3	38.9
1983[3]	13,427	8,534	4,273	2,251	21.8	17.0	46.2	37.7
1984	12,929	8,086	4,320	2,317	21.0	16.1	46.2	38.7
1985	12,483	7,838	4,057	2,512	20.1	15.6	43.1	39.6
1986	12,257	7,714	4,037	2,413	19.8	15.3	42.7	37.1
1987[4]	12,275	7,398	4,234	2,606	19.7	14.7	44.4	38.9
1988	11,935	7,095	4,148	2,576	19.0	14.0	42.8	37.3
1989	12,001	7,164	4,257	2,496	19.0	14.1	43.2	35.5
1990	12,715	7,696	4,412	2,750	19.9	15.1	44.2	37.7
1991	13,658	8,316	4,637	2,977	21.1	16.1	45.6	39.8
1992[5]	14,521	8,752	5,015	3,440	21.6	16.5	46.3	39.0
1993	14,961	9,123	5,030	3,666	22.0	17.0	45.9	39.9
1994	14,610	8,826	4,787	3,956	21.2	16.3	43.3	41.1
1995	13,999	8,474	4,644	3,938	20.2	15.5	41.5	39.3
1996	13,764	8,488	4,411	4,090	19.8	15.5	39.5	39.9
1997	13,422	8,441	4,116	3,865	19.2	15.4	36.8	36.4

NA Not available.

[1] Includes other races not shown separately.

[2] Persons of Hispanic origin may be of any race.

[3] Beginning 1983, data based on revised Hispanic population controls and not directly comparable with prior years.

[4] Beginning 1987, data based on revised processing procedures and not directly comparable with prior years.

[5] Beginning 1992, based on 1990 population controls.

SOURCE: *Statistical Abstract of the United States*. U.S. Bureau of the Census: Washington, D.C., 1999

programs in which recipients receive monthly checks from the government), Medicaid, food stamps, the school lunch program, and rent subsidies.

Aid to Families with Dependent Children

Aid to Families with Dependent Children's (AFDC) last year in operation was 1996. In that year, on average, 4,553,000 families were receiving AFDC assistance per month. More than 4.9 million recipients were adults, and nearly 9 million were children. Three of five AFDC families were members of minority races or ethnic groups. Black families accounted for 37 percent of AFDC families; White families made up 36 percent; and Hispanic families comprised 21 percent. Table 5.11 shows the state-by-state distribution of AFDC families based on the race of the parent. Table 5.12 shows the distribution of families by the race of the recipient children.

COMMUNICATIONS ACCESS

In the area of communications, the term "universal service" refers to the goal that all Americans should have affordable telephone service. The most commonly used method of measuring universal service is to determine the number of U.S. households with a telephone on the premises. In 1994, 93.8 percent of all households had

telephones. In 1998 at-home ownership of telephones rose slightly to 94.1 percent.

Because today's society dictates that people have to access, accumulate, and assimilate information, the federal government has expanded the measure of universal service to include computers and modems. The Commerce Department's National Telecommunications and Information Administration contracted with the Census Bureau to include questions on computer/modem ownership and usage in their *Current Population Surveys*. They found that most people who do not have these information-gathering tools live in rural areas as well as in central cities.

Non-Hispanic White urban households had more telephone coverage (95.9 percent) than any other group, while rural Native American households—which includes American Indians, Aleuts, and Eskimos—had the least (76.4 percent). Rural Hispanic (84.6 percent) and rural non-Hispanic Black (85.4 percent) households also had relatively low telephone penetration. As a group, Asians/Pacific Islanders (APIs) had the highest percentage of households with telephones. (See Figure 5.3.)

In 1998, overall, non-Hispanic Black households (23.2 percent) owned the fewest computers. About 18 percent of rural, 23.8 percent of urban, and 21.8 percent

TABLE 5.11

AFDC Families by Race of Natural or Adoptive Parent, October 1995–Sept. 1996

State	Total Families	Race of Parent[1]					
		White	Black	Hispanic	Asian	Native American	Unknown
U.S. Total	4,553,308	35.9%	36.9%	20.8%	3.0%	1.4%	2.0%
Alabama	42,393	26.3	72.9	0.1	0.3	0.2	0.1
Alaska	12,253	47.8	6.2	5.6	2.9	36.3	1.2
Arizona	63,404	35.8	8.l	39.7	0.6	15.4	0.5
Arkansas	22,747	41.4	58.1	0.5	-0-	-0-	-0-
California	895,960	31.2	16.8	37.9	8.3	0.8	5.1
Colorado	35,447	41.5	17.2	37.8	1.8	1.5	0.2
Connecticut	58,117	31.2	31.4	36.0	0.7	-0-	0.7
Delaware	10,388	25.8	70.0	3.9	-0-	-0-	0.3
District of Columbia	25,721	0.5	97.6	1.3	0.3	-0-	-0-
Florida	211,975	33.9	47.2	17.7	0.9	-0-	0.3
Georgia	130,387	25.9	72.3	1.1	0.5	0.1	0.1
Guam	2,137	2.2	-0-	-0-	97.8	-0-	-0-
Hawaii	21,960	24.2	1.6	1.2	71.4	0.4	1.2
Idaho	9,008	82.3	1.0	11.3	0.3	4.8	0.3
Illinois	224,148	28.4	57.8	12.8	0.7	0.2	0.1
Indiana	52,873	55.6	39.5	3.5	0.2	0.4	0.7
Iowa	32,785	81.2	14.3	2.7	1.4	0.1	0.3
Kansas	25,148	61.8	29.7	6.0	1.9	0.3	0.2
Kentucky	71,827	80.0	19.8	0.2	-0-	-0-	0.1
Louisiana	70,581	16.7	81.6	0.8	0.7	0.2	-0-
Maine	20,461	97.4	0.4	0.4	0.8	1.0	-0-
Maryland	74,106	21.7	73.9	1.4	0.6	0.3	2.1
Massachusetts	88,365	46.8	17.2	28.7	3.9	0.6	3.0
Michigan	178,002	42.6	53.5	2.6	0.3	0.7	0.3
Minnesota	58,250	55.8	22.6	5.9	8.3	7.3	0.1
Mississippi	47,954	13.3	86.2	0.2	0.1	0.2	-0-
Missouri	82,717	52.0	47.0	0.5	0.3	0.1	0.2
Montana	10,806	61.8	0.3	1.4	0.3	36.0	0.3
Nebraska	14,166	59.9	26.0	6.5	1.9	4.9	0.8
Nevada	14,827	55.0	30.0	11.1	1.1	2.4	0.5
New Hampshire	9,538	83.6	1.0	2.3	-0-	-0-	13.2
New Jersey	111,983	18.8	52.5	27.9	0.7	-0-	0.2
New Mexico	33,852	24.0	4.0	57.4	0.5	13.5	0.5
New York	433,325	19.9	34.6	37.2	1.1	0.2	6.9
North Carolina	113,127	31.2	63.4	1.8	0.6	2.5	0.4
North Dakota	4,892	54.7	1.2	0.3	0.9	42.9	-0-
Ohio	206,722	53.2	43.2	2.9	0.5	0.1	0.2
Oklahoma	38,809	56.4	28.9	2.3	0.4	12.1	-0-
Oregon	33,444	80.1	8.4	7.3	2.0	2.2	-0-
Pennsylvania	190,329	42.4	44.8	10.4	2.1	0.2	0.2
Puerto Rico	50,888	0.2	0.3	99.4	-0-	-0-	0.1
Rhode Island	21,226	52.0	13.9	24.0	8.1	0.4	1.5
South Carolina	45,770	26.3	72.5	0.7	0.3	-0-	0.1
South Dakota	5,995	38.0	1.6	0.6	-0-	59.7	-0-
Tennessee	99,096	44.0	55.2	0.6	0.2	0.1	-0-
Texas	254,953	19.9	32.1	46.6	1.1	0.4	-0-
Utah	14,767	74.9	2.9	14.9	1.2	5.9	0.2
Vermont	9,058	97.0	1.0	0.3	1.0	-0-	0.7
Virgin Islands	1,399	-0-	54.7	25.3	-0-	-0-	20.0
Virginia	64,937	31.0	65.0	2.0	1.7	0.2	0.1
Washington	98,933	68.2	11.0	8.8	6.6	3.9	1.4
West Virginia	36,562	89.6	9.4	0.1	0.1	-0-	0.7
Wisconsin	60,058	39.0	44.2	6.8	4.6	2.0	3.3
Wyoming	4,732	68.0	4.2	12.9	-0-	15.0	-0-

Note: -0- = Zero

[1] = Race of parents in the assistance unit.
If race is unknown or parent(s) are not in the assistance unit, race of youngest child is used.

SOURCE: *Characteristics and Financial Circumstances of AFDC Recipients: FY 1996–Aid to Families with Dependent Children*. U.S. Department of Health and Human Services: Washington, D.C., 1996

TABLE 5.12

Percent Distribution of AFDC Recipient Children by Race, October 1995–Sept. 1996

| State | Total Children | Race of Recipient Children | | | | | |
		White	Black	Hispanic	Asian	Native American	Unknown
U.S. Total	8,685,985	31.6%	38.4%	22.4%	3.8%	1.4%	2.4%

SOURCE: *Characteristics and Financial Circumstances of AFDC Recipients: FY 1996–Aid to Families with Dependent Children.* U.S. Department of Health and Human Services: Washington, D.C., 1996

FIGURE 5.4

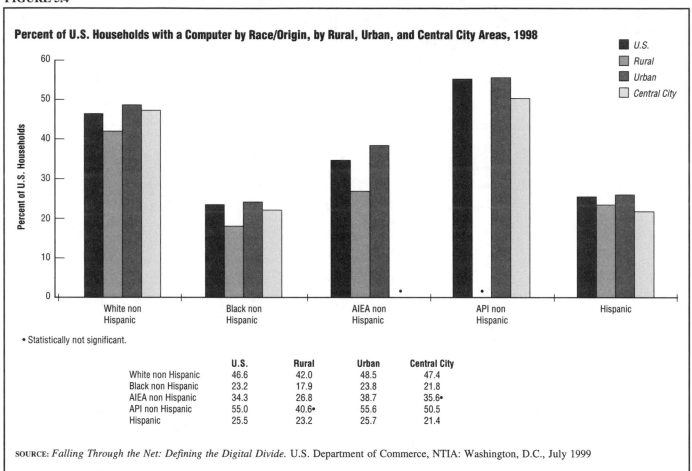

Percent of U.S. Households with a Computer by Race/Origin, by Rural, Urban, and Central City Areas, 1998

• Statistically not significant.

	U.S.	Rural	Urban	Central City
White non Hispanic	46.6	42.0	48.5	47.4
Black non Hispanic	23.2	17.9	23.8	21.8
AIEA non Hispanic	34.3	26.8	38.7	35.6•
API non Hispanic	55.0	40.6•	55.6	50.5
Hispanic	25.5	23.2	25.7	21.4

SOURCE: *Falling Through the Net: Defining the Digital Divide.* U.S. Department of Commerce, NTIA: Washington, D.C., July 1999

of central city Black households had computers. One-fourth (25.5 percent) of Hispanic households and one-third of American Indian households (34.3 percent) had computers, compared to nearly half (46.6 percent) of White households. API households had more computers than any other group (rural, 40.6 percent; urban, 55.6 percent; and central city, 50.5 percent). (See Figure 5.4.) Of the different racial and ethnic groups earning under $15,000, Black households (6.6 percent) were the least likely to have a computer. As the income rose for all groups, so did the proportion of computer ownership; at incomes of over $75,000, computer ownership rates ranged from 78 percent for Blacks to 85 percent for APIs. (See Figure 5.5.)

API households had the highest rate of Internet access (36 percent), followed by White households (29.8 percent). In central cities, White households had three times as much Internet access as non-Hispanic Black and Hispanic households (10.2 percent each). (See Figure 5.6.)

In 1998 most Americans who used the Internet used it to send e-mail—66 percent of American Indians, 68 percent of Blacks, 71.5 percent of Hispanics, 76.1 percent of Asians, and over 79 percent of Whites. Besides e-mail, however, Americans differed in the other ways they used the Internet. Blacks and Hispanics (43.5 percent each), followed by American Indians (43 percent) and APIs (40.3 percent) were more likely than Whites (35 percent)

FIGURE 5.5

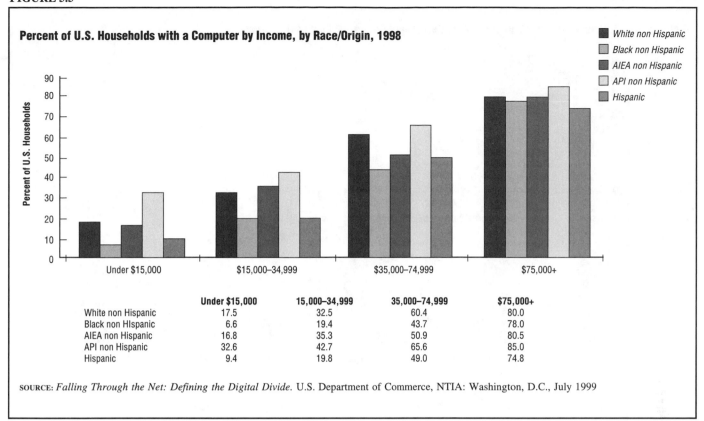

Percent of U.S. Households with a Computer by Income, by Race/Origin, 1998

Legend:
- White non Hispanic
- Black non Hispanic
- AIEA non Hispanic
- API non Hispanic
- Hispanic

	Under $15,000	15,000–34,999	35,000–74,999	$75,000+
White non Hispanic	17.5	32.5	60.4	80.0
Black non HIspanic	6.6	19.4	43.7	78.0
AIEA non Hispanic	16.8	35.3	50.9	80.5
API non Hispanic	32.6	42.7	65.6	85.0
Hispanic	9.4	19.8	49.0	74.8

SOURCE: *Falling Through the Net: Defining the Digital Divide.* U.S. Department of Commerce, NTIA: Washington, D.C., July 1999

FIGURE 5.6

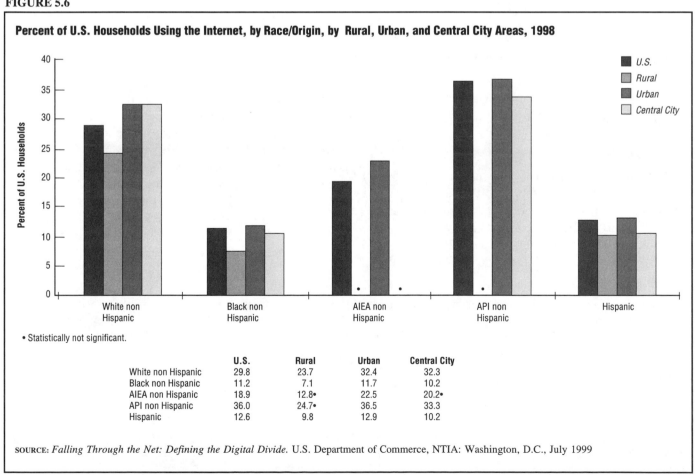

Percent of U.S. Households Using the Internet, by Race/Origin, by Rural, Urban, and Central City Areas, 1998

Legend:
- U.S.
- Rural
- Urban
- Central City

• Statistically not significant.

	U.S.	Rural	Urban	Central City
White non Hispanic	29.8	23.7	32.4	32.3
Black non Hispanic	11.2	7.1	11.7	10.2
AIEA non Hispanic	18.9	12.8•	22.5	20.2•
API non Hispanic	36.0	24.7•	36.5	33.3
Hispanic	12.6	9.8	12.9	10.2

SOURCE: *Falling Through the Net: Defining the Digital Divide.* U.S. Department of Commerce, NTIA: Washington, D.C., July 1999

FIGURE 5.7

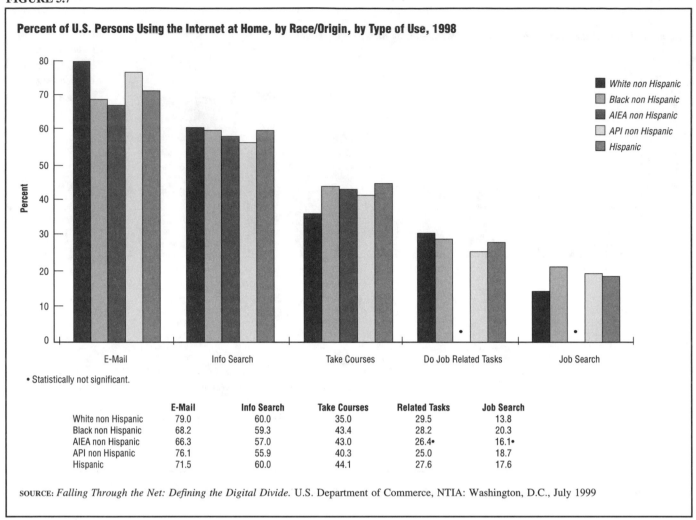

Percent of U.S. Persons Using the Internet at Home, by Race/Origin, by Type of Use, 1998

Legend:
- White non Hispanic
- Black non Hispanic
- AIEA non Hispanic
- API non Hispanic
- Hispanic

• Statistically not significant.

	E-Mail	Info Search	Take Courses	Related Tasks	Job Search
White non Hispanic	79.0	60.0	35.0	29.5	13.8
Black non Hispanic	68.2	59.3	43.4	28.2	20.3
AIEA non Hispanic	66.3	57.0	43.0	26.4•	16.1•
API non Hispanic	76.1	55.9	40.3	25.0	18.7
Hispanic	71.5	60.0	44.1	27.6	17.6

SOURCE: *Falling Through the Net: Defining the Digital Divide.* U.S. Department of Commerce, NTIA: Washington, D.C., July 1999

to take courses online. Minorities were also more likely to use the Internet to look for jobs. (See Figure 5.7.)

NET WORTH

Net worth, or wealth, is the amount of financial resources, or assets, minus debts. In 1993, according to the U.S. Census Bureau, the median net worth of American households was $37,587. The median net worth of a White household ($45,740) was 10 times that of a Black household ($4,418) or a Hispanic household ($4,656). (See Table 5.13.)

White households in every income quintile (one-fifth) had significantly higher levels of median measured net worth than Black and Hispanic households in the same income quintile. In the lowest quintile, the median measured net worth for White households was $7,605, while those of Hispanic ($499) and Black ($250) households were significantly lower. In the highest quintile, the median measured net worth for White households was $123,350, much higher than the median for Hispanic households ($55,923) and Black households ($45,023). (See Table 5.13.) Net worth is a very important figure. It tends to indicate how well a family can live financially, how able they are to help a child through college, and how much help they can give young people when they start out on their own.

TABLE 5.13

Median Measured Net Worth by Race and Hispanic Origin of Householder and Monthly Household Income Quintile, 1993 and 1991

[Excludes group quarters]

Monthly household income quintile	Total		White		Black		Hispanic origin[1]	
	1993	1991 (in 1993 dollars)	1993	1991 (in 1993 dollars)	1993	1991 (in 1993 dollars)	1993	1991 (in 1993 dollars)
All households (thousands)	96,468	94,692	82,190	81,409	11,248	10,768	7,403	6,407
Median measured net worth (dollars)	37,587	38,500	45,740	47,075	4,418	4,844	4,656	5,557
Measured Net Worth by Income Quintile[2]								
Lowest quintile:								
Households (thousands)	19,327	18,977	14,662	14,480	4,066	4,041	2,272	1,835
Median measured net worth (dollars)	4,249	5,406	7,605	10,743	250	0	499	529
Second quintile:								
Households (thousands)	19,306	18,912	16,162	16,006	2,663	2,436	1,760	1,557
Median measured net worth (dollars)	20,230	20,315	27,057	26,665	3,406	3,446	2,900	3,214
Third quintile:								
Households (thousands)	19,279	18,969	16,591	16,388	2,126	2,124	1,437	1,312
Median measured net worth (dollars)	30,788	30,263	36,341	35,510	8,480	8,302	6,313	7,501
Fourth quintile:								
Households (thousands)	19,304	18,928	17,218	17,043	1,454	1,353	1,115	1,009
Median measured net worth (dollars)	50,000	51,779	54,040	55,950	20,745	21,852	20,100	20,564
Highest quintile:								
Households (thousands)	19,252	18,905	17,558	17,492	937	814	819	694
Median measured net worth (dollars)	118,996	121,423	123,350	128,298	45,023	56,922	55,923	72,168

[1]Persons of Hispanic origin may be of any race.

[2]Quintile upper limits for 1993 were: lowest quintile - $1,071; second quintile - $1,963; third quintile - $2,995; fourth quintile - $4,635. Upper limits for 1991 were: lowest quintile - $1,135; second quintile - $2,027; third quintile - $3,089; fourth quintile - $4,721.

SOURCE: *Asset Ownership of Households: 1993*. U.S. Bureau of the Census: Washington, D.C., 1995

CHAPTER 6

HEALTH

In 1985 then-Secretary of Health and Human Services Margaret M. Heckler noted the continuing large differences between the health status of White and minority Americans. Heckler remarked that Blacks, Hispanics, and Native Americans "have not benefited fully or equitably from the fruits" of biomedical science. That same year, the Office of Minority Health was created (PL 101-527) to advocate culturally and linguistically competent services and prevention efforts for minority communities.

Toward Equality of Well-Being: Strategies for Improving Minority Health (Office of Minority Health, Washington, DC, 1993) reported that, in general, persons belonging to minority groups are not as healthy and die at a younger age than those of the White majority. It also concluded that poverty, inadequate health insurance or absence of health insurance, poor access to health care, high-risk behavior, and inadequate prenatal care were some of the major causes of minority health differences.

SOCIAL CHARACTERISTICS OF MINORITY POPULATIONS THAT AFFECT HEALTH

The demographic profiles of non-Hispanic Blacks, Hispanics, Asians/Pacific Islanders, and Native Americans/Alaska Natives differ considerably from those of the non-minority population. Because a high percentage of minorities live in urban areas, they are exposed to a greater number of environmental hazards, including pollution, traffic hazards, substandard and/or overcrowded housing, and crime. Occupational risks are also greater for minorities because a greater percentage of them are employed in potentially dangerous jobs. In addition, the amount of stress in changing cultural environments and the lack of resources for solving stressful situations can play a critical role in the mental health of minority groups.

Differences exist within each minority group concerning the number and status of native-born versus foreign-born persons, age at time of immigration, and how fully group members have assimilated into American society. Moreover, dietary patterns are different among the various minority groups and vary according to how thoroughly minorities have adopted non-minority eating patterns.

SELF-ASSESSMENT OF HEALTH

In addition to indicating physical and/or mental illnesses, the way people feel often reflects their attitudes toward themselves and society. In 1996, 15 percent of all Blacks reported their health as fair or poor, in comparison to 8.4 percent of all White individuals, virtually unchanged from 1991. (See Table 6.1.)

PREGNANCY AND BIRTH

The importance of early prenatal care cannot be overemphasized, as doctors are now better able to detect, and often correct, potential problems early in pregnancy. While every pregnant woman should receive prenatal care, the National Center for Health Statistics believes the United States is capable of guaranteeing that more than 90 percent of pregnant women receive prenatal care during the first trimester of pregnancy. The Centers for Disease Control and Prevention (CDC) is the Public Health Service agency headquartered in Atlanta, Georgia. In "Prenatal Care in the United States" (*Vital and Health Statistics,* Hyattsville, Maryland, July 1996), the CDC reported that certain women are more likely to delay prenatal care until after the third month or to receive no prenatal care at all. These women are often Black, Hispanic, not born in the United States, young, or unmarried, or have had little education.

In 1997 just over seven in 10 (72.1 percent) of Mexican American mothers received early prenatal care. Similarly, only 68.1 percent of American Indian/Alaskan Native (AI/AN) mothers, 72.3 percent of Black mothers,

TABLE 6.1

Respondent-Assessed Health Status, According to Selected Characteristics, U.S., 1991–96
[Data are based on household interviews of a sample of the civilian noninstitutionalized population]

	Percent with fair or poor health								
	Both sexes			Male			Female		
Characteristic	1991	1995	1996	1991	1995	1996	1991	1995	1996
Total[1,2]	9.2	9.3	9.2	8.9	8.9	8.7	9.6	9.8	9.7
Age									
Under 18 years	2.6	2.6	2.6	2.7	2.7	2.5	2.6	2.4	2.7
Under 6 years	2.7	2.7	2.6	2.9	3.1	2.6	2.4	2.2	2.5
6–17 years	2.6	2.5	2.6	2.5	2.4	2.4	2.6	2.6	2.8
18–44 years	6.1	6.6	6.7	5.2	5.5	5.6	6.9	7.7	7.7
45–54 years	13.4	13.4	13.1	12.5	12.5	12.3	14.2	14.3	13.9
55–64 years	20.7	21.4	21.2	20.7	20.6	21.4	20.8	22.2	21.1
65 years and over	29.0	28.3	27.0	29.2	28.8	26.6	28.9	28.0	27.4
65–74 years	26.0	25.6	23.8	26.7	26.3	23.2	25.5	25.0	24.4
75–84 years	32.6	31.4	30.2	33.2	31.7	31.3	32.3	31.2	29.4
85 years and over	37.3	35.3	36.2	36.5	38.5	34.9	37.6	33.8	36.8
Race[1,3]									
White	8.5	8.6	8.4	8.3	8.3	8.0	8.7	8.8	8.7
Black	15.0	15.3	15.0	14.0	13.7	13.7	15.9	16.6	16.0
American Indian or Alaska Native	16.8	15.9	18.9	16.1	16.1	19.2	17.0	16.0	17.8
Asian or Pacific Islander	6.7	8.2	8.3	5.9	7.0	6.5	7.3	9.2	10.0
Race and Hispanic origin[1]									
White, non-Hispanic	8.0	8.0	7.9	7.9	7.8	7.6	8.1	8.1	8.1
Black, non-Hispanic	15.0	15.4	14.9	14.1	13.8	13.7	15.9	16.6	15.9
Hispanic[3]	13.7	13.6	12.9	12.3	12.3	11.8	14.9	14.8	14.1
Mexican[3]	14.9	14.9	13.7	13.0	13.9	11.9	16.8	16.0	15.4
Poverty status[1,4]									
Poor	21.8	22.5	22.2	22.4	22.1	21.6	21.5	23.0	22.8
Near poor	13.5	14.2	14.1	13.5	14.9	14.4	13.5	13.8	14.0
Nonpoor	5.5	5.6	5.5	5.4	5.3	5.3	5.7	5.8	5.6
Race and Hispanic origin and poverty status[1,4]									
White, non-Hispanic:									
Poor	21.1	21.4	21.6	22.7	21.6	22.5	20.2	21.5	21.1
Near poor	12.9	13.6	13.8	13.5	15.0	14.7	12.5	12.5	13.2
Nonpoor	5.2	5.2	5.1	5.2	5.1	5.0	5.3	5.3	5.1
Black, non-Hispanic:									
Poor	24.9	26.7	26.9	25.2	26.2	26.0	24.8	27.1	27.8
Near poor	15.5	17.2	16.6	14.6	15.9	15.2	16.3	18.1	17.6
Nonpoor	8.5	8.1	8.5	7.6	7.3	7.6	9.5	8.9	9.3
Hispanic:[3]									
Poor	21.1	21.2	19.9	20.2	20.1	17.7	21.7	22.3	21.8
Near poor	15.8	15.5	14.7	14.3	14.1	14.3	17.4	16.9	15.5
Nonpoor	7.9	7.0	7.7	7.1	6.4	7.6	8.7	7.6	7.5
Geographic region[1]									
Northeast	7.4	8.0	8.2	7.2	7.7	7.7	7.6	8.3	8.7
Midwest	8.0	8.5	8.1	7.7	8.3	7.7	8.3	8.7	8.6
South	11.6	10.9	10.7	11.3	10.3	10.1	11.9	11.4	11.3
West	8.6	8.9	8.7	8.1	8.2	8.4	9.1	9.6	9.2
Location of residence[1]									
Within MSA[5]	8.8	8.9	8.4	8.3	8.4	7.8	9.3	9.4	9.0
Outside MSA[5]	10.6	11.1	11.8	10.9	10.8	11.5	10.4	11.4	12.1

[1]Age adjusted.

[2]Includes all other races not shown separately and unknown family income.

[3]The race groups, white, black, American Indian or Alaska Native, and Asian or Pacific Islander, include persons of Hispanic and non-Hispanic origin; persons of Hispanic origin may be of any race.

[4]Poverty status is based on family income and family size using Bureau of the Census poverty thresholds. Poor persons are defined as below the poverty threshold. Near poor persons have incomes of 100 percent to less than 200 percent of poverty threshold. Nonpoor persons have incomes of 200 percent or greater than the poverty threshold.

[5]Metropolitan statistical area.

SOURCE: *Health, United States, 1999.* National Center for Health Statistics: Hyattsville, Md., 1999

TABLE 6.2

Prenatal Care for Live Births, According to Detailed Race of Mother and Hispanic Origin of Mother: U.S., Selected Years 1970–97

[Data are based on the National Vital Statistics System]

Prenatal care, race of mother, and Hispanic origin of mother	1970	1975	1980	1985	1990	1991	1992	1993	1994	1995	1996	1997
Prenatal care began during 1st trimester					Percent of live births[1]							
All races	68.0	72.4	76.3	76.2	75.8	76.2	77.7	78.9	80.2	81.3	81.9	82.5
White	72.3	75.8	79.2	79.3	79.2	79.5	80.8	81.8	82.8	83.6	84.0	84.7
Black	44.2	55.5	62.4	61.5	60.6	61.9	63.9	66.0	68.3	70.4	71.4	72.3
American Indian or Alaska Native	38.2	45.4	55.8	57.5	57.9	59.9	62.1	63.4	65.2	66.7	67.7	68.1
Asian or Pacific Islander	- - -	- - -	73.7	74.1	75.1	75.3	76.6	77.6	79.7	79.9	81.2	82.1
Chinese	71.8	76.7	82.6	82.0	81.3	82.3	83.8	84.6	86.2	85.7	86.8	87.4
Japanese	78.1	82.7	86.1	84.7	87.0	87.7	88.2	87.2	89.2	89.7	89.3	89.3
Filipino	60.6	70.6	77.3	76.5	77.1	77.1	78.7	79.3	81.3	80.9	82.5	83.3
Hawaiian and part Hawaiian	- - -	- - -	68.8	67.7	65.8	68.1	69.9	70.6	77.0	75.9	78.5	78.0
Other Asian or Pacific Islander	- - -	- - -	67.4	69.9	71.9	71.9	72.8	74.4	76.2	77.0	78.4	79.7
Hispanic origin (selected States)[2,3]	- - -	- - -	60.2	61.2	60.2	61.0	64.2	66.6	68.9	70.8	72.2	73.7
Mexican	- - -	- - -	59.6	60.0	57.8	58.7	62.1	64.8	67.3	69.1	70.7	72.1
Puerto Rican	- - -	- - -	55.1	58.3	63.5	65.0	67.8	70.0	71.7	74.0	75.0	76.5
Cuban	- - -	- - -	82.7	82.5	84.8	85.4	86.8	88.9	90.1	89.2	89.2	90.4
Central and South American	- - -	- - -	58.8	60.6	61.5	63.4	66.8	68.7	71.2	73.2	75.0	76.9
Other and unknown Hispanic	- - -	- - -	66.4	65.8	66.4	65.6	68.0	70.0	72.1	74.3	74.6	76.0
White, non-Hispanic (selected States)[2]	- - -	- - -	81.2	81.4	83.3	83.7	84.9	85.6	86.5	87.1	87.4	87.9
Black, non-Hispanic (selected States)[2]	- - -	- - -	60.7	60.1	60.7	61.9	64.0	66.1	68.3	70.4	71.5	72.3
Prenatal care began during 3rd trimester or no prenatal care												
All races	7.9	6.0	5.1	5.7	6.1	5.8	5.2	4.8	4.4	4.2	4.0	3.9
White	6.3	5.0	4.3	4.8	4.9	4.7	4.2	3.9	3.6	3.5	3.3	3.2
Black	16.6	10.5	8.9	10.2	11.3	10.7	9.9	9.0	8.2	7.6	7.3	7.3
American Indian or Alaska Native	28.9	22.4	15.2	12.9	12.9	12.2	11.0	10.3	9.8	9.5	8.6	8.6
Asian or Pacific Islander	- - -	- - -	6.5	6.5	5.8	5.7	4.9	4.6	4.1	4.3	3.9	3.8
Chinese	6.5	4.4	3.7	4.4	3.4	3.4	2.9	2.9	2.7	3.0	2.5	2.4
Japanese	4.1	2.7	2.1	3.1	2.9	2.5	2.4	2.8	1.9	2.3	2.2	2.7
Filipino	7.2	4.1	4.0	4.8	4.5	5.0	4.3	4.0	3.6	4.1	3.3	3.3
Hawaiian and part Hawaiian	- - -	- - -	6.7	7.4	8.7	7.5	7.0	6.7	4.7	5.1	5.0	5.4
Other Asian or Pacific Islander	- - -	- - -	9.3	8.2	7.1	6.8	5.9	5.4	4.8	5.0	4.6	4.4
Hispanic origin (selected States)[2,3]	- - -	- - -	12.0	12.4	12.0	11.0	9.5	8.8	7.6	7.4	6.7	6.2
Mexican	- - -	- - -	11.8	12.9	13.2	12.2	10.5	9.7	8.3	8.1	7.2	6.7
Puerto Rican	- - -	- - -	16.2	15.5	10.6	9.1	8.0	7.1	6.5	5.5	5.7	5.4
Cuban	- - -	- - -	3.9	3.7	2.8	2.4	2.1	1.8	1.6	2.1	1.6	1.5
Central and South American	- - -	- - -	13.1	12.5	10.9	9.5	7.9	7.3	6.5	6.1	5.5	5.0
Other and unknown Hispanic	- - -	- - -	9.2	9.4	8.5	8.2	7.5	7.0	6.2	6.0	5.9	5.3
White, non-Hispanic (selected States)[2]	- - -	- - -	3.5	4.0	3.4	3.2	2.8	2.7	2.5	2.5	2.4	2.4
Black, non-Hispanic (selected States)[2]	- - -	- - -	9.7	10.9	11.2	10.7	9.8	9.0	8.2	7.6	7.3	7.3

- - - Data not available.

[1] Excludes live births for whom trimester when prenatal care began is unknown.

[2] Trend data for Hispanics and non-Hispanics are affected by expansion of the reporting area for an Hispanic-origin item on the birth certificate and by immigration. These two factors affect numbers of events, composition of the Hispanic population, and maternal and infant health characteristics. The number of States in the reporting area increased from 22 in 1980, to 23 and the District of Columbia (DC) in 1983–87, 30 and DC in 1988, 47 and DC in 1989, 48 and DC in 1990, 49 and DC in 1991–92, and 50 and DC in 1993 and later years.

[3] Includes mothers of all races.

NOTES: Data for 1970 and 1975 exclude births that occurred in States not reporting prenatal care. The race groups, white, black, American Indian or Alaska Native, and Asian or Pacific Islander, include persons of Hispanic and non-Hispanic origin. Conversely, persons of Hispanic origin may be of any race. Data for additional years are available.

SOURCE: *Health, United States, 1999*. National Center for Health Statistics: Hyattsville, Md., 1999

76.9 percent of Central and South American-origin mothers, and 76.5 percent of Puerto Rican mothers received early care. In contrast, 84.7 percent of White women, 90.4 percent of Cuban-origin women, 89.3 percent of Japanese-origin women, and 87.4 percent of Chinese-origin mothers received prenatal care. (See Table 6.2.)

Amniocentesis, the insertion of a needle through the abdominal wall into the uterus, allows medical specialists to obtain a sample of the amniotic fluid surrounding a fetus. Laboratory testing of this fluid can detect chromosomal abnormalities, metabolic disorders, and physical abnormalities in the growing fetus. Pregnant women over the age of 35 are often advised to undergo this procedure, since they are more likely than younger women to have babies with chromosomal abnormalities. About 17 percent of pregnant Black women over the age of 35 have amniocentesis testing, compared to 30 percent of pregnant White women; Black women living in non-metropolitan areas and/or the South are the least likely to use this procedure.

TABLE 6.3

Maternal Mortality for Complications of Pregnancy, Childbirth, and the Pueperium, According to Race and Age: United States, Selected Years, 1950–97

[Data are based on the National Vital Statistics System]

Race, Hispanic origin, and age	1950[1]	1960[1]	1970	1980	1985	1990	1994	1995	1996	1997
					Number of deaths					
All persons	2,960	1,579	803	334	295	343	328	277	294	327
White	1,873	936	445	193	156	177	193	129	159	179
Black	1,041	624	342	127	124	153	118	133	121	125
American Indian or Alaska Native	- - -	- - -	- - -	3	7	4	–	1	6	2
Asian or Pacific Islander	- - -	- - -	- - -	11	8	9	17	14	8	21
Hispanic[2]	- - -	- - -	- - -	- - -	29	47	64	43	39	57
White, non-Hispanic[2]	- - -	- - -	- - -	- - -	60	125	127	84	114	121
All persons					**Deaths per 100,000 live births**					
All ages, age adjusted	73.7	32.1	21.5	9.4	7.6	7.6	7.9	6.3	6.4	7.6
All ages, crude	83.3	37.1	21.5	9.2	7.8	8.2	8.3	7.1	7.6	8.4
Under 20 years	70.7	22.7	18.9	7.6	6.9	7.5	6.9	3.9	*	5.7
20–24 years	47.6	20.7	13.0	5.8	5.4	6.1	7.6	5.7	5.0	6.6
25–29 years	63.5	29.8	17.0	7.7	6.4	6.0	7.1	6.0	6.6	7.9
30–34 years	107.7	50.3	31.6	13.6	8.9	9.5	6.5	7.3	7.6	8.3
35 years and over[3]	222.0	104.3	81.9	36.3	25.0	20.7	18.3	15.9	19.0	16.1
White										
All ages, age adjusted	53.1	22.4	14.4	6.7	4.9	5.1	5.8	3.6	4.1	5.2
All ages, crude	61.1	26.0	14.3	6.6	5.1	5.4	6.2	4.2	5.1	5.8
Under 20 years	44.9	14.8	13.8	5.8	*	*	6.2	*	*	*
20–24 years	35.7	15.3	8.4	4.2	3.3	3.9	4.7	3.5	*	4.2
25–29 years	45.0	20.3	11.1	5.4	4.6	4.8	6.1	4.0	4.0	5.4
30–34 years	75.9	34.3	18.7	9.3	5.1	5.0	5.0	4.0	5.0	5.4
35 years and over[3]	174.1	73.9	59.3	25.5	17.5	12.6	12.0	9.1	14.9	11.5
Black										
All ages, age adjusted	- - -	92.0	65.5	24.9	22.1	21.7	18.1	20.9	19.9	20.1
All ages, crude	- - -	103.6	60.9	22.4	21.3	22.4	18.5	22.1	20.3	20.8
Under 20 years	- - -	54.8	32.3	13.1	*	*	*	*	*	*
20–24 years	- - -	56.9	41.9	13.9	14.6	14.7	18.2	15.3	15.1	15.3
25–29 years	- - -	92.8	65.2	22.4	19.4	14.9	*	21.0	25.5	24.3
30–34 years	- - -	150.6	117.8	44.0	38.0	44.2	*	31.2	28.6	32.9
35 years and over[3]	- - -	299.5	207.5	100.6	77.2	79.7	64.5	61.4	49.9	40.4
Hispanic[2,4]										
All ages, age adjusted	- - -	- - -	- - -	- - -	7.1	7.4	9.1	5.4	4.8	7.6
All ages, crude	- - -	- - -	- - -	- - -	7.8	7.9	9.6	6.3	5.6	8.0
White, non-Hispanic[2]										
All ages, age adjusted	- - -	- - -	- - -	- - -	4.0	4.4	4.9	3.3	3.9	4.4
All ages, crude	- - -	- - -	- - -	- - -	4.3	4.8	5.2	3.5	4.8	5.2

- - - Data not available.

– Quantity zero.

* Based on fewer than 20 deaths.

[1]Includes deaths of persons who were not residents of the 50 States and the District of Columbia.

[2]Hispanic and White, non-Hispanic data exclude data from States lacking an Hispanic-origin item on their death and birth certificates.

[3]Rates computed by relating deaths of women 35 years and over to live births to women 35–49 years.

[4]Age-specific maternal mortality rates are not calculated because rates based on fewer than 20 deaths are unreliable.

NOTES: For data years shown, the code numbers for cause of death are based on the then current *International Classification of Diseases*. The race groups, white, black, Asian or Pacific Islander, and American Indian or Alaska Native, include persons of Hispanic and non-Hispanic origin. Conversely, persons of Hispanic origin may be of any race. For 1950 and 1960, rates are based on live births by race of child; for all other years, rates are based on live births by race of mother. Rates are not calculated for American Indian or Alaska Native and Asian or Pacific Islander mothers because rates based on fewer than 20 deaths are unreliable. Data for additional years are available.

SOURCE: *Health, United States, 1999*. National Center for Health Statistics: Hyattsville, Md., 1999

The goal of the U.S. Department of Health and Human Services (DHHS) for 2000 was for the maternal mortality rate (the number of deaths of women from complications of pregnancy and childbirth) not to exceed five deaths per 100,000 live births. In 1997 the rate for White women approached that goal at 5.2 per 100,000. The rate for Black women, however, which has fluctuated from year to year, reaching a low of 18.1 per 100,000 in 1994, jumped to 20.9 per 100,000 in 1995, and remained at 20.1 in 1997. While this rate represents a huge drop from 92 deaths per 100,000 live births in 1960, the maternal mortality rate for Black women in 1997 was almost the same as the rate for White women in 1960. (See Table 6.3.)

Low Birth Weight and Infant Mortality

Between 1990 and 1997 the overall percentage of babies born weighing less than 2,500 grams (5.5 pounds) increased somewhat from 6.97 percent to 7.51 percent. The percentage of Black low-birth-weight babies stayed at about the same level during the same period, 13.25 per-

TABLE 6.4

Low-Birthweight Live Births, According to Mother's Detailed Race, Hispanic Origin, and Smoking Status: United States, Selected Years 1970–97

[Data are based on the National Vital Statistics System]

Birthweight, race of mother, Hispanic origin of mother, and smoking status of mother	1970	1975	1980	1985	1990	1991	1992	1993	1994	1995	1996	1997
Low birthweight (less than 2,500 grams)					Percent of live births[1]							
All races	7.93	7.38	6.84	6.75	6.97	7.12	7.08	7.22	7.28	7.32	7.39	7.51
White	6.85	6.27	5.72	5.65	5.70	5.80	5.80	5.98	6.11	6.22	6.34	6.46
Black	13.90	13.19	12.69	12.65	13.25	13.55	13.31	13.34	13.24	13.13	13.01	13.01
American Indian or Alaska Native	7.97	6.41	6.44	5.86	6.11	6.15	6.22	6.42	6.45	6.61	6.49	6.75
Asian or Pacific Islander	- - -	- - -	6.68	6.16	6.45	6.54	6.57	6.55	6.81	6.90	7.07	7.23
Chinese	6.67	5.29	5.21	4.98	4.69	5.10	4.98	4.91	4.76	5.29	5.03	5.06
Japanese	9.03	7.47	6.60	6.21	6.16	5.90	7.00	6.53	6.91	7.26	7.27	6.82
Filipino	10.02	8.08	7.40	6.95	7.30	7.31	7.43	6.99	7.77	7.83	7.92	8.33
Hawaiian and part Hawaiian	- - -	- - -	7.23	6.49	7.24	6.73	6.89	6.76	7.20	6.84	6.77	7.20
Other Asian or Pacific Islander	- - -	- - -	6.83	6.19	6.65	6.74	6.68	6.89	7.06	7.05	7.42	7.54
Hispanic origin (selected States)[2,3]	- - -	- - -	6.12	6.16	6.06	6.15	6.10	6.24	6.25	6.29	6.28	6.42
Mexican	- - -	- - -	5.62	5.77	5.55	5.60	5.61	5.77	5.80	5.81	5.86	5.97
Puerto Rican	- - -	- - -	8.95	8.69	8.99	9.42	9.19	9.23	9.13	9.41	9.24	9.39
Cuban	- - -	- - -	5.62	6.02	5.67	5.57	6.10	6.18	6.27	6.50	6.46	6.78
Central and South American	- - -	- - -	5.76	5.68	5.84	5.87	5.77	5.94	6.02	6.20	6.03	6.26
Other and unknown Hispanic.	- - -	- - -	6.96	6.83	6.87	7.25	7.24	7.51	7.54	7.55	7.68	7.93
White, non-Hispanic (selected States)[2]	- - -	- - -	5.67	5.60	5.61	5.72	5.73	5.92	6.06	6.20	6.36	6.47
Black, non-Hispanic (selected States)[2]	- - -	- - -	12.71	12.61	13.32	13.62	13.40	13.43	13.34	13.21	13.12	13.11
Cigarette smoker[4]	- - -	- - -	- - -	- - -	11.25	11.41	11.49	11.84	12.28	12.18	12.13	12.06
Nonsmoker[4]	- - -	- - -	- - -	- - -	6.14	6.36	6.35	6.56	6.71	6.79	6.91	7.07
Very low birthweight (less than 1,500 grams)												
All races	1.17	1.16	1.15	1.21	1.27	1.29	1.29	1.33	1.33	1.35	1.37	1.42
White	0.95	0.92	0.90	0.94	0.95	0.96	0.96	1.01	1.02	1.06	1.09	1.13
Black	2.40	2.40	2.48	2.71	2.92	2.96	2.96	2.96	2.96	2.97	2.99	3.04
American Indian or Alaska Native	0.98	0.95	0.92	1.01	1.01	1.07	0.95	1.05	1.10	1.10	1.21	1.19
Asian or Pacific Islander	- - -	- - -	0.92	0.85	0.87	0.85	0.91	0.86	0.93	0.91	0.99	1.05
Chinese	0.80	0.52	0.66	0.57	0.51	0.65	0.67	0.63	0.58	0.67	0.64	0.74
Japanese	1.48	0.89	0.94	0.84	0.73	0.62	0.85	0.74	0.92	0.87	0.81	0.78
Filipino	1.08	0.93	0.99	0.86	1.05	0.97	1.05	0.95	1.19	1.13	1.20	1.29
Hawaiian and part Hawaiian	- - -	- - -	1.05	1.03	0.97	1.02	1.02	1.14	1.20	0.94	0.97	1.41
Other Asian or Pacific Islander	- - -	- - -	0.96	0.91	0.92	0.87	0.93	0.89	0.93	0.91	1.04	1.07
Hispanic origin (selected States)[2,3]	- - -	- - -	0.98	1.01	1.03	1.02	1.04	1.06	1.08	1.11	1.12	1.13
Mexican	- - -	- - -	0.92	0.97	0.92	0.92	0.94	0.97	0.99	1.01	1.01	1.02
Puerto Rican	- - -	- - -	1.29	1.30	1.62	1.66	1.70	1.66	1.63	1.79	1.70	1.85
Cuban	- - -	- - -	1.02	1.18	1.20	1.15	1.24	1.23	1.31	1.19	1.35	1.36
Central and South American	- - -	- - -	0.99	1.01	1.05	1.02	1.02	1.02	1.06	1.13	1.14	1.17
Other and unknown Hispanic	- - -	- - -	1.01	0.96	1.09	1.09	1.10	1.23	1.29	1.28	1.48	1.35
White, non-Hispanic (selected States)[2]	- - -	- - -	0.86	0.90	0.93	0.94	0.94	1.00	1.01	1.04	1.08	1.12
Black, non-Hispanic (selected States)[2]	- - -	- - -	2.46	2.66	2.93	2.97	2.97	2.99	2.99	2.98	3.02	3.05
Cigarette smoker[4]	- - -	- - -	- - -	- - -	1.73	1.73	1.74	1.77	1.81	1.85	1.85	1.83
Nonsmoker[4]	- - -	- - -	- - -	- - -	1.18	1.21	1.22	1.28	1.30	1.31	1.35	1.40

- - - Data not available.

[1]Excludes live births with unknown birthweight. Percent based on live births with known birthweight.

[2]Trend data for Hispanics and non-Hispanics are affected by expansion of the reporting area for an Hispanic-origin item on the birth certificate and by immigration These two factors affect numbers of events, composition of the Hispanic population, and maternal and infant health characteristics. The number of States in the reporting area increased from 22 in 1980, to 23 and the District of Columbia (DC) in 1983–87, 30 and DC in 1988, 47 and DC in 1989, 48 and DC in 1990, 49 and DC in 1991–92, and 50 and DC in 1993 and later years.

[3]Includes mothers of all races.

[4]Percent based on live births with known smoking status of mother and known birthweight. Includes data for 43 States and the District of Columbia (DC) in 1989, 45 States and DC in 1990, 46 States and DC in 1991–93, and 46 States, DC, and New York City (NYC) in 1994–97. Excludes data for California, Indiana, New York (but includes NYC in 1994–97), and South Dakota (1989–97), Oklahoma (1989–90), and Louisiana and Nebraska (1989), which did not require the reporting of mother's tobacco use during pregnancy on the birth certificate.

NOTES: The race groups, white, black, American Indian or Alaska Native, and Asian or Pacific Islander, include persons of Hispanic and non-Hispanic origin. Conversely, persons of Hispanic origin may be of any race. Data for additional years are available.

SOURCE: *Health, United States, 1999.* National Center for Health Statistics: Hyattsville, Md., 1999

TABLE 6.5

Infant Mortality Rates, According to Detailed Race of Mother and Hispanic Origin of Mother: United States, Selected Birth Cohorts, 1983-96

[Data are based on National Linked Birth/Infant Death Data Sets]

Race of mother and Hispanic origin of mother	Birth cohort								
	1983	1987	1990	1991	1995[1]	1996[1]	1983–85	1986–88	1989–91
	Infant deaths per 1,000 live births								
All mothers	10.9	9.8	8.9	8.6	7.6	7.3	10.6	9.8	9.0
White	9.3	8.2	7.3	7.1	6.3	6.1	9.0	8.2	7.4
Black	19.2	17.8	16.9	16.6	14.6	14.1	18.7	17.9	17.1
American Indian or Alaska Native	15.2	13.0	13.1	11.3	9.0	10.0	13.9	13.2	12.6
Asian or Pacific Islander	8.3	7.3	6.6	5.8	5.3	5.2	8.3	7.3	6.6
Chinese	9.5	6.2	4.3	4.6	3.8	3.2	7.4	5.8	5.1
Japanese	*	*6.6	*5.5	*4.2	*5.3	*4.2	6.0	6.9	5.3
Filipino	8.4	6.6	6.0	5.1	5.6	5.8	8.2	6.9	6.4
Hawaiian and part Hawaiian	*	*	*	*	*	*	11.3	11.1	9.0
Other Asian or Pacific Islander	8.1	7.6	7.4	6.3	5.5	5.7	8.6	7.6	7.0
Hispanic origin[2,3]	9.5	8.2	7.5	7.1	6.3	6.1	9.2	8.3	7.6
Mexican	9.1	8.0	7.2	6.9	6.0	5.8	8.8	7.9	7.2
Puerto Rican	12.9	9.9	9.9	9.7	8.9	8.6	12.3	11.1	10.4
Cuban	*7.5	7.1	7.2	5.2	5.3	5.1	8.0	7.3	6.2
Central and South American	8.5	7.8	6.8	5.9	5.5	5.0	8.2	7.6	6.6
Other and unknown Hispanic	10.6	8.7	8.0	8.2	7.4	7.7	9.9	9.0	8.2
White, non-Hispanic[3]	9.2	8.1	7.2	7.0	6.3	6.0	8.9	8.1	7.3
Black, non-Hispanic[3]	19.1	17.4	16.9	16.6	14.7	14.2	18.5	17.9	17.2
	Neonatal deaths per 1,000 live births								
All mothers	7.1	6.2	5.7	5.4	4.9	4.8	6.9	6.3	5.7
White	6.1	5.2	4.6	4.4	4.1	4.0	5.9	5.2	4.7
Black	12.5	11.8	11.1	10.7	9.6	9.4	12.2	11.7	11.1
American Indian or Alaska Native	7.5	6.2	6.1	5.5	4.0	4.7	6.7	5.9	5.9
Asian or Pacific Islander	5.2	4.5	3.9	3.6	3.4	3.3	5.2	4.5	3.9
Chinese	5.5	3.7	2.3	2.3	2.3	1.9	4.3	3.3	2.7
Japanese	*	*4.0	*3.5	*3.2	*3.3	*2.2	3.4	4.4	3.0
Filipino	5.6	4.1	3.5	3.4	3.4	4.1	5.3	4.5	4.0
Hawaiian and part Hawaiian	*	*	*	*	*	*	7.4	7.1	4.8
Other Asian or Pacific Islander	5.0	4.6	4.4	4.1	3.7	3.7	5.5	4.7	4.2
Hispanic origin[2,3]	6.2	5.3	4.8	4.5	4.1	4.0	6.0	5.3	4.8
Mexican	5.9	5.1	4.5	4.3	3.9	3.8	5.7	5.0	4.5
Puerto Rican	8.7	6.7	6.9	6.1	6.1	5.6	8.3	7.2	7.0
Cuban	*5.0	5.3	5.3	4.0	3.6	3.6	5.9	5.3	4.6
Central and South American	5.8	5.0	4.4	4.0	3.7	3.4	5.7	5.0	4.4
Other and unknown Hispanic	6.4	5.6	5.0	5.1	4.8	5.3	6.2	5.8	5.2
White, non-Hispanic[3]	6.0	5.0	4.5	4.3	4.0	3.9	5.8	5.1	4.6
Black, non-Hispanic[3]	12.1	11.3	11.0	10.7	9.6	9.4	11.8	11.4	11.1
	Postneonatal deaths per 1,000 live births								
All mothers	3.8	3.5	3.2	3.2	2.6	2.5	3.7	3.5	3.3
White	3.2	3.0	2.7	2.6	2.2	2.1	3.1	3.0	2.7
Black	6.7	6.1	5.9	5.9	5.0	4.8	6.4	6.2	6.0
American Indian or Alaska Native	7.7	6.8	7.0	5.8	5.1	5.3	7.2	7.3	6.7
Asian or Pacific Islander	3.1	2.8	2.7	2.2	1.9	1.9	3.1	2.8	2.6
Chinese	*	*2.5	2.0	2.3	1.5	1.2	3.1	2.5	2.4
Japanese	*	*	*	*	*	*	2.6	2.5	2.2
Filipino	*2.8	2.5	2.5	1.8	2.2	1.8	2.9	2.4	2.3
Hawaiian and part Hawaiian	*	*	*	*	*	*	*	*4.0	*4.1
Other Asian or Pacific Islander	3.0	2.9	3.0	2.3	1.9	2.0	3.1	2.9	2.8
Hispanic origin[2,3]	3.3	2.9	2.7	2.6	2.1	2.1	3.2	3.0	2.7
Mexican	3.2	2.9	2.7	2.6	2.1	2.1	3.2	2.9	2.7
Puerto Rican	4.2	3.2	3.0	3.5	2.8	3.0	4.0	3.9	3.4
Cuban	*	*	*	*	*	*	2.2	2.0	1.6
Central and South American	2.6	2.8	2.4	1.9	1.9	1.6	2.5	2.6	2.2
Other and unknown Hispanic	4.1	3.2	3.0	3.1	2.6	2.5	3.7	3.2	3.0
White, non-Hispanic[3]	3.2	3.0	2.7	2.7	2.2	2.1	3.1	3.0	2.7
Black, non-Hispanic[3]	7.0	6.2	5.9	5.9	5.0	4.8	6.7	6.4	6.1

* Infant and neonatal mortality rates for groups with fewer than 10,000 births are considered unreliable. Postneonatal mortality rates for groups with fewer than 20,000 births are considered unreliable. Infant and neonatal mortality rates for groups with fewer than 7,500 births are considered highly unreliable and are not shown.

Postneonatal mortality rates for groups with fewer than 15,000 births are considered highly unreliable and are not shown.

[1]Rates based on a period file using weighted data. Data for 1995 and 1996 not strictly comparable with unweighted birth cohort data for earlier years. The 1995 and 1996 weighted mortality rates shown in this table are less than 1 percent to 5 percent higher than unweighted rates for 1995 and 1996.

[2]Persons of Hispanic origin may be of any race.

[3]Data shown only for States with an Hispanic-origin item on their birth certificates. The number of States reporting the item increased from 23 and the District of Columbia (DC) in 1983–87, to 30 and DC in 1988, 47 and DC in 1989, 48 and DC in 1990, 49 and DC in 1991, and 50 and DC in 1995–96.

NOTES: The race groups, white, black, American Indian or Alaska Native, and Asian or Pacific Islander, include persons of Hispanic and non-Hispanic origin. National linked files do not exist for 1992–94 birth cohorts. Data for additional years are available.

SOURCE: *Health, United States, 1999.* National Center for Health Statistics: Hyattsville, Md., 1999

TABLE 6.6

Persons with a Dental Visit Within the Past Year Among Persons 25 Years of Age and Over, According to Selected Patient Characteristics: United States, Selected Years 1983—1993

[Data are based on household interviews of a sample of the civilian noninstitutionalized population]

Characteristic	1983[1]	1989[1]	1990	1991	1993
	Percent of persons with a visit within the past year				
Total[2,3]	53.9	58.9	62.3	58.2	60.8
Age					
25-34 years	59.0	60.9	65.1	59.1	60.3
35-44 years	60.3	65.9	69.1	64.8	66.9
45-64 years	54.1	59.9	62.8	59.2	62.0
65 years and over	39.3	45.8	49.6	47.2	51.7
65-74 years	43.8	50.0	53.5	51.1	56.3
75 years and over	31.8	39.0	43.4	41.3	44.9
Sex[3]					
Male	51.7	56.2	58.8	55.5	58.2
Female	55.9	61.4	65.6	60.8	63.4
Poverty status[3,4]					
Below poverty	30.4	33.3	38.2	33.0	35.9
At or above poverty	55.8	62.1	65.4	61.9	64.3
Race and Hispanic origin[3]					
White, non-Hispanic	56.6	61.8	64.9	61.5	64.0
Black, non-Hispanic	39.1	43.3	49.1	44.3	47.3
Hispanic	42.1	48.9	53.8	43.1	46.2
Education[3]					
Less than 12 years	35.1	36.9	41.2	35.2	38.0
12 years	54.8	58.2	61.3	56.7	58.7
13 years or more	70.9	73.9	75.7	72.2	73.8
Education, race, and Hispanic origin[3]					
Less than 12 years:					
White, non-Hispanic	36.1	39.1	41.8	38.1	41.2
Black, non-Hispanic	31.7	32.0	37.9	33.0	33.1
Hispanic	33.8	36.5	42.7	28.9	33.0
12 years:					
White, non-Hispanic	56.6	59.8	62.8	58.8	60.4
Black, non-Hispanic	40.5	44.8	51.1	43.1	48.2
Hispanic	48.7	56.5	59.9	49.5	54.6
13 years or more:					
White, non-Hispanic	72.6	75.8	77.3	74.2	75.8
Black, non-Hispanic	54.4	57.2	64.4	61.7	61.3
Hispanic	58.4	66.2	67.9	61.2	61.8

[1]Data for 1983 and 1989 are not strictly comparable with data for later years. Data for 1983 and 1989 are based on responses to the question "About how long has it been since you last went to a dentist?" Starting in 1990 data are based on the question "During the past 12 months, how many visits did you make to a dentist?"

[2]Includes all other races not shown separately and unknown poverty status and education level.

[3]Age adjusted.

[4]Poverty status is based on family income and family size using Bureau of the Census poverty thresholds.

NOTES: Denominators exclude persons with unknown dental data. Estimates for 1983 and 1989 are based on data for all members of the sample household.

Beginning in 1990 estimates are based on one adult member per sample household. Estimates for 1993 are based on responses during the last half of the year only.

SOURCE: *Health, United States, 1996-97.* National Center for Health Statistics: Hyattsville, Md., 1997

---

cent in 1990 and 13.01 percent in 1997. In 1997 the percentage of Black low-birth-weight babies was nearly twice the White percentage. Chinese American women had the lowest rate at 5.06 percent. Hispanics had a lower rate (6.42 percent) than the general population, although 9.39 percent of Puerto Rican births were low-birthweight babies. (See Table 6.4.)

Blacks suffer the highest rates of infant mortality (deaths before one year of age). In 1996 the mortality rate of non-Hispanic Black births (14.1 per 1,000 live births) was more than twice the rate of non-Hispanic White

infants and Hispanic infants (6.1 per 1,000 live births each). (See Table 6.5.)

DOCTOR AND DENTIST VISITS

Over the past 20 years, as more outpatient clinics and other outreach health facilities have opened, most Americans have had increased opportunities to seek medical help. The National Center for Health Statistics (NCHS) reported that, in 1997, overall visits to physician offices averaged 286 visits per 100 persons. Blacks (242 visits per 100 persons) were less likely than Whites (297 visits per 100 persons) to

TABLE 6.7

Health Care Coverage for Persons Under 65 Years of Age, According to Type of Coverage and Selected Characteristics: United States, Selected Years 1984-97

[Data are based on household interviews of a sample of the civilian noninstitutionalized population]

Characteristic	Private insurance						Private insurance obtained through workplace[1]					
	1984	1989	1994[2]	1995	1996	1997[2,3]	1984	1989	1994[2]	1995	1996	1997[2,3]
	Number in millions											
Total[4]	157.5	162.7	160.7	165.0	165.9	165.8	141.8	146.3	146.7	151.4	151.4	152.5
	Percent of population											
Total, age adjusted[4]	76.6	75.7	69.9	71.2	71.1	70.4	68.9	68.1	63.8	65.4	64.8	64.7
Total, crude[4]	76.8	75.9	70.3	71.6	71.4	70.7	69.1	68.3	64.2	65.7	65.1	65.0
Age												
Under 18 years	72.6	71.8	63.8	65.7	66.4	66.1	66.5	65.8	59.0	60.9	61.1	61.3
Under 6 years	68.1	67.9	58.3	60.1	61.1	61.3	62.1	62.3	53.9	55.6	56.5	57.3
6–17 years	74.9	74.0	66.8	68.7	69.1	68.5	68.7	67.7	61.8	63.7	63.4	63.4
18–44 years	76.5	75.5	69.8	71.2	70.6	69.4	69.6	68.4	63.9	65.6	64.7	64.4
18–24 years	67.4	64.5	58.3	61.2	60.4	59.3	58.7	55.3	50.7	53.9	52.3	53.8
25–34 years	77.4	75.9	69.4	70.3	69.5	68.1	71.2	69.5	64.1	65.3	64.4	63.6
35–44 years	83.9	82.7	77.1	78.0	77.5	76.4	77.4	76.2	71.6	72.9	72.0	71.2
45–64 years	83.3	82.5	80.3	80.4	79.5	79.1	71.8	71.6	71.8	72.4	71.4	70.8
45–54 years	83.3	83.4	81.3	81.1	80.4	80.4	74.6	74.4	74.6	74.9	74.0	73.6
55–64 years	83.3	81.6	78.8	79.3	78.1	76.9	69.0	68.3	67.9	68.6	67.5	66.6
Sex[5]												
Male	77.1	76.0	70.4	71.6	71.4	70.7	69.7	68.6	64.3	65.9	65.2	65.0
Female	76.0	75.4	69.5	70.8	70.8	70.1	68.1	67.6	63.4	64.8	64.4	64.4
Race[5,6]												
White	79.7	79.0	73.5	74.4	74.2	74.1	71.9	71.1	67.0	68.4	67.6	67.9
Black	58.3	57.8	51.5	54.2	54.9	54.9	52.4	52.9	48.8	50.4	51.8	52.6
Asian or Pacific Islander	69.8	71.1	67.3	68.0	67.8	68.0	63.6	60.2	57.4	59.8	59.3	60.4
Hispanic origin and race[5,6]												
All Hispanic	56.3	52.6	48.6	47.3	47.5	47.3	52.3	48.0	44.5	44.0	43.8	44.0
Mexican	54.3	48.0	45.7	43.9	43.8	43.3	51.1	45.2	43.7	41.9	40.9	41.2
Puerto Rican	48.8	45.9	48.3	47.9	50.7	47.2	46.4	42.6	45.2	44.7	48.1	44.6
Cuban	71.7	69.0	63.9	62.4	65.4	70.5	57.7	55.8	46.5	53.1	54.4	56.0
Other Hispanic	61.6	61.9	52.3	52.2	52.6	50.7	57.4	55.4	46.2	47.1	47.6	47.1
White, non-Hispanic	82.3	82.4	77.3	78.6	78.5	77.9	74.0	74.1	70.4	72.1	71.5	71.4
Black, non-Hispanic	58.5	57.9	51.9	54.6	55.4	55.1	52.6	53.0	49.2	50.9	52.2	52.8
Age and percent of poverty level[6,7]												
All ages:[5]												
Below 100 percent	32.4	26.7	21.3	21.9	20.0	22.7	23.7	19.4	16.1	17.0	15.5	18.9
100–149 percent	62.4	54.9	46.8	47.8	47.1	42.1	51.9	45.8	40.9	41.9	40.8	37.0
150–199 percent	77.7	71.3	65.7	66.5	67.9	64.0	69.5	62.9	59.0	60.4	60.9	58.7
200 percent or more	91.7	91.2	88.9	89.3	89.5	87.7	85.2	84.2	83.0	83.7	83.2	82.0
Under 18 years:												
Below 100 percent	28.7	22.3	14.9	16.8	16.1	17.4	23.2	17.5	12.4	13.4	13.4	15.4
100–149 percent	66.2	59.6	47.8	48.5	49.5	42.5	58.3	52.5	43.2	43.6	43.7	38.5
150–199 percent	80.9	75.9	69.3	68.5	73.0	66.8	75.8	70.1	64.0	63.0	67.4	63.1
200 percent or more	92.3	92.7	89.7	90.4	90.7	88.9	86.9	86.7	84.5	85.5	84.6	83.7
Geographic region[5]												
Northeast	80.1	81.8	74.8	75.1	74.9	74.0	73.8	74.9	69.5	69.5	68.7	69.4
Midwest	80.4	81.4	77.2	77.2	78.4	76.9	71.9	73.3	71.0	71.1	72.3	71.1
South	74.0	71.1	65.0	66.7	65.9	66.8	65.9	63.3	59.1	61.7	60.4	61.0
West	71.8	71.3	65.2	67.9	67.1	65.3	64.5	63.9	58.1	60.7	59.6	58.9
Location of residence[5]												
Within MSA[8]	77.2	76.3	70.4	72.1	72.5	71.0	70.6	69.5	64.8	66.6	66.5	65.6
Outside MSA[8]	75.1	73.6	68.1	67.7	65.8	68.0	65.1	63.4	60.4	60.5	58.6	61.4

have contact with a physician in his or her office. Blacks (56 visits per 100 persons), however, were more than twice as likely as Whites (26 visits per 100 persons) to use a hospital outpatient department. Blacks (60 visits per 100 persons) also tended to visit a hospital emergency department more often than Whites (32 visits per 100 persons).

Non-Hispanic Blacks' visits to dentists have increased significantly, although they still do not go as often as non-Hispanic Whites. In 1993 non-Hispanic Whites were more likely to make dental visits (64 percent) than non-Hispanic Blacks (47.3 percent) and Hispanics (46.2 percent). (See Table 6.6.)

HEALTH INSURANCE

According to the NCHS, in 1997, 54.9 percent of Black individuals under the age of 65 were covered by

TABLE 6.7

Health Care Coverage for Persons Under 65 Years of Age, According to Type of Coverage and Selected Characteristics: United States, Selected Years 1984-97 [CONTINUED]

[Data are based on household interviews of a sample of the civilian noninstitutionalized population]

Characteristic	Medicaid[9]						Not covered[10]					
	1984	1989	1994[2]	1995	1996	1997[2,3]	1984	1989	1994[2]	1995	1996	1997[2,3]
	Number in millions											
Total[4]	14.0	15.4	24.1	25.3	25.0	22.9	29.8	33.4	40.4	37.4	38.9	41.0
	Percent of population											
Total, age adjusted[4]	7.3	7.8	11.5	12.0	11.7	10.7	14.2	15.2	17.1	15.6	16.1	16.8
Total, crude[4]	6.8	7.2	10.6	11.0	10.8	9.7	14.5	15.6	17.7	16.2	16.7	17.5
Age												
Under 18 years	11.9	12.6	20.0	20.6	20.1	18.4	13.9	14.7	15.3	13.6	13.4	14.0
Under 6 years	15.5	15.7	27.2	28.3	27.4	24.7	14.9	15.1	13.7	11.9	11.9	12.5
6–17 years	10.1	10.9	16.2	16.6	16.4	15.2	13.4	14.5	16.2	14.5	14.1	14.7
18–44 years	5.1	5.2	7.3	7.4	7.3	6.6	17.1	18.4	21.9	20.5	21.2	22.4
18–24 years	6.4	6.8	9.6	9.7	9.2	8.8	25.0	27.1	31.1	28.2	29.6	30.1
25–34 years	5.3	5.2	7.7	7.7	7.5	6.8	16.2	18.3	22.1	21.3	22.5	23.8
35–44 years	3.5	4.0	5.4	5.6	6.0	5.2	11.2	12.3	16.0	15.2	15.2	16.7
45–64 years	3.4	4.3	4.5	5.3	5.2	4.6	9.6	10.5	12.0	11.0	12.1	12.4
45–54 years	3.2	3.8	3.8	4.9	4.8	4.0	10.5	11.0	12.6	11.7	12.5	12.8
55–64 years	3.6	4.9	5.5	6.0	5.7	5.6	8.7	10.0	11.2	10.0	11.6	11.8
Sex[5]												
Male	6.1	6.5	9.8	10.3	10.1	9.4	14.8	16.1	18.1	16.7	17.2	17.8
Female	8.5	9.1	13.2	13.6	13.3	11.9	13.6	14.3	16.1	14.6	15.1	15.9
Race[5,6]												
White	5.0	5.6	8.7	9.4	9.3	8.2	13.3	14.1	16.4	15.0	15.4	15.8
Black	20.5	19.3	27.0	27.0	24.5	22.7	19.5	21.0	19.5	17.9	19.0	19.3
Asian or Pacific Islander	10.1	11.8	10.2	11.4	12.4	10.3	17.8	18.2	19.9	17.8	18.6	18.8
Hispanic origin and race[5,6]												
All Hispanic	13.1	13.5	19.6	21.2	20.1	17.8	29.0	32.4	31.4	30.8	31.6	33.2
Mexican	11.8	12.3	18.3	20.1	19.0	17.1	33.1	38.6	35.7	35.4	36.7	38.1
Puerto Rican	31.1	28.0	36.2	32.7	33.8	30.9	17.9	23.3	15.4	17.8	14.4	18.5
Cuban	5.0	8.0	9.8	15.3	13.9	9.2	21.6	21.8	26.1	21.6	17.6	19.8
Other Hispanic	8.0	11.2	16.2	18.4	16.3	15.6	27.1	24.8	30.2	29.0	29.8	31.8
White, non-Hispanic	4.0	4.6	7.1	7.5	7.5	6.8	11.6	11.7	14.2	12.7	12.9	13.3
Black, non-Hispanic	20.8	19.4	27.0	26.7	24.2	22.5	19.2	20.8	19.1	17.8	18.9	19.3
Age and percent of poverty level[6,7]												
All ages:[5]												
Below 100 percent	32.1	37.0	45.0	46.9	46.8	41.6	34.0	35.2	32.7	30.9	32.7	32.8
100–149 percent	7.7	11.2	16.0	18.4	17.2	19.1	26.4	30.6	34.0	31.2	32.8	34.8
150–199 percent	3.3	5.1	5.9	7.7	7.7	8.0	16.7	21.0	24.9	22.8	22.5	25.1
200 percent or more	0.6	1.1	1.4	1.6	1.6	1.9	5.6	6.5	8.4	7.8	7.4	8.5
Under 18 years:												
Below 100 percent	43.1	47.8	63.6	65.6	65.9	59.9	28.9	31.6	23.3	20.6	21.3	22.4
100–149 percent	9.0	12.3	22.9	26.3	24.8	30.2	22.8	26.1	27.7	25.5	25.2	26.1
150–199 percent	4.4	6.1	8.6	11.7	10.8	12.2	12.7	15.8	19.0	17.7	16.1	19.7
200 percent or more	0.8	1.6	2.2	2.7	2.6	2.9	4.2	4.4	6.8	6.0	5.3	6.1
Geographic region[5]												
Northeast	9.4	7.4	12.0	12.5	12.3	12.4	9.8	10.5	13.3	12.7	13.2	12.8
Midwest	7.9	8.2	10.4	11.0	9.4	9.2	10.9	10.2	11.9	11.8	11.9	12.6
South	5.5	7.0	11.3	11.6	12.0	9.8	17.4	19.4	20.9	19.1	19.7	20.3
West	7.5	9.1	12.6	13.2	13.4	12.5	17.6	18.1	20.2	17.3	18.1	19.8
Location of residence[5]												
Within MSA[8]	7.8	7.7	11.7	11.8	11.1	10.6	13.2	14.7	16.6	14.9	15.3	16.2
Outside MSA[8]	6.4	8.3	11.1	12.8	13.9	11.0	16.3	16.7	18.8	18.4	19.2	19.4

[1]Private insurance originally obtained through a present or former employer or union.

[2]The questionnaire changed compared with previous years.

[3]Preliminary data. [4]Includes all other races not shown separately and unknown poverty level.

[5]Age adjusted.

[6]The race groups white, black, and Asian or Pacific Islander include persons of Hispanic and non-Hispanic origin; persons of Hispanic origin may be of any race.

[7]Poverty level is based on family income and family size using Bureau of the Census poverty thresholds.

[8]Metropolitan statistical area.

[9]Includes other public assistance through 1996. In 1997 includes state-sponsored health plans. In 1997 the age-adjusted percent of the population under 65 years of age covered by Medicaid was 9.5 percent, and 1.2 percent were covered by state-sponsored health plans.

[10]Includes persons not covered by private insurance, Medicaid, public assistance (through 1996), state-sponsored or other government-sponsored health plans (1997), Medicare, or military plans. Estimates of the percentage of persons lacking health care coverage based on the National Health Interview Survey (NHIS) are slightly higher than those based on the March Current Population Survey (CPS).

NOTE: Percents do not add to 100 because the percent with other types of health insurance (for example, Medicare, military) is not shown, and because persons with both private insurance and Medicaid appear in both columns.

SOURCE: *Health, United States, 1999.* National Center for Health Statistics: Hyattsville, MD, 1999

TABLE 6.8

Health Care Coverage for Persons 65 Years of Age or Over, According to Type of Coverage and Selected Characteristics: United States, Selected Years 1984–97

[Data are based on household interviews of a sample of the civilian noninstitutionalized population]

Characteristic	Medicare and private insurance				Medicare and Medicaid				Medicare only[1]			
	1989	1993[2]	1994	1995[3]	1989	1993[2]	1994	1995[3]	1989	1993[2]	1994	1995[3]
						Number in millions						
Total[4]	21.5	23.7	23.3	22.6	1.7	1.7	1.7	2.2	4.9	4.8	4.6	5.1
						Percent of population						
Total, age adjusted[4]	73.5	75.5	75.1	72.0	5.7	5.2	5.3	7.0	16.8	15.3	14.8	16.2
Total, crude[4]	73.5	75.4	75.1	72.1	5.7	5.3	5.4	7.1	16.9	15.4	14.8	16.2
Age												
65-74 years	74.2	76.0	74.9	71.6	5.0	4.6	4.5	6.1	15.5	14.2	14.4	16.3
75 years and over	72.3	74.5	75.3	72.8	6.8	6.4	6.9	8.6	19.0	17.2	15.4	16.0
75-84 years	74.1	76.5	77.3	74.1	6.4	5.8	5.8	8.1	17.4	15.6	14.4	15.0
85 years and over	64.8	66.7	67.4	68.2	8.5	8.5	11.0	10.3	26.1	23.7	19.5	19.2
Sex[5]												
Male	73.9	76.5	75.8	72.5	4.0	3.0	3.0	4.6	17.2	15.7	15.8	17.3
Female	73.4	74.7	74.7	71.8	6.8	6.9	7.0	8.8	16.4	15.0	13.9	15.3
Race[5]												
White	77.3	79.1	78.8	75.6	4.5	4.2	4.4	5.5	14.7	13.2	12.9	14.8
Black	39.3	43.6	42.4	40.1	16.5	13.3	14.9	22.2	37.9	36.2	34.5	31.3
Hispanic origin and race[5]												
All Hispanic	38.8	38.1	49.2	33.8	20.4	23.6	19.5	27.9	24.1	31.7	23.2	28.4
Mexican American	33.5	30.2	41.8	24.1	23.5	15.7	22.0	25.1	26.7	45.8	29.5	37.3
Puerto Rican	*18.5	*6.3	48.4	41.3	*30.6	*21.9	17.5	26.6	*27.6	59.0	28.3	28.5
Cuban	45.7	59.0	55.9	41.7	*20.6	39.7	*24.8	44.1	*23.7	*3.2	12.9	*14.1
Other Hispanic	49.5	42.6	56.3	40.3	13.0	*19.1	12.9	19.8	19.2	27.9	17.9	25.1
White, non-Hispanic	78.5	80.9	80.3	77.8	3.9	3.4	3.7	4.4	14.4	12.4	12.3	14.0
Black, non-Hispanic	39.3	43.8	42.9	39.9	16.3	13.2	14.4	22.3	38.0	36.1	34.6	31.4
Family income[5]												
Less than $14,000	64.8	58.3	59.0	54.9	11.4	14.1	15.0	19.6	21.5	24.3	22.8	23.1
$14,000-$24,999	81.2	82.8	82.5	79.5	2.6	1.6	2.0	3.4	13.4	13.1	12.3	13.7
$25,000-$34,999	80.0	85.7	83.5	80.6	2.4	1.5	1.4	2.1	12.5	9.4	9.5	12.1
$35,000-$49,999	80.3	83.6	83.9	80.9	*1.9	*2.1	*2.0	*1.4	10.2	9.4	9.3	11.4
$50,000 or more	76.5	81.3	79.1	78.4	*1.1	*2.4	*1.4	*2.0	12.6	8.5	8.4	10.4
Geographic region[5]												
Northeast	73.1	79.0	75.5	72.8	4.0	3.5	4.3	5.1	18.0	12.1	15.6	16.9
Midwest	79.6	81.7	82.4	81.4	2.9	3.5	2.5	3.9	14.1	12.3	11.3	11.4
South	70.6	70.8	69.8	69.1	7.7	7.4	7.7	9.8	18.3	19.0	18.1	17.1
West	71.4	71.7	74.0	63.5	7.6	5.7	6.1	8.2	16.0	16.3	12.7	20.2
Location of residence[5]												
Within MSA[6]	73.6	75.2	75.3	71.9	5.1	5.1	5.0	6.6	16.8	15.1	14.4	15.9
Outside MSA[6]	73.4	76.3	74.5	72.6	7.2	5.8	6.3	8.5	16.8	15.9	15.9	17.0

*Relative standard error greater than 30 percent.

[1]Includes persons not covered by private insurance or Medicaid and a small proportion of persons with other types of coverage, such as CHAMPUS or public assistance.

[2]July 1 to Dec. 31, 1993. The questionnaire changed in 1993 compared with previous years.

[3]January 1 to June 30, 1995, preliminary data.

[4]Includes all other races not shown separately and unknown family income.

[5]Age adjusted.

[6]Metropolitan statistical area.

NOTES: Percents do not add to 100 because the percent without Medicare is not shown, and because persons with Medicare, private insurance, and Medicaid appear in both columns. In 1995, 5.5 percent of all persons 65 years of age and over had no Medicare, but only 0.8 percent were without health insurance.

SOURCE: *Health, United States, 1999.* National Center for Health Statistics: Hyattsville, MD, 1999

private health insurance, compared to 74.1 percent of their White counterparts. Fewer than half (47.3 percent) of all Hispanics had private insurance, and two-thirds (68 percent) of Asians/Pacific Islanders (APIs) carried private insurance. Employers often provide private health insurance. In 1997 Whites (67.9 percent) and APIs (60.4 percent) were more likely than Blacks (52.6 percent) and

Hispanics (44 percent) to have insurance coverage through their jobs. (See Table 6.7.)

In 1997, among individuals under 65 years old, 15.8 percent of Whites, 19.3 percent of Blacks, 18.8 percent of APIs, and 33.2 percent of Hispanics had no insurance coverage. Among Hispanics, 38.1 percent of Mexican

TABLE 6.9

Percentages Reporting Past Month Use of Any Illicit Drug, by Age Group, Race/Ethnicity, and Gender, 1979–1998

Demographic Characteristics	1979	1985	1991	1992	1993	1994	1995	1996	1997	1998
TOTAL	14.1[b]	12.1[b]	6.6	5.8	5.9	6.0	6.1	6.1	6.4	6.2
AGE GROUP										
12-17	16.3[a]	13.2	5.8[b]	5.3[b]	5.7[b]	8.2[a]	10.9	9.0	11.4[a]	9.9
18-25	38.0[b]	25.3[b]	15.4	13.1	13.6	13.3[a]	14.2	15.6	14.7	16.1
26-34	20.8[b]	23.1[b]	10.0[a]	11.4[b]	9.5	8.5[a]	8.3	8.4[a]	7.4	7.0
>35	2.8	3.9	3.4	2.5	3.0	3.2	2.8	2.9	3.6	3.3
RACE/ETHNICITY										
White, non-Hispanic	14.2[b]	12.3[b]	6.5	6.1	6.1	6.0	6.0	6.1	6.4	6.1
Black, non-Hispanic	13.3[a]	12.7[a]	8.1	5.6[b]	5.8[a]	7.3	7.9	7.5	7.5	8.2
Hispanic	12.9[a]	8.9[a]	5.3	4.4[a]	5.2	5.4	5.1	5.2	5.9	6.1
Other, non-Hispanic	15.1[b]	10.7	6.0	3.9	4.3	3.1	4.0	4.8	5.4	3.8
GENDER										
Male	19.2[b]	14.9[b]	7.9	7.6	7.7	7.9	7.8	8.1	8.5	8.1
Female	9.4[b]	9.5[b]	5.4	4.2	4.3	4.3	4.5	4.2	4.5	4.5

*Low precision; no estimate reported.

— Not available.

NOTE: Any Illicit Drug indicates use at least once of marijuana/hashish, cocaine (including crack), inhalants, hallucinogens (including PCP and LSD), heroin, or any prescription-type psychotherapeutic used nonmedically. Any Illicit Drug Other than Marijuana indicates use at least once of any of these listed drugs, regardless of marijuana/hashish use; marijuana/hashish users who also have used any of the other listed drugs are included.

NOTE: The population distributions for the 1993 through 1998 NHSDAs are post-stratified to population projections of totals based on the 1990 decennial census. The 1979 NHSDA used population projections based on the 1970 census; NHSDAs from 1982 through 1992 used projections based on the 1980 census. The change from one census base to another has little effect on estimated percentages reporting drug use, but may have a significant effect on estimates of number of drug users in some subpopulation groups.

NOTE: Estimates for 1979 through 1993 may differ from estimates for these survey years that were published in other NHSDA reports. The estimates shown here for 1979 through 1993 have been adjusted to improve their comparability with estimates based on the new version of the NHSDA instrument that was fielded in 1994 and subsequent NHSDAs. For 1979 and 1982, estimates are not shown (as indicated by —) where (a) the relevant data were not collected, or (b) the data for those drugs were based on measures that differed appreciably from those used in the other survey years. Consequently, adjustments to the 1979 and 1982 data were made only for those drugs whose measures were comparable to those in the other survey years.

Because of the methodology used to adjust the 1979 through 1993 estimates, some logical inconsistency may exist between estimates for a given drug within the same survey year. For example, some adjusted estimates of past year use may appear to be greater then adjusted lifetime estimates. These inconsistencies tend to be small, rare and not statistically significant.

[a]Difference between estimate and 1998 estimate is statistically significant at the .05 level.

[b]Difference between estimate and 1998 estimate is statistically significant at the .01 level.

SOURCE: *Summary of Findings from the 1998 National Household Survey on Drug Abuse.* U.S. Department of Health and Human Services, Substance Abuse and Mental Health Services Administration

Americans had no coverage, while only 18.5 percent of Puerto Ricans were not covered. Medicaid (the federally funded health-care program for low-income people) covered 8.2 percent of Whites, 22.7 percent of Blacks, and 10.3 percent of APIs. Nearly 18 percent of all Hispanics were covered by Medicaid, including 30.9 percent of all Puerto Ricans. (See Table 6.7.)

In 1997, among persons 65 and older, 43.5 percent of Blacks had private insurance, compared to 72.9 percent of Whites. A lower proportion (31.9 percent) of Hispanics were covered by private insurance. About 32 percent of Blacks and 19 percent of Hispanics had private insurance through their workplace, compared to 39.1 percent of Whites. More Blacks (33.9 percent) than Whites (19.2 percent) were covered by Medicare only, the government health-care program for people age 65 and over. Medicare has two parts, Part A for hospital bills and Part B for physician care. Of those people in the Medicare program, most are covered by both parts either through their own payments or assistance from Medicaid. In contrast, 19.3 percent of elderly Blacks had Medicaid coverage, com-

pared to 6.4 percent of Whites. Larger proportions of elderly Hispanics were covered by Medicare only (34.9 percent) and Medicaid (27.6 percent). (See Table 6.8.)

DRUG ABUSE AMONG MINORITY POPULATIONS

Each year the Substance Abuse and Mental Health Services Administration (SAMHSA) of the U.S. Department of Health and Human Services surveys American households on drug use. The 1998 *National Household Survey on Drug Abuse* (Office of Applied Studies, SAMHSA, Washington, DC, 1999) found that, in 1998, 6.2 percent of Americans age 12 and over used illicit drugs in the month prior to the survey. Blacks (8.2 percent) were somewhat more likely to have used illegal drugs than Whites or Hispanics (6.1 percent each). (See Table 6.9.)

In 1998 half (51.7 percent) the population reported alcohol use in the past month. More Whites (55.3 percent) than either Hispanics (45.4 percent) or Blacks (39.8 percent) reported drinking alcohol in the month before

TABLE 6.10

Percentages Reporting Past Month Use of Alcohol, by Age Group, Race/Ethnicity, and Gender, 1979–1998

Demographic Characteristics	1979	1985	1991	1992	1993	1994	1995	1996	1997	1998
TOTAL	63.2[b]	60.2[b]	52.2	49.0	50.8	53.9	52.2	51.0	51.4	51.7
AGE GROUP										
12-17	49.6[b]	41.2[b]	27.0[b]	20.9	23.9[a]	21.6[a]	21.1	18.8	20.5	19.1
18-25	75.1[b]	70.1[a]	63.1	58.6	58.7	63.1	61.3	60.0	58.4	60.0
26-34	71.6[b]	70.6[a]	62.7	62.3	63.8	65.3[b]	63.0	61.6	60.2	60.9
>35	59.7	57.5	50.4	47.4	49.8	54.1	52.6	51.7	52.8	53.1
RACE/ETHNICITY										
White, non-Hispanic	64.4[b]	62.8[a]	54.0	50.9	54.0	56.7	55.6	54.2	55.1	55.3
Black, non-Hispanic	58.8[b]	50.6[b]	47.2[a]	42.8	40.5	43.8[a]	40.8	41.9	40.4	39.8
Hispanic	58.6[b]	49.3	46.3	43.7	44.3	47.7	45.2	43.1	42.4	45.4
Other, non-Hispanic	50.9[a]	*	42.4	39.2	33.0	42.0	36.9	35.6	37.0	35.8
GENDER										
Male	72.4[b]	69.2[b]	59.6	57.2	58.7	60.3	60.1	58.9	58.2	58.7
Female	54.9[b]	52.0[a]	45.4	41.4	43.6	47.9	45.0	43.6	45.1	45.1

*Low precision; no estimate reported.

— Not available.

NOTE: The population distributions for the 1993 through 1998 NHSDAs are post-stratified to population projections of totals based on the 1990 decennial census. The 1979 NHSDA used population projections based on the 1970 census; NHSDAs from 1982 through 1992 used projections based on the 1980 census. The change from one census base to another has little effect on estimated percentages reporting drug use, but may have a significant effect on estimates of number of drug users in some subpopulation groups.

NOTE: Estimates for 1979 through 1993 may differ from estimates for these survey years that were published in other NHSDA reports. The estimates shown here for 1979 through 1993 have been adjusted to improve their comparability with estimates based on the new version of the NHSDA instrument that was fielded in 1994 and subsequent NHSDAs. For 1979 and 1982, estimates are not shown (as indicated by —) where (a) the relevant data were not collected, or (b) the data for those drugs were based on measures that differed appreciably from those used in the other survey years. Consequently, adjustments to the 1979 and 1982 data were made only for those drugs whose measures were comparable to those in the other survey years.

    Because of the methodology used to adjust the 1979 through 1993 estimates, some logical inconsistency may exist between estimates for a given drug within the same survey year. For example, some adjusted estimates of past year use may appear to be greater then adjusted lifetime estimates. These inconsistencies tend to be small, rare and not statistically significant.

[a]Difference between estimate and 1998 estimate is statistically significant at the .05 level.

[b]Difference between estimate and 1998 estimate is statistically significant at the .01 level.

SOURCE: *Summary of Findings from the 1998 National Household Survey on Drug Abuse.* U.S. Department of Health and Human Services, Substance Abuse and Mental Health Services Administration

the survey. In 1979 nearly two-thirds (63.2 percent) of Americans age 12 and over reported past-month use of alcohol, with nearly three in five Blacks and Hispanics reporting alcohol consumption. (See Table 6.10.)

In 1998, 27.9 percent of Whites, 29.4 percent of Blacks, and 25.8 percent of Hispanics 12 years old and over smoked cigarettes in the month preceding the survey. (See Table 6.11.) That same year, 17.2 percent of survey respondents indicated using smokeless tobacco at some time during their lives, while 3.1 percent said they used it in the last month prior to the survey. More Whites (3.7 percent) than Blacks (2 percent) or Hispanics (.8 percent) used smokeless tobacco.

Cocaine Use

In 1998 the *National Household Survey on Drug Abuse* reported that .8 percent of the population used cocaine in the month preceding the survey. Over 1 percent of the Black and Hispanic population had used it in the month prior to the survey, compared to .7 percent of the White population. These rates of cocaine use were down significantly from 1985, when 3.4 percent of Blacks, 2.5 percent of

Hispanics, and 3 percent of Whites had used cocaine in the month preceding the survey. (See Table 6.12.)

The introduction, especially into the minority community, of "crack"—a highly addictive, cheaper form of cocaine that can be smoked—changed the drug-use situation. Sold in vials for about $10, crack gave the poor access to the previously expensive cocaine, which had been the drug of choice for young, successful, generally White professionals. Crack took hold of inner-city minority communities and fostered the proliferation of gangs that sold crack and increased violence and high-risk behaviors, such as unprotected sex. Crack is powerfully addictive, often overwhelming any other needs and wreaking havoc on the lives of those living in these communities.

Crack use, however, has not been restricted to minority neighborhoods. According to the National Institute on Drug Abuse, the rates of cocaine use (including crack) in 1998 in large and small metropolitan areas (.9 and .8 percent, respectively) were virtually the same percentage. Non-metropolitan areas had a .5 percent cocaine use. These rates, however, were down considerably from 1985, when the rate for large metropolitan areas was 3.6

TABLE 6.11

Percentages Reporting Past Month Use of Cigarettes, by Age group, Race/Ethnicity, and Gender, 1979–1998

Demographic Characteristics	1979	1985	1991	1992	1993	1994	1995	1996	1997	1998
TOTAL	—	38.7[b]	33.0[b]	31.9[a]	29.6	28.6	28.8	28.9	29.6[a]	27.7
AGE GROUP										
12-17	—	29.4[b]	20.9	18.4	18.5	18.9	20.2	18.3	19.9	18.2
18-25	—	47.4	41.7	41.5	37.9	34.6[b]	35.3[b]	38.3[a]	40.6	41.6
26-34	—	45.7[b]	37.3	38.2[a]	34.2	32.4	34.7	35.0	33.7	32.5
>35	—	35.5[b]	31.6[a]	30.0	28.2	27.9[a]	27.2	27.0	27.9[b]	25.1
RACE/ETHNICITY										
White, non-Hispanic	—	38.9[b]	33.5[a]	32.8[a]	30.3	29.4	29.7	29.8	30.5[b]	27.9
Black, non-Hispanic	—	38.0[a]	31.2	29.8	26.2	28.4	28.1	30.4	29.8	29.4
Hispanic	—	40.0[b]	33.6[b]	29.2	29.0	25.8	24.7	24.7	27.4	25.8
Other, non-Hispanic	—	*	28.0	25.4	27.6	20.5	23.5	17.2[a]	18.8	23.8
GENDER										
Male	—	43.4[b]	35.2[a]	34.1	32.2	31.5	31.0	31.1	31.2	29.7
Female	—	34.5[b]	31.1[b]	30.0[a]	27.3	26.0	26.8	26.7	28.2[a]	25.7

*Low precision; no estimate reported.

— Not available.

NOTE: The population distributions for the 1993 through 1998 NHSDAs are post-stratified to population projections of totals based on the 1990 decennial census. The 1979 NHSDA used population projections based on the 1970 census; NHSDAs from 1982 through 1992 used projections based on the 1980 census. The change from one census base to another has little effect on estimated percentages reporting drug use, but may have a significant effect on estimates of number of drug users in some subpopulation groups.

NOTE: Estimates for 1979 through 1993 may differ from estimates for these survey years that were published in other NHSDA reports. The estimates shown here for 1979 through 1993 have been adjusted to improve their comparability with estimates based on the new version of the NHSDA instrument that was fielded in 1994 and subsequent NHSDAs. For 1979 and 1982, estimates are not shown (as indicated by —) where (a) the relevant data were not collected, or (b) the data for those drugs were based on measures that differed appreciably from those used in the other survey years. Consequently, adjustments to the 1979 and 1982 data were made only for those drugs whose measures were comparable to those in the other survey years.

Because of the methodology used to adjust the 1979 through 1993 estimates, some logical inconsistency may exist between estimates for a given drug within the same survey year. For example, some adjusted estimates of past year use may appear to be greater then adjusted lifetime estimates. These inconsistencies tend to be small, rare and not statistically significant.

[a]Difference between estimate and 1998 estimate is statistically significant at the .05 level.

[b]Difference between estimate and 1998 estimate is statistically significant at the .01 level.

SOURCE: *Summary of Findings from the 1998 National Household Survey on Drug Abuse.* U.S. Department of Health and Human Services, Substance Abuse and Mental Health Services Administration

percent, compared to 2.3 percent for small metropolitan and 1.7 percent for non-metropolitan areas.

Marijuana Use

In 1998, 5 percent of the total population 12 years and older claimed to have used marijuana at least once during the 30 days prior to the survey. In 1985, 10 percent each of Whites and of Blacks, and 6.4 percent of Hispanics were current users. In 1995, 4.7 percent of Whites, 5.9 percent of Blacks, and 3.9 percent of Hispanics used marijuana during the month before the survey. (See Table 6.13.)

HEALTH OF BLACK AMERICANS

Cancer

According to the American Cancer Society (*Cancer Facts & Figures—2000,* Atlanta, Georgia, 2000), in 2000, about 1,220,100 new cancer cases were expected to be diagnosed in the United States and about 552,200 Americans were expected to die of cancer. Nonetheless, this number of deaths from cancer is down from 564,800 in 1998. Since 1990 there have been nearly 5 million deaths from cancer. Cancer distribution among various population groups varies according to racial and ethnic background. Risk factors, such as occupation, use of tobacco and alcohol, sexual and reproductive behaviors, and nutritional and dietary habits, influence the development of cancer. Socioeconomic status is an important factor in receiving and surviving cancer treatment.

Cancer incidence and mortality rates are generally higher for Black Americans than White Americans. The Surveillance, Epidemiology, and End Results (SEER) Program of the National Cancer Institute (NCI) is the most authoritative source of information on cancer incidence, mortality, and survival in the United Sates. In *SEER Cancer Statistics Review, 1973–1997* (Bethesda, Maryland, 2000), the NCI reported that the incidence rates between 1993 and 1997 were 455.2 per 100,000 Blacks and 401.9 per 100,000 Whites. The five-year survival rate for cancer in Blacks diagnosed between 1989 and 1996 was about 48.9 percent, compared to 61.5 percent for Whites. Much of this difference in survival can be attributed to late diagnosis. Types of cancer for which Blacks have significantly higher incidence and mortality rates include stomach, colon, rectum, pancreas, lung and bronchus, breast, prostate, kidney and renal pelvis, non-Hodgkin's lymphoma, and multiple myeloma.

TABLE 6.12

Percentages Reporting Past Month Use of Cocaine, by Age group, Race/Ethnicity, and Gender, 1979–1998

Demographic Characteristics	1979	1985	1991	1992	1993	1994	1995	1996	1997	1998
TOTAL	2.6[b]	3.0[b]	1.0	0.7	0.7	0.7	0.7	0.8	0.7	0.8
AGE GROUP										
12-17	1.5	1.5	0.4	0.3[b]	0.4	0.3[a]	0.8	0.6	1.0	0.8
18-25	9.9[b]	8.1[b]	2.2	2.0	1.6	1.2[a]	1.3	2.0	1.2[a]	2.0
26-34	3.0[a]	6.3[b]	1.9	1.5	1.0	1.3	1.2	1.5	0.9	1.2
>35	0.2	0.5	0.5	0.2[a]	0.4	0.4	0.4	0.4	0.5	0.5
RACE/ETHNICITY										
White, non-Hispanic	2.4[b]	3.0[b]	0.7	0.6	0.5	0.5	0.6	0.8	0.6	0.7
Black, non-Hispanic	2.8	3.4[b]	1.9	1.0	1.4	1.3	1.1	1.0	1.4	1.3
Hispanic	4.8	2.5[a]	1.7	1.3	1.2	1.1	0.7[a]	1.1	0.8[a]	1.3
Other, non-Hispanic	3.5[a]	*	2.1	0.1	*	*	0.3	0.5	0.5	0.3
GENDER										
Male	3.5[b]	3.9[b]	1.4	1.0	1.0	0.9	1.0	1.1	0.9	1.1
Female	1.8[b]	2.1[b]	0.6	0.4	0.4	0.4	0.4	0.5	0.5	0.5

*Low precision; no estimate reported.

— Not available.

NOTE: The population distributions for the 1993 through 1998 NHSDAs are post-stratified to population projections of totals based on the 1990 decennial census. The 1979 NHSDA used population projections based on the 1970 census; NHSDAs from 1982 through 1992 used projections based on the 1980 census. The change from one census base to another has little effect on estimated percentages reporting drug use, but may have a significant effect on estimates of number of drug users in some subpopulation groups.

NOTE: Estimates for 1979 through 1993 may differ from estimates for these survey years that were published in other NHSDA reports. The estimates shown here for 1979 through 1993 have been adjusted to improve their comparability with estimates based on the new version of the NHSDA instrument that was fielded in 1994 and subsequent NHSDAs. For 1979 and 1982, estimates are not shown (as indicated by —) where (a) the relevant data were not collected, or (b) the data for those drugs were based on measures that differed appreciably from those used in the other survey years. Consequently, adjustments to the 1979 and 1982 data were made only for those drugs whose measures were comparable to those in the other survey years.

    Because of the methodology used to adjust the 1979 through 1993 estimates, some logical inconsistency may exist between estimates for a given drug within the same survey year. For example, some adjusted estimates of past year use may appear to be greater then adjusted lifetime estimates. These inconsistencies tend to be small, rare and not statistically significant.

[a]Difference between estimate and 1998 estimate is statistically significant at the .05 level.

[b]Difference between estimate and 1998 estimate is statistically significant at the .01 level.

SOURCE: *Summary of Findings from the 1998 National Household Survey on Drug Abuse.* U.S. Department of Health and Human Services, Substance Abuse and Mental Health Services Administration

BREAST CANCER. While White women suffer breast cancer more often than Black women, Black women are more likely to die from the disease. The *SEER* review found that, between 1993 and 1997, 115 incidences of breast cancer occurred per 100,000 White women, compared to 103 incidences per 100,000 Black women. The survival rates between 1989 and 1996, however, were 86 and 71 per 100,000, respectively.

For years experts assumed that the difference was due to poor health care and late treatment for Black women. Recent studies, however, indicate that Black women may be more susceptible to a more deadly form of the cancer. Tumors from Black women were found to have more actively dividing cells than tumors from White women. The Black tumor cells also lacked hormone receptors, another indicator of a poor prognosis. Breast cancer seems to strike Black women under the age of 45 at a particularly high rate and to be especially deadly. It is only at age 65 or older that White women die of breast cancer at a faster rate than Black women. Experts now think that poor access to medical care for Blacks accounts for about half the increased death rate for Black women.

PROSTATE CANCER. The NCI *SEER* review found that between 1993 and 1997, at ages 40 to 44, the incidence rate for prostate cancer (a cancer that occurs only in males) was 4.2 incidences per 100,000 individuals. At ages 50 and 54, the rate had climbed to 111.4 per 100,000. Men between the ages of 60 and 64 had a rate of 662.6 per 100,000, and for those between 70 and 74 years of age, the rate reached 1,149.2 per 100,000.

Black men are more likely to develop prostate cancer at all ages. In 1997 Black men (214.6 per 100,000) were one and one-half times as likely to develop prostate cancer as White men (132.5 per 100,000). Blacks (49.9 per 100,000) were nearly two and one-half times as likely as Whites (20.6 per 100,000) to die from the disease. (See Table 6.14.)

Incidences of prostate cancer rose during the late 1980s, but declined in 1993, when testing for prostate cancer became more commonly used. Due to the now-widespread use of prostate-specific antigen screening, earlier detection and treatment are possible. Therefore, mortality rates are expected to continue to fall. (See Table 6.14.)

TABLE 6.13

Percentages Reporting Past Month Use of Marijuana, by Age group, Race/Ethnicity, and Gender, 1979–1998

Demographic Characteristics	1979	1985	1991	1992	1993	1994	1995	1996	1997	1998
TOTAL	13.2[b]	9.7[b]	5.1	4.7	4.6	4.8	4.7	4.7	5.1	5.0
AGE GROUP										
12-17	14.2[a]	10.2	3.6[b]	3.4[b]	4.0[b]	6.0[b]	8.2	7.1	9.4	8.3
18-25	35.6[b]	21.7[a]	12.9	10.9	11.1	12.1	12.0	13.2	12.8	13.8
26-34	19.7[b]	19.0[b]	7.7	9.3[a]	7.5	6.9a	6.7a	6.3	6.0	5.5
>35	2.9	2.6	2.6	2.0	2.4	2.3	1.8a	2.0	2.6	2.5
RACE/ETHNICITY										
White, non-Hispanic	13.6[b]	10.0[b]	5.2	5.1	4.9	4.8	4.7	4.6	5.2	5.0
Black, non-Hispanic	11.0	9.9[a]	5.5	3.9[b]	4.2[b]	5.9	5.9	6.6	6.1	6.6
Hispanic	11.4[a]	6.4	3.6	3.0[a]	3.9	4.1	3.9	3.7	4.0	4.5
Other, non-Hispanic	12.2[b]	7.6	4.2	2.6	3.2	3.0	2.8	3.7	4.6	3.4
GENDER										
Male	18.1[b]	12.6[b]	6.8	6.4	6.4	6.7	6.2	6.5	7.0	6.7
Female	8.7[b]	7.1[b]	3.6	3.1	3.0	3.1	3.3	3.1	3.5	3.5

*Low precision; no estimate reported.

— Not available.

NOTE: The population distributions for the 1993 through 1998 NHSDAs are post-stratified to population projections of totals based on the 1990 decennial census. The 1979 NHSDA used population projections based on the 1970 census; NHSDAs from 1982 through 1992 used projections based on the 1980 census. The change from one census base to another has little effect on estimated percentages reporting drug use, but may have a significant effect on estimates of number of drug users in some subpopulation groups.

NOTE: Estimates for 1979 through 1993 may differ from estimates for these survey years that were published in other NHSDA reports. The estimates shown here for 1979 through 1993 have been adjusted to improve their comparability with estimates based on the new version of the NHSDA instrument that was fielded in 1994 and subsequent NHSDAs. For 1979 and 1982, estimates are not shown (as indicated by —) where (a) the relevant data were not collected, or (b) the data for those drugs were based on measures that differed appreciably from those used in the other survey years. Consequently, adjustments to the 1979 and 1982 data were made only for those drugs whose measures were comparable to those in the other survey years.

Because of the methodology used to adjust the 1979 through 1993 estimates, some logical inconsistency may exist between estimates for a given drug within the same survey year. For example, some adjusted estimates of past year use may appear to be greater then adjusted lifetime estimates. These inconsistencies tend to be small, rare and not statistically significant.

[a]Difference between estimate and 1998 estimate is statistically significant at the .05 level.

[b]Difference between estimate and 1998 estimate is statistically significant at the .01 level.

SOURCE: *Summary of Findings from the 1998 National Household Survey on Drug Abuse.* U.S. Department of Health and Human Services, Substance Abuse and Mental Health Services Administration

Heart Disease and Stroke

According to the National Center for Health Statistics, rates of heart disease vary considerably by race, with higher rates for Blacks, particularly Black men. In 1997 the age-adjusted death rate for heart disease among Black males (236.2 per 100,000 population) was significantly higher than the rate for White males (168.7 per 100,000). The rate for Black females (147.6 per 100,000) was far higher than for White females (90.4 per 100,000). (See Table 6.15.) The American Heart Association has found that from ages 45 to 74, the death rate from heart attack for Black women is about twice that of White and Hispanic women and three times that of American Indian/Alaskan Native and Asian/Pacific Islander women.

In 1997 the age-adjusted death rates from strokes (cerebrovascular disease) were: Black males, 48.6 per 100,000 population; Black females, 37.9 per 100,000; White males, 25.7 per 100,000; and White females, 22.5 per 100,000. While strokes among all Americans increased dramatically from 1970 to 1980, the number of deaths from strokes has dropped. One of the reasons for the decline in deaths from strokes is the better management of hypertension (high blood pressure), a disease that has always been more prevalent in Blacks.

The American Heart Association reported that the prevalence of hypertension in both Black males and females is significantly higher than in White males and females. In addition, persons living in the southeastern United States, where Black Americans are most concentrated, have a greater prevalence of high blood pressure and higher death rates from stroke than those in other parts of the country. From 1988 to 1994, 31.5 percent of Black men and 30.6 percent of Black women had hypertension, compared to 24.3 percent of White men and 20.4 percent of White women. Blacks develop high blood pressure at younger ages than Whites do. Hypertension is also generally more severe in Blacks than in Whites and, as a result, Blacks have greater rates of both nonfatal and fatal strokes.

Scientists are not yet sure why Blacks have a tendency to have high blood pressure, but researchers at the Postgraduate School of Medicine in Los Angeles suggested a possible genetic predisposition toward high blood pressure in Blacks because of an unusually strong tendency to

TABLE 6.14

Prostate Cancer—Incidence and Mortality Rates by Race, U.S., 1973–1997

	All Races		Whites		Blacks	
	Year	APC	Year	APC	Year	APC
SEER Cancer Incidence						
Age - All Ages	1973-88	2.8*	1973-88	3.0*	1973-89	2.2*
	1988-92	17.5*	1988-92	17.5*	1989-92	21.8*
	1992-95	-10.3*	1992-95	-11.7*	1992-97	-4.7*
	1995-97	0.7	1995-97	1.0		
Age - Under 65	1973-85	2.9*	1973-85	3.1*	1973-89	2.1*
	1985-89	7.2*	1985-89	8.3*	1989-93	26.6*
	1989-92	26.8*	1989-92	25.8*	1993-97	-0.4
	1992-97	1.6	1992-97	0.7		
Age - 65 and Over	1973-88	2.7*	1973-88	2.9*	1973-89	2.3*
	1988-92	16.0*	1988-92	15.8*	1989-92	19.1*
	1992-95	-14.2*	1992-95	-15.5*	1992-97	-8.5*
	1995-97	-1.0	1995-97	-1.0		
U.S. Cancer Mortality						
Age - All Ages	1973-87	0.8*	1973-85	0.6*	1973-93	1.9*
	1987-91	2.8*	1985-91	2.2*	1993-97	-2.3*
	1991-94	-1.2	1991-94	-1.1		
	1994-97	-4.4*	1994-97	-4.6*		
Age - Under 65	1973-87	0.3	1973-87	0.4*	1973-87	0.0
	1987-90	3.8	1987-90	3.7	1987-92	2.0
	1990-97	-3.4*	1990-97	-3.9*	1992-97	-2.9*
Age - 65 and Over	1973-87	0.8*	1973-87	0.7*	1973-93	2.1*
	1987-91	2.9*	1987-91	3.1*	1993-97	-2.3*
	1991-94	-0.9	1991-94	-1.2		
	1994-97	-4.4*	1994-97	-4.5*		

The APC is the Annual Percent Change based on rates age-adjusted to the 1970 U.S. standard population using the Joinpoint Regression Program.

*The APC is significantly different from zero (p<.05).

SOURCE: L.A.G. Ries et al., eds. *SEER Cancer Statistics Review, 73–97*. National Cancer Institute: Bethesda, Md., 2000

retain salt in their bodies. The scientists hypothesized that this developed as an adaptation to living in a very hot climate where excessive salt loss could result in death.

Sickle-Cell Anemia

Sickle-cell anemia, a hereditary disease that primarily strikes Black people, creates a major blood infection that can lead to death. Scientists believe the genetic trait arose randomly in Africa and survived as a defense against malaria. The disease can be inherited only when both parents have the sickle-cell trait. One of every 12 Blacks is a carrier for sickle-cell anemia, and about one of every 500 Black infants is born with it. According to the National Institutes of Health, many non-Blacks with ancestors from malaria regions—parts of Greece, Italy, the Near East, and India—also have the disease. Most of the 50,000 to 60,000 Americans with sickle-cell anemia, however, are of African descent.

Alzheimer's Disease

The results of a study, "The APOE-4 Allele and the Risk of Alzheimer Disease among African Americans, Whites, and Hispanics," conducted between 1991 and 1996 by Columbia University, were published in the *Journal of the American Medical Association* (March 1998). The findings indicated that Blacks and Hispanics may be at greater risk for Alzheimer's disease than Whites. In 1992 scientists first discovered that people with the apolipoprotein-E gene, or APOE-4 (approximately 25 percent of the total population), are at greater risk for developing the disease. The Columbia University research, however, showed that the increased risk associated with the APOE-4 gene applies only to Whites. The study showed that Blacks and a group of Hispanic Americans, mainly from the Caribbean, who do not have the gene, are still at greater risk for Alzheimer's disease than Whites.

The researchers surveyed 1,079 elderly men and women and found that Blacks who lacked the APOE-4 gene were four times more likely than Whites to get Alzheimer's disease. Since the APOE-4 could not account for the increased cases in Blacks and Hispanics, researchers now believe that there are other genetic or environmental factors affecting minorities that increase their risk of developing Alzheimer's disease. None of the subjects of the study had the disease when the study began, but 221 developed Alzheimer's by the time the study ended.

Life Expectancy

Women tend to live longer than men, and Whites are likely to live longer than Blacks. In 1997 Black men (67.2 years) had the shortest life expectancy, while White women (79.9 years) had the longest life expectancy. Black females had a life expectancy of 74.7 years, and White men could expect to live for 74.3 years.

Causes of Death

In 1997 the National Center for Health Statistics reported six causes of death for Black persons that together accounted for more than 65 percent of all deaths among Blacks. These are heart disease, cerebrovascular disease, cancer, human immunodeficiency virus (HIV) infection, unintentional injuries (accidents), and homicide and legal (police) intervention. The most dramatic difference in causes of death between White and Black Americans were in homicide and police intervention and HIV. In 1997 Blacks died of homicide and police intervention at a rate six times (28.1 deaths per 100,000 population) that of Whites (4.7 deaths per 100,000 population). HIV caused seven and one-half times more deaths among Blacks (24.9 deaths per 100,000 population) than among Whites (3.3 deaths per 100,000 population). (See Table 6.16.)

SUICIDE. Black individuals are significantly less likely than Whites to die from suicide. In 1997 White males (18.4 per 100,000) were more likely to commit suicide than Black males (11.2 per 100,000). White females (4.4 per 100,000) committed suicide twice as often as Black females (1.9 per 100,000).

TABLE 6.15

Death Rates for Diseases of Heart, According to Sex, Detailed Race, Hispanic Origin, and Age: United States, Selected Years 1950-97

[Data are based on the National Vital Statistics System]

Sex, race, Hispanic origin, and age	1950[1]	1960[1]	1970	1980	1985	1990	1994	1995	1996	1997	1995-97[2]
All persons					Deaths per 100,000 resident population						
All ages, age adjusted	307.2	286.2	253.6	202.0	181.4	152.0	140.4	138.3	134.5	130.5	134.4
All ages, crude	355.5	369.0	362.0	336.0	324.1	289.5	281.3	280.7	276.4	271.6	276.2
Under 1 year	3.5	6.6	13.1	22.8	25.0	20.1	17.7	17.1	16.6	16.4	16.7
1–4 years	1.3	1.3	1.7	2.6	2.2	1.9	1.8	1.6	1.4	1.4	1.5
5–14 years	2.1	1.3	0.8	0.9	1.0	0.9	0.9	0.8	0.9	0.8	0.8
15–24 years	6.8	4.0	3.0	2.9	2.8	2.5	2.8	2.9	2.7	3.0	2.9
25–34 years	19.4	15.6	11.4	8.3	8.3	7.6	8.5	8.5	8.3	8.3	8.4
35–44 years	86.4	74.6	66.7	44.6	38.1	31.4	31.8	32.0	30.5	30.1	30.8
45–54 years	308.6	271.8	238.4	180.2	153.8	120.5	112.6	111.0	108.2	104.9	108.0
55–64 years	808.1	737.9	652.3	494.1	443.0	367.3	329.9	322.9	315.2	302.4	313.4
65–74 years	1,839.8	1,740.5	1,558.2	1,218.6	1,089.8	894.3	817.4	799.9	776.2	753.7	776.7
75–84 years	4,310.1	4,089.4	3,683.8	2,993.1	2,693.1	2,295.7	2,093.0	2,064.7	2,010.2	1,943.6	2,005.2
85 years and over	9,150.6	9,317.8	7,891.3	7,777.1	7,384.1	6,739.9	6,494.9	6,484.1	6,314.5	6,198.9	6,329.4
Male											
All ages, age adjusted	383.8	375.5	348.5	280.4	250.1	206.7	188.5	184.9	178.8	173.1	178.9
All ages, crude	423.4	439.5	422.5	368.6	344.1	297.6	284.3	282.7	277.4	272.2	277.4
Under 1 year	4.0	7.8	15.1	25.5	27.8	21.9	18.6	17.5	17.4	18.0	17.6
1–4 years	1.4	1.4	1.9	2.8	2.2	1.9	1.8	1.7	1.4	1.5	1.5
5–14 years	2.0	1.4	0.9	1.0	0.9	0.9	0.9	0.8	0.9	0.9	0.9
15–24 years	6.8	4.2	3.7	3.7	3.5	3.1	3.4	3.6	3.3	3.6	3.5
25–34 years	22.9	20.1	15.2	11.4	11.6	10.3	11.0	11.4	11.0	10.8	11.1
35–44 years	118.4	112.7	103.2	68.7	58.6	48.1	46.6	47.2	44.2	43.7	45.0
45–54 years	440.5	420.4	376.4	282.6	237.8	183.0	170.6	168.6	161.8	157.7	162.6
55–64 years	1,104.5	1,066.9	987.2	746.8	659.1	537.3	478.1	465.4	453.8	434.6	451.1
65–74 years	2,292.3	2,291.3	2,170.3	1,728.0	1,535.8	1,250.0	1,133.1	1,102.3	1,065.0	1,031.1	1,066.2
75–84 years	4,825.0	4,742.4	4,534.8	3,834.3	3,496.9	2,968.2	2,655.1	2,615.0	2,529.4	2,443.6	2,527.4
85 years and over	9,659.8	9,788.9	8,426.2	8,752.7	8,251.8	7,418.4	7,123.0	7,039.6	6,834.0	6,658.5	6,838.3
Female											
All ages, age adjusted	233.9	205.7	175.2	140.3	127.4	108.9	101.6	100.4	98.2	95.4	98.0
All ages, crude	288.4	300.6	304.5	305.1	305.2	281.8	278.5	278.8	275.5	271.1	275.1
Under 1 year	2.9	5.4	10.9	20.0	22.0	18.3	16.7	16.7	15.7	14.7	15.7
1–4 years	1.2	1.1	1.6	2.5	2.2	1.9	1.8	1.5	1.4	1.2	1.4
5–14 years	2.2	1.2	0.8	0.9	1.0	0.8	0.8	0.7	0.8	0.7	0.7
15–24 years	6.7	3.7	2.3	2.1	2.1	1.8	2.1	2.2	2.0	2.4	2.2
25–34 years	16.2	11.3	7.7	5.3	5.0	5.0	6.0	5.6	5.6	5.8	5.6
35–44 years	55.1	38.2	32.2	21.4	18.3	15.1	17.2	17.1	16.8	16.5	16.8
45–54 years	177.2	127.5	109.9	84.5	74.4	61.0	57.1	56.0	56.9	54.3	55.7
55–64 years	510.0	429.4	351.6	272.1	252.1	215.7	195.8	193.9	189.3	182.1	188.4
65–74 years	1,419.3	1,261.3	1,082.7	828.6	746.1	616.8	566.3	557.8	543.8	529.4	543.8
75–84 years	3,872.0	3,582.7	3,120.8	2,497.0	2,220.4	1,893.8	1,741.3	1,715.2	1,674.7	1,616.6	1,668.2
85 years and over	8,796.1	9,016.8	7,591.8	7,350.5	7,037.6	6,478.1	6,252.7	6,267.8	6,108.0	6,013.7	6,127.5
White male											
All ages, age adjusted	381.1	375.4	347.6	277.5	246.2	202.0	183.8	179.7	174.5	168.7	174.2
All ages, crude	433.0	454.6	438.3	384.0	360.3	312.7	300.1	297.9	293.3	287.7	292.9
45–54 years	423.6	413.2	365.7	269.8	225.5	170.6	157.7	155.7	149.8	145.4	150.2
55–64 years	1,081.7	1,056.0	979.3	730.6	640.1	516.7	458.6	443.0	431.8	411.2	428.5
65–74 years	2,308.3	2,297.9	2,177.2	1,729.7	1,522.7	1,230.5	1,114.7	1,080.5	1,049.5	1,015.1	1,048.5
75–84 years	4,907.3	4,839.9	4,617.6	3,883.2	3,527.0	2,983.4	2,661.8	2,616.1	2,536.0	2,453.7	2,533.5
85 years and over	9,950.5	10,135.8	8,818.0	8,958.0	8,481.7	7,558.7	7,262.2	7,165.5	7,014.5	6,829.7	6,998.6
Black male											
All ages, age adjusted	415.5	381.2	375.9	327.3	310.8	275.9	254.0	255.9	242.6	236.2	244.7
All ages, crude	348.4	330.6	330.3	301.0	288.6	256.8	240.4	244.2	234.8	230.8	236.5
45–54 years	624.1	514.0	512.8	433.4	385.2	328.9	316.5	317.1	297.7	293.7	302.4
55–64 years	1,434.0	1,236.8	1,135.4	987.2	935.3	824.0	742.3	757.8	740.9	727.8	742.0
65–74 years	2,140.1	2,281.4	2,237.8	1,847.2	1,839.2	1,632.9	1,479.3	1,482.9	1,381.3	1,335.4	1,399.3
75–84 years	- - -	3,533.6	3,783.4	3,578.8	3,436.6	3,107.1	2,874.5	2,881.4	2,762.0	2,641.6	2,759.4
85 years and over	- - -	6,037.9	5,367.6	6,819.5	6,393.5	6,479.6	5,919.4	5,985.7	5,675.4	5,538.7	5,727.3

TABLE 6.15

Death Rates for Diseases of Heart, According to Sex, Detailed Race, Hispanic Origin, and Age: United States, Selected Years 1950-97

[CONTINUED]

[Data are based on the National Vital Statistics System]

Sex, race, Hispanic origin, and age	1950[1]	1960[1]	1970	1980	1985	1990	1994	1995	1996	1997	1995–97[2]
American Indian or Alaska Native male[3]					Deaths per 100,000 resident population						
All ages, age adjusted	- - -	- - -	- - -	180.9	162.2	144.6	145.5	136.7	131.6	136.5	135.0
All ages, crude	- - -	- - -	- - -	130.6	117.9	108.0	116.7	110.4	110.7	116.8	112.7
45–54 years	- - -	- - -	- - -	238.1	209.1	173.8	181.2	151.4	157.5	171.8	160.5
55–64 years	- - -	- - -	- - -	496.3	438.3	411.0	414.2	403.2	404.9	427.2	412.0
65–74 years	- - -	- - -	- - -	1,009.4	984.6	839.1	937.5	918.5	778.0	828.1	840.9
75–84 years	- - -	- - -	- - -	2,062.2	2,118.2	1,788.8	1,628.4	1,534.9	1,546.5	1,513.8	1,531.3
85 years and over	- - -	- - -	- - -	4,413.7	2,766.7	3,860.3	3,072.1	2,308.7	2,660.1	2,764.2	2,593.9
Asian or Pacific Islander male[4]											
All ages, age adjusted	- - -	- - -	- - -	136.7	123.4	102.6	107.6	106.2	98.1	95.9	99.4
All ages, crude	- - -	- - -	- - -	119.8	103.5	88.7	96.9	96.9	97.3	97.4	97.2
45–54 years	- - -	- - -	- - -	112.0	81.1	70.4	80.4	73.4	75.4	72.1	73.6
55–64 years	- - -	- - -	- - -	306.7	291.2	226.1	229.1	214.3	220.7	218.3	217.9
65–74 years	- - -	- - -	- - -	852.4	753.5	623.5	623.5	605.8	581.2	585.1	590.4
75–84 years	- - -	- - -	- - -	2,010.9	2,025.6	1,642.2	1,576.3	1,680.5	1,534.8	1,432.1	1,541.0
85 years and over	- - -	- - -	- - -	5,923.0	4,937.5	4,617.8	6,158.3	6,372.3	4,338.0	4,392.5	4,850.5
Hispanic male[5]											
All ages, age adjusted	- - -	- - -	- - -	- - -	152.3	136.3	123.5	121.9	117.6	113.4	117.4
All ages, crude	- - -	- - -	- - -	- - -	92.1	91.0	87.4	87.5	85.8	83.9	85.7
45–54 years	- - -	- - -	- - -	- - -	128.0	116.4	102.1	103.0	98.7	96.2	99.1
55–64 years	- - -	- - -	- - -	- - -	398.8	363.0	308.3	306.0	310.0	276.9	297.2
65–74 years	- - -	- - -	- - -	- - -	972.6	829.9	769.4	750.0	725.7	737.2	737.5
75–84 years	- - -	- - -	- - -	- - -	2,160.8	1,971.3	1,770.0	1,734.5	1,688.6	1,628.7	1,680.9
85 years and over	- - -	- - -	- - -	- - -	4,791.2	4,711.9	4,726.9	4,699.7	4,078.6	3,844.6	4,172.2
White, non-Hispanic male[5]											
All ages, age adjusted	- - -	- - -	- - -	- - -	240.3	204.1	185.3	181.2	176.2	171.1	176.1
All ages, crude	- - -	- - -	- - -	- - -	362.8	336.5	324.2	322.0	318.9	315.0	318.6
45–54 years	- - -	- - -	- - -	- - -	219.9	172.8	160.1	157.5	152.1	148.5	152.6
55–64 years	- - -	- - -	- - -	- - -	610.6	521.3	464.2	448.0	435.1	418.1	433.5
65–74 years	- - -	- - -	- - -	- - -	1,471.3	1,243.4	1,123.6	1,088.3	1,056.4	1,025.1	1,056.6
75–84 years	- - -	- - -	- - -	- - -	3,514.1	3,007.7	2,674.1	2,635.6	2,559.8	2,477.3	2,555.5
85 years and over	- - -	- - -	- - -	- - -	8,539.3	7,663.4	7,260.9	7,166.3	7,109.2	6,954.2	7,073.5
White female											
All ages, age adjusted	223.6	197.1	167.8	134.6	121.7	103.1	96.1	94.9	92.9	90.4	92.7
All ages, crude	289.4	306.5	313.8	319.2	321.8	298.4	296.8	297.4	294.2	289.8	293.8
45–54 years	141.9	103.4	91.4	71.2	62.5	50.2	47.0	45.9	46.9	44.9	45.9
55–64 years	460.2	383.0	317.7	248.1	227.1	192.4	174.7	173.1	167.8	162.5	167.8
65–74 years	1,400.9	1,229.8	1,044.0	796.7	713.3	583.6	535.6	526.3	515.1	500.7	514.1
75–84 years	3,925.2	3,629.7	3,143.5	2,493.6	2,207.5	1,874.3	1,717.6	1,689.8	1,652.9	1,595.9	1,645.6
85 years and over	9,084.7	9,280.8	7,839.9	7,501.6	7,170.0	6,563.4	6,342.8	6,352.6	6,211.4	6,108.0	6,222.0
Black female											
All ages, age adjusted	349.5	292.6	251.7	201.1	188.3	168.1	158.0	156.3	153.4	147.6	152.4
All ages, crude	289.9	268.5	261.0	249.7	250.3	237.0	230.6	231.1	229.0	224.2	228.1
45–54 years	526.8	360.7	290.9	202.4	176.2	155.3	146.4	143.1	144.7	134.8	140.7
55–64 years	1,210.7	952.3	710.5	530.1	510.7	442.0	392.2	384.9	388.4	364.8	379.2
65–74 years	1,659.4	1,680.5	1,553.2	1,210.3	1,149.9	1,017.5	941.7	933.7	890.0	871.6	898.3
75–84 years	- - -	2,926.9	2,964.1	2,707.2	2,533.4	2,250.9	2,158.1	2,163.1	2,097.7	2,030.5	2,096.3
85 years and over	- - -	5,650.0	5,003.8	5,796.5	5,686.5	5,766.1	5,531.8	5,614.8	5,493.6	5,542.5	5,549.4

Suicide rates among Black teens, however, have increased sharply, according to a study reported by the Centers for Disease Control and Prevention. The study, "Suicide among Black Youths—United States, 1980–1995" (*Morbidity and Mortality Weekly Report,* Washington, DC, March 1998), found that the suicide rates for Blacks between the ages of 15 and 19 more than doubled between 1980 (3.6 per 100,000) and 1995 (8.1 per 100,000), a 126 percent increase, compared to a 19 percent increase among Whites of the same age group. Among Black males ages 15 to 19, the suicide rate increased 146 percent, compared to a 22 percent increase among White males in the same age group. In 1995 suicide was the third-leading cause of death for Blacks ages 15 to 19, after homicides and accidents.

Experts theorize that this increase reflects the stress that some Black families feel as they make the transition

TABLE 6.15

Death Rates for Diseases of Heart, According to Sex, Detailed Race, Hispanic Origin, and Age: United States, Selected Years 1950-97

[CONTINUED]

[Data are based on the National Vital Statistics System]

Sex, race, Hispanic origin, and age	1950[1]	1960[1]	1970	1980	1985	1990	1994	1995	1996	1997	1995–97[2]
American Indian or Alaska Native female[3]				Deaths per 100,000 resident population							
All ages, age adjusted	- - -	- - -	- - -	88.4	83.7	76.6	71.3	77.3	74.9	73.9	75.3
All ages, crude	- - -	- - -	- - -	80.3	84.3	77.5	82.1	87.0	86.7	88.6	87.4
45–54 years	- - -	- - -	- - -	65.2	59.2	62.0	48.7	69.2	61.1	59.7	63.2
55–64 years	- - -	- - -	- - -	193.5	230.8	197.0	196.8	210.2	192.5	172.8	191.5
65–74 years	- - -	- - -	- - -	577.2	472.7	492.8	429.9	503.3	512.8	473.8	496.5
75–84 years	- - -	- - -	- - -	1,364.3	1,258.8	1,050.3	1,055.6	1,045.6	1,030.0	1,115.2	1,064.5
85 years and over	- - -	- - -	- - -	2,893.3	3,180.0	2,868.7	2,490.9	2,209.8	2,108.8	2,019.5	2,106.8
Asian or Pacific Islander female[4]											
All ages, age adjusted	- - -	- - -	- - -	55.8	59.6	58.3	57.7	57.7	50.9	49.3	52.2
All ages, crude	- - -	- - -	- - -	57.0	60.3	62.0	66.7	68.2	66.8	66.9	67.3
45–54 years	- - -	- - -	- - -	28.6	23.8	17.5	22.1	21.6	17.2	18.8	19.1
55–64 years	- - -	- - -	- - -	92.9	103.0	99.0	93.3	93.0	82.3	80.5	85.0
65–74 years	- - -	- - -	- - -	313.3	341.0	323.9	295.7	294.9	282.0	272.8	282.8
75–84 years	- - -	- - -	- - -	1,053.2	1,056.5	1,130.9	1,110.7	1,063.0	1,009.8	944.0	1,001.5
85 years and over	- - -	- - -	- - -	3,211.0	4,208.3	4,161.2	4,376.5	4,717.9	3,394.7	3,326.2	3,701.8
Hispanic female[5]											
All ages, age adjusted	- - -	- - -	- - -	- - -	86.5	76.0	67.0	68.1	64.7	64.7	65.7
All ages, crude	- - -	- - -	- - -	- - -	75.0	79.4	75.6	78.9	77.0	78.3	78.1
45–54 years	- - -	- - -	- - -	- - -	46.6	43.5	31.8	32.0	31.3	31.5	31.6
55–64 years	- - -	- - -	- - -	- - -	184.8	153.2	134.3	137.3	125.1	129.5	130.5
65–74 years	- - -	- - -	- - -	- - -	534.0	460.4	399.3	402.4	387.6	391.9	393.9
75–84 years	- - -	- - -	- - -	- - -	1,456.5	1,259.7	1,163.5	1,150.1	1,152.8	1,102.4	1,134.2
85 years and over	- - -	- - -	- - -	- - -	4,523.4	4,440.3	3,783.1	4,243.9	3,673.8	3,748.7	3,870.3
White, non-Hispanic female[5]											
All ages, age adjusted	- - -	- - -	- - -	- - -	120.2	103.7	96.5	95.4	93.6	91.3	93.4
All ages, crude	- - -	- - -	- - -	- - -	334.2	320.0	320.6	321.4	318.9	315.6	318.6
45–54 years	- - -	- - -	- - -	- - -	61.3	50.2	47.5	46.6	47.5	45.7	46.6
55–64 years	- - -	- - -	- - -	- - -	219.6	193.6	175.5	173.6	169.0	163.9	168.8
65–74 years	- - -	- - -	- - -	- - -	700.4	584.7	537.2	529 1	518.0	504.0	517.1
75–84 years	- - -	- - -	- - -	- - -	2,201.4	1,890.2	1,728.0	1,697.8	1,663.5	1,609.4	1,656.2
85 years and over	- - -	- - -	- - -	- - -	7,164.7	6,615.2	6,354.2	6,384.5	6,285.4	6,176.4	6,280.0

- - - Data not available.

[1]Includes deaths of persons who were not residents of the 50 States and the District of Columbia.

[2]Average annual death rate.

[3]Interpretation of trends should take into account that population estimates for American Indians increased by 45 percent between 1980 and 1990, partly due to better enumeration techniques in the 1990 decennial census and to the increased tendency for people to identify themselves as American Indian in 1990.

[4]Interpretation of trends should take into account that the Asian population in the United States more than doubled between 1980 and 1990, primarily due to immigration.

[5]Excludes data from States lacking an Hispanic-origin item on their death certificates.

NOTES: For data years shown, the code numbers for cause of death are based on the then current *International Classification of Diseases*. Age groups were selected to minimize the presentation of unstable age-specific death rates based on small numbers of deaths and for consistency among comparison groups. The race groups, white, black, Asian or Pacific Islander, and American Indian or Alaska Native, include persons of Hispanic and non-Hispanic origin. Conversely, persons of Hispanic origin may be of any race. Consistency of race identification between the death certificate (source of data for numerator of death rates) and data from the Census Bureau (denominator) is high for individual white and black persons; however, persons identified as American Indian, Asian, or Hispanic origin in data from the Census Bureau are sometimes misreported as white or non-Hispanic on the death certificate, causing death rates to be underestimated by 22–30 percent for American Indians, about 12 percent for Asians, and about 7 percent for persons of Hispanic origin. (Sorlie PD, Rogot E, and Johnson NJ: Validity of demographic characteristics on the death certificate, *Epidemiology* 3(2):181–184, 1992).

SOURCE: *Health, United States, 1999*. National Center for Health Statistics: Hyattsville, MD, 1999

---

to the middle class. Black youths in this situation may feel a loss of community and family support networks, weaker religious bonds, and the pressure of trying to compete in professions and social circles dominated by Whites. Other risk factors include hopelessness; depression; family history of suicide; impulsive and aggressive behavior; social isolation; a previous suicide attempt; and easier access to alcohol, illicit drugs, and lethal suicide methods.

DIABETES. In 1997 Black persons (28.9 per 100,000) died of diabetes at more than twice the rate of the White population (11.9 per 100,000). (See Table 6.16.)

HISPANICS AND HEALTH

In 1999, 25.6 percent of all Hispanics lived below the poverty level, compared to 8.2 percent of non-Hispanic Whites. Hispanics 16 years and older had an unemploy-

TABLE 6.16

Age-Adjusted Death Rates for Selected Causes of Death, According to Sex, Detailed Race, and Hispanic Origin: United States, Selected Years 1950–97

[Data are based on the National Vital Statistics System]

Sex, race, Hispanic origin, and cause of death	1950[1]	1960[1]	1970	1980	1985	1990	1994	1995	1996	1997
All persons				Deaths per 100,000 resident population						
All causes	841.5	760.9	714.3	585.8	548.9	520.2	507.4	503.9	491.6	479.1
Natural causes	766.6	695.2	636.9	519.7	493.0	465.1	454.4	451.7	440.6	429.2
Diseases of heart	307.2	286.2	253.6	202.0	181.4	152.0	140.4	138.3	134.5	130.5
Ischemic heart disease	- - -	- - -	- - -	149.8	126.1	102.6	91.4	89.5	86.7	82.9
Cerebrovascular diseases	88.8	79.7	66.3	40.8	32.5	27.7	26.5	26.7	26.4	25.9
Malignant neoplasms	125.4	125.8	129.8	132.8	134.4	135.0	131.5	129.9	127.9	125.6
Respiratory system	12.8	19.2	28.4	36.4	39.1	41.4	40.1	39.7	39.3	38.7
Colorectal	- - -	17.7	16.8	15.5	14.9	13.6	12.8	12.7	12.2	12.0
Prostate[2]	13.4	13.1	13.3	14.4	14.7	16.7	16.0	15.4	14.9	13.9
Breast[3]	22.2	22.3	23.1	22.7	23.3	23.1	21.3	21.0	20.2	19.4
Chronic obstructive pulmonary diseases	4.4	8.2	13.2	15.9	18.8	19.7	21.0	20.8	21.0	21.1
Pneumonia and influenza	26.2	28.0	22.1	12.9	13.5	14.0	13.0	12.9	12.8	12.9
Chronic liver disease and cirrhosis	8.5	10.5	14.7	12.2	9.7	8.6	7.9	7.6	7.5	7.4
Diabetes mellitus	14.3	13.6	14.1	10.1	9.7	11.7	12.9	13.3	13.6	13.5
Human immunodeficiency virus infection	- - -	- - -	- - -	- - -	- - -	9.8	15.4	15.6	11.1	5.8
External causes	73.9	65.7	77.4	66.1	55.9	55.1	53.0	52.2	50.9	49.9
Unintentional injuries	57.5	49.9	53.7	42.3	34.8	32.5	30.3	30.5	30.4	30.1
Motor vehicle-related injuries	23.3	22.5	27.4	22.9	18.8	18.5	16.1	16.3	16.2	15.9
Suicide	11.0	10.6	11.8	11.4	11.5	11.5	11.2	11.2	10.8	10.6
Homicide and legal intervention	5.4	5.2	9.1	10.8	8.3	10.2	10.3	9.4	8.5	8.0
Male										
All causes	1,001.6	949.3	931.6	777.2	723.0	680.2	654.6	646.3	623.7	602.8
Natural causes	- - -	- - -	- - -	675.5	637.9	595.8	573.6	567.0	547.2	528.0
Diseases of heart	383.8	375.5	348.5	280.4	250.1	206.7	188.5	184.9	178.8	173.1
Ischemic heart disease.	- - -	- - -	- - -	214.8	179.6	144.0	127.0	123.9	119.3	114.2
Cerebrovascular diseases	91.9	85.4	73.2	44.9	35.5	30.2	29.0	28.9	28.5	27.9
Malignant neoplasms	130.8	143.0	157.4	165.5	166.1	166.3	159.6	156.8	153.8	150.4
Respiratory system	21.3	34.8	50.6	59.7	60.7	61.0	56.5	55.3	54.2	52.8
Colorectal	- - -	18.6	18.7	18.3	17.9	16.8	15.6	15.3	14.8	14.6
Prostate	13.4	13.1	13.3	14.4	14.7	16.7	16.0	15.4	14.9	13.9
Chronic obstructive pulmonary diseases	6.0	13.7	23.4	26.1	28.1	27.2	26.9	26.3	25.9	26.1
Pneumonia and influenza	30.6	35.0	28.8	17.4	18.4	18.5	16.7	16.5	16.2	16.2
Chronic liver disease and cirrhosis	11.4	14.5	20.2	17.1	13.7	12.2	11.3	11.0	10.7	10.5
Diabetes mellitus	11.4	12.0	13.5	10.2	10.0	12.3	13.9	14.4	14.9	14.8
Human immunodeficiency virus infection	- - -	- - -	- - -	- - -	- - -	17.7	26.4	26.2	18.1	9.1
External causes	- - -	- - -	- - -	101.7	85.2	84.4	81.0	79.3	76.5	74.8
Unintentional injuries	83.7	73.9	80.7	64.0	51.8	47.7	44.0	44.1	43.3	42.9
Motor vehicle-related injuries	36.4	34.5	41.1	34.3	27.3	26.3	22.5	22.7	22.3	21.7
Suicide	17.3	16.6	17.3	18.0	18.8	19.0	18.7	18.6	18.0	17.4
Homicide and legal intervention	8.4	7.9	14.9	17.4	12.8	16.3	16.4	14.7	13.3	12.5
Female										
All causes	688.4	590.6	532.5	432.6	410.3	390.6	385.2	385.2	381.0	375.7
Natural causes	- - -	- - -	- - -	400.1	382.2	363.5	359.2	359.1	354.8	349.8
Diseases of heart	233.9	205.7	175.2	140.3	127.4	108.9	101.6	100.4	98.2	95.4
Ischemic heart disease	- - -	- - -	- - -	98.8	84.2	70.2	63.1	61.9	60.4	57.6
Cerebrovascular diseases	86.0	74.7	60.8	37.6	30.0	25.7	24.5	24.8	24.6	24.2
Malignant neoplasms	120.8	111.2	108.8	109.2	111.7	112.7	111.1	110.4	108.8	107.3
Respiratory system	4.6	5.2	10.1	18.3	22.5	26.2	27.3	27.5	27.5	27.5
Colorectal	- - -	16.9	15.4	13.4	12.6	11.3	10.6	10.6	10.2	10.0
Breast	22.2	22.3	23.1	22.7	23.3	23.1	21.3	21.0	20.2	19.4
Chronic obstructive pulmonary diseases	2.9	3.5	5.4	8.9	12.5	14.7	17.1	17.1	17.6	17.7
Pneumonia and influenza	22.0	21.8	16.7	9.8	10.1	11.0	10.4	10.4	10.4	10.5
Chronic liver disease and cirrhosis	5.8	6.9	9.8	7.9	6.1	5.3	4.8	4.6	4.5	4.5
Diabetes mellitus	17.1	15.0	14.4	10.0	9.4	11.1	12.1	12.4	12.5	12.4
Human immunodeficiency virus infection	- - -	- - -	- - -	- - -	- - -	2.1	4.8	5.2	4.2	2.6
External causes	- - -	- - -	- - -	32.5	28.1	27.0	26.1	26.1	26.2	25.9
Unintentional injuries	31.7	26.8	28.2	21.8	18.7	17.9	17.2	17.5	17.9	17.8
Motor vehicle-related injuries	10.7	11.0	14.4	11.8	10.5	10.7	9.9	10.0	10.2	10.2
Suicide	4.9	5.0	6.8	5.4	4.9	4.5	4.2	4.1	4.0	4.1
Homicide and legal intervention	2.5	2.6	3.7	4.5	3.9	4.2	4.0	4.0	3.6	3.3
White										
All causes	800.4	727.0	679.6	559.4	524.9	492.8	479.8	476.9	466.8	456.5
Natural causes	- - -	- - -	- - -	497.7	471.9	442.0	431.4	428.5	419.2	409.7
Diseases of heart	300.5	281.5	249.1	197.6	176.6	146.9	135.4	133.1	129.8	125.9
Ischemic heart disease	- - -	- - -	- - -	150.6	126.6	102.5	91.1	89.0	86.4	82.5

TABLE 6.16

Age-Adjusted Death Rates for Selected Causes of Death, According to Sex, Detailed Race, and Hispanic Origin: United States, Selected Years 1950–97 [CONTINUED]

[Data are based on the National Vital Statistics System]

Sex, race, Hispanic origin, and cause of death	1950[1]	1960[1]	1970	1980	1985	1990	1994	1995	1996	1997
White					Deaths per 100,000 resident population					
Cerebrovascular diseases	83.2	74.2	61.8	38.0	30.1	25.5	24.5	24.7	24.5	24.0
Malignant neoplasms	124.7	124.2	127.8	129.6	131.2	131.5	128.6	127.0	125.2	122.9
Respiratory system	13.0	19.1	28.0	35.6	38.4	40.6	39.7	39.3	38.9	38.4
Colorectal	- - -	17.9	16.9	15.4	14.7	13.3	12.5	12.3	11.8	11.6
Prostate[2]	13.1	12.4	12.3	13.2	13.4	15.3	14.6	14.0	13.5	12.6
Breast[3]	22.5	22.4	23.4	22.8	23.4	22.9	20.9	20.5	19.8	18.9
Chronic obstructive pulmonary diseases	4.3	8.2	13.4	16.3	19.2	20.1	21.6	21.3	21.5	21.7
Pneumonia and influenza	22.9	24.6	19.8	12.2	12.9	13.4	12.5	12.4	12.2	12.4
Chronic liver disease and cirrhosis	8.6	10.3	13.4	11.0	8.9	8.0	7.5	7.4	7.3	7.3
Diabetes mellitus	13.9	12.8	12.9	9.1	8.6	10.4	11.5	11.7	12.0	11.9
Human immunodeficiency virus infection.	- - -	- - -	- - -	- - -	- - -	8.0	11.2	11.1	7.2	3.3
External causes	- - -	- - -	- - -	61.9	53.0	50.8	48.5	48.4	47.5	46.8
Unintentional injuries	55.7	47.6	51.0	41.5	34.2	31.8	29.5	29.9	29.9	29.6
Motor vehicle-related injuries	23.1	22.3	26.9	23.4	19.1	18.6	16.2	16.4	16.3	15.9
Suicide	11.6	11.1	12.4	12.1	12.3	12.2	11.9	11.9	11.6	11.3
Homicide and legal intervention	2.6	2.7	4.7	6.9	5.4	5.9	5.8	5.5	4.9	4.7
Black										
All causes	1,236.7	1,073.3	1,044.0	842.5	793.6	789.2	772.1	765.7	738.3	705.3
Natural causes	- - -	- - -	- - -	740.2	713.5	701.3	686.5	685.8	662.3	632.7
Diseases of heart	379.6	334.5	307.6	255.7	240.6	213.5	198.8	198.8	191.5	185.7
Ischemic heart disease	- - -	- - -	- - -	150.5	130.9	113.2	103.8	103.4	99.4	96.3
Cerebrovascular diseases	150.9	140.3	114.5	68.5	55.8	48.4	45.4	45.0	44.2	42.5
Malignant neoplasms	129.1	142.3	156.7	172.1	176.6	182.0	173.8	171.6	167.8	165.2
Respiratory system	10.4	20.3	33.5	46.5	50.3	54.0	50.6	49.9	48.9	47.9
Colorectal.	- - -	15.2	16.6	16.9	17.9	17.9	17.2	17.3	16.8	16.8
Prostate[2]	16.9	22.2	25.4	29.1	31.2	35.3	35.3	34.0	33.8	31.4
Breast[3]	19.3	21.3	21.5	23.3	25.5	27.5	26.9	27.5	26.5	26.7
Chronic obstructive pulmonary diseases	- - -	- - -	- - -	12.5	15.3	16.9	17.7	17.6	17.8	17.4
Pneumonia and influenza	57.0	56.4	40.4	19.2	18.8	19.8	17.5	17.8	17.8	17.2
Chronic liver disease and cirrhosis	7.2	11.7	24.8	21.6	16.3	13.7	10.7	9.9	9.2	8.7
Diabetes mellitus	17.2	22.0	26.5	20.3	20.1	24.8	27.4	28.5	28.8	28.9
Human immunodeficiency virus infection	- - -	- - -	- - -	- - -	- - -	25.7	49.4	51.8	41.4	24.9
External causes	- - -	- - -	- - -	101.2	80.1	87.8	85.6	79.8	76.0	72.6
Unintentional injuries	70.9	66.4	74.4	51.2	42.3	39.7	38.1	37.4	36.7	36.1
Motor vehicle-related injuries	24.7	23.4	30.6	19.7	17.4	18.4	16.6	16.6	16.7	16.8
Suicide	4.2	4.7	6.1	6.4	6.4	7.0	7.1	6.9	6.6	6.3
Homicide and legal intervention	30.5	27.4	46.1	40.6	29.2	39.5	38.2	33.4	30.6	28.1
American Indian or Alaska Native										
All causes	- - -	- - -	- - -	564.1	468.2	445.1	460.7	468.5	456.7	465.3
Natural causes	- - -	- - -	- - -	436.5	375.1	360.3	374.9	385.4	374.5	381.1
Diseases of heart	- - -	- - -	- - -	131.2	119.6	107.1	104.9	104.5	100.8	102.6
Ischemic heart disease	- - -	- - -	- - -	87.4	77.3	66.6	65.8	65.4	63.8	64.2
Cerebrovascular diseases	- - -	- - -	- - -	26.6	22.5	19.3	20.2	21.6	21.1	19.9
Malignant neoplasms	- - -	- - -	- - -	70.6	72.0	75.0	78.1	80.8	84.9	86.6
Respiratory system	- - -	- - -	- - -	15.0	18.8	20.5	23.7	23.7	24.4	25.3
Colorectal	- - -	- - -	- - -	5.6	6.3	6.4	7.5	7.6	8.5	9.1
Prostate[2]	- - -	- - -	- - -	9.6	8.9	7.7	9.2	8.8	9.8	8.6
Breast[3]	- - -	- - -	- - -	8.1	8.0	10.0	10.4	10.4	12.7	9.4
Chronic obstructive pulmonary diseases	- - -	- - -	- - -	7.5	9.8	12.8	13.3	13.8	12.6	15.3
Pneumonia and influenza	- - -	- - -	- - -	19.4	14.9	15.2	14.8	14.2	14.0	13.4
Chronic liver disease and cirrhosis	- - -	- - -	- - -	38.6	23.6	19.8	21.4	24.3	20.7	20.6
Diabetes mellitus	- - -	- - -	- - -	20.0	18.7	20.8	25.9	27.3	27.8	30.4
Human immunodeficiency virus infection	- - -	- - -	- - -	- - -	- - -	1.8	5.4	7.0	4.2	2.4
External causes	- - -	- - -	- - -	127.6	93.1	84.8	85.8	83.0	82.1	84.3
Unintentional injuries	- - -	- - -	- - -	95.1	66.2	59.0	58.3	56.7	57.6	58.5
Motor vehicle-related injuries	- - -	- - -	- - -	54.4	36.3	33.2	31.4	33.1	34.0	32.3
Suicide	- - -	- - -	- - -	12.8	12.1	12.4	14.0	12.2	13.0	12.9
Homicide and legal intervention	- - -	- - -	- - -	16.0	12.2	11.1	11.9	11.9	10.1	11.0
Asian or Pacific Islander										
All causes	- - -	- - -	- - -	315.6	305.7	297.6	299.2	298.9	277.4	274.8
Natural causes	- - -	- - -	- - -	280.7	274.4	266.7	269.5	269.2	250.3	247.0
Diseases of heart	- - -	- - -	- - -	93.9	88.6	78.5	79.7	78.9	71.7	69.8
Ischemic heart disease	- - -	- - -	- - -	67.5	58.8	49.7	50.5	49.3	44.8	43.5
Cerebrovascular diseases	- - -	- - -	- - -	29.0	25.5	25.0	25.4	25.8	23.9	24.4

TABLE 6.16

Age-Adjusted Death Rates for Selected Causes of Death, According to Sex, Detailed Race, and Hispanic Origin: United States, Selected Years 1950–97 [CONTINUED]

[Data are based on the National Vital Statistics System]

Sex, race, Hispanic origin, and cause of death	1950[1]	1960[1]	1970	1980	1985	1990	1994	1995	1996	1997
Asian or Pacific Islander				Deaths per 100,000 resident population						
Malignant neoplasms	- - -	- - -	- - -	77.2	80.2	79.8	81.8	81.1	76.3	75.4
Respiratory system	- - -	- - -	- - -	18.1	17.2	18.3	18.5	18.5	17.4	17.4
Colorectal	- - -	- - -	- - -	9.3	9.6	8.3	8.4	8.2	7.7	7.6
Prostate[2]	- - -	- - -	- - -	4.0	5.9	6.9	6.4	7.4	5.8	5.3
Breast[3]	- - -	- - -	- - -	9.2	9.6	10.0	10.5	11.0	8.9	9.2
Chronic obstructive pulmonary diseases	- - -	- - -	- - -	5.9	8.4	8.7	8.5	9.0	8.6	8.6
Pneumonia and influenza	- - -	- - -	- - -	9.1	9.1	10.4	10.5	10.8	9.9	10.1
Chronic liver disease and cirrhosis	- - -	- - -	- - -	4.5	4.2	3.7	3.2	2.7	2.6	2.4
Diabetes mellitus	- - -	- - -	- - -	6.9	6.1	7.4	8.0	9.2	8.8	9.3
Human immunodeficiency virus infection	- - -	- - -	- - -	- - -	- - -	2.1	3.5	3.1	2.2	0.9
External causes	- - -	- - -	- - -	34.9	31.4	30.9	29.7	29.7	27.1	27.7
Unintentional injuries	- - -	- - -	- - -	21.7	20.1	19.3	17.2	17.1	16.1	16.7
Motor vehicle-related injuries	- - -	- - -	- - -	12.6	12.0	12.5	10.3	10.8	9.5	9.7
Suicide	- - -	- - -	- - -	6.7	6.4	6.0	6.6	6.6	6.0	6.2
Homicide and legal intervention	- - -	- - -	- - -	5.6	4.2	5.2	5.4	5.4	4.6	4.3
Hispanic[4]										
All causes	- - -	- - -	- - -	- - -	397.4	400.2	383.8	386.8	365.9	350.3
Natural causes	- - -	- - -	- - -	- - -	342.7	342.4	330.3	334.0	316.9	304.5
Diseases of heart	- - -	- - -	- - -	- - -	116.0	102.8	91.9	92.1	88.6	86.8
Ischemic heart disease	- - -	- - -	- - -	- - -	77.8	68.0	59.9	60.1	58.2	56.8
Cerebrovascular diseases	- - -	- - -	- - -	- - -	23.8	21.0	19.5	20.3	19.5	19.4
Malignant neoplasms	- - -	- - -	- - -	- - -	75.8	82.4	79.5	79.7	77.8	76.4
Respiratory system	- - -	- - -	- - -	- - -	14.3	16.9	15.5	15.6	15.4	15.2
Colorectal	- - -	- - -	- - -	- - -	7.5	8.2	7.9	7.6	7.3	7.5
Prostate[2]	- - -	- - -	- - -	- - -	8.5	9.5	11.0	10.9	9.9	8.6
Breast[3]	- - -	- - -	- - -	- - -	11.8	14.1	12.6	12.7	12.8	12.6
Chronic obstructive pulmonary diseases	- - -	- - -	- - -	- - -	8.2	8.7	9.0	9.4	8.9	8.7
Pneumonia and influenza	- - -	- - -	- - -	- - -	12.0	11.5	9.8	9.9	9.7	10.0
Chronic liver disease and cirrhosis	- - -	- - -	- - -	- - -	16.3	14.2	13.7	12.9	12.6	12.0
Diabetes mellitus	- - -	- - -	- - -	- - -	12.8	15.7	18.0	19.3	18.8	18.7
Human immunodeficiency virus infection	- - -	- - -	- - -	- - -	- - -	15.5	23.6	23.9	16.3	8.2
External causes	- - -	- - -	- - -	- - -	54.7	57.8	53.6	52.9	49.0	45.8
Unintentional injuries	- - -	- - -	- - -	- - -	31.8	32.2	29.2	29.8	29.0	27.7
Motor vehicle-related injuries	- - -	- - -	- - -	- - -	16.9	19.3	16.6	16.6	16.1	15.2
Suicide	- - -	- - -	- - -	- - -	6.1	7.3	7.2	7.2	6.7	6.1
Homicide and legal intervention	- - -	- - -	- - -	- - -	15.7	17.7	16.1	15.0	12.4	11.1
White, non-Hispanic[4]										
All causes	- - -	- - -	- - -	- - -	510.7	493.1	478.1	475.2	466.7	458.5
Natural causes	- - -	- - -	- - -	- - -	460.7	444.2	431.7	428.8	420.7	412.6
Diseases of heart	- - -	- - -	- - -	- - -	173.0	148.2	136.4	134.1	131.0	127.5
Ischemic heart disease	- - -	- - -	- - -	- - -	125.4	103.7	91.9	89.8	87.4	83.6
Cerebrovascular diseases	- - -	- - -	- - -	- - -	29.2	25.7	24.4	24.6	24.4	24.0
Malignant neoplasms	- - -	- - -	- - -	- - -	128.3	134.2	130.7	129.2	127.6	125.3
Respiratory system	- - -	- - -	- - -	- - -	38.0	41.9	40.9	40.5	40.2	39.8
Colorectal	- - -	- - -	- - -	- - -	14.4	13.6	12.7	12.5	12.1	11.8
Prostate[2]	- - -	- - -	- - -	- - -	13.0	15.6	14.7	14.1	13.6	12.7
Breast[3]	- - -	- - -	- - -	- - -	23.3	23.5	21.3	20.9	20.1	19.2
Chronic obstructive pulmonary diseases	- - -	- - -	- - -	- - -	19.7	20.7	22.1	21.8	22.1	22.4
Pneumonia and influenza	- - -	- - -	- - -	- - -	13.2	13.3	12.4	12.3	12.2	12.4
Chronic liver disease and cirrhosis	- - -	- - -	- - -	- - -	8.5	7.5	6.9	6.8	6.7	6.7
Diabetes mellitus	- - -	- - -	- - -	- - -	8.0	10.1	11.0	11.2	11.5	11.3
Human immunodeficiency virus infection	- - -	- - -	- - -	- - -	- - -	7.0	9.6	9.4	6.0	2.6
External causes	- - -	- - -	- - -	- - -	50.0	48.9	46.4	46.4	46.0	45.9
Unintentional injuries	- - -	- - -	- - -	- - -	31.9	31.3	28.9	29.3	29.3	29.4
Motor vehicle-related injuries	- - -	- - -	- - -	- - -	17.8	18.4	15.8	16.0	16.0	15.8
Suicide	- - -	- - -	- - -	- - -	12.7	12.7	12.2	12.2	12.0	11.8
Homicide and legal intervention	- - -	- - -	- - -	- - -	4.5	4.2	4.1	3.8	3.5	3.5

- - - Data not available.

[1] Includes deaths of persons who were not residents of the 50 States and the District of Columbia.

[2] Male only.

[3] Female only.

[4] Excludes data from States lacking an Hispanic-origin item on their death certificates.

NOTES: For data years shown, code numbers for cause of death are based on the current revision of *International Classification of Diseases*. Categories for coding human immunodeficiency virus infection deaths were introduced in the United States in 1987. Consistency of race identification between the death certificate (source of data for numerator of death rates) and data from the Census Bureau (denominator) is high for individual white and black persons; however, persons identified as American Indian, Asian, or Hispanic origin in data from the Census Bureau are sometimes misreported as white or non-Hispanic on the death certificate, causing death rates to be underestimated by 22–30 percent for American Indians, about 12 percent for Asians, and about 7 percent for persons of Hispanic origin. (Sorlie PD, Rogot E, and Johnson NJ: Validity of demographic characteristics on the death certificate, *Epidemiology* 3(2):181–184, 1992.)

SOURCE: *Health, United States, 1999.* National Center for Health Statistics: Hyattsville, MD, 1999

TABLE 6.17

Death Rates for Malignant Neoplasms, According to Sex, Detailed Race, Hispanic Origin, and Age: United States, Selected Years 1950–97

[Data are based on the National Vital Statistics System]

Sex, race, Hispanic origin, and age	1950[1]	1960[1]	1970	1980	1985	1990	1994	1995	1996	1997	1995–97[2]
All persons					Deaths per 100,000 resident population						
All ages, age adjusted	125.4	125.8	129.8	132.8	134.4	135.0	131.5	129.9	127.9	125.6	127.8
All ages, crude	139.8	149.2	162.8	183.9	194.0	203.2	205.2	204.9	203.4	201.6	203.3
Under 1 year	8.7	7.2	4.7	3.2	3.1	2.3	1.5	1.8	2.3	2.4	2.2
1–4 years	11.7	10.9	7.5	4.5	3.8	3.5	3.3	3.1	2.7	2.9	2.9
5–14 years	6.7	6.8	6.0	4.3	3.5	3.1	2.8	2.7	2.7	2.7	2.7
15–24 years	8.6	8.3	8.3	6.3	5.4	4.9	4.8	4.6	4.5	4.5	4.5
25–34 years	20.0	19.5	16.5	13.7	13.2	12.6	12.2	11.9	12.0	11.6	11.9
35–44 years	62.7	59.7	59.5	48.6	45.9	43.3	40.4	40.3	39.3	38.9	39.5
45–54 years	175.1	177.0	182.5	180.0	170.1	158.9	145.9	142.2	137.9	135.1	138.3
55–64 years	390.7	396.8	423.0	436.1	454.6	449.6	424.6	416.0	406.5	395.7	405.9
65–74 years	698.8	713.9	751.2	817.9	845.5	872.3	875.4	868.2	861.6	847.3	859.1
75–84 years	1,153.3	1,127.4	1,169.2	1,232.3	1,271.8	1,348.5	1,367.4	1,364.8	1,351.5	1,335.2	1,350.3
85 years and over	1,451.0	1,450.0	1,320.7	1,594.6	1,615.4	1,752.9	1,789.0	1,823.8	1,798.3	1,805.0	1,808.8
Male											
All ages, age adjusted	130.8	143.0	157.4	165.5	166.1	166.3	159.6	156.8	153.8	150.4	153.6
All ages, crude	142.9	162.5	182.1	205.3	213.4	221.3	220.7	219.5	217.2	214.6	217.0
Under 1 year	9.7	7.7	4.4	3.7	3.0	2.4	1.4	1.8	2.2	2.3	2.1
1–4 years	12.5	12.4	8.3	5.2	4.3	3.7	3.5	3.6	3.1	3.1	3.3
5–14 years	7.4	7.6	6.7	4.9	3.9	3.5	3.1	3.0	3.0	2.8	2.9
15–24 years	9.7	10.2	10.4	7.8	6.4	5.7	5.8	5.5	5.1	5.2	5.3
25–34 years	17.7	18.8	16.3	13.4	13.2	12.6	12.1	11.7	11.5	11.5	11.5
35–44 years	45.6	48.9	53.0	44.0	42.4	38.5	36.7	36.5	35.6	34.5	35.5
45–54 years	156.2	170.8	183.5	188.7	175.2	162.5	148.8	143.7	140.7	138.0	140.7
55–64 years	413.1	459.9	511.8	520.8	536.9	532.9	495.3	480.5	469.1	453.4	467.5
65–74 years	791.5	890.5	1,006.8	1,093.2	1,105.2	1,122.2	1,102.5	1,089.9	1,080.9	1,058.4	1,076.4
75–84 years	1,332.6	1,389.4	1,588.3	1,790.5	1,839.7	1,914.4	1,862.6	1,842.3	1,802.7	1,770.2	1,804.3
85 years and over	1,668.3	1,741.2	1,720.8	2,369.5	2,451.8	2,739.9	2,805.8	2,837.3	2,733.1	2,712.5	2,759.1
Female											
All ages, age adjusted	120.8	111.2	108.8	109.2	111.7	112.7	111.1	110.4	108.8	107.3	108.8
All ages, crude	136.8	136.4	144.4	163.6	175.7	186.0	190.5	191.0	190.2	189.2	190.1
Under 1 year.	7.6	6.8	5.0	2.7	3.2	2.2	1.6	1.8	2.4	2.5	2.2
1–4 years	10.8	9.3	6.7	3.7	3.4	3.2	3.0	2.6	2.3	2.6	2.5
5–14 years	6.0	6.0	5.2	3.6	3.1	2.8	2.4	2.4	2.4	2.5	2.4
15–24 years	7.6	6.5	6.2	4.8	4.3	4.1	3.9	3.6	3.8	3.7	3.7
25–34 years	22.2	20.1	16.7	14.0	13.2	12.6	12.3	12.2	12.6	11.7	12.2
35–44 years	79.3	70.0	65.6	53.1	49.2	48.1	44.1	44.0	42.9	43.1	43.4
45–54 years	194.0	183.0	181.5	171.8	165.3	155.5	143.1	140.7	135.2	132.3	136.0
55–64 years	368.2	337.7	343.2	361.7	381.8	375.2	360.7	357.5	349.6	343.2	350.0
65–74 years	612.3	560.2	557.9	607.1	645.3	677.4	694.7	690.7	685.2	676.8	684.3
75–84 years	1,000.7	924.1	891.9	903.1	937.8	1,010.3	1,057.5	1,061.5	1,060.0	1,050.6	1,057.3
85 years and over	1,299.7	1,263.9	1,096.7	1,255.7	1,281.4	1,372.1	1,397.1	1,429.1	1,426.8	1,439.2	1,431.8
White male											
All ages, age adjusted	130.9	141.6	154.3	160.5	160.4	160.3	154.4	151.8	149.2	145.9	148.9
All ages, crude	147.2	166.1	185.1	208.7	218.1	227.7	228.9	228.1	225.8	223.3	225.7
25–34 years	17.7	18.8	16.2	13.6	13.1	12.3	11.8	11.3	11.3	11.2	11.3
35–44 years	44.5	46.3	50.1	41.1	39.8	35.8	34.5	34.2	33.5	32.3	33.3
45–54 years	150.8	164.1	172.0	175.4	162.0	149.9	138.0	134.3	131.8	129.0	131.6
55–64 years	409.4	450.9	498.1	497.4	512.0	508.2	474.7	460.0	448.9	432.4	446.9
65–74 years	798.7	887.3	997.0	1,070.7	1,076.5	1,090.7	1,074.6	1,064.6	1,057.3	1,038.7	1,053.6
75–84 years	1,367.6	1,413.7	1,592.7	1,779.7	1,817.1	1,883.2	1,831.2	1,810.9	1,771.0	1,746.1	1,775.3
85 years and over	1,732.7	1,791.4	1,772.2	2,375.6	2,449.1	2,715.1	2,780.3	2,805.2	2,723.9	2,695.5	2,740.1
Black male											
All ages, age adjusted	126.1	158.5	198.0	229.9	239.9	248.1	232.6	226.8	221.9	214.8	221.1
All ages, crude	106.6	136.7	171.6	205.5	214.9	221.9	212.1	209.1	207.3	203.0	206.5
25–34 years	18.0	18.4	18.8	14.1	14.9	15.7	15.5	15.2	14.0	14.5	14.6
35–44 years	55.7	72.9	81.3	73.8	69.9	64.3	57.2	57.5	55.0	54.3	55.6
45–54 years	211.7	244.7	311.2	333.0	315.9	302.6	269.5	250.7	242.7	235.3	242.7
55–64 years	490.8	579.7	689.2	812.5	851.3	859.2	772.7	755.3	741.2	723.3	739.8
65–74 years	636.4	938.5	1,168.9	1,417.2	1,532.8	1,613.9	1,547.8	1,509.6	1,473.2	1,412.4	1,464.7
75–84 years	- - -	1,053.3	1,624.8	2,029.6	2,229.6	2,478.3	2,456.3	2,426.8	2,421.8	2,298.4	2,381.1
85 years and over	- - -	1,155.2	1,387.0	2,393.9	2,629.0	3,238.3	3,274.6	3,338.2	3,209.7	3,306.2	3,284.0

See footnotes at end of table.

TABLE 6.17

Death Rates for Malignant Neoplasms, According to Sex, Detailed Race, Hispanic Origin, and Age: United States, Selected Years 1950–97 [CONTINUED]

[Data are based on the National Vital Statistics System]

Sex, race, Hispanic origin, and age	1950[1]	1960[1]	1970	1980	1985	1990	1994	1995	1996	1997	1995–97[2]
American Indian or Alaska Native male[3]					Deaths per 100,000 resident population						
All ages, age adjusted	- - -	- - -	- - -	82.1	87.1	83.5	91.3	94.0	94.0	104.0	97.4
All ages, crude	- - -	- - -	- - -	58.1	62.8	61.4	70.7	74.2	75.9	84.7	78.3
25–34 years	- - -	- - -	- - -	*	*	*	*	*	*	*	6.8
35–44 years	- - -	- - -	- - -	*	28.8	22.8	18.9	16.0	18.4	25.0	19.9
45–54 years	- - -	- - -	- - -	86.9	89.4	86.9	79.8	88.0	76.0	109.3	91.4
55–64 years	- - -	- - -	- - -	213.4	276.6	246.2	287.8	300.3	325.5	336.2	321.0
65–74 years	- - -	- - -	- - -	613.0	584.6	530.6	728.3	670.4	680.1	761.6	704.5
75–84 years	- - -	- - -	- - -	936.4	963.6	1,038.4	892.8	1,111.9	1,036.6	1,041.1	1,061.6
85 years and over	- - -	- - -	- - -	1,471.2	1,133.3	1,654.4	1,135.4	1,081.5	1,284.2	1,011.3	1,124.0
Asian or Pacific Islander male[4]											
All ages, age adjusted	- - -	- - -	- - -	96.4	101.0	99.6	100.9	98.3	93.8	91.7	94.3
All ages, crude	- - -	- - -	- - -	81.9	82.6	82.7	88.1	87.1	87.1	87.0	87.1
25–34 years	- - -	- - -	- - -	6.3	10.0	9.2	9.9	8.8	7.8	9.4	8.7
35–44 years	- - -	- - -	- - -	29.4	25.7	27.7	27.8	27.4	27.4	26.1	27.0
45–54 years	- - -	- - -	- - -	108.2	98.0	92.6	95.4	86.6	85.7	89.0	87.1
55–64 years	- - -	- - -	- - -	298.5	315.0	274.6	270.3	255.4	247.5	261.6	254.9
65–74 years	- - -	- - -	- - -	581.2	631.3	687.2	659.5	640.6	663.6	596.2	632.9
75–84 years	- - -	- - -	- - -	1,147.6	1,251.2	1,229.9	1,288.8	1,278.9	1,199.8	1,160.3	1,209.0
85 years and over	- - -	- - -	- - -	1,798.7	1,800.0	1,837.0	2,385.5	2,712.8	1,668.4	1,674.0	1,922.8
Hispanic male[5]											
All ages, age adjusted	- - -	- - -	- - -	- - -	92.1	99.8	97.4	98.6	93.1	91.4	94.2
All ages, crude	- - -	- - -	- - -	- - -	56.1	65.5	67.4	68.9	65.8	65.4	66.6
25–34 years	- - -	- - -	- - -	- - -	9.7	8.0	9.3	9.2	8.0	8.8	8.7
35–44 years	- - -	- - -	- - -	- - -	23.0	22.5	22.5	25.4	22.0	22.5	23.3
45–54 years	- - -	- - -	- - -	- - -	83.4	96.6	85.5	85.8	81.6	87.3	84.9
55–64 years	- - -	- - -	- - -	- - -	259.0	294.0	269.9	276.8	262.2	256.0	264.7
65–74 years	- - -	- - -	- - -	- - -	599.1	655.5	663.9	667.1	647.9	627.2	646.9
75–84 years	- - -	- - -	- - -	- - -	1,216.6	1,233.4	1,241.4	1,272.1	1,178.3	1,123.5	1,187.1
85 years and over	- - -	- - -	- - -	- - -	1,700.7	2,019.4	1,962.5	1,858.7	1,637.8	1,658.8	1,709.4
White, non-Hispanic male[5]											
All ages, age adjusted	- - -	- - -	- - -	- - -	156.0	163.3	156.8	154.0	151.7	148.6	151.4
All ages, crude	- - -	- - -	- - -	- - -	217.4	246.2	248.1	247.1	246.2	244.7	246.0
25–34 years	- - -	- - -	- - -	- - -	13.5	12.8	12.1	11.4	11.8	11.5	11.6
35–44 years	- - -	- - -	- - -	- - -	39.1	36.8	35.4	34.7	34.4	33.1	34.1
45–54 years	- - -	- - -	- - -	- - -	159.9	153.9	141.0	137.0	134.9	131.9	134.5
55–64 years	- - -	- - -	- - -	- - -	496.4	520.6	486.4	469.9	458.6	443.3	457.1
65–74 years	- - -	- - -	- - -	- - -	1,044.2	1,109.0	1,091.2	1,081.1	1,073.6	1,057.8	1,070.9
75–84 years	- - -	- - -	- - -	- - -	1,766.1	1,906.6	1,846.0	1,825.6	1,791.6	1,765.7	1,793.6
85 years and over	- - -	- - -	- - -	- - -	2,327.6	2,744.4	2,776.3	2,814.6	2,764.3	2,738.3	2,771.4
White female											
All ages, age adjusted	119.4	109.5	107.6	107.7	110.5	111.2	109.9	108.9	107.6	106.0	107.5
All ages, crude	139.9	139.8	149.4	170.3	184.4	196.1	201.9	202.4	201.8	200.4	201.6
25–34 years	20.9	18.8	16.3	13.5	12.7	11.9	11.8	11.5	12.1	11.2	11.6
35–44 years	74.5	66.6	62.4	50.9	47.3	46.2	41.8	42.0	40.5	40.6	41.0
45–54 years	185.8	175.7	177.3	166.4	161.6	150.9	139.4	136.1	131.0	128.4	131.8
55–64 years	362.5	329.0	338.6	355.5	376.3	368.5	356.5	352.6	347.3	339.6	346.4
65–74 years	616.5	562.1	554.7	605.2	644.9	675.1	694.3	689.6	684.6	674.6	683.0
75–84 years	1,026.6	939.3	903.5	905.4	938.2	1,011.8	1,056.5	1,060.2	1,059.9	1,049.7	1,056.5
85 years and over	1,348.3	1,304.9	1,126.6	1,266.8	1,285.4	1,372.3	1,395.6	1,428.2	1,430.1	1,435.8	1,431.4

See footnotes at end of table.

ment rate of 6.7 percent, compared to 3.6 percent for non-Hispanic Whites. Hispanic Americans are overrepresented in the manufacturing and construction industries, as well as farming and metal mining, all of which report a high number of work-related injuries. The Social Security Administration reported that severe disability resulting from work-related injuries was almost twice as high among Hispanics as among other non-minority workers.

Hispanics are more likely than non-Hispanics to suffer from stroke, cirrhosis, obesity, and certain types of cancer. Hispanics are also two to three times more likely than non-Hispanics to have diabetes and to suffer complications, such as blindness and amputation, because of lack of regular treatment. A General Accounting Office study of Texas border counties, "Hispanic Access to Health Care" (Washington, DC, 1992), found that 60

TABLE 6.17

Death Rates for Malignant Neoplasms, According to Sex, Detailed Race, Hispanic Origin, and Age: United States, Selected Years 1950–97 [CONTINUED]

[Data are based on the National Vital Statistics System]

Sex, race, Hispanic origin, and age	1950[1]	1960[1]	1970	1980	1985	1990	1994	1995	1996	1997	1995–97[2]
Black female					Deaths per 100,000 resident population						
All ages, age adjusted	131.9	127.8	123.5	129.7	131.8	137.2	133.7	134.1	130.7	131.2	132.0
All ages, crude	111.8	113.8	117.3	136.5	145.2	156.1	157.6	159.1	157.9	160.5	159.2
25–34 years	34.3	31.0	20.9	18.3	17.2	18.7	16.3	16.8	16.4	16.2	16.5
35–44 years	119.8	102.4	94.6	73.5	69.0	67.4	64.6	62.2	62.8	62.9	62.6
45–54 years	277.0	254.8	228.6	230.2	212.4	209.9	192.0	192.7	182.8	180.6	185.2
55–64 years	484.6	442.7	404.8	450.4	474.9	482.4	445.8	443.6	422.2	426.4	430.6
65–74 years	477.3	541.6	615.8	662.4	704.2	773.2	794.5	799.6	790.6	789.7	793.3
75–84 years	- - -	696.3	763.3	923.9	986.3	1,059.9	1,139.3	1,154.1	1,150.9	1,166.5	1,157.2
85 years and over	- - -	728.9	791.5	1,159.9	1,284.2	1,431.3	1,469.2	1,490.3	1,507.2	1,602.3	1,534.3
American Indian or Alaska Native female[3]											
All ages, age adjusted	- - -	- - -	- - -	62.1	60.5	69.6	68.0	70.7	78.6	72.8	74.0
All ages, crude	- - -	- - -	- - -	50.4	52.5	62.1	65.8	69.9	77.1	71.8	73.0
25–34 years	- - -	- - -	- - -	*	*	*	*	11.1	*	11.0	9.8
35–44 years	- - -	- - -	- - -	36.9	23.4	31.0	24.1	33.5	38.5	36.8	36.3
45–54 years	- - -	- - -	- - -	96.9	90.1	104.5	86.4	85.2	111.2	88.3	94.9
55–64 years	- - -	- - -	- - -	198.4	192.3	213.3	224.9	223.2	249.2	245.5	239.5
65–74 years	- - -	- - -	- - -	350.8	378.8	438.9	440.7	427.7	487.3	467.5	461.0
75–84 years	- - -	- - -	- - -	446.4	505.9	554.3	618.5	723.9	721.4	613.4	684.8
85 years and over	- - -	- - -	- - -	786.5	700.0	843.7	708.6	736.6	638.0	561.9	640.0
Asian or Pacific Islander female[4]											
All ages, age adjusted	- - -	- - -	- - -	59.8	62.8	63.6	67.3	68.4	63.2	63.0	64.7
All ages, crude	- - -	- - -	- - -	54.1	57.5	60.5	69.7	71.5	69.7	71.1	70.8
25–34 years	- - -	- - -	- - -	9.5	9.9	7.3	10.1	10.6	9.6	7.0	9.0
35–44 years	- - -	- - -	- - -	38.7	33.1	29.8	30.1	28.6	29.9	31.5	30.0
45–54 years	- - -	- - -	- - -	99.8	91.3	93.9	90.2	98.0	88.7	81.1	88.9
55–64 years	- - -	- - -	- - -	174.7	195.5	196.2	198.4	211.4	179.6	176.7	188.6
65–74 years	- - -	- - -	- - -	301.9	330.8	346.2	352.2	351.2	347.8	376.4	358.8
75–84 years	- - -	- - -	- - -	522.1	589.1	641.4	769.7	722.6	703.6	662.1	694.1
05 years and over	- - -	- - -	- - -	800.0	908.3	971.7	1,214.4	1,307.7	917.8	1,014.0	1,053.6
Hispanic female[5]											
All ages, age adjusted	- - -	- - -	- - -	- - -	64.1	70.0	67.1	66.1	66.7	65.4	66.1
All ages, crude	- - -	- - -	- - -	- - -	49.8	60.7	60.7	60.5	62.1	61.4	61.4
25–34 years	- - -	- - -	- - -	- - -	9.7	9.7	10.3	9.2	10.3	10.3	9.9
35–44 years	- - -	- - -	- - -	- - -	30.9	34.8	33.4	31.2	30.0	30.5	30.6
45–54 years	- - -	- - -	- - -	- - -	90.1	100.5	95.2	89.7	85.3	84.7	86.5
55–64 years	- - -	- - -	- - -	- - -	199.4	205.4	200.0	197.6	202.4	201.6	200.6
65–74 years	- - -	- - -	- - -	- - -	356.3	404.8	384.5	382.3	405.3	388.2	392.0
75–84 years	- - -	- - -	- - -	- - -	599.7	663.0	628.4	659.6	637.8	622.4	639.3
85 years and over	- - -	- - -	- - -	- - -	906.1	1,022.7	912.9	938.2	913.9	888.6	911.9

See footnotes at end of table.

percent of Hispanic cases of blindness, 51 percent of kidney failures, and 67 percent of diabetes-related amputations of feet and legs could have been prevented with proper treatment.

Health Insurance

Having health insurance is commonly associated with employment, retirement, and income. Hispanics are less likely than any other population group to have medical insurance. In comparison with Whites and Blacks, Hispanics are more likely to work in industries such as personal services and agriculture that are less likely to provide health insurance. (See Table 6.7 for information on insurance coverage among Hispanics.)

Hispanic Infant Mortality

Recent studies question the commonly assumed connection between lower levels of income and education and high infant mortality. Mexican Americans, whose prenatal health care is poor and whose education and income levels are low, generally have a lower infant mortality rate than non-Hispanic Whites. In 1996, although only 70.7 percent of Mexican Americans (nearly 17 percent lower than non-Hispanic White women) received prenatal care in the first trimester, they had a lower infant mortality rate (5.8 infant deaths per 1,000 live births) than that of non-Hispanic White women (6 per 1,000). (See Tables 6.2 and 6.5.) Researchers have speculated that greater social support, less high-risk behavior, and dietary factors may explain the differences.

TABLE 6.17

Death Rates for Malignant Neoplasms, According to Sex, Detailed Race, Hispanic Origin, and Age: United States, Selected Years 1950–97 [CONTINUED]

[Data are based on the National Vital Statistics System]

Sex, race, Hispanic origin, and age	1950[1]	1960[1]	1970	1980	1985	1990	1994	1995	1996	1997	1995–97[2]
White, non-Hispanic female[5]					Deaths per 100,000 resident population						
All ages, age adjusted	- - -	- - -	- - -	- - -	108.9	113.6	111.7	111.1	109.8	108.1	109.6
All ages, crude	- - -	- - -	- - -	- - -	187.1	210.6	217.5	218.4	218.3	217.3	218.0
25–34 years	- - -	- - -	- - -	- - -	12.2	11.9	11.8	11.7	12.2	11.2	11.7
35–44 years	- - -	- - -	- - -	- - -	47.2	47.0	42.1	42.7	41.2	41.4	41.8
45–54 years	- - -	- - -	- - -	- - -	158.8	154.9	141.7	139.3	133.9	131.2	134.7
55–64 years	- - -	- - -	- - -	- - -	372.7	379.5	366.1	362.7	356.6	348.5	355.8
65–74 years	- - -	- - -	- - -	- - -	638.3	688.5	706.8	703.1	697.9	688.7	696.6
75–84 years	- - -	- - -	- - -	- - -	917.7	1,027.2	1,069.6	1,070.5	1,075.3	1,063.9	1,069.8
85 years and over	- - -	- - -	- - -	- - -	1,241.6	1,385.7	1,397.7	1,438.4	1,448.8	1,452.5	1,446.7

- - - Data not available.

*Based on fewer than 20 deaths.

[1]Includes deaths of persons who were not residents of the 50 States and the District of Columbia.

[2]Average annual death rate.

[3]Interpretation of trends should take into account that population estimates for American Indians increased by 45 percent between 1980 and 1990, partly due to better enumeration techniques in the 1990 decennial census and to the increased tendency for people to identify themselves as American Indian in 1990.

[4]Interpretation of trends should take into account that the Asian population in the United States more than doubled between 1980 and 1990, primarily due to immigration.

[5]Excludes data from States lacking an Hispanic-origin item on their death certificates.

NOTES: For data years shown, the code numbers for cause of death are based on the then current *International Classification of Diseases*. Age groups were selected to minimize the presentation of unstable age-specific death rates based on small numbers of deaths and for consistency among comparison groups. The race groups, white, black, Asian or Pacific Islander, and American Indian or Alaska Native, include persons of Hispanic and non-Hispanic origin. Conversely, persons of Hispanic origin may be of any race. Consistency of race identification between the death certificate (source of data for numerator of death rates) and data from the Census Bureau (denominator) is high for individual white and black persons; however, persons identified as American Indian, Asian, or Hispanic origin in data from the Census Bureau are sometimes misreported as white or non-Hispanic on the death certificate, causing death rates to be underestimated by 22–30 percent for American Indians, about 12 percent for Asians, and about 7 percent for persons of Hispanic origin. (Sorlie PD, Rogot E, and Johnson NJ: Validity of demographic characteristics on the death certificate, *Epidemiology* 3(2):181–184, 1992.)

SOURCE: *Health, United States, 1999*. National Center for Health Statistics: Hyattsville, MD, 1999

Cancer

Overall, death rates from cancer for Hispanics are considerably lower than for non-Hispanic Blacks and non-Hispanic Whites. In 1997 the age-adjusted mortality rate was 91.4 deaths per 100,000 for Hispanic males and 65.4 per 100,000 for Hispanic females. These compare to a Black male rate of 214.8 per 100,000, a Black female rate of 131.2, a non-Hispanic White male rate of 148.6 per 100,000, and a non-Hispanic White female rate of 108.1. (See Table 6.17.)

Types of cancer that are more likely to be found among Hispanic populations include stomach, prostate, esophagus, pancreas, and cervical cancers. Hispanics living in New Mexico have pancreatic cancer rates higher than those of Whites; excess risk for pancreatic cancer has been found among cigarette smokers. In addition, the risk of cervical cancer is twice as high for Hispanics from Puerto Rico and New Mexico as it is for Hispanics from other areas. The overall cancer survival rate for Hispanic males is nearly the same as for Whites. On the other hand, Hispanic females have a somewhat lower survival rate than that of Whites.

Heart Disease

Even though Hispanics have a lower death rate from heart disease than most groups, it is the leading killer of Hispanics, having caused 113.4 deaths per 100,000 males and 64.7 per 100,000 females in 1997. The only minority group with lower death rates from heart diseases was Asians/Pacific Islanders, with a male death rate of 95.9 per 100,000 and a female rate of 49.3 per 100,000. As with all groups, the death rate from heart disease increases with age. (See Table 6.15.)

Other Causes of Death

In 1997 the third-leading cause of death for Hispanic women was cerebrovascular diseases (strokes), followed by diabetes and injuries and accidents. For Hispanic men, unintentional injuries were the third-leading cause of death, followed by homicide and legal intervention. (See Table 6.18 for the 10 leading causes of death for Hispanics.)

Diabetes and the Hispanic Population

Diabetes mellitus is a major problem for Hispanics, especially for Mexican Americans and Puerto Ricans. In Mexico diabetes appears to be only slightly more common than among the worldwide population. In the United States, however, Mexican Americans apparently exercise less and eat more. These changes in living patterns seem to increase their risk of developing diabetes. Among persons 45 to 74 years old, diabetes is about twice as likely in

TABLE 6.18

Leading Causes of Death and Numbers of Deaths, According to Sex, Detailed Race, and Hispanic Origin, United States, 1980 and 1997

[Data are based on the National Vital Statistics System]

Sex, race, Hispanic origin, and rank order	1980 Cause of death	Deaths	1997 Cause of death	Deaths
All persons				
. . .	All causes	1,989,841	All causes	2,314,245
1	Diseases of heart	761,085	Diseases of heart	726,974
2	Malignant neoplasms	416,509	Malignant neoplasms	539,577
3	Cerebrovascular diseases	170,225	Cerebrovascular diseases	159,791
4	Unintentional injuries	105,718	Chronic obstructive pulmonary diseases	109,029
5	Chronic obstructive pulmonary diseases	56,050	Unintentional injuries	95,644
6	Pneumonia and influenza	54,619	Pneumonia and influenza	86,449
7	Diabetes mellitus	34,851	Diabetes mellitus	62,636
8	Chronic liver disease and cirrhosis	30,583	Suicide	30,535
9	Atherosclerosis	29,449	Nephritis, nephrotic syndrome, and nephrosis	25,331
10	Suicide	26,869	Chronic liver disease and cirrhosis	25,175
Male				
. . .	All causes	1,075,078	All causes	1,154,039
1	Diseases of heart	405,661	Diseases of heart	356,598
2	Malignant neoplasms	225,948	Malignant neoplasms	281,110
3	Unintentional injuries	74,180	Cerebrovascular diseases	62,564
4	Cerebrovascular diseases	69,973	Unintentional injuries	61,963
5	Chronic obstructive pulmonary diseases	38,625	Chronic obstructive pulmonary diseases	55,984
6	Pneumonia and influenza	27,574	Pneumonia and influenza	39,284
7	Suicide	20,505	Diabetes mellitus	28,187
8	Chronic liver disease and cirrhosis	19,768	Suicide	24,492
9	Homicide and legal intervention	19,088	Chronic liver disease and cirrhosis	16,260
10	Diabetes mellitus	14,325	Homicide and legal intervention	15,449
Female				
. . .	All causes	914,763	All causes	1,160,206
1	Diseases of heart	355,424	Diseases of heart	370,376
2	Malignant neoplasms	190,561	Malignant neoplasms	258,467
3	Cerebrovascular diseases	100,252	Cerebrovascular diseases	97,227
4	Unintentional injuries	31,538	Chronic obstructive pulmonary diseases	53,045
5	Pneumonia and influenza	27,045	Pneumonia and influenza	47,165
6	Diabetes mellitus	20,526	Diabetes mellitus	34,449
7	Atherosclerosis	17,848	Unintentional injuries	33,681
8	Chronic obstructive pulmonary diseases	17,425	Alzheimer's disease	15,437
9	Chronic liver disease and cirrhosis	10,815	Nephritis, nephrotic syndrome, and nephrosis	13,191
10	Certain conditions originating in the perinatal period	9,815	Septicemia	12,741
White				
. . .	All causes	1,738,607	All causes	1,996,393
1	Diseases of heart	683,347	Diseases of heart	639,225
2	Malignant neoplasms	368,162	Malignant neoplasms	468,521
3	Cerebrovascular diseases	148,734	Cerebrovascular diseases	138,324
4	Unintentional injuries	90,122	Chronic obstructive pulmonary diseases	100,770
5	Chronic obstructive pulmonary diseases	52,375	Unintentional injuries	79,922
6	Pneumonia and influenza	48,369	Pneumonia and influenza	76,875
7	Diabetes mellitus	28,868	Diabetes mellitus	49,850
8	Atherosclerosis	27,069	Suicide	27,513
9	Chronic liver disease and cirrhosis	25,240	Chronic liver disease and cirrhosis	21,683
10	Suicide	24,829	Alzheimer's disease	21,192
Black				
. . .	All causes	233,135	All causes	276,520
1	Diseases of heart	72,956	Diseases of heart	77,174
2	Malignant neoplasms	45,037	Malignant neoplasms	61,333
3	Cerebrovascular diseases	20,135	Cerebrovascular diseases	18,131
4	Unintentional injuries	13,480	Unintentional injuries	12,665
5	Homicide and legal intervention	10,283	Diabetes mellitus	11,130
6	Certain conditions originating in the perinatal period	6,961	Homicide and legal intervention	9,253
7	Pneumonia and influenza	5,648	Human immunodeficiency virus infection	8,525
8	Diabetes mellitus	5,544	Pneumonia and influenza	7,920
9	Chronic liver disease and cirrhosis	4,790	Chronic obstructive pulmonary diseases	6,908
10	Nephritis, nephrotic syndrome, and nephrosis	3,416	Certain conditions originating in the perinatal period	4,714

See footnotes at end of table.

TABLE 6.18

Leading Causes of Death and Numbers of Deaths, According to Sex, Detailed Race, and Hispanic Origin, United States, 1980 and 1997 [CONTINUED]

[Data are based on the National Vital Statistics System]

Sex, race, Hispanic origin, and rank order	1980 Cause of death	1980 Deaths	1997 Cause of death	1997 Deaths
American Indian or Alaska Native				
...	All causes	6,923	All causes	10,576
1	Diseases of heart	1,494	Diseases of heart	2,383
2	Unintentional injuries	1,290	Malignant neoplasms	1,817
3	Malignant neoplasms	770	Unintentional injuries	1,330
4	Chronic liver disease and cirrhosis	410	Diabetes mellitus	645
5	Cerebrovascular diseases	322	Cerebrovascular diseases	497
6	Pneumonia and influenza	257	Chronic liver disease and cirrhosis	426
7	Homicide and legal intervention	219	Pneumonia and influenza	354
8	Diabetes mellitus	210	Chronic obstructive pulmonary diseases	349
9	Certain conditions originating in the perinatal period	199	Suicide	290
10	Suicide	181	Homicide and legal intervention	251
Asian or Pacific Islander				
...	All causes	11,071	All causes	30,756
1	Diseases of heart	3,265	Diseases of heart	8,192
2	Malignant neoplasms	2,522	Malignant neoplasms	7,906
3	Cerebrovascular diseases	1,028	Cerebrovascular diseases	2,839
4	Unintentional injuries	810	Unintentional injuries	1,727
5	Pneumonia and influenza	342	Pneumonia and influenza	1,300
6	Suicide	249	Diabetes mellitus	1,011
7	Certain conditions originating in the perinatal period	246	Chronic obstructive pulmonary diseases	1,002
8	Diabetes mellitus	227	Suicide	629
9	Homicide and legal intervention	211	Homicide and legal intervention	429
10	Chronic obstructive pulmonary diseases	207	Congenital anomalies	309
Hispanic				
...	- - -	- - -	All causes	95,460
1	- - -	- - -	Diseases of heart	23,824
2	- - -	- - -	Malignant neoplasms	18,635
3	- - -	- - -	Unintentional injuries	7,932
4	- - -	- - -	Cerebrovascular diseases	5,306
5	- - -	- - -	Diabetes mellitus	4,538
6	- - -	- - -	Homicide and legal intervention	3,248
7	- - -	- - -	Pneumonia and influenza	3,119
8	- - -	- - -	Chronic liver disease and cirrhosis	2,793
9	- - -	- - -	Chronic obstructive pulmonary diseases	2,477
10	- - -	- - -	Human immunodeficiency virus infection	2,300
White male				
...	All causes	933,878	All causes	986,884
1	Diseases of heart	364,679	Diseases of heart	313,316
2	Malignant neoplasms	198,188	Malignant neoplasms	243,192
3	Unintentional injuries	62,963	Cerebrovascular diseases	53,158
4	Cerebrovascular diseases	60,095	Unintentional injuries	51,396
5	Chronic obstructive pulmonary diseases	35,977	Chronic obstructive pulmonary diseases	51,184
6	Pneumonia and influenza	23,810	Pneumonia and influenza	34,386
7	Suicide	18,901	Diabetes mellitus	22,968
8	Chronic liver disease and cirrhosis	16,407	Suicide	22,042
9	Diabetes mellitus	12,125	Chronic liver disease and cirrhosis	14,045
10	Atherosclerosis	10,543	Nephritis, nephrotic syndrome, and nephrosis	10,002
Black male				
...	All causes	130,138	All causes	144,110
1	Diseases of heart	37,877	Diseases of heart	37,212
2	Malignant neoplasms	25,861	Malignant neoplasms	32,719
3	Unintentional injuries	9,701	Unintentional injuries	8,582
4	Cerebrovascular diseases	9,194	Cerebrovascular diseases	7,794
5	Homicide and legal intervention	8,385	Homicide and legal intervention	7,601
6	Certain conditions originating in the perinatal period	3,869	Human immunodeficiency virus infection	6,078
7	Pneumonia and influenza	3,386	Diabetes mellitus	4,440
8	Chronic liver disease and cirrhosis	3,020	Pneumonia and influenza	3,978
9	Chronic obstructive pulmonary diseases	2,429	Chronic obstructive pulmonary diseases	3,966
10	Diabetes mellitus	2,010	Certain conditions originating in the perinatal period	2,624

See footnotes at end of table.

TABLE 6.18

Leading Causes of Death and Numbers of Deaths, According to Sex, Detailed Race, and Hispanic Origin, United States, 1980 and 1997 [CONTINUED]

[Data are based on the National Vital Statistics System]

Sex, race, Hispanic origin, and rank order	1980 Cause of death	1980 Deaths	1997 Cause of death	1997 Deaths
American Indian or Alaska Native male				
. . .	All causes	4,193	All causes	5,985
1	Unintentional injuries	946	Diseases of heart	1,347
2	Diseases of heart	917	Malignant neoplasms	977
3	Malignant neoplasms	408	Unintentional injuries	927
4	Chronic liver disease and cirrhosis	239	Diabetes mellitus	291
5	Homicide and legal intervention	164	Chronic liver disease and cirrhosis	244
6	Cerebrovascular diseases	163	Suicide	241
7	Pneumonia and influenza	148	Cerebrovascular diseases	213
8	Suicide	147	Chronic obstructive pulmonary diseases	206
9	Certain conditions originating in the perinatal period	107	Homicide and legal intervention	189
10	Diabetes mellitus	86	Pneumonia and influenza	186
Asian or Pacific Islander male				
. . .	All causes	6,809	All causes	17,060
1	Diseases of heart	2,174	Diseases of heart	4,723
2	Malignant neoplasms	1,485	Malignant neoplasms	4,222
3	Unintentional injuries	556	Cerebrovascular diseases	1,399
4	Cerebrovascular diseases	521	Unintentional injuries	1,058
5	Pneumonia and influenza	227	Pneumonia and influenza	734
6	Suicide	159	Chronic obstructive pulmonary diseases	628
7	Chronic obstructive pulmonary diseases	158	Diabetes mellitus	488
8	Homicide and legal intervention	151	Suicide	445
9	Certain conditions originating in the perinatal period	128	Homicide and legal intervention	316
10	Diabetes mellitus	103	Certain conditions originating in the perinatal period	177
Hispanic male				
. . .	- - -	- - -	All causes	54,348
1	- - -	- - -	Diseases of heart	12,654
2	- - -	- - -	Malignant neoplasms	9,865
3	- - -	- - -	Unintentional injuries	5,978
4	- - -	- - -	Homicide and legal intervention	2,800
5	- - -	- - -	Cerebrovascular diseases	2,510
6	- - -	- - -	Diabetes mellitus	2,083
7	- - -	- - -	Chronic liver disease and cirrhosis	2,003
8	- - -	- - -	Human immunodeficiency virus infection	1,856
9	- - -	- - -	Pneumonia and influenza	1,608
10	- - -	- - -	Suicide	1,479
White female				
. . .	All causes	804,729	All causes	1,009,509
1	Diseases of heart	318,668	Diseases of heart	325,909
2	Malignant neoplasms	169,974	Malignant neoplasms	225,329
3	Cerebrovascular diseases	88,639	Cerebrovascular diseases	85,166
4	Unintentional injuries	27,159	Chronic obstructive pulmonary diseases	49,586
5	Pneumonia and influenza	24,559	Pneumonia and influenza	42,489
6	Diabetes mellitus	16,743	Unintentional injuries	28,526
7	Atherosclerosis	16,526	Diabetes mellitus	26,882
8	Chronic obstructive pulmonary diseases	16,398	Alzheimer's disease	14,613
9	Chronic liver disease and cirrhosis	8,833	Nephritis, nephrotic syndrome, and nephrosis	10,676
10	Certain conditions originating in the perinatal period	6,512	Septicemia	10,199
Black female				
. . .	All causes	102,997	All causes	132,410
1	Diseases of heart	35,079	Diseases of heart	39,962
2	Malignant neoplasms	19,176	Malignant neoplasms	28,614
3	Cerebrovascular diseases	10,941	Cerebrovascular diseases	10,337
4	Unintentional injuries	3,779	Diabetes mellitus	6,690
5	Diabetes mellitus	3,534	Unintentional injuries	4,083
6	Certain conditions originating in the perinatal period	3,092	Pneumonia and influenza	3,942
7	Pneumonia and influenza	2,262	Chronic obstructive pulmonary diseases	2,942
8	Homicide and legal intervention	1,898	Human immunodeficiency virus infection	2,447
9	Chronic liver disease and cirrhosis	1,770	Septicemia	2,370
10	Nephritis, nephrotic syndrome, and nephrosis	1,722	Nephritis, nephrotic syndrome, and nephrosis	2,295

See footnotes at end of table.

TABLE 6.18

Leading Causes of Death and Numbers of Deaths, According to Sex, Detailed Race, and Hispanic Origin, United States, 1980 and 1997 [CONTINUED]

[Data are based on the National Vital Statistics System]

Sex, race, Hispanic origin, and rank order	1980		1997	
	Cause of death	Deaths	Cause of death	Deaths
American Indian or Alaska Native female				
. . .	All causes	2,730	All causes	4,591
1	Diseases of heart	577	Diseases of heart	1,036
2	Malignant neoplasms	362	Malignant neoplasms	840
3	Unintentional injuries	344	Unintentional injuries	403
4	Chronic liver disease and cirrhosis	171	Diabetes mellitus	354
5	Cerebrovascular diseases	159	Cerebrovascular diseases	284
6	Diabetes mellitus	124	Chronic liver disease and cirrhosis	182
7	Pneumonia and influenza	109	Pneumonia and influenza	168
8	Certain conditions originating in the perinatal period	92	Chronic obstructive pulmonary diseases	143
9	Nephritis, nephrotic syndrome, and nephrosis	56	Nephritis, nephrotic syndrome, and nephrosis	68
10	Homicide and legal intervention	55	Homicide and legal intervention	62
Asian or Pacific Islander female				
. . .	All causes	4,262	All causes	13,696
1	Diseases of heart	1,091	Malignant neoplasms	3,684
2	Malignant neoplasms	1,037	Diseases of heart	3,469
3	Cerebrovascular diseases	507	Cerebrovascular diseases	1,440
4	Unintentional injuries	254	Unintentional injuries	669
5	Diabetes mellitus	124	Pneumonia and influenza	566
6	Certain conditions originating in the perinatal period	118	Diabetes mellitus	523
7	Pneumonia and influenza	115	Chronic obstructive pulmonary diseases	374
8	Congenital anomalies	104	Suicide	184
9	Suicide	90	Nephritis, nephrotic syndrome, and nephrosis	152
10	Homicide and legal intervention	60	Congenital anomalies	149
Hispanic female				
. . .	- - -	- - -	All causes	41,112
1	- - -	- - -	Diseases of heart	11,170
2	- - -	- - -	Malignant neoplasms	8,770
3	- - -	- - -	Cerebrovascular diseases	2,796
4	- - -	- - -	Diabetes mellitus	2,455
5	- - -	- - -	Unintentional injuries	1,954
6	- - -	- - -	Pneumonia and influenza	1,511
7	- - -	- - -	Chronic obstructive pulmonary diseases	1,120
8	- - -	- - -	Certain conditions originating in the perinatal period	831
9	- - -	- - -	Chronic liver disease and cirrhosis	790
10	- - -	- - -	Congenital anomalies	759

. . . Category not applicable.

- - - Data not available.

NOTES: For data years shown, the code numbers for cause of death are based on the *International Classification of Diseases, 9th Revision*. Categories for the coding and classification of human immunodeficiency virus infection were introduced in the United States beginning with mortality data for 1987.

SOURCE: *Health, United States, 1999*. National Center for Health Statistics: Hyattsville, MD, 1999

Mexican Americans (24 per 100,000) and Puerto Ricans (26 per 100,000) as in the general population (12 per 100,000). By the year 2000 an estimated 2.5 to 3 million Hispanics in the United States will suffer from diabetes.

HEALTH CARE FOR NATIVE AMERICANS

Native American diets have been harmed by the introduction of nonnative foods. Although there are considerable tribal variations in diet, studies show that the less American Indians eat of their traditional foods, the greater the levels of obesity and adult-onset diabetes. High carbohydrate, high sodium, and high saturated fat contents can characterize most current Indian diets. In addition, current Indian diets are relatively low in meat and dairy products. Factors contributing to these eating habits include food availability, preference for nonnative food, and place of residence.

The customs and patterns of White culture imposed on Native Americans have disrupted their traditional way of life. As a result, the Native American population has been plagued by a sense of powerlessness and hopelessness. According to social researchers, the high incidence of alcohol abuse, suicide, and depression is likely to be related to this.

Indian Health Service

Federal funding for American Indian health care is provided through the Indian Health Service (IHS), which is "charged with raising Indians' health status to the highest possible level." Delivery of health care to Native Americans is complicated by the lack of services and the long distances that sometimes must be traveled to receive care. Alaska Natives are often able to get preventive medical care only by flying to a medical facility, and, while transportation costs are covered for emergency care, transportation costs are not provided for routine care.

The General Accounting Office, in "Indian Health Service" (Washington, DC, 1993), studied the care provided by the IHS and found that although emergency and diagnostic care was generally available, preventive, dental, and substance abuse/mental health services needed improvement.

UNMET NEEDS. While preventive services have been a primary focus of the health strategy of the IHS, the survey found that in some areas preventive care was not available and in others was underutilized. Pap smears (a test for cervical cancer) were generally available. Nonetheless, the estimated percentage of women 50 years and older who had a Pap smear in 1991 ranged from 22 percent on the Navajo reservation to 54 percent among Native Americans living in California. This low rate of Pap smears is of particular concern since the rate of cervical cancer among Native American women is more than twice that of non-Indians. Prenatal care is another underutilized service. Teenage pregnancy rates are relatively high among Native Americans, and pregnant teens tend to delay getting prenatal care.

Alcohol and substance abuse treatment was the greatest unmet need. The alcoholism mortality rate for Native Americans ages 15 to 44 was about 6.5 times the rate of the general population. The IHS estimated that 75 percent of accidents and 80 percent of suicides among Native Americans ages 15 to 24 involved alcohol abuse. In 49 IHS and tribal-operated hospitals, about 21 percent of all adult cases (35 percent male, 12 percent female) and 3 percent of pediatric cases admitted to the hospital in one day were admitted for alcohol-related reasons.

Alcohol and substance abuse treatment facilities were inadequate and waiting lists were so long that many providers reported that by the time space was available, the clients had lost interest in seeking help. In addition, about one-fourth of the user population was served by facilities that reported that mental health services were available to less than 50 percent of those seeking care.

Using Gambling Profits to Improve Health Services

Approximately one-third of American Indian tribes have invested some of the money earned from their casinos to improve health services. The Sandia Pueblo in New Mexico, for example, now has a $3 million medical complex on the pueblo. This saves the residents the long drives to distant clinics that provide medical and dental care through the Indian Health Service. The 10,400-square foot health-care center includes seven exam rooms, three dental rooms, and state-of-the-art equipment. There is also a wellness and education center. After the health complex was built, the Sandia Pueblo used federal funds to hire a part-time doctor and a full-time nurse. Other medical personnel help staff the facility.

American Indians experience some health problems, such as diabetes (see below), at three times the rate of the total U.S. population. At the Sandia Pueblo, nearly 20 percent of the tribe is being treated for diabetes. In addition, in the Albuquerque area (where the Sandia Pueblo is located), death rates from unintentional injury, diabetes, and liver disease are higher than for the general population.

Indian Infant Mortality

The infant mortality rate for American Indians/Alaska Natives (AIs/ANs) fell from 15.2 deaths per 1,000 live births in 1983 to 10 per 1,000 live births in 1996. (See Table 6.5.) The most common, single cause of death was sudden infant death syndrome (SIDS). Also called crib death, SIDS is the sudden death of an infant while sleeping, occurring without any warning. Some of the factors associated with SIDS are low birth weight and smoking by the mother. In 1997, 7.2 percent of AI/AN babies were born with low birth weight. The AI/AN rate is lower than the overall population average of 7.5 percent and is only somewhat higher than the 6.5 percent of White babies. (See Table 6.4.) Among the various racial and ethnic categories, AI/AN mothers were the least likely to get prenatal care in the first trimester. Only two-thirds (68.1 percent) of AI/AN births were to women who had received early prenatal care. (See Table 6.2.)

Fetal Alcohol Syndrome

Native Americans appear to be at higher risk for fetal alcohol syndrome/fetal alcohol effects (FAS/FAE) than other population groups. Experts believe that the number of FAS babies is underestimated because children who do not receive follow-up health care or have been placed in adoption or foster care may be more likely to have FAS than other infants. In addition, clinicians are reluctant to label infants as FAS babies because the defects can be hard to diagnose or may not be apparent until later in life, mothers may not be honest about their alcohol consumption during pregnancy, and infants with FAS may die before the FAS is diagnosed.

Diabetes among American Indians

Before the 1930s diabetes was not frequently diagnosed among Native Americans. Over the past 25 years, however, diabetes has become highly prevalent among this population, and diabetes-related mortality rates are 2.4 times higher than for the general population. In 1997 dia-

TABLE 6.19

AIDS Cases by Sex, Age at Diagnosis, and Race/Ethnicity, Reported Through December 1999, United States

Male Age at diagnosis (years)	White, not Hispanic No.	(%)	Black, not Hispanic No.	(%)	Hispanic No.	(%)	Asian/Pacific Islander No.	(%)	American Indian/ Alaska Native No.	(%)	Total[1] No.	(%)
Under 5	517	(0)	2,093	(1)	758	(1)	16	(0)	12	(1)	3,400	(1)
5-12	338	(0)	451	(0)	278	(0)	9	(0)	5	(0)	1,083	(0)
13-19	840	(0)	829	(0)	483	(0)	25	(1)	21	(1)	2,201	(0)
20-24	7,573	(3)	6,785	(3)	4,083	(4)	166	(4)	78	(4)	18,711	(3)
25-29	37,490	(13)	24,474	(12)	15,884	(15)	587	(13)	318	(18)	78,846	(13)
30-34	67,733	(23)	41,979	(21)	25,995	(24)	1,024	(22)	466	(26)	137,333	(23)
35-39	66,370	(23)	45,576	(23)	24,239	(22)	1,020	(22)	385	(22)	137,789	(23)
40-44	48,405	(17)	36,041	(18)	17,069	(16)	806	(17)	265	(15)	102,729	(17)
45-49	29,209	(10)	20,997	(10)	9,504	(9)	490	(10)	107	(6)	60,387	(10)
50-54	15,766	(5)	10,744	(5)	5,044	(5)	263	(6)	46	(3)	31,910	(5)
55-59	8,536	(3)	5,893	(3)	2,796	(3)	158	(3)	29	(2)	17,440	(3)
60-64	4,722	(2)	3,232	(2)	1,542	(1)	65	(1)	18	(1)	9,591	(2)
65 or older	3,893	(1)	2,698	(1)	1,228	(1)	66	(1)	10	(1)	7,906	(1)
Male subtotal	**291,392**	**(100)**	**201,792**	**(100)**	**108,903**	**(100)**	**4,695**	**(100)**	**1,760**	**(100)**	**609,326**	**(100)**
Female **Age at diagnosis (years)**												
Under 5	482	(2)	2,080	(3)	758	(3)	15	(2)	13	(4)	3,353	(3)
5-12	180	(1)	480	(1)	211	(1)	8	(1)	–	–	882	(1)
13-19	247	(1)	1,001	(1)	264	(1)	7	(1)	4	(1)	1,524	(1)
20-24	1,581	(6)	4,097	(6)	1,441	(6)	37	(6)	29	(8)	7,193	(6)
25-29	4,440	(16)	10,295	(14)	3,935	(16)	89	(14)	54	(15)	18,829	(15)
30-34	6,097	(23)	15,551	(22)	5,751	(23)	119	(18)	86	(23)	27,656	(22)
35-39	5,372	(20)	15,605	(22)	5,073	(20)	123	(19)	76	(20)	26,287	(21)
40-44	3,536	(13)	10,805	(15)	3,316	(13)	96	(15)	43	(12)	17,812	(14)
45-49	1,882	(7)	5,341	(8)	1,820	(7)	63	(10)	30	(8)	9,159	(7)
50-54	1,078	(4)	2,646	(4)	1,004	(4)	27	(4)	16	(4)	4,776	(4)
55-59	692	(3)	1,460	(2)	625	(3)	21	(3)	12	(3)	2,811	(2)
60-64	451	(2)	868	(1)	317	(1)	24	(4)	5	(1)	1,667	(1)
65 or older	922	(3)	860	(1)	285	(1)	23	(4)	3	(1)	2,096	(2)
Female subtotal	**26,960**	**(100)**	**71,089**	**(100)**	**24,800**	**(100)**	**652**	**(100)**	**371**	**(100)**	**124,045**	**(100)**
Total[2]	**318,354**		**272,881**		**133,703**		**5,347**		**2,132**		**733,374**	

[1]Includes 784 males and 173 females whose race/ethnicity is unknown.
[2]Includes 3 persons whose sex is unknown.

SOURCE: *HIV/AIDS Surveillance Report*, Centers for Disease Control and Prevention, October 1999

betes was the fourth-leading cause of death among American Indians and Alaska Natives. (See Table 6.18.) Among the more than 500 federally recognized tribes of Native Americans, diabetes was found most often among the Pima Indians, who have the highest diabetes rate in the world.

Causes of Death

The causes of death among American Indians and Alaska Natives differ in many ways from that of the general American population. In 1997 unintentional injuries accounted for a far greater proportion of deaths among the AI/AN population. Cirrhosis of the liver caused by alcoholism was five times higher than the national rate. Suicide was the sixth-leading cause of death among AI/AN men, receiving a higher ranking than for any other race. (See Table 6.18 for the 10 leading causes of death for AI/AN men.)

In 1997 heart disease was the leading killer of AI/AN women. Unintentional injuries were the third-leading cause of death, while liver disease and cirrhosis ranked

sixth. In 1997 homicide and legal intervention were responsible for 62 female deaths and 189 male deaths. Diabetes claimed the lives of 291 males and 354 females. (See Table 6.18.) As indicated earlier, these causes of death are frequently associated with alcohol and drug abuse.

ASIAN AMERICAN HEALTH CARE

The Asian/Pacific Islander (API) diet is generally healthful; it is low in fat and cholesterol. The primary food source for most APIs is rice. Consumption of vegetables is relatively high; pork and fish are also commonly eaten. Dairy products are used less frequently. The traditional sources of calcium are soybean curd, sardines, or green, leafy vegetables. Many Asian Americans, however, pride themselves on their independence and self-sufficiency. Consequently, some are particularly reluctant to seek health services outside of their own community.

Infant Mortality

Infant mortality rates in the Asian community are generally lower than for any other race. In 1996 the rate

TABLE 6.20

AIDS Cases and Annual Rates per 100,000 Population, by Race/Ethnicity, Age Group and Sex, Reported in 1999, United States

| | Adults/adolescents | | | | | | Children <13 years | | Total | |
| | Males | | Females | | Total | | | | | |
Race/ethnicity	No.	Rate	No.	Rate	No.	Rate	No.	Rate	No.	Rate
White, not Hispanic	12,855	16.2	1,924	2.3	14,779	9.0	34	0.1	14,813	7.6
Black, not Hispanic	14,946	124.8	6,784	49.0	21,730	84.2	170	2.3	21,900	66.0
Hispanic	7,019	54.4	1,948	14.9	8,967	34.6	54	0.6	9,021	25.6
Asian/Pacific Islander	303	7.6	63	1.4	366	4.3	2	0.1	368	3.4
American Indian/Alaska Native	136	18.0	40	5.0	176	11.3	2	0.4	178	8.8
Total[1]	35,357	32.4	10,780	9.3	46,137	20.5	263	0.5	46,400	16.7

[1]Totals include 120 persons whose race/ethnicity is unknown.

SOURCE: *HIV/AIDS Surveillance Report*. Centers for Disease Control and Prevention, October 1999

was 5.8 deaths per 1,000 live births. Japanese Americans had the lowest infant mortality rate (4.2 per 1,000 births), but the Centers for Disease Control and Prevention warns that rates for groups with fewer than 10,000 births are considered unreliable. (See Table 6.5.)

In 1997 Asian/Pacific Islander women had relatively low rates of low-birth-weight babies (7.2 percent of live births). Chinese-origin women had the lowest rate (5 percent) and Filipino Americans had the highest rate (8.3 percent) of births that were below 2,500 grams. (See Table 6.4.) Asian American mothers are also less likely than any other group to be teenage mothers or unwed mothers. Maternal education and socioeconomic status are relatively high among many Asian Americans. In 1997, 82.1 percent of all Asian-origin mothers (and as high as 89.3 percent of Japanese-origin mothers) sought prenatal care during the first trimester. (See Table 6.2.)

Cancer

API women make up the only group for which cancer is the leading cause of death. Cancer incidence varies widely among Americans of Chinese, Japanese, Filipino, and Hawaiian descent, with Hawaiians having the second-highest incidence of cancer for minority populations. Hawaiians are most likely to have cancer of the breast and lung, while Japanese Americans are most likely to have stomach cancer. Chinese Americans have excess rates of cervical and nasopharyngeal (nose and throat) cancer. Among the Chinese and Japanese American populations, cancer is found more often among males than females. In 1997 the death rate for cancer among API males was 91.7 per 100,000 population. Among API females, the rate was 64.7 per 100,000. (See Table 6.17.)

Cardiovascular Disease

Heart disease is the leading cause of death for API men. Americans of Korean, Filipino, and Chinese descent generally have a lower risk of heart disease than Japanese Ameri-

cans. Stroke mortality rates in Asian-origin populations are generally similar to the rates for Whites, with strokes being the third-leading cause of death. Japanese American men, however, have very high stroke mortality rates.

Causes of Death

In 1997 the four most common causes of death for APIs were the same as those for Whites—heart disease, cancer, cerebrovascular disease, and accidents. (See Table 6.18.)

AIDS AND MINORITIES

Acquired immune deficiency syndrome (AIDS) is caused by a virus that affects the body's immune system, making it difficult to fight invasions from infection or other foreign substances. As a result, persons infected with the AIDS virus are subject to a number of opportunistic infections, primarily *Pneumocystis carinii* pneumonia (PCP) and Kaposi's sarcoma, a form of skin cancer. AIDS, which is caused by the human immunodeficiency virus (HIV), is not transmitted casually, but only through bodily fluids, such as blood and semen. The Centers for Disease Control and Prevention (CDC) reports only four methods of transmission: contaminated blood, sexual transmission, contaminated syringes from intravenous drug use, and perinatal (around the time of birth) transmission from a mother to her child or through breast milk.

Minorities have been especially hit hard by the AIDS epidemic. The CDC noted that, of the 711,344 cases reported through June 1999, 37 percent (262,317) were among non-Hispanic Blacks and 18 percent (129,555) were among Hispanics, proportions dramatically higher than their representation in the general population (12 percent and 8 percent, respectively). (See Table 6.19.)

The rate per 100,000 population shows how prevalent AIDS is in the Black and Hispanic populations. By year-end 1999, the rate of AIDS cases among non-Hispanic Black adults and adolescents (84.2 per 100,000 popula-

TABLE 6.21

Male Adult/Adolescent AIDS cases by Exposure Category and Race/Ethnicity, Reported Through June 1999, United States

	White, not Hispanic				Black, not Hispanic				Hispanic			
	1999		Cumulative total		1999		Cumulative total		1999		Cumulative total	
Exposure category	No.	(%)	No.	(%)	No.	(%)	No.	(%)	No.	(%)	No.	(%)
Men who have sex with men	8,106	(63)	216,564	(75)	4,511	(30)	74,434	(37)	2,584	(37)	45,867	(43)
Injecting drug use	1,485	(12)	26,856	(9)	3,770	(25)	68,491	(34)	1,899	(27)	38,338	(36)
Men who have sex with men and inject drugs	895	(7)	23,880	(8)	616	(4)	14,965	(8)	271	(4)	7,253	(7)
Hemophilia/coagulation disorder	108	(1)	3,725	(1)	19	(0)	551	(0)	9	(0)	424	(0)
Heterosexual contact:	476	(4)	5,181	(2)	1,736	(12)	15,121	(8)	615	(9)	5,986	(6)
Sex with injecting drug user	125		1,849		381		5,079		123		1,704	
Sex with person with hemophilia	2		29		7		18		1		10	
Sex with transfusion recipient with HIV infection	6		153		11		148		–		87	
Sex with HIV-infected person, risk not specified	343		3,150		1,337		9,876		491		4,185	
Receipt of blood transfusion, blood components, or tissue	63	(0)	3,133	(1)	42	(0)	1,028	(1)	25	(0)	574	(1)
Risk not reported or identified	1,722	(13)	11,198	(4)	4,252	(28)	24,658	(12)	1,616	(23)	9,425	(9)
Total	12,855	(100)	290,537	(100)	14,946	(100)	199,248	(100)	7,019	(100)	107,867	(100)

	Asian/Pacific Islander				American Indian/Alaska Native				Cumulative totals[2]			
	1999		Cumulative total		1999		Cumulative total		1999		Cumulative total	
Exposure category	No.	(%)	No.	(%)	No.	(%)	No.	(%)	No.	(%)	No.	(%)
Men who have sex with men	168	(55)	3,389	(73)	63	(46)	987	(57)	15,464	(44)	341,597	(56)
Injecting drug use	14	(5)	244	(5)	22	(16)	273	(16)	7,207	(20)	134,356	(22)
Men who have sex with men and inject drugs	5	(2)	172	(4)	16	(12)	295	(17)	1,806	(5)	46,582	(8)
Hemophilia/coagulation disorder	2	(1)	67	(1)	1	(1)	30	(2)	139	(0)	4,803	(1)
Heterosexual contact:	24	(8)	165	(4)	4	(3)	47	(3)	2,858	(8)	26,530	(4)
Sex with injecting drug user	6		45		–		14		635		8,696	
Sex with person with hemophilia	1		1		–		–		11		58	
Sex with transfusion recipient with HIV infection	1		8		1		2		19		398	
Sex with HIV-infected person, risk not specified	16		111		3		31		2,193		17,378	
Receipt of blood transfusion, blood components, or tissue	6	(2)	112	(2)	1	(1)	8	(0)	137	(0)	4,863	(1)
Risk not reported or identified	84	(28)	521	(11)	29	(21)	103	(6)	7,746	(22)	46,112	(8)
Total	303	(100)	4,670	(100)	136	(100)	1,743	(100)	35,357	(100)	604,843	(100)

[2]Includes 778 men whose race/ethnicity is unknown.

SOURCE: *HIV/AIDS Surveillance Report*. Centers for Disease Control and Prevention, October 1999

tion) was over nine times that of non-Hispanic Whites (9 per 100,000), while the Hispanic rate (34.6 per 100,000 population) was nearly four times higher than the non-Hispanic White rate. (See Table 6.20.)

By year-end 1999, the pediatric AIDS (younger than age 13) cases were far fewer than the adult numbers, but the non-Hispanic Black pediatric rate (2.3 per 100,000) was over 20 times higher than the non-Hispanic White rate (.1 per 100,000). The Hispanic pediatric rate (.6 per 100,000) was six times higher than the non-Hispanic White rate. (See Table 6.20.)

Although everyone can become infected with AIDS in the same ways, the proportions of the methods of transmission differ considerably by race. For non-Hispanic White men who have AIDS, 75 percent resulted

from homosexual contact and 9 percent from intravenous drug use. While most non-Hispanic Black (38 percent) and Hispanic (43 percent) men acquired AIDS through homosexual activity, a significant proportion of Black men (35 percent) and Hispanic men (36 percent) with AIDS contracted the disease through intravenous drug use. (See Table 6.21.)

Women of all racial and ethnic groups except Asians and Pacific Islanders seemed to contract AIDS in similar ways. More than half (58 percent) of all non-Hispanic White women with AIDS were either intravenous drug users or had partners who were drug users, as were 57 percent of all non-Hispanic Black women and 63 percent of all Hispanic women with AIDS. Non-Hispanic Black women accounted for 56.9 percent and non-Hispanic

TABLE 6.22

Female Adult/Adolescent AIDS Cases by Exposure Category and Race/Ethnicity Reported Through June 1999, United States

Exposure category	White, not Hispanic 1999 No.	White, not Hispanic 1999 (%)	White, not Hispanic Cumulative total No.	White, not Hispanic Cumulative total (%)	Black, not Hispanic 1999 No.	Black, not Hispanic 1999 (%)	Black, not Hispanic Cumulative total No.	Black, not Hispanic Cumulative total (%)	Hispanic 1999 No.	Hispanic 1999 (%)	Hispanic Cumulative total No.	Hispanic Cumulative total (%)
Injecting drug use	646	(34)	11,074	(42)	1,718	(25)	29,059	(42)	539	(28)	9,613	(40)
Hemophilia/coagulation disorder	4	(0)	102	(0)	5	(0)	108	(0)	3	(0)	53	(0)
Heterosexual contact:	762	(40)	10,528	(40)	2,565	(38)	25,719	(38)	906	(47)	11,222	(47)
Sex with injecting drug user	249		4,294		628		9,916		267		5,159	
Sex with bisexual male	78		1,452		72		1,311		23		513	
Sex with person with hemophilia	8		281		7		80		3		39	
Sex with transfusion recipient with HIV infection	7		300		9		162		5		96	
Sex with HIV-infected person, risk not specified	420		4,201		1,849		14,250		608		5,415	
Receipt of blood transfusion, blood components, or tissue	25	(1)	1,789	(7)	75	(1)	1,230	(2)	15	(1)	536	(2)
Risk not reported or identified[1]	487	(25)	2,805	(11)	2,421	(36)	12,413	(18)	485	(25)	2,407	(10)
Total	**1,924**	**(100)**	**26,298**	**(100)**	**6,784**	**(100)**	**68,529**	**(100)**	**1,948**	**(100)**	**23,831**	**(100)**

Exposure category	Asian/Pacific Islander 1999 No.	Asian/Pacific Islander 1999 (%)	Asian/Pacific Islander Cumulative total No.	Asian/Pacific Islander Cumulative total (%)	American Indian/Alaska Native 1999 No.	American Indian/Alaska Native 1999 (%)	American Indian/Alaska Native Cumulative total No.	American Indian/Alaska Native Cumulative total (%)	Cumulative totals[2] 1999 No.	Cumulative totals[2] 1999 (%)	Cumulative totals[2] Cumulative total No.	Cumulative totals[2] Cumulative total (%)
Injecting drug use	7	(11)	107	(17)	12	(30)	164	(46)	2,931	(27)	50,073	(42)
Hemophilia/coagulation disorder	–	–	5	(1)	–	–	2	(1)	12	(0)	272	(0)
Heterosexual contact:	32	(51)	310	(49)	12	(30)	127	(35)	4,281	(40)	47,946	(40)
Sex with injecting drug user	4		80		5		62		1,155		19,523	
Sex with bisexual male	3		69		1		17		177		3,368	
Sex with person with hemophilia	–		5		1		2		19		407	
Sex with transfusion recipient with HIV infection	–		19		2		3		23		581	
Sex with HIV-infected person, risk not specified	25		137		3		43		2,907		24,067	
Receipt of blood transfusion, blood components, or tissue	3	(5)	96	(15)	1	(3)	14	(4)	119	(1)	3,668	(3)
Risk not reported or identified	21	(33)	111	(18)	15	(38)	51	(14)	3,437	(32)	17,851	(15)
Total	**63**	**(100)**	**629**	**(100)**	**40**	**(100)**	**358**	**(100)**	**10,780**	**(100)**	**119,810**	**(100)**

[2]Includes 165 women whose race/ethnicity is unknown.

SOURCE: *HIV/AIDS Surveillance Report.* Centers for Disease Control and Prevention, October 1999

White women accounted for 22.2 percent of all female AIDS cases. Hispanic women comprised 20 percent of all cases among women. Asians/Pacific Islanders (.5 percent) and American Indian/Alaska Natives (.3 percent) made up a very small proportion of total female AIDS cases. (See Table 6.22.)

Many minority women pass this fatal disease on to their children at birth. According to the CDC, by June 1999, 81.5 percent of all children (under age 13) with AIDS were either non-Hispanic Black or Hispanic. Ninety-six percent of non-Hispanic Black children and 92 percent of Hispanic children with AIDS were infected by their mothers. (See Table 6.23.)

TABLE 6.23

Pediatric AIDS Cases by Exposure Category and Race/Ethnicity Reported Through June 1999, United States

Exposure category	White, not Hispanic				Black, not Hispanic				Hispanic			
	1999		Cumulative total		1999		Cumulative total		1999		Cumulative total	
	No.	(%)	No.	(%)	No.	(%)	No.	(%)	No.	(%)	No.	(%)
Hemophilia/coagulation disorder	1	(3)	158	(10)	–	–	34	(1)	1	(2)	38	(2)
Mother with/at risk for HIV infection:	28	(82)	1,144	(75)	154	(91)	4,881	(96)	48	(89)	1,846	(92)
Injecting drug use	9		477		39		1,880		17		737	
Sex with injecting drug user	7		223		18		718		8		489	
Sex with bisexual male	1		66		2		63		1		39	
Sex with person with hemophilia	–		17		1		7		1		8	
Sex with transfusion recipient with HIV infection	–		8		–		8		–		9	
Sex with HIV-infected person, risk not specified	3		140		32		777		9		254	
Receipt of blood transfusion, blood components, or tissue	–		42		2		77		–		33	
Has HIV infection, risk not specified	8		171		60		1,351		12		277	
Receipt of blood transfusion, blood components, or tissue	1	(3)	189	(12)	1	(1)	89	(2)	–	–	91	(5)
Risk not reported or identified[1]	4	(12)	26	(2)	15	(9)	100	(2)	5	(9)	30	(1)
Total	34	(100)	1,517	(100)	170	(100)	5,104	(100)	54	(100)	2,005	(100)

Exposure category	Asian/Pacific Islander				American Indian/ Alaska Native				Cumulative totals[2]			
	1999		Cumulative total		1999		Cumulative total		1999		Cumulative total	
	No.	(%)	No.	(%)	No.	(%)	No.	(%)	No.	(%)	No.	(%)
Hemophilia/coagulation disorder	–	–	3	(6)	1	(50)	2	(7)	3	(1)	235	(3)
Mother with/at risk for HIV infection:	–	–	31	(65)	1	(50)	27	(90)	232	(88)	7,943	(91)
Injecting drug use	–		4		1		13		66		3,116	
Sex with injecting drug user	–		5		–		7		33		1,443	
Sex with bisexual male	–		2		–		–		5		171	
Sex with person with hemophilia	–		–		–		–		2		32	
Sex with transfusion recipient with HIV infection	–		–		–		–		–		25	
Sex with HIV-infected person, risk not specified	–		9		–		3		44		1,185	
Receipt of blood transfusion, blood components, or tissue	–		1		–		–		2		153	
Has HIV infection, risk not specified	–		10		–		4		80		1,818	
Receipt of blood transfusion, blood components, or tissue	–	–	10	(21)	–	–	–	–	2	(1)	379	(4)
Risk not reported or identified	2	(100)	4	(8)	–	–	1	(3)	26	(10)	161	(2)
Total	2	(100)	48	(100)	2	(100)	30	(100)	263	(100)	8,718	(100)

[2]Includes 14 children whose race/ethnicity is unknown.

SOURCE: *HIV/AIDS Surveillance Report*, Centers for Disease Control and Prevention, October 1999

CHAPTER 7

MINORITIES AND EDUCATION

STUDENT DEMOGRAPHICS

In the United States, in the fall of 1997 about 52 million young people were enrolled in kindergarten through grade 12—37.6 million in elementary school (grades K through 8), and 14.4 million in high school (grades 9 through 12). (See Table 7.1.) In 1986 approximately 30 percent of the total school population were Hispanic, Black, or a member of another racial group other than White; by 1995 this group had grown to 36.5 percent. In the 11 years between 1986 and 1997, the Hispanic proportion of school enrollment grew from 9.9 percent to 14.4 percent of all students, while those of "other races" increased from 3.7 percent to 5.1 percent. The Black proportion of the school population rose from 16.1 percent to 17 percent, while the White proportion declined from 70.4 percent to 63.5 percent. (See Table 7.2.)

In 1997, 14.3 million students were enrolled in colleges or graduate schools. About 73 percent were non-Hispanic White; 11 percent, non-Hispanic Black; 8.6 percent, Hispanic; 6.1 percent, Asian or Pacific Islander; and 1 percent, American Indian/Alaskan Native. (See Table 7.3.)

EDUCATIONAL ATTAINMENT

In the United States, education is often presented as a way out of poverty to a better life. Many observers believe education is the key to narrowing the economic gap between the races. Unfortunately, minority students are generally more likely to drop out of school than their White counterparts.

Progress for Black Students

Black students make up nearly 17 percent of the nation's public-school population, and their proportion is expected to grow into the next century. They are currently about 90 percent of the students in the school districts of Atlanta, Georgia; Detroit, Michigan; and Washington,

DC; and nearly 40 percent of the school population in New York City.

While the average academic performance of Black children, in general, remains below that of Whites, school attendance and high school graduation among Blacks have risen considerably. In 1890, while two-thirds of White school-age youth attended school, only about one-third of Black school-age youth did. The difference has narrowed over the years until, by the mid-1970s, a similar proportion of Black and White school-age children were enrolled in school.

Blacks made notable progress in attaining an education during the 1980s. In 1980, 51.2 percent of Black males 25 years and older had at least completed high school; by 1998 the proportion had increased to 75.4 percent. In comparison, 72.4 percent of White males in 1980 and 87.1 percent in 1998 had at least completed high school. Far fewer Blacks, however, continue past high school to get a bachelor's degree or more. In 1998, 14 percent of Black males and 15.5 percent of Black females did, compared to 29.3 percent of White males and 24.1 percent of White females. (See Table 7.4.)

Hispanic Educational Attainment

Although Hispanics have made modest gains in education in the past decade, low educational attainment has been a major hindrance to their economic advancement in the United States. In 1980 about 44.9 percent of Hispanics age 25 years and over had completed four years or more of high school. In 1998 just over one-half (55.7 percent) had, compared to 87.1 percent of White non-Hispanics and 76.4 percent of Blacks in the same age group. (See Table 7.4.)

Non-Hispanic Whites (26.6 percent) and non-Hispanic Blacks (14.8 percent) age 25 and older were much more likely to have completed four or more years of college than Hispanics (11 percent). (See Table 7.4.)

TABLE 7.1

Enrollment in Educational Institutions, by Level and Control of Institution: Fall 1980–Fall 2005

[In thousands]

Level of instruction and type of control	Fall 1980	Fall 1985	Fall 1990	Fall 1991	Fall 1992	Fall 1993	Fall 1994	Fall 1995	Fall 1996	Fall 1997[1]	Projected fall 1998	Projected fall 1999	Projected fall 2000	Projected fall 2005
1	2	3	4	5	6	7	8	9	10	11	12	13	14	15
All levels	58,305	57,226	60,267	61,605	62,686	63,241	63,986	64,764	65,694	66,334	67,376	68,096	68,611	70,003
Public	50,335	48,901	52,061	53,356	54,208	54,654	55,245	55,933	56,701	57,273	58,234	58,846	59,283	60,511
Private	7,971	8,325	8,206	8,248	8,478	8,587	8,741	8,831	8,993	9,060	9,142	9,250	9,328	9,523
Elementary and secondary education[2]	46,208	44,979	46,448	47,246	48,198	48,936	49,707	50,502	51,394	51,987	52,768	53,215	53,539	54,477
Public	40,877	39,422	41,217	42,047	42,823	43,465	44,111	44,840	45,611	46,127	46,844	47,244	47,533	48,392
Private	5,331	5,557	5,232	5,199	5,375	5,471	[3]5,596	[3]5,662	[3]5,783	[3]5,860	5,924	5,971	6,006	6,086
Grades K-8[4]	31,639	31,229	33,973	34,580	35,300	35,784	36,258	36,806	37,250	37,625	38,110	38,323	38,521	38,348
Public	27,647	27,034	29,878	30,506	31,088	31,504	31,898	32,341	32,764	33,073	33,514	33,701	33,875	33,723
Private	3,992	4,195	4,095	[3]4,074	[3]4,212	[3]4,280	[3]4,360	4,465	[3]4,486	[3]4,552	4,597	4,622	4,646	4,625
Grades 9-12	14,570	13,750	12,475	12,666	12,898	13,152	13,449	13,697	14,144	14,362	14,658	14,891	15,018	16,129
Public	13,231	12,388	11,338	11,541	11,735	11,961	12,213	12,500	12,847	13,054	13,330	13,543	13,658	14,669
Private	1,339	1,362	1,137	[3]1,125	[3]1,163	[3]1,191	[3]1,236	[3]1,197	[3]1,297	[3]1,308	1,327	1,348	1,360	1,461
Higher education[5]	12,097	12,247	13,819	14,359	14,487	14,305	14,279	14,262	14,300	14,345	14,608	14,881	15,072	15,556
Public	9,457	9,479	10,845	11,310	11,385	11,189	11,134	11,092	11,090	11,146	11,390	11,602	11,750	12,119
Undergraduate[6]	8,442	8,477	9,710	10,148	10,216	10,012	9,945	9,904	9,905	9,958	10,193	10,398	10,548	10,914
First-professional	114	112	112	111	111	114	114	115	116	118	109	108	107	109
Graduate[7]	901	890	1,023	1,050	1,058	1,064	1,075	1,074	1,068	1,070	1,089	1,096	1,094	1,096
Private	2,640	2,768	2,974	3,049	3,103	3,116	3,145	3,169	3,210	3,199	3,218	3,279	3,322	3,437
Undergraduate[6]	2,033	2,120	2,250	2,291	2,321	2,312	2,317	2,328	2,354	2,340	2,385	2,444	2,489	2,601
First-professional	163	162	162	169	170	179	181	183	181	178	171	171	170	171
Graduate[7]	443	486	563	589	611	625	647	659	675	681	661	665	664	665

[1]Higher education data are preliminary.

[2]Includes enrollments in local public school systems and in most private schools (religiously affiliated and nonsectarian). Excludes subcollegiate departments of institutions of higher education, residential schools for exceptional children, federal schools, and home-schooled children. Based on Department estimates, the home-schooled children numbered approximately 800,000 to 1,000,000 in 1997–98. Excludes preprimary pupils in schools that do not offer first grade or above.

[3]Estimated.

[4]Includes kindergarten and some nursery school pupils.

[5]Includes full-time and part-time students enrolled in degree-credit and nondegree-credit programs in universities, other 4-year colleges, and 2-year colleges.

[6]Includes unclassified students below the baccalaureate level.

[7]Includes unclassified postbaccalaureate students.

NOTE.—Higher education enrollment projections are based on the middle alternative projections published by the National Center for Education Statistics. Because of rounding, details may not add to totals. Some data have been revised from previously published figures.

SOURCE: *Digest of Education Statistics 1999*. National Center for Education Statistics, May 2000

TABLE 7.2

Enrollment in Public Elementary and Secondary Schools, by Race or Ethnicity, United States, Fall 1986–Fall 1997

State or other area	Total	White[1]	Black[1]	Hispanic	Asian or Pacific Islander	American Indian/ Alaskan Native	Total	White[1]	Black[1]	Hispanic	Asian or Pacific Islander	American Indian/ Alaskan Native
				Percent distribution, fall 1986						Percent distribution, fall 1997		
1	2	3	4	5	6	7	8	9	10	11	12	13
United States	**100.0**	**70.4**	**16.1**	**9.9**	**2.8**	**0.9**	**100.0**	**63.5**	**17.0**	**14.4**	**3.9**	**1.2**
Alabama	100.0	62.0	37.0	0.1	0.4	0.5	100.0	61.7	36.0	0.8	0.7	0.8
Alaska	100.0	65.7	4.3	1.7	3.3	25.1	100.0	62.8	4.7	3.0	4.8	24.8
Arizona	100.0	62.2	4.0	26.4	1.3	6.1	100.0	56.0	4.4	30.8	1.8	7.0
Arkansas	100.0	74.7	24.2	0.4	0.6	0.2	100.0	73.1	23.5	2.2	0.8	0.4
California	100.0	53.7	9.0	27.5	9.1	0.7	100.0	38.8	8.8	40.5	11.1	0.9
Colorado	100.0	78.7	4.5	13.7	2.0	1.0	100.0	71.3	5.6	19.3	2.7	1.1
Connecticut	100.0	77.2	12.1	8.9	1.5	0.2	100.0	71.5	13.7	12.1	2.5	0.2
Delaware	100.0	68.3	27.7	2.5	1.4	0.2	100.0	63.2	30.1	4.6	1.9	0.2
District of Columbia	100.0	4.0	91.1	3.9	0.9	0.1	100.0	4.0	87.0	7.5	1.5	(2)
Florida	100.0	65.4	23.7	9.5	1.2	0.2	100.0	56.2	25.4	16.4	1.8	0.2
Georgia	100.0	60.7	37.9	0.6	0.8	(2)	100.0	57.1	38.0	2.9	1.9	0.1
Hawaii	100.0	23.5	2.3	2.2	71.7	0.3	100.0	21.6	2.6	4.7	70.7	0.4
Idaho	100.0	92.6	0.3	4.9	0.8	1.3	100.0	87.6	0.7	9.2	1.2	1.3
Illinois	100.0	69.8	18.7	9.2	2.3	0.1	100.0	62.0	21.3	13.4	3.1	0.2
Indiana	100.0	88.7	9.0	1.7	0.5	0.1	100.0	85.1	11.3	2.6	0.8	0.2
Iowa	100.0	94.6	3.0	0.9	1.2	0.3	100.0	91.8	3.6	2.6	1.6	0.5
Kansas	100.0	85.6	7.6	4.4	1.9	0.6	100.0	81.3	8.6	7.0	2.0	1.1
Kentucky	100.0	89.2	10.2	0.1	0.5	(2)	100.0	88.6	10.3	0.5	0.5	0.1
Louisiana	100.0	56.5	41.3	0.8	1.1	0.3	100.0	50.2	46.7	1.2	1.3	0.6
Maine	100.0	98.3	0.5	0.2	0.8	0.2	100.0	97.1	0.9	0.5	0.9	0.6
Maryland	100.0	59.7	35.3	1.7	3.1	0.2	100.0	55.9	36.1	3.7	4.0	0.3
Massachusetts	100.0	83.7	7.4	6.0	2.8	0.1	100.0	77.5	8.5	9.7	4.1	0.2
Michigan	100.0	76.4	19.8	1.8	1.2	0.8	100.0	75.6	18.8	2.9	1.6	1.0
Minnesota	100.0	93.9	2.1	0.9	1.7	1.5	100.0	85.5	5.6	2.5	4.4	2.0
Mississippi	100.0	43.9	55.5	0.1	0.4	0.1	100.0	47.8	51.0	0.4	0.6	0.1
Missouri	100.0	83.4	14.9	0.7	0.8	0.2	100.0	80.7	16.7	1.3	1.1	0.3
Montana	100.0	92.7	0.3	0.9	0.5	5.5	100.0	87.1	0.6	1.4	0.8	10.0
Nebraska	100.0	91.4	4.4	2.4	0.8	1.0	100.0	85.7	6.2	5.3	1.4	1.5
Nevada	100.0	77.4	9.6	7.5	3.2	2.3	100.0	63.2	9.7	20.5	4.8	1.9
New Hampshire	100.0	98.0	0.7	0.5	0.8	0.1	100.0	96.3	1.0	1.4	1.1	0.2
New Jersey	100.0	69.1	17.4	10.7	2.7	0.1	100.0	61.9	18.3	14.0	5.7	0.2
New Mexico	100.0	43.1	2.3	45.1	0.8	8.7	100.0	38.0	2.4	48.0	1.0	10.6
New York	100.0	68.4	16.5	12.3	2.7	0.2	100.0	55.9	20.4	17.8	5.4	0.5
North Carolina	100.0	68.4	28.9	0.4	0.6	1.7	100.0	63.2	31.0	2.7	1.6	1.5
North Dakota	100.0	92.4	0.6	1.1	0.8	5.0	100.0	88.9	0.9	1.1	0.8	8.3
Ohio	100.0	83.1	15.0	1.0	0.7	0.1	100.0	81.7	15.6	1.5	1.0	0.1
Oklahoma	100.0	79.0	7.8	1.6	1.0	10.6	100.0	68.1	10.6	4.5	1.3	15.5
Oregon	100.0	89.8	2.2	3.9	2.4	1.7	100.0	83.7	2.6	8.1	3.5	2.1
Pennsylvania	100.0	84.4	12.6	1.8	1.2	0.1	100.0	79.7	14.5	3.9	1.8	0.1
Rhode Island	100.0	87.9	5.6	3.7	2.4	0.3	100.0	77.2	7.5	11.5	3.4	0.5
South Carolina	100.0	54.6	44.5	0.2	0.6	0.1	100.0	55.7	42.3	1.0	0.8	0.2
South Dakota	100.0	90.6	0.5	0.6	0.7	7.6	100.0	82.9	1.0	0.9	0.8	14.4
Tennessee	100.0	76.5	22.6	0.2	0.6	(2)	100.0	74.0	23.7	1.1	1.0	0.1
Texas	100.0	51.0	14.4	32.5	2.0	0.2	100.0	45.0	14.4	37.9	2.4	0.3
Utah	100.0	93.7	0.4	3.0	1.5	1.5	100.0	88.7	0.8	6.5	2.5	1.5
Vermont	100.0	98.4	0.3	0.2	0.6	0.6	100.0	97.1	0.9	0.4	1.1	0.5
Virginia	100.0	72.6	23.7	1.0	2.6	0.1	100.0	65.5	27.0	3.6	3.6	0.2
Washington	100.0	84.5	4.2	3.8	5.1	2.3	100.0	76.8	4.9	8.6	6.9	2.8
West Virginia	100.0	95.9	3.7	0.1	0.3	(2)	100.0	95.1	4.1	0.5	0.3	0.1
Wisconsin	100.0	86.6	8.9	1.9	1.7	1.0	100.0	82.2	9.8	3.6	3.0	1.4
Wyoming	100.0	90.7	0.9	5.9	0.6	1.9	100.0	88.6	1.1	6.6	0.8	2.9

While a language barrier handicaps many Hispanic students, this does not completely explain their poor academic progress. For example, Cuban-origin students are most likely to speak Spanish at home, yet with the exception of those who are of "other Hispanic origin," they have the highest educational achievement levels among the Hispanic-origin population. Cuban-origin students are also more likely to have greater economic advantages and other benefits of a middle- or upper-class background, which often outweigh the difficulty of having to learn English as a second language.

Asian American Attainment

In recent years, many Asian American students have accomplished stunning academic achievements. It is not

TABLE 7.2

Enrollment in Public Elementary and Secondary Schools, by Race or Ethnicity, United States, Fall 1986–Fall 1997 [CONTINUED]

	Percent distribution, fall 1986						Percent distribution, fall 1997					
State or other area	Total	White[1]	Black[1]	Hispanic	Asian or Pacific Islander	American Indian/ Alaskan Native	Total	White[1]	Black[1]	Hispanic	Asian or Pacific Islander	American Indian/ Alaskan Native
1	2	3	4	5	6	7	8	9	10	11	12	13
Outlying areas												
American Samoa	—	—	—	—	—	—	100.0	—	—	—	100.0	—
Guam	—	—	—	—	—	—	100.0	3.1	0.6	0.3	95.9	0.1
Northern Marianas	—	—	—	—	—	—	100.0	0.9	—	—	99.1	—
Puerto Rico	—	—	—	—	—	—	100.0	—	—	100.0	—	—
Virgin Islands	—	—	—	—	—	—	100.0	0.9	84.8	14.0	0.3	(2)

[1]Excludes persons of Hispanic origin.
[2]Less than 0.05 percent.
—Data not available.
NOTE.—The 1986–87 data were derived from the 1986 Elementary and Secondary School Civil Rights sample survey of public school districts. Because of rounding, details may not add to totals.

SOURCE: *Digest of Education Statistics 1999.* National Center for Education Statistics, May 2000

---

unusual for high school graduations to have students with Asian names as valedictorians and salutatorians. Educators often point with pride to these high-achieving students, who have often overcome both language and cultural barriers.

In 1994, 85 percent of adult Asian Americans age 25 and over had completed high school, the same proportion as non-Hispanic Whites. Even more significant was Asian American performance at the college and university levels. In 1994, 41 percent of Asian Americans had earned at least a bachelor's degree, nearly double the non-Hispanic White rate of 24 percent.

In 1999, 84.6 percent of Asian Americans age 25 years and over had completed high school, a lower proportion than non-Hispanic Whites (87.7 percent), but slightly higher than all races and ethnic groups as a whole (83.4 percent). Asian Americans (42 percent) were more likely than non-Hispanic Whites (27.7 percent) to have a bachelor's degree or higher. (See Table 7.5.)

Native American Attainment

Native Americans—which includes American Indians, Eskimos, and Aleuts—have the lowest educational attainment of all minority groups. In 1990, 65.5 percent of Native Americans 25 years and over had completed high school, compared to 75 percent of the total population. Only 9 percent of Native Americans had been graduated from college, compared to 20 percent of the total population, in 1990. (See Figure 7.1.)

While poverty and low educational attainment tend to limit the number of Native Americans who continue on to post-secondary education, the number being graduated from high school has improved significantly. High school

graduation increased from 51 percent in 1970 to 56 percent in 1980 to 65.5 percent in 1990.

NATIONAL ASSESSMENT OF EDUCATIONAL PROGRESS

The National Assessment of Educational Progress (NAEP) is a series of reading, writing, and mathematics tests given to fourth-, eighth-, and twelfth-grade students. The National Institute of Education, under a grant to the Educational Testing Service, funds NAEP. Student performance is measured on a scale from 0 to 500, and the results are reported according to three achievement levels—basic, proficient, and advanced.

Reading Performance

The ability to read is fundamental to virtually all aspects of education. When students cannot read well, they usually cannot succeed in other subject areas and will eventually have additional problems in a society requiring increasingly sophisticated job skills. In 1996 the NAEP tested the reading performance of students in grades 4, 8, and 12 in public and private schools. They assessed students on:

• Initial understanding (comprehension of the overall or general meaning)

• Development of an interpretation (ability to extend the ideas in the text by making inferences and connections)

• Personal response (ability to make connections between the text and the student's own experience)

• Critical stance (ability to judge and determine how the author crafted a text)

TABLE 7.3

Total Fall Enrollment in Institutions of Higher Education, by Level of Study, Sex, and Race/Ethnicity of Student, 1976–1997

Level of study, sex, and race/ethnicity of student	Institutions of higher education, in thousands						Degree-granting institutions, in thousands[1]		Percentage distribution of students[2] — Institutions of higher education						Percentage distribution — Degree-granting institutions[1]	
	1976	1980	1990	1995	1996	1997	1996	1997	1976	1980	1990	1995	1996	1997	1996	1997
1	2	3	4	5	6	7	8	9	10	11	12	13	14	15	16	17
All students																
Total	10,985.6	12,086.8	13,818.6	14,261.8	14,300.3	14,345.4	14,367.5	14,502.3	100.0	100.0	100.0	100.0	100.0	100.0	100.0	100.0
White, non-Hispanic	9,076.1	9,833.0	10,722.5	10,311.2	10,226.0	10,160.9	10,263.9	10,266.1	84.3	83.5	79.9	74.7	73.9	73.2	73.8	73.1
Total minority	1,690.8	1,948.8	2,704.7	3,496.2	3,609.3	3,723.2	3,637.4	3,771.2	15.7	16.5	20.1	25.3	26.1	26.8	26.2	26.9
Black, non-Hispanic	1,033.0	1,106.8	1,247.0	1,473.7	1,499.4	1,532.8	1,505.6	1,551.0	9.6	9.4	9.3	10.7	10.8	11.0	10.8	11.0
Hispanic	383.8	471.7	782.4	1,093.8	1,152.2	1,200.1	1,166.1	1,218.5	3.6	4.0	5.8	7.9	8.3	8.6	8.4	8.7
Asian or Pacific Islander	197.9	286.4	572.4	797.4	823.6	851.5	828.2	859.2	1.8	2.4	4.3	5.8	6.0	6.1	6.0	6.1
American Indian/Alaskan Native	76.1	83.9	102.8	131.3	134.0	138.8	137.6	142.5	0.7	0.7	0.8	1.0	1.0	1.0	1.0	1.0
Nonresident alien	218.7	305.0	391.5	454.4	464.9	461.3	466.3	465.0	—	—	—	—	—	—	—	—
Men	5,794.4	5,868.1	6,283.9	6,342.5	6,344.0	6,330.0	6,352.8	6,396.0	100.0	100.0	100.0	100.0	100.0	100.0	100.0	100.0
White, non-Hispanic	4,813.7	4,772.9	4,861.0	4,594.1	4,553.0	4,504.8	4,552.2	4,548.8	85.3	84.4	80.5	75.6	74.9	74.3	74.8	74.2
Total minority	826.6	884.4	1,176.6	1,484.2	1,524.3	1,562.2	1,533.4	1,582.3	14.7	15.6	19.5	24.4	25.1	25.7	25.2	25.8
Black, non-Hispanic	469.9	463.7	484.7	555.9	563.6	572.5	564.1	579.8	8.3	8.2	8.0	9.1	9.3	9.4	9.3	9.5
Hispanic	209.7	231.6	353.9	480.2	501.3	518.1	506.6	525.8	3.7	4.1	5.9	7.9	8.2	8.5	8.3	8.6
Asian or Pacific Islander	108.4	151.3	294.9	393.3	403.6	414.0	405.5	417.7	1.9	2.7	4.9	6.5	6.6	6.8	6.7	6.8
American Indian/Alaskan Native	38.5	37.8	43.1	54.8	55.7	57.6	57.2	59.0	0.7	0.7	0.7	0.9	0.9	0.9	0.9	1.0
Nonresident alien	154.1	210.8	246.3	264.3	266.7	262.9	267.2	264.9	—	—	—	—	—	—	—	—
Women	5,191.2	6,218.7	7,534.7	7,919.2	7,956.3	8,015.5	8,014.7	8,106.3	100.0	100.0	100.0	100.0	100.0	100.0	100.0	100.0
White, non-Hispanic	4,262.4	5,060.1	5,861.5	5,717.2	5,673.1	5,656.1	5,711.7	5,717.4	83.1	82.6	79.3	74.0	73.1	72.4	73.1	72.3
Total minority	864.2	1,064.4	1,528.1	2,012.0	2,085.0	2,161.0	2,104.0	2,188.9	16.9	17.4	20.7	26.0	26.9	27.6	26.9	27.7
Black, non-Hispanic	563.1	643.0	762.3	917.8	935.8	960.2	941.4	971.3	11.0	10.5	10.3	11.9	12.1	12.3	12.0	12.3
Hispanic	174.1	240.1	428.5	613.7	650.9	682.0	659.5	692.7	3.4	3.9	5.8	7.9	8.4	8.7	8.4	8.8
Asian or Pacific Islander	89.4	135.2	277.5	404.1	420.0	437.4	422.6	441.5	1.7	2.2	3.8	5.2	5.4	5.6	5.4	5.6
American Indian/Alaskan Native	37.6	46.1	59.7	76.5	78.2	81.3	80.4	83.4	0.7	0.8	0.8	1.0	1.0	1.0	1.0	1.1
Nonresident alien	64.6	94.2	145.2	190.1	198.2	198.4	199.0	200.1	—	—	—	—	—	—	—	—
Full-time	6,703.6	7,088.9	7,821.0	8,128.8	8,213.5	8,322.4	8,303.0	8,438.1	100.0	100.0	100.0	100.0	100.0	100.0	100.0	100.0
White, non-Hispanic	5,512.6	5,717.0	6,016.5	5,833.8	5,847.5	5,886.7	5,906.1	5,960.1	84.2	83.4	79.9	74.9	74.4	73.9	74.3	73.8
Total minority	1,030.9	1,137.5	1,514.9	1,955.3	2,017.2	2,079.8	2,046.8	2,118.7	15.8	16.6	20.1	25.1	25.6	26.1	25.7	26.2
Black, non-Hispanic	659.9	685.6	718.9	840.4	861.0	880.7	871.9	896.6	10.1	10.0	9.5	10.8	10.9	11.1	11.0	11.1
Hispanic	211.1	247.0	394.7	553.2	577.1	599.6	588.8	614.0	3.2	3.6	5.2	7.1	7.3	7.5	7.4	7.6
Asian or Pacific Islander	117.7	162.0	347.4	488.7	503.9	520.6	508.5	526.6	1.8	2.4	4.6	6.3	6.4	6.5	6.4	6.5
American Indian/Alaskan Native	43.0	43.0	54.4	73.0	75.2	79.0	77.5	81.5	0.7	0.6	0.7	0.9	1.0	1.0	1.0	1.0
Nonresident alien	160.0	234.4	289.6	339.7	348.7	355.9	350.1	359.2	—	—	—	—	—	—	—	—
Part-time	4,282.1	4,997.9	5,997.7	6,133.0	6,086.8	6,023.1	6,064.6	6,064.3	100.0	100.0	100.0	100.0	100.0	100.0	100.0	100.0
White, non-Hispanic	3,563.5	4,116.0	4,706.0	4,477.4	4,378.5	4,274.3	4,357.8	4,306.0	84.4	83.5	79.8	74.4	73.3	72.2	73.3	72.3
Total minority	659.9	811.3	1,189.8	1,540.9	1,592.1	1,643.4	1,590.6	1,652.5	15.6	16.5	20.2	25.6	26.7	27.8	26.7	27.7
Black, non-Hispanic	373.8	421.2	528.7	633.3	638.4	652.1	633.6	654.5	8.9	8.5	9.0	10.5	10.7	11.0	10.7	11.0
Hispanic	172.7	224.8	387.7	540.7	575.1	600.6	577.3	604.5	4.1	4.6	6.6	9.0	9.6	10.1	9.7	10.1
Asian or Pacific Islander	80.2	124.4	225.1	308.6	319.7	330.9	319.6	332.6	1.9	2.5	3.8	5.1	5.4	5.6	5.4	5.6
American Indian/Alaskan Native	33.1	40.9	48.4	58.3	58.8	59.9	60.0	61.0	0.8	0.8	0.8	1.0	1.0	1.0	1.0	1.0
Nonresident alien	58.7	70.6	101.8	114.7	116.2	105.4	116.2	105.8	—	—	—	—	—	—	—	—

TABLE 7.3

Total Fall Enrollment in Institutions of Higher Education, by Level of Study, Sex, and Race/Ethnicity of Student, 1976–1997 (CONTINUED)

Level of study, sex, and race/ethnicity of student	Institutions of higher education, in thousands						Degree-granting institutions, in thousands[1]		Percentage distribution of students[2]							
									Institutions of higher education						Degree-granting institutions[1]	
	1976	1980	1990	1995	1996	1997	1996	1997	1976	1980	1990	1995	1996	1997	1996	1997
1	2	3	4	5	6	7	8	9	10	11	12	13	14	15	16	17
Undergraduate																
Total	9,419.0	10,469.1	11,959.1	12,231.7	12,259.4	12,298.3	12,326.9	12,450.6	100.0	100.0	100.0	100.0	100.0	100.0	100.0	100.0
White, non-Hispanic	7,740.5	8,480.7	9,272.6	8,805.6	8,730.9	8,681.8	8,769.5	8,783.9	83.4	82.7	79.0	73.6	72.8	72.1	72.8	72.1
Total minority	1,535.3	1,778.5	2,467.7	3,158.5	3,254.4	3,351.5	3,282.1	3,398.5	16.6	17.3	21.0	26.4	27.2	27.9	27.2	27.9
Black, non-Hispanic	943.4	1,018.8	1,147.2	1,333.6	1,352.6	1,379.9	1,358.6	1,398.1	10.2	9.9	9.8	11.1	11.3	11.5	11.3	11.5
Hispanic	352.9	433.1	724.6	1,012.0	1,065.6	1,107.8	1,079.4	1,125.9	3.8	4.2	6.2	8.5	8.9	9.2	9.0	9.2
Asian or Pacific Islander	169.3	248.7	500.5	692.2	713.2	736.6	717.6	743.7	1.8	2.4	4.3	5.8	6.0	6.1	6.0	6.1
American Indian/Alaskan Native	69.7	77.9	95.5	120.7	122.9	127.2	126.5	130.8	0.8	0.8	0.8	1.0	1.0	1.1	1.0	1.1
Nonresident alien	143.2	209.9	218.7	267.6	274.1	265.0	275.3	268.2	—	—	—	—	—	—	—	—
Men																
Total	4,896.8	4,997.4	5,379.8	5,401.1	5,411.1	5,405.4	5,420.7	5,468.5	100.0	100.0	100.0	100.0	100.0	100.0	100.0	100.0
White, non-Hispanic	4,052.2	4,054.9	4,184.4	3,918.1	3,890.7	3,857.3	3,890.8	3,899.3	84.4	83.5	79.6	74.5	73.9	73.3	73.8	73.2
Total minority	748.2	802.7	1,069.3	1,339.3	1,375.0	1,408.4	1,384.1	1,427.9	15.6	16.5	20.4	25.5	26.1	26.7	26.2	26.8
Black, non-Hispanic	430.7	428.2	448.0	506.8	513.1	520.6	513.6	527.1	9.0	8.8	8.5	9.6	9.7	9.9	9.7	9.9
Hispanic	191.7	211.2	326.9	444.2	464.0	479.1	469.2	486.7	4.0	4.3	6.2	8.4	8.8	9.1	8.9	9.1
Asian or Pacific Islander	91.1	128.5	254.5	338.1	346.9	356.1	348.8	359.4	1.9	2.6	4.8	6.4	6.6	6.8	6.6	6.7
American Indian/Alaskan Native	34.8	34.8	39.9	50.2	51.0	52.6	52.4	54.1	0.7	0.7	0.8	1.0	1.0	1.0	1.0	1.0
Nonresident alien	96.4	139.8	126.1	143.8	145.3	139.6	145.8	141.4	0.8	0.8	—	—	—	—	—	—
Women																
Total	4,522.1	5,471.7	6,579.3	6,830.6	6,848.4	6,892.9	6,906.3	6,982.1	100.0	100.0	100.0	100.0	100.0	100.0	100.0	100.0
White, non-Hispanic	3,688.3	4,425.8	5,088.2	4,887.5	4,840.2	4,824.5	4,878.7	4,884.6	82.4	81.9	78.4	72.9	72.0	71.3	72.0	71.3
Total minority	787.0	975.8	1,398.5	1,819.2	1,879.3	1,943.0	1,898.1	1,970.6	17.6	18.1	21.6	27.1	28.0	28.7	28.0	28.7
Black, non-Hispanic	512.7	590.6	699.2	826.9	839.5	859.3	845.0	870.3	11.5	10.9	10.8	12.3	12.5	12.7	12.5	12.7
Hispanic	161.2	221.8	397.6	567.8	601.6	628.7	610.1	639.3	3.6	4.1	6.1	8.5	9.0	9.3	9.0	9.3
Asian or Pacific Islander	78.2	120.2	246.0	354.1	366.3	380.5	368.8	384.4	1.7	2.2	3.8	5.3	5.5	5.6	5.4	5.6
American Indian/Alaskan Native	34.9	43.1	55.5	70.5	71.9	74.5	74.1	76.7	0.8	0.8	0.9	1.1	1.1	1.0	1.1	1.1
Nonresident alien	46.8	70.1	92.6	123.8	128.8	125.4	129.5	126.8	—	—	—	—	—	—	—	—
Graduate																
Total	1,322.5	1,340.9	1,586.2	1,732.5	1,743.1	1,750.6	1,742.3	1,753.5	100.0	100.0	100.0	100.0	100.0	100.0	100.0	100.0
White, non-Hispanic	1,115.6	1,104.7	1228.4	1,282.3	1,273.9	1,260.2	1,272.6	1,261.8	89.2	88.5	86.6	82.6	81.7	80.7	81.6	80.7
Total minority	134.5	144.0	190.5	270.7	286.0	301.6	286.3	302.3	10.8	11.5	13.4	17.4	18.3	19.3	18.4	19.3
Black, non-Hispanic	78.5	75.1	83.9	118.6	125.5	131.7	125.5	131.6	6.3	6.0	5.9	7.6	8.0	8.4	8.0	8.4
Hispanic	26.4	32.1	47.2	68.0	72.7	78.4	72.8	78.7	2.1	2.6	3.3	4.4	4.7	5.0	4.7	5.0
Asian or Pacific Islander	24.5	31.6	53.2	75.6	79.0	82.1	79.1	82.6	2.0	2.5	3.8	4.9	5.1	5.3	5.1	5.3
American Indian/Alaskan Native	5.1	5.2	6.2	8.5	8.9	9.4	8.9	9.4	0.4	0.4	0.4	0.5	0.6	0.6	0.6	0.6
Nonresident alien	72.4	92.2	167.3	179.5	183.2	188.8	183.3	189.4	—	—	—	—	—	—	—	—
Men																
Total	707.9	672.2	737.4	767.5	760.5	756.1	759.4	757.9	100.0	100.0	100.0	100.0	100.0	100.0	100.0	100.0
White, non-Hispanic	589.1	538.5	538.8	541.6	530.2	519.5	529.0	520.4	90.2	89.2	86.8	83.1	82.3	81.5	82.3	81.4
Total minority	63.7	65.0	82.1	110.4	113.9	118.2	114.0	118.8	9.8	10.8	13.2	16.9	17.7	18.5	17.7	18.6
Black, non-Hispanic	32.0	28.2	29.3	39.8	41.2	42.8	41.2	42.8	4.9	4.7	4.7	6.1	6.4	6.7	6.4	6.7
Hispanic	14.6	15.7	20.6	28.2	29.5	31.3	29.6	31.5	2.2	2.6	3.3	4.3	4.6	4.9	4.6	4.9
Asian or Pacific Islander	14.4	18.6	29.7	39.0	39.7	40.4	39.7	40.7	2.2	3.1	4.8	6.0	6.2	6.3	6.2	6.4
American Indian/Alaskan Native	2.7	2.5	2.6	3.4	3.6	3.7	3.6	3.7	0.4	0.4	0.4	0.5	0.6	0.6	0.6	0.6
Nonresident alien	55.1	68.7	116.4	115.6	116.3	118.4	116.4	118.7	—	—	—	—	—	—	—	—

TABLE 7.3
Total Fall Enrollment in Institutions of Higher Education, by Level of Study, Sex, and Race/Ethnicity of Student, 1976–1997 [CONTINUED]

Level of study, sex, and race/ethnicity of student	Institutions of higher education, in thousands						Degree-granting institutions, in thousands[1]		Percentage distribution of students[2] — Institutions of higher education						Percentage distribution of students[2] — Degree-granting institutions[1]	
	1976	1980	1990	1995	1996	1997	1996	1997	1976	1980	1990	1995	1996	1997	1996	1997
	2	3	4	5	6	7	8	9	10	11	12	13	14	15	16	17
Graduate																
Women	10,614.6	668.7	848.8	965.0	982.6	994.5	982.8	995.6	100.0	100.0	100.0	100.0	100.0	100.0	100.0	100.0
White, non-Hispanic	526.5	566.2	689.5	740.7	743.7	740.7	743.6	741.4	88.1	87.8	86.4	82.2	81.2	80.2	81.2	80.2
Total minority	70.8	79.0	108.3	160.3	172.1	183.3	172.3	183.5	11.9	12.2	13.6	17.8	18.8	19.8	18.8	19.8
Black, non-Hispanic	46.5	46.9	54.6	78.8	84.3	88.8	84.3	88.8	7.8	7.3	6.8	8.7	9.2	9.6	9.2	9.6
Hispanic	11.8	16.4	26.6	39.9	43.1	47.1	43.2	47.2	2.0	2.5	3.3	4.4	4.7	5.1	4.7	5.1
Asian or Pacific Islander	10.1	13.0	23.6	36.6	39.3	41.7	39.4	41.8	1.7	2.0	3.0	4.1	4.3	4.5	4.3	4.5
American Indian/Alaskan Native	2.4	2.7	3.6	5.0	5.3	5.7	5.3	5.7	0.4	0.4	0.5	0.6	0.6	0.6	0.6	0.6
Nonresident alien	17.3	23.5	50.9	63.9	66.9	70.4	66.9	70.7	—	—	—	—	—	—	—	—
First-professional																
Total	244.1	276.8	273.4	297.6	297.7	296.5	298.3	298.3	100.0	100.0	100.0	100.0	100.0	100.0	100.0	100.0
White, non-Hispanic	220.0	247.7	221.5	223.3	221.2	218.9	221.7	220.4	91.3	90.4	82.6	76.9	76.2	75.7	76.3	75.8
Total minority	21.1	26.3	46.5	67.0	68.9	70.1	69.0	70.4	8.7	9.6	17.4	23.1	23.8	24.3	23.7	24.2
Black, non-Hispanic	11.2	12.8	15.9	21.4	21.4	21.2	21.5	21.4	4.6	4.7	5.9	7.4	7.4	7.3	7.4	7.3
Hispanic	4.5	6.5	10.7	13.8	14.0	13.9	13.9	13.9	1.9	2.4	4.0	4.8	4.8	4.8	4.8	4.8
Asian or Pacific Islander	4.1	6.1	18.7	29.6	31.4	32.8	31.4	32.9	1.7	2.2	7.0	10.2	10.8	11.4	10.8	11.3
American Indian/Alaskan Native	1.3	0.8	1.1	2.1	2.2	2.3	2.2	2.3	0.5	0.3	0.4	0.7	0.7	0.8	0.7	0.8
Nonresident alien	3.1	2.9	5.4	7.3	7.7	7.5	7.6	7.5	—	—	—	—	—	—	—	—
Men	189.6	198.5	166.8	173.9	172.5	168.4	172.7	169.6	100.0	100.0	100.0	100.0	100.0	100.0	100.0	100.0
White, non-Hispanic	172.4	179.5	137.8	134.4	132.0	128.0	132.3	129.1	92.1	91.5	84.5	79.5	78.9	78.3	78.9	78.3
Total minority	14.7	16.7	25.3	34.6	35.3	35.5	35.4	35.7	7.9	8.5	15.5	20.5	21.1	21.7	21.1	21.7
Black, non-Hispanic	7.2	7.4	7.4	9.4	9.4	9.1	9.4	9.2	3.9	3.8	4.5	5.5	5.6	5.6	5.6	5.6
Hispanic	3.5	4.6	6.4	7.8	7.8	7.6	7.7	7.6	1.9	2.4	3.9	4.6	4.6	4.7	4.6	4.6
Asian or Pacific Islander	2.9	4.1	10.8	16.2	17.0	17.6	17.1	17.6	1.6	2.1	6.6	9.6	10.2	10.7	10.2	10.7
American Indian/Alaskan Native	1.0	0.5	0.6	1.2	1.2	1.2	1.2	1.2	0.6	0.3	0.4	0.7	0.7	0.7	0.7	0.7
Nonresident alien	2.5	2.3	3.8	4.9	5.1	4.9	5.1	4.9	—	—	—	—	—	—	—	—
Women	54.5	78.4	106.6	123.7	125.3	128.1	125.6	128.6	100.0	100.0	100.0	100.0	100.0	100.0	100.0	100.0
White, non-Hispanic	47.6	68.1	83.7	88.9	89.1	90.9	89.4	91.3	88.2	87.6	79.7	73.3	72.6	72.4	72.7	72.5
Total minority	6.4	9.6	21.3	32.4	33.6	34.6	33.6	34.7	11.8	12.4	20.3	26.7	27.4	27.6	27.3	27.5
Black, non-Hispanic	3.9	5.5	8.5	12.1	12.0	12.0	12.1	12.1	7.3	7.0	8.1	10.0	9.8	9.6	9.8	9.6
Hispanic	1.0	1.9	4.3	6.0	6.2	6.2	6.2	6.2	1.9	2.4	4.1	5.0	5.1	5.0	5.0	4.9
Asian or Pacific Islander	1.1	2.0	7.9	13.4	14.4	15.3	14.4	15.3	2.1	2.6	7.6	11.0	11.7	12.2	11.7	12.1
American Indian/Alaskan Native	0.2	0.3	0.5	0.9	1.0	1.1	1.0	1.1	0.4	0.3	0.5	0.8	0.8	0.8	0.8	0.8
Nonresident alien	0.5	0.6	1.6	2.4	2.6	2.6	2.6	2.6	—	—	—	—	—	—	—	—

[1] Data are for 4-year and 2-year degree-granting institutions that were eligible to participate in Title IV federal financial aid programs.

[2] Distribution for U.S. citizens only.

—Not applicable.

NOTE: Because of underreporting and nonreporting of racial/ethnic data, some figures are slightly lower than corresponding data in other tables. Trend tabulations of institutions of higher education data are based on institutions that were accredited by an agency or association that was recognized by the U.S. Department of Education. The Department of Education no longer distinguishes between those institutions and other institutions that are eligible to the earlier higher education classification, except that it includes some additional institutions, primarily 2-year colleges, and excludes a few higher education institutions that did not award degrees. Because of rounding, details may not add to totals.

SOURCE: *Digest of Education Statistics 1999.* National Center for Education Statistics, May 2000

TABLE 7.4

Years of School Completed by Persons Age 25 and Over and 25 to 29, by Race/Ethnicity and Sex, 1910–1998

Percent, by years of school completed

Age and year	All races			White, non-Hispanic[1]			Black, non-Hispanic[1]			Hispanic		
	Less than 5 years of elementary school	High school completion or higher[2]	4 or more years of college[3]	Less than 5 years of elementary school	High school completion or higher[2]	4 or more years of college[3]	Less than 5 years of elementary school	High school completion or higher[2]	4 or more years of college[3]	Less than 5 years of elementary school	High school completion or higher[2]	4 or more years of college[3]
1	2	3	4	5	6	7	8	9	10	11	12	13
25 and over								Males and females				
1910[4]	23.8	13.5	2.7	—	—	—	—	—	—	—	—	—
1920[4]	22.0	16.4	3.3	—	—	—	—	—	—	—	—	—
1930[4]	17.5	19.1	3.9	—	—	—	—	—	—	—	—	—
April 1940	13.7	24.5	4.6	10.9	26.1	4.9	41.8	7.7	1.3	—	—	—
April 1950	11.1	34.3	6.2	8.9	36.4	6.6	32.6	13.7	2.2	—	—	—
April 1960	8.3	41.1	7.7	6.7	43.2	8.1	23.5	21.7	3.5	—	—	—
March 1970	5.3	55.2	11.0	4.2	57.4	11.6	14.7	36.1	6.1	—	—	—
March 1980	3.4	68.6	17.0	1.9	71.9	18.4	9.1	51.4	7.9	15.8	44.5	7.6
March 1985	2.7	73.9	19.4	1.4	77.5	20.8	6.1	59.9	11.1	13.5	47.9	8.5
March 1986	2.7	74.7	19.4	1.4	78.2	20.1	5.3	62.5	10.9	12.9	48.5	8.4
March 1987	2.4	75.6	19.9	1.3	79.0	20.5	4.9	63.6	10.8	11.9	50.9	8.6
March 1988	2.5	76.2	20.3	1.2	79.8	21.8	4.8	63.5	11.2	12.2	51.0	10.0
March 1989	2.5	76.9	21.1	1.2	80.7	22.8	5.2	64.7	11.7	12.2	50.9	9.9
March 1990	2.5	77.6	21.3	1.1	81.4	23.1	5.1	66.2	11.3	12.3	50.8	9.2
March 1991	2.4	78.4	21.4	1.1	82.4	23.3	4.7	66.8	11.5	12.5	51.3	9.7
March 1992	2.1	79.4	21.4	0.9	83.4	23.2	3.9	67.7	11.9	11.8	52.6	9.3
March 1993	2.1	80.2	21.9	0.8	84.1	23.8	3.7	70.5	12.2	11.8	53.1	9.0
March 1994	1.9	80.9	22.2	0.8	84.9	24.3	2.7	73.0	12.9	10.8	53.3	9.1
March 1995	1.9	81.7	23.0	0.7	85.9	23.4	2.5	73.8	13.3	10.6	53.4	9.3
March 1996	1.8	81.7	23.6	0.6	86.0	25.9	2.2	74.6	13.8	10.4	53.1	9.3
March 1997	1.7	82.1	23.9	0.6	86.3	26.2	2.0	75.3	13.3	9.4	54.7	10.3
March 1998	1.7	82.8	24.4	0.6	87.1	26.6	1.7	76.4	14.8	9.3	55.5	11.0
25 to 29												
1920[4]	5.9	—	—	12.9	22.0	4.5	44.6	6.3	1.2	—	—	—
April 1940	4.6	38.1	5.9	3.4	41.2	6.4	27.0	12.3	1.6	—	—	—
April 1950	2.8	52.8	7.7	3.3	56.3	8.2	16.1	23.6	2.8	—	—	—
April 1960	1.1	60.7	11.0	2.2	63.7	11.8	7.2	38.6	5.4	—	—	—
March 1970	0.8	75.4	16.4	0.9	77.8	17.3	2.2	58.4	10.0	—	—	—
March 1980	0.7	85.4	22.5	0.3	89.2	25.0	0.7	76.7	11.6	6.7	58.0	7.7
March 1985	0.9	86.1	22.2	0.2	89.5	24.4	0.4	80.5	11.6	6.0	60.9	11.1
March 1986	0.9	86.1	22.4	0.4	89.6	25.2	0.5	83.5	11.8	5.6	59.1	9.0
March 1987	1.0	86.0	22.0	0.4	89.4	24.7	0.4	83.5	11.5	4.8	59.8	8.7
March 1988	1.0	85.9	22.7	0.3	89.7	25.1	0.3	80.9	12.0	6.0	62.3	11.3
March 1989	1.2	85.5	23.4	0.3	89.3	26.3	0.5	82.3	12.7	5.4	61.0	10.1
March 1990	1.0	85.7	23.2	0.3	90.1	26.4	1.0	81.7	13.4	7.3	58.2	8.2
March 1991	0.9	85.4	23.2	0.3	89.8	26.7	0.5	81.8	11.0	5.8	56.7	9.2
March 1992	0.7	86.3	23.6	0.3	90.7	27.2	0.8	80.9	11.1	5.2	60.9	9.5
March 1993	0.8	86.7	23.7	0.3	91.2	27.2	0.2	82.7	13.3	4.0	60.9	8.3
March 1994	1.0	86.1	23.3	0.3	91.1	27.1	0.6	84.1	13.6	3.6	60.3	8.0
March 1995	0.8	86.9	24.7	0.3	92.5	28.8	0.2	86.7	15.4	4.9	57.2	8.9
March 1996	0.8	87.3	27.1	0.2	92.6	31.6	0.4	86.0	14.6	4.3	61.1	10.0
March 1997	0.8	87.4	27.8	0.1	92.9	32.6	0.6	86.9	14.2	4.2	61.8	11.0
March 1998	0.7	88.1	27.3	0.1	93.6	32.3	0.4	88.3	15.8	3.7	62.8	10.4

TABLE 7.4

Years of School Completed by Persons Age 25 and Over and 25 to 29, by Race/Ethnicity and Sex, 1910–1998 (CONTINUED)

	All races			White, non-Hispanic[1]			Black, non-Hispanic[1]			Hispanic		
Age and year	Less than 5 years of elementary school	High school completion or higher[2]	4 or more years of college[3]	Less than 5 years of elementary school	High school completion or higher[2]	4 or more years of college[3]	Less than 5 years of elementary school	High school completion or higher[2]	4 or more years of college[3]	Less than 5 years of elementary school	High school completion or higher[2]	4 or more years of college[3]
1	2	3	4	5	6	7	8	9	10	11	12	13
25 and over						**Males**						
April 1940	15.1	22.7	5.5	12.0	24.2	5.9	46.2	6.9	1.4	—	—	—
April 1950	12.2	32.6	7.3	9.8	34.6	7.9	36.9	12.6	2.1	—	—	—
April 1960	9.4	39.5	9.7	7.4	41.6	10.3	27.7	20.0	3.5	—	—	—
March 1970	5.9	55.0	14.1	4.5	57.2	15.0	17.9	35.4	6.8	—	—	—
March 1980	3.6	69.2	20.9	2.0	72.4	22.8	11.3	51.2	7.7	16.5	44.9	9.2
March 1990	2.7	77.7	24.4	1.3	81.6	26.7	6.4	65.8	11.9	12.9	50.3	9.8
March 1994	2.1	81.1	25.1	0.8	85.1	27.8	3.9	71.8	12.7	11.4	53.4	9.6
March 1995	2.0	81.7	26.0	0.8	86.0	28.9	3.4	73.5	13.7	10.8	52.9	10.1
March 1996	1.9	81.9	26.0	0.7	86.1	28.8	2.9	74.6	12.5	10.2	53.0	10.3
March 1997	1.8	82.0	26.2	0.6	86.3	29.0	2.9	73.8	12.5	9.2	54.9	10.6
March 1998	1.7	82.8	26.5	0.7	87.1	29.3	2.3	75.4	14.0	9.3	55.7	11.1
25 and over						**Females**						
April 1940	12.4	26.3	3.8	9.8	28.1	4.0	37.5	8.4	1.2	—	—	—
April 1950	10.0	36.0	5.2	8.1	38.2	5.4	28.6	14.7	2.4	—	—	—
April 1960	7.4	42.5	5.8	6.0	44.7	6.0	19.7	23.1	3.6	—	—	—
March 1970	4.7	55.4	8.2	3.9	57.7	8.6	11.9	36.6	5.6	—	—	—
March 1980	3.2	68.1	13.6	1.8	71.5	14.4	7.4	51.5	8.1	15.3	44.2	6.2
March 1990	2.2	77.5	18.4	1.0	81.3	19.8	4.1	66.5	10.8	11.7	51.3	8.7
March 1994	1.7	80.8	19.6	0.7	84.7	21.1	1.8	73.9	13.1	10.3	53.2	8.6
March 1995	1.7	81.6	20.2	0.6	85.8	22.2	1.8	74.1	13.0	10.4	53.8	8.4
March 1996	1.7	81.6	21.4	0.5	85.9	23.2	1.6	74.6	14.8	10.6	53.3	8.3
March 1997	1.6	82.2	21.7	0.5	86.3	23.7	1.3	76.5	14.0	9.5	54.6	10.1
March 1998	1.6	82.9	22.4	0.6	87.1	24.1	1.2	77.1	15.5	9.2	55.3	10.9

[1] Includes persons of Hispanic origin for years prior to 1980.

[2] Data for years prior to 1993 include all persons with at least 4 years of high school.

[3] Data for 1993 and later years are for persons with a bachelor's degree or higher.

[4] Estimates based on Bureau of the Census retrojection of 1940 Census data on education by age.

—Data not available.

NOTE—Data for 1980 and subsequent years are for the noninstitutional population.

SOURCE: *Digest of Education Statistics 1999.* National Center for Education Statistics, May 2000

TABLE 7.5

Percent of Persons 25 years Old and Over who are High School and College Graduates, by Race and Hispanic Origin: March 1999

(Numbers in thousands.)

Population Age 25 Years and Over	Total		Asian or Pacific Islander		Non-Hispanic, White		Other Groups[2]	
	Number	Percent	Number	Percent	Number	Percent	Number	Percent
Total	**173,754**	**100.0**	**6,594**	**100.0**	**130,411**	**100.0**	**36,749**	**100.0**
Less than 9th grade	12,397	7.1	539	8.2	5,828	4.5	6,030	16.4
9th to 12th grade (no diploma)	16,443	9.5	478	7.3	10,215	7.8	5,751	15.6
High school graduate	57,935	33.3	1,478	22.4	44,733	34.3	11,723	31.9
Some college or associate degree	43,175	24.8	1,326	20.1	33,528	25.7	8,322	22.6
Bachelor's degree	29,495	17.0	1,822	27.6	24,178	18.5	3,495	9.5
Advanced degree	14,308	8.2	950	14.4	11,930	9.1	1,429	3.9
Less than high school diploma	28,841	16.6	1,018	15.4	16,043	12.3	11,780	32.1
High school graduate or more	144,913	83.4	5,576	84.6	114,368	87.7	24,969	67.9
Less than Bachelor's degree	129,951	74.8	3,822	58.0	94,304	72.3l	31,825	86.6
Bachelor's degree or more	43,803	25.2	2,772	42.0	36,107	27.7	4,924	13.4l
Male								
Total	**82,917**	**100.0**	**3,095**	**100.0**	**62,710**	**100.0**	**17,112**	**100.0**
Less than 9th grade	5,990	7.2	189	6.1	2,819	4.5	2,982	17.4
9th to 12th grade (no diploma)	7,736	9.3	224	7.2	4,900	7.8	2,612	15.3
High school graduate	26,368	31.8	607	19.6	20,128	32.1	5,633	32.9
Some college or associate degree	20,042	24.2	654	21.1	15,654	25.0	3,734	21.8
Bachelor's degree	14,808	17.9	855	27.6	12,439	19.8	1,513	8.8
Advanced degree	7,974	9.6	566	18.3	6,769	10.8	638	3.7
Less than high school diploma	13,726	16.6	413	13.3	7,719	12.3	5,594	32.7
High school graduate or more	69,191	83.4	2,682	86.7	54,991	87.7	11,518	67.3
Less than Bachelor's degree	60,136	72.5	1,674	54.1	43,501l	69.4	14,961	87.4
Bachelor's degree or more	22,781	27.5	1,421	45.9	19,209	30.6	2,151	12.6
Female								
Total	**90,837**	**100.0**	**3,499**	**100.0**	**67,701**	**100.0**	**19,637**	**100.0**
Less than 9th grade	6,408	7.1	350	10.0	3,010	4.4	3,048	15.5
9th to 12th grade (no diploma)	8,707	9.6	254	7.3	5,314	7.8	3,139	16.0
High school graduate	31,566	34.8	872	24.9	24,605	36.3	6,090	31.0
Some college or associate degree	23,134	25.5	673	19.2	17,873	26.4	4,588	23.4
Bachelor's degree	14,687	16.2	967	27.6	11,738	17.3	1,982	10.1
Advanced degree	6,335	7.0	383	11.0	5,160	7.6	791	4.0
Less than high school diploma	15,115	16.6	604	17.3	8,324	12.3	6,186	31.5
High school graduate or more	75,722	83.4	2,894	82.7	59,377	87.7	13,450	68.5
Less than Bachelor's degree	69,815	76.9	2,148	61.4	50,803	75.0	16,864	85.9
Bachelor's degree or more	21,022	23.1	1,350	38.6	16,898	25.0	2,773	14.1

Race and Hispanic Origin[1]

[1] Hispanic refers to people whose origin are Mexican, Puerto Rican, Cuban, South or Central American, or other Spanish, regardless of race.

[2] This category includes people who are American Indian or Alaska Native, African American, or Hispanic (except for those Hispanics that are Asian or Pacific Islander).

SOURCE: *The Asian and Pacific Islander Population in the United States: March 1999 (Update)*. PPL-131. U.S. Bureau of the Census: Washington, D.C.

The National Center for Education Statistics compared reading proficiency for 9-, 13-, and 17-year olds from 1971 to 1996. Average reading ability for Black students was higher in 1996 than in 1971 at all three age levels, narrowing the gap between White and Black performance. Black students tended to improve their scores in the older grades. Twelfth-grade Hispanic students improved their reading skills between 1975 and 1990, slipped in 1992 and 1994, but improved in 1996. The younger Hispanic students made no appreciable gains between 1971 and 1994 but improved significantly in 1996. The performance of White students changed little over the 25 years studied. (See Table 7.6.)

Writing Ability

The NAEP found the writing ability for students of all races/ethnicity very poor. Whites scored consistently higher than either Blacks or Hispanics at all grade levels. Few students, however, achieved more than a minimal rating, defined as knowing the elements needed to complete the task, but not well enough to ensure the intended purpose. (See Table 7.7.) The report concluded that American students, on the whole, could not express themselves well enough through their writing to accomplish an intended purpose.

Mathematics Performance

In a time when science and technology are considered vital to the nation's economy and position in the international community, education observers have been concerned about the generally poor American performance in mathematics and science. Since 1971 the NAEP has tested fourth, eighth, and twelfth graders to determine their mathematical knowledge, skills, and aptitudes.

In 1996 White and Asian/Pacific Islander fourth- and twelfth-grade students and White eighth graders scored higher than their Black and Hispanic counterparts. Fourth-grade American Indians and Alaskan Natives scored higher than Blacks and Hispanics in the same grade. Eighth-grade Hispanics outscored their Black counterparts. (See Table 7.8.)

Science Ability

In 1996 science proficiency scores for 17-year olds showed that students of all races could apply general scientific information. The average scores were 28.4 percent for Whites, 28.7 percent for Blacks, and 30 percent Hispanics. Test scores for White and Black students fell between 1970 and 1982, but began to rise in 1986 and have continued to improve. Test scores for Hispanic students followed the same patterns, beginning in 1977. (See Table 7.9.)

RISK FACTORS IN EDUCATION

The U.S. Department of Education's *National Education Longitudinal Study of 1988* (NELS; 1988) studied a set of students throughout their education. The goal of the study was to identify early student, school, and parental experiences that promote student learning. NELS asked, "Under what circumstances do our children flourish and succeed?"

In addition to many academic measures, NELS compared the following risk factors against educational problems: single-parent family, low parent education, limited English proficiency, low family income, sibling dropout, and being home alone more than three hours on weekdays. Minorities were more at risk from all these factors than non-minorities. Students with two or more factors were more than twice as likely to be in the lowest grade quartile (fourth) and almost three times as likely to be in the lowest test quartile. These students were over six times as likely to think that they would not finish high school. (See Table 7.10.)

Overcoming Risk Factors

Nathan Caplan and others, in "Why Asian Children Excel in School" (*Scientific American,* February 1992), found that despite hardships and severe traumatic experiences in their native countries and attending schools in low-income inner cities, the majority of Indochinese refugee children performed well in school. The authors found that strong family traditions and values were the important influences in these children's lives. The families were committed to a love of learning. They placed a high value on homework and did it as a family activity, with the older children helping the younger. Furthermore, parents read regularly to their children either in English or their

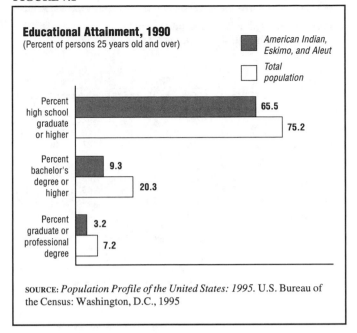

FIGURE 7.1

Educational Attainment, 1990
(Percent of persons 25 years old and over)

■ *American Indian, Eskimo, and Aleut*
□ *Total population*

- Percent high school graduate or higher: 65.5 / 75.2
- Percent bachelor's degree or higher: 9.3 / 20.3
- Percent graduate or professional degree: 3.2 / 7.2

SOURCE: *Population Profile of the United States: 1995.* U.S. Bureau of the Census: Washington, D.C., 1995

native language. The Refugee families were linked not only to their past traditions, but also to the reality of the present and to future possibilities, which appears to have given a sense of continuity and direction to their lives.

The Indochinese are not the only group to have accomplished this kind of academic success. For the most part, Japanese and Jewish immigrants (two groups with strong family traditions and values of learning) have also had high academic success. Ninety percent of third-generation Jews in the United States have attended college, even though most of the first-generation Jews had little or no education when they came to the United States. Japanese students overcame long-time prejudice and excelled in school. In schools that emphasize parental involvement and structure the children's learning environment at home as well as in school, Blacks have also had outstanding achievement.

DROPPING OUT

When students drop out or fail to complete high school, both the individual and society suffer. Dropping out of school often results in limited occupational and economic opportunities for the individual. For society, it may result in increased costs of government assistance programs to the individuals and their families, the running of costly public training programs, and higher crime rates.

Education is a major factor that can lead to higher earnings. Based on 1996 data from the Bureau of the Census, Black workers with high school diplomas earned 32 percent more than Blacks who were not graduated from high school. Hispanic graduates earned 40 percent more than Hispanics who did not have high school diplomas.

TABLE 7.6

Average Reading Performance (scale score), by Race/Ethnicity and Age: Selected Years 1971–96

	White			Black			Hispanic		
Year	Age 9	Age 13	Age 17	Age 9	Age 13	Age 17	Age 9	Age 13	Age 17
1971	214	261	291	170	222	239	—	—	—
1975	217	262	293	181	226	241	183	232	252
1980	221	264	293	189	233	243	190	237	261
1984	218	263	295	186	236	264	187	240	268
1988	218	261	295	189	243	274	194	240	271
1990	217	262	297	182	242	267	189	238	275
1992	218	266	297	185	238	261	192	239	271
1994	218	265	296	185	234	266	186	235	263
1996	220	267	294	190	236	265	194	240	265

—Not available.

NOTE: The reading performance scale has a range from 0 to 500.

SOURCE: *The Condition of Education 1999*. National Center for Education Statistics

In 1998 typical Black high school graduates increased their earnings by 35 percent if they earned an associate's degree, while it meant an additional 30 percent for Hispanic high school graduates. Black men with a bachelor's degree earned 60 percent more than Black men with only a high school diploma, while Black women with a bachelor's degree earned 65 percent more than Black women who had only been graduated from high school. Hispanic men with a bachelor's degree earned 71 percent more than their high school counterparts, and Hispanic women with a bachelor's degree earned 85 percent more than Hispanic females with only high school diplomas. (See Table 7.11.)

The Dropout Rate

In 1998, 11.8 percent of all persons 16 to 24 years old had dropped out of high school. Non-Hispanic White stu-

TABLE 7.7

Average Writing Performance (scale score), by Race/Ethnicity and Age: Selected Years 1984–96

	White			Black			Hispanic		
Year	Grade 4	Grade 8	Grade 11	Grade 4	Grade 8	Grade 11	Grade 4	Grade 8	Grade 11
1984	211	272	297	182	247	270	189	247	259
1988	215	269	296	173	246	275	190	250	274
1990	211	262	293	171	239	268	184	246	277
1992	217	279	294	175	258	263	189	265	274
1994	214	272	291	173	245	267	189	252	271
1996	216	271	289	182	242	267	191	246	269

NOTE: The writing performance scale has a range from 0 to 500.

SOURCE: *The Condition of Education 1999*. National Center for Education Statistics

TABLE 7.8

Average Mathematics Performance (scale score), by Grade and Race/Ethnicity, Selected Years 1990, 1992, and 1996

	Grade 4			Grade 8			Grade 12		
Selected student characteristics	1990	1992	1996	1990	1992	1996	1990	1992	1996
Total	213	220	224	263	268	272	294	300	304
Sex									
Male	214	221	226	263	268	272	297	301	305
Female	213	219	222	262	269	272	292	298	303
Race–ethnicity									
White	220	228	232	270	278	282	301	306	311
Black	189	193	200	238	238	243	268	276	280
Hispanic	198	202	206	244	247	251	276	284	287
Asian/Pacific Islander	228	232	232	279	289	274	311	316	319
American Indian/Alaskan Native	208	211	216	246	255	264	—	—	297
Parents' highest education level									
Less than high school	202	205	205	242	249	254	272	279	282
Graduated high school	209	215	219	255	257	261	283	288	294
Some education after high school	222	225	232	268	271	279	297	299	302
Graduated college	221	227	232	274	281	282	306	311	314
Type of school									
Public	212	219	222	262	267	271	294	297	303
Nonpublic	224	228	237	272	281	284	300	314	315

—Too few sample observations for a reliable estimate.

NOTE: The mathematics performance scale has a range of 0 to 500.

SOURCE: *The Condition of Education 1999*. National Center for Education Statistics

dents dropped out at a rate of 7.7 percent, down from 12 percent in 1976. Non-Hispanic Blacks dropped out at a rate of 13.8 percent, a decline from 20.5 percent in 1976. The Hispanic dropout rate varied only slightly, from 31.4 percent in 1976 to 29.5 percent in 1998. Hispanics were more than twice as likely as Blacks and four times as likely as Whites to never finish high school. (See Table 7.12.)

Table 7.12 also shows how much improvement Blacks have made in dropout rates. The dropout rate for Black males declined from 21.2 percent in 1976 to 15.5 percent in 1998, while the rate for Black females dropped from 19.9 percent in 1976 to 12.2 percent in 1998.

MINORITIES AND COLLEGE

SAT and ACT Scores

Students wishing to enter most colleges and universities in the United States must take the Scholastic Assessment Test (SAT) or the American College Test (ACT). These are standardized tests intended to measure verbal and mathematical ability in terms of readiness for college-level work. More students take the SAT than the ACT. The ACT is graded on a scale of 1 to 36. The average score in 1999 for all college-bound seniors was 21. (See Table 7.13.) Performance on the SAT is measured in two areas, each on a scale of 200 to 800. In 1999 the average SAT scores for all college-bound seniors were 505 for the verbal section and 511 for the mathematics segment. (See Table 7.14.)

RACIAL AND ETHNIC DIFFERENCES IN TEST SCORES. The College Board reported that minority students made up about one-third of all students taking the SAT in 1999, up from 25 percent in 1989 and just 13 percent in 1973. The number of Black students who took the SAT rose to its highest level, a total of 119,394 students, or 11 percent of all test takers. More than 96,100 Asian/Pacific Islander (API) students took the test in 1999, nine percent of the total SAT takers (Asian Americans represent four percent of the total population). About 9 percent of the test takers were Hispanic, while only 1 percent were American Indian/Alaskan Native. (See Table 7.14.) In every ethnic group listed in Table 7.14, more women than men took the test.

In 1999 API students achieved the highest SAT scores (a total score of 1,058). White students (1,055) and students who described themselves as "other" (1,024) also ranked high. (See Table 7.15.) For the past several years, API students have surpassed all students on the average mathematics score.

Between 1991 and 1996 the verbal and math scores rose for all ethnic groups, except for Mexican Americans, who had fluctuations in scores between 1991 and 1995 but improved in 1996. The increase was greatest among Asian American, Black, and American Indian students. (See Table 7.16.) Nonetheless, despite gains made by all

TABLE 7.9

Average Science Performance (scale score), by Race/Ethnicity and Age, Selected Years 1970–96

Year	White			Black			Hispanic		
	Age 9	Age 13	Age 17	Age 9	Age 13	Age 17	Age 9	Age 13	Age 17
1970	236	263	312	179	215	258	—	—	—
1973	231	259	304	177	205	250	—	—	—
1977	230	256	298	175	208	240	192	213	262
1982	229	257	293	187	217	235	189	226	249
1986	232	259	298	196	222	253	199	226	259
1990	238	264	301	196	226	253	206	232	262
1992	239	267	304	200	224	256	205	238	270
1994	240	267	306	201	224	257	201	232	261
1996	239	266	307	202	226	260	207	232	269

—Not available.

NOTE: The science performance scale has a range from 0 to 500.

SOURCE: *The Condition of Education 1999*. National Center for Education Statistics

TABLE 7.10

Comparison of Children of Different Ethnic Backgrounds Who Were At Risk on Various Risk Items

Risk Item	White N = 15,035 %	Black 3,574 %	Hispanic 1,514 %	Native American 505 %	Asian 598 %
Suspended from school	5	11	6	8	2
Attempted suicide	1	0	1	3	1
Involved in pregnancy	0	1	1	1	1
Student sold drugs	1	1	0	1	0
Student used drugs	3	2	3	11	2
Family used drugs	3	3	4	14	1
Student used alcohol	5	3	4	16	2
Parent alcoholic	4	3	4	14	1
Student arrested	1	2	1	3	1
Student abused	2	2	2	6	1
Low grades in school	11	22	16	12	5
Failed courses	7	15	15	14	3
Overage in grade	14	24	22	23	15
Retained in grade	12	24	18	21	7
Excessive absences	6	10	8	10	4
Low self-esteem	12	14	15	14	7
Special education	10	10	10	12	5
Low reading scores	7	17	16	10	9
Parent sick last year	4	5	5	11	3
Parent died last year	1	1	1	3	1
Parent lost job last year	4	4	6	5	3
Friend died last year	4	6	5	11	3
Student ill last year	3	4	3	9	4
Sibling died last year	0	1	1	4	1
Father low-level job	15	19	25	26	25
Father not high school graduate	6	9	19	12	11
Mother low-level job	18	25	24	22	26
Mother not high school graduate	6	10	20	13	14
Parents' attitude negative	5	7	6	6	2
Language not English	1	1	41	5	36
Broken home	30	55	43	45	2
Moved frequently	14	19	20	19	21
Changed schools frequently	23	23	23	23	36
Parents divorced last year	6	10	7	8	4

*480 students did not specify ethnic background

SOURCE: Jack Frymier. *Growing Up is Risky Business, and Schools Are Not to Blame*. Phi Delta Kappa: Bloomington, Ind., 1992

TABLE 7.11

Earnings, by Highest Degree Earned, 1998

Characteristic	Total persons	Level of highest degree							
		Not a high school graduate	High school graduate only	Some college, no degree	Asso- ciate's	Bachelor's	Master's	Profes- sional	Doctorate
MEAN EARNINGS (dol)									
All persons[1]	29,514	16,124	22,895	24,804	29,872	40,478	51,183	95,148	77,445
Age:									
18 to 24 years old	11,264	7,737	12,001	9,813	15,931	19,444	23,007	14,045	4,158
25 to 34 years old	26,462	16,262	21,637	23,489	25,978	35,027	40,798	58,079	47,779
35 to 44 years old	34,081	18,532	26,235	30,353	32,429	45,298	53,594	103m,418	77,982
45 to 54 years old	37,242	20,800	26,925	35,090	34,606	46,773	56,922	115,697	86,237
65 years old and over	21,588	13,482	13,734	21,880	33,313	29,958	26,154	54,246	65,543
Sex:									
Male	36,556	19,575	28,307	31,268	36,392	50,056	63,220	109,206	87,426
Female	21,528	10,725	16,906	18,104	24,009	30,119	38,337	62,113	51,189
White	30,515	16,596	23,618	25,442	30,509	41,439	52,475	97,487	79,947
Male	37,933	20,071	29,298	32,294	37,362	51,678	65,421	110,977	89,110
Female	21,799	10,700	17,166	18,083	24,059	30,041	38,428	63,450	54,587
Black	21,909	13,185	18,980	22,105	25,527	32,062	40,610	51,004	(B)
Male	25,080	15,423	22,440	26,743	29,099	35,792	46,729	(B)	(B)
Female	19,161	10,607	15,789	18,346	23,416	29,091	37,425	(B)	(B)
Hispanic[2]	20,766	15,069	19,558	20,825	25,478	33,465	46,556	(B)	(B)
Male	23,520	17,447	22,253	24,807	29,627	37,963	54,790	(B)	(B)
Female	16,781	10,503	15,747	16,258	21,705	29,173	35,425	(B)	(B)

B Base figure too small to meet statistical standards for reliability of a derived figure.

[1]Includes other races, not shown separately.

[2]Persons of Hispanic origin may be of any race.

SOURCE: *Statistical Abstract of the United States.* U.S. Bureau of the Census, 1999

ethnic groups in verbal and math scores, minority scores (with the exception of Asian American math scores) still lag behind White scores.

In 1999 American Indian/Alaskan Native SAT takers had the largest one-year increase, 4 points, in verbal average, followed by Puerto Ricans (3 points), and Hispanics/Latinos (2 points). In the mathematics score, Asian American women dropped 5 points from 1998, followed by Black and Mexican women (a decline of 4 points each). Among male test takers, Puerto Rican men gained 5 points within a one-year period. Other ethnic groups showed a decline—Mexicans (5 points), Blacks (2 points), and Hispanics/Latinos (1 point).

Among students who took the ACT in 1999, Whites and APIs scored the highest averages at 21.7 each. Black students earned the lowest average score—17.1. All other racial/ethnic groups placed in the middle range of about 19. (See Table 7.13.)

Minority College Attendance

Minority enrollment in higher education more than doubled between 1976 and 1997, from 1.7 million (16 percent of the total student body) to 3.7 million (26 percent). In 1997 non-Hispanic Whites accounted for 73.2

percent of those attending college; Blacks, 11 percent; Hispanics, 8.6 percent; Asians/Pacific Islanders, 6.1 percent; and American Indians/Alaskan Natives, 1 percent. (See Table 7.3.)

Generally, minority enrollment has grown ever since racial and ethnic enrollment statistics were first reported in 1976. This is due primarily to increases in the Asian and Hispanic populations. Though these gains are encouraging, they must be viewed in the context of overall participation rates and degree completion rates, which have been relatively low for Blacks and Hispanics.

Between 1976 and 1997 the number of Asian/Pacific Islander students enrolled in college more than quadrupled, while the number of Hispanics more than tripled. The number of American Indian/Alaskan Native college students rose 82.3 percent, while the number of Black students grew 48.3 percent. (See Table 7.3.)

Affirmative Action

In the 1978 landmark reverse discrimination case of *Regents of the University of California v. Bakke* (438 U.S. 265), the Supreme Court allowed race and ethnicity to be considered in college admissions in the interest of racial and ethnic diversity on American college campuses. This

TABLE 7.12

Percent of High School Dropouts Among Persons 16 to 24 Years Old, by Sex and Race/Ethnicity, April 1960–October 1998

Year	Total				Men				Women			
	All races	White, non-Hispanic	Black, non-Hispanic	Hispanic origin	All races	White, non-Hispanic	Black, non-Hispanic	Hispanic origin	All races	White, non-Hispanic	Black, non-Hispanic	Hispanic origin
1	2	3	4	5	6	7	8	9	10	11	12	13
1960[1]	27.2	—	—	—	27.8	—	—	—	26.7	—	—	—
1967[2]	17.0	15.4	28.6	—	16.5	14.7	30.6	—	17.3	16.1	26.9	—
1968[2]	16.2	14.7	27.4	—	15.8	14.4	27.1	—	16.5	15.0	27.6	—
1969[2]	15.2	13.6	26.7	—	14.3	12.6	26.9	—	16.0	14.6	26.7	—
1970[2]	15.0	13.2	27.9	—	14.2	12.2	29.4	—	15.7	14.1	26.6	—
1971[2]	14.7	13.4	23.7	—	14.2	12.6	25.5	—	15.2	14.2	22.1	—
1972	14.6 (0.3)	12.3 (0.3)	21.3 (1.1)	34.3 (2.2)	14.1 (0.4)	11.6 (0.4)	22.3 (1.6)	33.7 (3.2)	15.1 (0.4)	12.8 (0.4)	20.5 (1.4)	34.8 (3.1)
1973	14.1 (0.3)	11.6 (0.3)	22.2 (1.1)	33.5 (2.2)	13.7 (0.4)	11.5 (0.4)	21.5 (1.5)	30.4 (3.2)	14.5 (0.4)	11.8 (0.4)	22.8 (1.5)	36.4 (3.2)
1974	14.3 (0.3)	11.9 (0.3)	21.2 (1.0)	33.0 (2.1)	14.2 (0.4)	12.0 (0.4)	20.1 (1.5)	33.8 (3.0)	14.3 (0.4)	11.8 (0.4)	22.1 (1.5)	32.2 (2.9)
1975	13.9 (0.3)	11.4 (0.3)	22.9 (1.1)	29.2 (2.0)	13.3 (0.4)	11.0 (0.4)	23.0 (1.6)	26.7 (2.8)	14.5 (0.4)	11.8 (0.4)	22.9 (1.4)	31.6 (2.9)
1976	14.1 (0.3)	12.0 (0.3)	20.5 (1.0)	31.4 (2.0)	14.1 (0.4)	12.1 (0.4)	21.2 (1.5)	30.3 (2.9)	14.2 (0.4)	11.8 (0.4)	19.9 (1.4)	32.3 (2.8)
1977	14.1 (0.3)	11.9 (0.3)	19.8 (1.0)	33.0 (2.0)	14.5 (0.4)	12.6 (0.4)	19.5 (1.5)	31.6 (2.9)	13.8 (0.4)	11.2 (0.4)	20.0 (1.4)	34.3 (2.8)
1978	14.2 (0.3)	11.9 (0.3)	20.2 (1.0)	33.3 (2.0)	14.6 (0.4)	12.2 (0.4)	22.5 (1.5)	33.6 (2.9)	13.9 (0.4)	11.6 (0.4)	18.3 (1.3)	33.1 (2.8)
1979	14.6 (0.3)	12.0 (0.3)	21.1 (1.0)	33.8 (2.0)	15.0 (0.4)	12.6 (0.4)	22.4 (1.5)	33.0 (2.8)	14.2 (0.4)	11.5 (0.4)	20.0 (1.3)	34.5 (2.8)
1980	14.1 (0.3)	11.4 (0.3)	19.1 (1.0)	35.2 (1.9)	15.1 (0.4)	12.3 (0.4)	20.8 (1.5)	37.2 (2.7)	13.1 (0.4)	10.5 (0.4)	17.7 (1.3)	33.2 (2.6)
1981	13.9 (0.3)	11.3 (0.3)	18.4 (0.9)	33.2 (1.8)	15.1 (0.4)	12.5 (0.4)	19.9 (1.4)	36.0 (2.6)	12.8 (0.4)	10.2 (0.4)	17.1 (1.2)	30.4 (2.5)
1982	13.9 (0.3)	11.4 (0.3)	18.4 (1.0)	31.7 (1.9)	14.5 (0.4)	12.0 (0.4)	21.2 (1.5)	30.5 (2.7)	13.3 (0.4)	10.8 (0.4)	15.9 (1.3)	32.8 (2.7)
1983	13.7 (0.3)	11.1 (0.3)	18.0 (1.0)	31.6 (1.9)	14.9 (0.4)	12.2 (0.4)	19.9 (1.5)	34.3 (2.8)	12.5 (0.4)	10.1 (0.4)	16.2 (1.3)	29.1 (2.6)
1984	13.1 (0.3)	11.0 (0.3)	15.5 (0.9)	29.8 (1.9)	14.0 (0.4)	11.9 (0.4)	16.8 (1.4)	30.6 (2.8)	12.3 (0.4)	10.1 (0.4)	14.3 (1.2)	29.0 (2.6)
1985	12.6 (0.3)	10.4 (0.3)	15.2 (0.9)	27.6 (1.9)	13.4 (0.4)	11.1 (0.4)	16.1 (1.4)	29.9 (2.8)	11.8 (0.4)	9.8 (0.4)	14.3 (1.2)	25.2 (2.7)
1986	12.2 (0.3)	9.7 (0.3)	14.2 (0.9)	30.1 (1.9)	13.1 (0.4)	10.3 (0.4)	15.0 (1.3)	32.8 (2.7)	11.4 (0.4)	9.1 (0.4)	13.5 (1.2)	27.2 (2.6)
1987	12.6 (0.3)	10.4 (0.3)	14.1 (0.9)	28.6 (1.8)	13.2 (0.4)	10.8 (0.4)	15.0 (1.3)	29.1 (2.6)	12.1 (0.4)	10.0 (0.4)	13.3 (1.2)	28.1 (2.6)
1988	12.9 (0.3)	9.6 (0.3)	14.5 (1.0)	35.8 (2.3)	13.5 (0.4)	10.3 (0.5)	15.0 (1.5)	36.0 (3.2)	12.2 (0.4)	8.9 (0.4)	14.0 (1.4)	35.4 (3.3)
1989	12.6 (0.3)	9.4 (0.3)	13.9 (1.0)	33.0 (2.2)	13.6 (0.5)	10.3 (0.5)	14.9 (1.5)	34.4 (3.1)	11.7 (0.4)	8.5 (0.4)	13.0 (1.3)	31.6 (3.1)
1990	12.1 (0.3)	9.0 (0.3)	13.2 (0.9)	32.4 (1.9)	12.3 (0.4)	9.3 (0.4)	11.9 (1.3)	34.3 (2.7)	11.8 (0.4)	8.7 (0.4)	14.4 (1.3)	30.3 (2.7)
1991	12.5 (0.3)	8.9 (0.3)	13.6 (0.9)	35.3 (1.9)	13.0 (0.4)	8.9 (0.4)	13.5 (1.4)	39.2 (2.7)	11.9 (0.4)	8.9 (0.4)	13.7 (1.3)	31.1 (2.7)
1992[3]	11.0 (0.3)	7.7 (0.3)	13.7 (0.9)	29.4 (1.9)	11.3 (0.4)	8.0 (0.4)	12.5 (1.3)	32.1 (2.7)	10.7 (0.4)	7.4 (0.4)	14.8 (1.4)	26.6 (2.6)
1993[3]	11.0 (0.3)	7.9 (0.3)	13.6 (0.9)	27.5 (1.8)	11.2 (0.4)	8.2 (0.4)	12.6 (1.3)	28.1 (2.5)	10.9 (0.4)	7.6 (0.4)	14.4 (1.3)	26.9 (2.5)
1994[3]	11.4 (0.3)	7.7 (0.3)	12.6 (0.8)	30.0 (1.2)	12.3 (0.4)	8.0 (0.4)	14.1 (1.1)	31.6 (1.6)	10.6 (0.4)	7.5 (0.4)	11.3 (1.0)	28.1 (1.7)
1995[3]	12.0 (0.3)	8.6 (0.3)	12.1 (0.7)	30.0 (1.1)	12.2 (0.4)	9.0 (0.4)	11.1 (1.0)	30.0 (1.6)	11.7 (0.4)	8.2 (0.4)	12.9 (1.1)	30.0 (1.7)
1996[3]	11.1 (0.3)	7.3 (0.3)	13.0 (0.8)	29.4 (1.2)	11.4 (0.4)	7.3 (0.4)	13.5 (1.2)	30.3 (1.7)	10.9 (0.4)	7.3 (0.4)	12.5 (1.1)	28.3 (1.7)
1997[3]	11.0 (0.3)	7.6 (0.3)	13.4 (0.8)	25.3 (1.1)	11.9 (0.4)	8.5 (0.4)	13.3 (1.2)	27.0 (1.6)	10.1 (0.4)	6.7 (0.4)	13.5 (1.1)	23.4 (1.6)
1998[3]	11.8 (0.3)	7.7 (0.3)	13.8 (0.8)	29.5 (1.1)	13.3 (0.4)	8.6 (0.4)	15.5 (1.2)	33.5 (1.6)	10.3 (0.4)	6.9 (0.4)	12.2 (1.1)	25.0 (1.6)

[1]Based on the April 1960 decennial census.

[2]White and black include persons of Hispanic origin.

[3]Because of changes in data collection procedures, data may not be comparable with figures for earlier years.

—Data not available

NOTE– "Status" dropouts are 16- to 24-year-olds who are not enrolled in school and who have not completed a high school program regardless of when they left school. People who have received GED credentials are counted as high school completers. All data except for 1960 are based on October counts. Data are based upon sample surveys of the civilian noninstitutional population. Standard errors appear in parentheses.

SOURCE: U.S. Bureau of the Census, National Center for Education Statistics, October 1999

TABLE 7.13

1999 College Bound Seniors ACT Test Scores
Total Test-takers: 1,019,053 of whom 56.9% are female

ALL TEST-TAKERS	21.0
Gender	
All Males	21.1
All Females	20.9
Ethnicity	
African-American/Black	17.1
American Indian/Alaskan Native	18.9
Caucasian American/White	21.7
Mexican American/Chicano	18.6
Asian American/Pacific Islander	21.7
Puerto Rican/Hispanic	19.6
Other	19.5
Multiracial	21.2
Household Income	
Less than $18,000/year	18.4
$18,000 - $24,000/year	19.2
$24,000 - $30,000/year	19.9
$30,000 - $36,000/year	20.5
$36,000 - $42,000/year	20.8
$42,000 - $50,000/year	21.2
$50,000 - $60,000/year	21.6
$60,000 - $80,000/year	22.1
$80,000 - $100,000/year	22.7
More than $100,000/year	23.4

SOURCE: *ACT High School Profile Report: H.S. Graduating Class of 1999. National Report.* The National Center for Fair and Open Testing

led many schools to take special steps to boost the number of minorities that they admitted, a process commonly called affirmative action.

Over time, many people came to see affirmative action as a bad policy. Their reasons were varied, but a common complaint was that affirmative action unfairly allowed some minority students to get into colleges even when their test scores and high school grade points than those colleges would accept from White students. In June 1996 California governor Pete Wilson urged Californian voters to support the California Civil Rights Initiative (Proposition 209), a proposal to eliminate affirmative action in higher-education enrollment. His critics disagreed. Jesse Jackson, a former Democratic presidential nominee and a defender of civil rights for minorities, observed that affirmative action supporters abrace fairness. He went on to say that affirmative action is a conservative remedy to generations of unfair practices that favored White men. On the other hand, Joanne Corday Kozberg, the state's secretary of state, said that Wilson's initiative would start a new era toward a colorblind society.

In November 1996 California voters approved Proposition 209, prohibiting public universities from considering race and ethnicity when deciding on admissions. In 1997, the last year during which the University of California considered race and ethnicity in its admissions process, 7,236 underrepresented minority groups (American Indians, Blacks, and Hispanics) were admitted, accounting for 18.8 percent of total admissions. Asian/Pacific Islander freshmen, numbering nearly 12,800, comprised 33.2 percent of new admissions, compared to 40.4 percent of Whites.

In 1998, the first year of admissions after Proposition 209 went into effect, the proportion of underrepresented minorities dropped to 16.7 percent. The University of California reported that, in 1999, the proportion of this group rose to 16.9 percent, and climbed to 17.6 percent in 2000. In 2000 Whites made up 38.2 percent and Asian Americans made up 34.2 percent of freshmen admissions. Of the underrepresented minorities, 13.8 percent

TABLE 7.14

Number and Percent of SAT I Test Takers for Males, Females, and Total by Ethnic Group

SAT I Test Takers Who Described Themselves as:	Number			Percent		Percent Responding		
	Males	Females	Total	Male	Female	Male	Female	Total
American Indian or Alaskan Native	3,760	4,501	8,261	46	54	1	1	1
Asian, Asian American, or Pacific Islander	46,319	49,789	96,108	48	52	10	8	9
African American or Black	48,861	70,533	119,394	41	59	10	12	11
Hispanic or Latino Background:								
Mexican or Mexican American	18,349	24,811	43,160	43	57	4	4	4
Puerto Rican	5,862	8,124	13,986	42	58	1	1	1
Latin American, South American, Central American, or Other Hispanic or Latino	15,803	21,718	37,521	42	58	3	4	3
White	326,799	390,833	717,632	46	54	68	66	67
Other	16,371	21,759	38,130	43	57	3	4	4
No Response	80,787	65,151	145,938	55	45	—	—	—
Total	**482,124**	**592,068**	**1,074,192**	**—**	**—**	**100**	**100**	**100**

SOURCE: SAT College Board Online

were Hispanics, 3.2 percent were Blacks, and .6 percent were American Indians.

In March 1996, in the case of *Hopwood v. Texas* (78 F.3d 932), often called Bakke II, the Fifth Circuit Court of Appeals unanimously ruled that the University of Texas (UT) School of Law was discriminating against White students by using race or ethnicity as a factor in admissions. Four White applicants charged that less-qualified Black and Hispanic students had been accepted instead of them due to racial preference on UT's part. The appeals court ruled that colleges could not give preferences to minority students, even for what it called "the wholesome practice of correcting perceived racial imbalance in the student body." In the opinion of the appeals court, "any consideration of race or ethnicity by the law school for the purpose of achieving a diverse student body is not a compelling interest under the Fourteenth Amendment." The *Hopwood* decision applies to all public universities in Texas, Louisiana, and Mississippi. In Texas, then-Attorney General Dan Morales applied the admissions ruling to include financial aid and scholarships.

The UT School of Law admits 500 students per year. In 1997, following the decision affecting the law school, only three Black students sent in tuition deposits, and none actually joined the class. (There were 31 Black students admitted in the previous class.) Only 20 Hispanic students joined the first-year class in 1997, down from 42 the previous year. At the undergraduate levels, public universities throughout Texas also saw a drop in minority applications. UT registered 4 percent fewer Hispanics and nearly 33 percent fewer Blacks. Texas A&M University welcomed nearly 13 percent fewer Hispanics and 29 percent fewer Blacks.

PUBLIC UNIVERSITIES RESPOND. In 1998 the University of Texas (UT) system became the first public university to grant automatic admission to first-time freshmen based on class rank. Under Texas Education Code 51.803, students who are graduated in the top 10 percent of their class from an accredited Texas high school are guaranteed admission to UT. Since some high schools have large minority populations, state officials hope that more minority students will be admitted to state universities.

In March 1999 University of California (UC) regents approved a similar admission policy called Eligibility in the Local Context (ELC). Under ELC, students graduating in the top 4 percent of their class in California high schools will be eligible for admission to one of UC's undergraduate campuses. ELC will be implemented starting with freshmen applicants in the fall of 2001. Persons who oppose UC's new policy claim that such a step may send a negative message to minority students who do not excel in class.

TABLE 7.15

1999 College Bound Seniors SAT Test Scores
Total Test-Takers: 1,220,130 of whom 53.9% are female

	Verbal	Math	Total
Ethnic Group			
American Indian or Alaskan Native	484	481	965
Asian, Asian Amer., or Pacific Islander	498	560	1,058
African American or Black	434	422	856
Mexican or Mexican American	453	456	909
Puerto Rican	455	448	903
Other Hispanic or Latino	463	464	927
White	527	528	1,055
Other	511	513	1,024
Family Income			
Less than $10,000/year	427	444	871
$10,000 - $20,000/year	449	458	907
$20,000 - $30,000/year	476	478	954
$30,000 - $40,000/year	493	493	986
$40,000 - $50,000/year	505	506	1,011
$50,000 - $60,000/year	514	516	1,030
$60,000 - $70,000/year	520	523	1,043
$70,000 - $80,000/year	527	531	1,058
$80,000 - $100,000/year	539	543	1,082
More than $100,000/year	559	571	1,130
Gender			
Female	502	495	997
Male	509	531	1,040
All Test-Takers	**505**	**511**	**1,016**

SOURCE: *College-Bound Seniors National Report, 1999.* College Board

Increasing Enrollment Rates for Women

The proportion of women in institutions of higher education rose from 48 percent in 1976 to 54.4 percent in 1997. Asian/Pacific Islander (a 386 percent increase from 1976 to 1997) and Hispanic (a 292 percent increase) women made the greatest gains in the numbers enrolled over those years. American Indian (116.2 percent) and Black (70.5 percent) women also saw significant increases. (See Table 7.3.) With the exception of "nonresident aliens," women in institutions of higher learning significantly outnumbered men in their racial/ethnic category.

Between 1976 and 1997 the proportion of White men enrolled in higher education fell from 43.8 percent to 31.4 percent of all students, while the number of enrolled men from all other racial/ethnic groups increased during the same period. Asian/Pacific Islander men increased their numbers 282 percent; Hispanic men, 147 percent; Blacks, 21.8 percent; and Native American men, 49.6 percent. (See Table 7.3.)

Earning Bachelor's Degrees

Although minority attendance increased in institutions of higher learning, not all minorities finish college and receive a bachelor's degree. The overall number of minority students who received degrees rose 145 percent between 1976–77 and 1996–97, from 94,498 to 231,372. There were, however, large differences within groups during this period. The number of bachelor's degrees

TABLE 7.16

Trends in Average SAT Mathematics and Verbal Scores, by Race/Ethnicity, 1991–1996

Race/ethnicity	1991	1992	1993	1994	1995	1996	1991 to 1996 change Number	Percent
Total								
Number of students	1,032,685	1,034,131	1,044,465	1,050,386	1,067,993	1,084,725	52,040	5
SAT V - mean	499	500	500	499	504	505	6	-
SAT M - mean	500	501	503	504	506	508	8	-
White								
Number of students	687,231	680,806	670,965	662,107	674,343	681,053	(6,178)	-1
SAT V - mean	518	519	520	520	525	526	8	-
SAT M - mean	.513	515	517	519	521	523	10	-
Asian American								
Number of students	76,703	78,387	78,693	81,097	81,514	84,319	7,616	10
SAT V - mean	485	487	489	489	492	496	11	-
SAT M - mean	548	551	553	553	555	558	10	-
Black								
Number of students	100,209	99,126	102,939	102,679	103,872	106,573	6,364	6
SAT V - mean	427	428	429	428	432	434	7	-
SAT M - mean	419	419	421	421	422	422	3	-
Mexican American								
Number of students	28,602	30,336	32,355	35,397	36,323	36,689	8,087	28
SAT V - mean	454	449	451	448	453	455	1	-
SAT M - mean	459	457	459	458	458	459	0	-
Puerto Rican[1]								
Number of students	12,065	12,091	12,645	13,036	13,056	13,103	1,038	9
SAT V - mean	436	442	443	444	448	452	16	-
SAT M - mean	439	438	440	442	444	445	6	-
Latin American								
Number of students	25,584	26,766	28,420	29,395	30,713	32,193	6,609	26
SAT V - mean	458	459	460	460	465	465	7	-
SAT M - mean	462	463	463	464	468	466	4	-
American Indian								
Number of students	7,843	7,412	7,488	8,150	8,936	8,737	894	11
SAT V - mean	470	472	477	473	480	483	13	-
SAT M - mean	468	471	476	470	476	477	9	-
Other								
Number of students	16,300	17,771	19,614	22,198	25,113	28,099	11,799	72
SAT V - mean	486	491	497	500	507	511	25	-
SAT M - mean	492	498	501	504	510	512	20	-

[1] Excludes students in Puerto Rico.
NOTES: - = not applicable. V = verbal, M = mathematics. Total includes persons of unknown race/ethnicity.
SOURCE: *Trends in Average (mean) SAT Mathematics and Verbal Scores, by Race/Ethnicity: 1991–1996.* National Science Foundation: 1998

earned by non-Hispanic Black men increased 33.3 percent, while the number of degrees awarded to non-Hispanic Black women grew 80.8 percent. The number of degrees earned by Asian/Pacific Islander men more than quadrupled, while the number earned by their female counterparts increased nearly sixfold. The number of Hispanic women receiving a college degree more than quadrupled, while the number of American Indian/Alaskan Native women earning a college degree more than tripled. (See Table 7.17.)

Tribal Colleges

Special post-secondary institutions, collectively known as Tribal Colleges, were established to prepare students with the skills most needed on Indian reservations, while at the same time preserving their culture. Usually situated in areas where the students cannot oth-erwise pursue education beyond high school, these colleges all offer associate's degrees. In addition, four offer bachelor's degrees and two offer master's degrees. The American Indian Higher Education Consortium (AIHEC) and the Institute for Higher Education Policy, in *Tribal Colleges: An Introduction* (Alexandria, Virginia, and Washington, DC, February 1999) report that in the academic period 1995–96, 25,000 students were enrolled in 31 U.S. Tribal Colleges in 12 states, up from 2,100 students in 1982.

Tribal Colleges offer courses—ranging from teaching and nursing to secretarial skills and computer science—to meet the needs of specific communities. Besides tribal languages, traditional subjects are a part of the curricula. According to AIHEC, an example is a traditional tribal literature class offered only in the winter term by Bay Mills Community College in Brimley,

TABLE 7.17

Bachelor's Degrees Conferred by Institutions of Higher Education, by Racial/Ethnic Group and Sex of Student: 1976–77 to 1996–97

	Number of degrees conferred							Percentage distribution of degrees conferred to U.S. citizens					
Year	Total	White, non-Hispanic	Black, non-Hispanic	Hispanic	Asian/Pacific Islander	American Indian/Alaskan Native	Non-resident alien	Total	White, non-Hispanic	Black, non-Hispanic	Hispanic	Asian/Pacific Islander	American Indian/Alaskan Native
1	2	3	4	5	6	7	8	9	10	11	12	13	14
				Total						Total			
1976-77[1]	917,900	807,688	58,636	18,743	13,793	3,326	15,714	100.0	89.5	6.5	2.1	1.5	0.4
1978-79[2]	919,540	802,542	60,246	20,096	15,407	3,410	17,839	100.0	89.0	6.7	2.2	1.7	0.4
1980-81[3]	934,800	807,319	60,673	21,832	18,794	3,593	22,589	100.0	88.5	6.7	2.4	2.1	0.4
1984-85[4]	968,311	826,106	57,473	25,874	25,395	4,246	29,217	100.0	88.0	6.1	2.8	2.7	0.5
1986-87[5]	991,264	841,818	56,560	26,988	32,624	3,968	29,306	100.0	87.5	5.9	2.8	3.4	0.4
1988-89[5,6]	1,016,350	859,703	58,078	29,918	37,674	3,951	27,026	100.0	86.9	5.9	3.0	3.8	0.4
1989-90[5,7]	1,048,631	884,376	61,063	32,844	39,248	4,392	26,708	100.0	86.5	6.0	3.2	3.8	0.4
1990-91[5,8]	1,081,280	904,062	65,341	36,612	41,618	4,513	29,134	100.0	85.9	6.2	3.5	4.0	0.4
1991-92[5,9]	1,129,833	936,771	72,326	40,761	46,720	5,176	28,079	100.0	85.0	6.6	3.7	4.2	0.5
1992-93[5,10]	1,159,931	947,309	77,872	45,376	51,463	5,671	32,240	100.0	84.0	6.9	4.0	4.6	0.5
1993-94[5,11]	1,165,973	936,227	83,576	50,241	55,660	6,189	34,080	100.0	82.7	7.4	4.4	4.9	0.5
1994-95[5,12]	1,158,788	913,377	87,203	54,201	60,478	6,606	36,923	100.0	81.4	7.8	4.8	5.4	0.6
1995-96[5,13]	1,163,036	904,709	91,166	58,288	64,359	6,970	37,544	100.0	80.4	8.1	5.2	5.7	0.6
1996-97[5,14]	1,168,023	898,224	94,053	61,941	67,969	7,409	38,427	100.0	79.5	8.3	5.5	6.0	0.7
				Men						Men			
1976-77[1]	494,424	438,161	25,147	10,318	7,638	1,804	11,356	100.0	90.7	5.2	2.1	1.6	0.4
1978-79[2]	476,065	418,215	24,659	10,418	8,261	1,736	12,776	100.0	90.3	5.3	2.2	1.8	0.4
1980-81[3]	469,625	406,173	24,511	10,810	10,107	1,700	16,324	100.0	89.6	5.4	2.4	2.2	0.4
1984-85[4]	476,148	405,085	23,018	12,402	13,554	1,998	20,091	100.0	88.8	5.0	2.7	3.0	0.4
1986-87[5]	480,782	406,749	22,501	12,865	17,253	1,817	19,597	100.0	88.2	4.9	2.8	3.7	0.4
1988-89[5,6]	481,946	407,154	22,370	13,950	19,260	1,730	17,482	100.0	87.7	4.8	3.0	4.1	0.4
1989-90[5,7]	490,317	413,573	23,262	14,941	19,721	1,859	16,961	100.0	87.4	4.9	3.2	4.2	0.4
1990-91[5,8]	496,424	415,505	24,328	16,158	20,678	1,901	17,854	100.0	86.8	5.1	3.4	4.3	0.4
1991-92[5,9]	516,976	429,842	26,956	17,976	23,248	2,182	16,772	100.0	85.9	5.4	3.6	4.6	0.4
1992-93[5,10]	530,541	435,084	28,883	19,865	25,293	2,449	18,967	100.0	85.0	5.6	3.9	4.9	0.5
1993-94[5,11]	530,804	429,121	30,648	21,807	26,938	2,616	19,674	100.0	84.0	6.0	4.3	5.3	0.5
1994-95[5,12]	525,174	417,006	31,775	23,600	28,973	2,736	21,084	100.0	82.7	6.3	4.7	5.7	0.5
1995-96[5,13]	521,439	408,829	32,852	24,994	30,630	2,885	21,249	100.0	81.7	6.6	5.0	6.1	0.6
1996-97[5,14]	517,901	401,878	33,509	26,007	32,111	2,988	21,408	100.0	80.9	6.7	5.2	6.5	0.6

TABLE 7.17
Bachelor's Degrees Conferred by Institutions of Higher Education, by Racial/Ethnic Group and Sex of Student: 1976–77 to 1996–97 [CONTINUED]

Year	Number of degrees conferred							Percentage distribution of degrees conferred to U.S. citizens					
	Total	White, non-Hispanic	Black, non-Hispanic	Hispanic	Asian/Pacific Islander	American Indian/Alaskan Native	Non-resident alien	Total	White, non-Hispanic	Black, non-Hispanic	Hispanic	Asian/Pacific Islander	American Indian/Alaskan Native
1	2	3	4	5	6	7	8	9	10	11	12	13	14
				Women						Women			
1976–77[1]	423,476	369,527	33,489	8,425	6,155	1,522	4,358	100.0	88.2	8.0	2.0	1.5	0.4
1978–79[2]	443,475	384,327	35,587	9,678	7,146	1,674	5,063	100.0	87.7	8.1	2.2	1.6	0.4
1980–81[3]	465,175	401,146	36,162	11,022	8,687	1,893	6,265	100.0	87.4	7.9	2.4	1.9	0.4
1984–85[4]	492,163	421,021	34,455	13,472	11,841	2,248	9,126	100.0	87.2	7.1	2.8	2.5	0.5
1986–87[5]	510,482	435,069	34,059	14,123	15,371	2,151	9,709	100.0	86.9	6.8	2.8	3.1	0.4
1988–89[5,6]	534,404	452,549	35,708	15,968	18,414	2,221	9,544	100.0	86.2	6.8	3.0	3.5	0.4
1989–90[5,7]	558,314	470,803	37,801	17,903	19,527	2,533	9,747	100.0	85.8	6.9	3.3	3.6	0.5
1990–91[5,8]	584,856	488,557	41,013	20,454	20,940	2,612	11,280	100.0	85.2	7.2	3.6	3.7	0.5
1991–92[5,9]	612,857	506,929	45,370	22,785	23,472	2,994	11,307	100.0	84.3	7.5	3.8	3.9	0.5
1992–93[5,10]	629,390	512,225	48,989	25,511	26,170	3,222	13,273	100.0	83.1	8.0	4.1	4.2	0.5
1993–94[5,11]	635,169	507,106	52,928	28,434	28,722	3,573	14,406	100.0	81.7	8.5	4.6	4.6	0.6
1994–95[5,12]	633,614	496,371	55,428	30,601	31,505	3,870	15,839	100.0	80.3	9.0	5.0	5.1	0.6
1995–96[5,13]	641,597	495,880	58,314	33,294	33,729	4,085	16,295	100.0	79.3	9.3	5.3	5.4	0.7
1996–97[5,14]	650,122	496,346	60,544	35,934	35,858	4,421	17,019	100.0	78.4	9.6	5.7	5.7	0.7

[1] Excludes 1,121 men and 528 women whose racial/ethnic group was not available.
[2] Excludes 1,279 men and 571 women whose racial/ethnic group was not available.
[3] Excludes 258 men and 82 women whose racial/ethnic group was not available.
[4] Excludes 6,380 men and 4,786 women whose racial/ethnic group was not available.
[5] Reported racial/ethnic distributions of students by level of degree, field of degree, and sex were used to estimate race/ethnicity for students whose race/ethnicity was not reported.
[6] Excludes 1,400 men and 1,005 women whose racial/ethnic group and field of study were not available.
[7] Excludes 1,379 men and 1,334 women whose racial/ethnic group and field of study were not available.
[8] Excludes 7,621 men and 5,637 women whose racial/ethnic group and field of study were not available.
[9] Excludes 3,835 men and 2,885 women whose racial/ethnic group and field of study were not available.
[10] Excludes 2,340 men and 2,907 women whose racial/ethnic group and field of study were not available.
[11] Excludes 1,618 men and 1,684 women whose racial/ethnic group and field of study were not available.
[12] Excludes 957 men and 389 women whose racial/ethnic group and field of study were not available.
[13] Excludes 1,015 men and 741 women whose racial/ethnic group and field of study were not available.
[14] Excludes 2,614 men and 2,242 women whose racial/ethnic group and field of study were not available.

NOTE—For years 1984–85 to 1996–97, reported racial/ethnic distributions of students by level of degree, field of degree, and sex were used to estimate race/ethnicity for students whose race/ethnicity was not reported. Because of rounding, percents may not add to 100.0.

SOURCE: *Digest of Education Statistics 1999,* National Center for Education Statistics

TABLE 7.18

Selected Statistics on Historically Black Colleges and Universities, 1980, 1990, 1996, and 1997

		Public		Private	
Item	Total	4-year	2-year	4-year	2-year
1	2	3	4	5	6
Number of institutions, fall 1997	**101**	**41**	**10**	**47**	**3**
Total enrollment, fall 1980	233,557	155,085	13,132	62,924	2,416
Men	106,387	70,236	6,758	28,352	1,041
Men, black	81,818	53,654	2,781	24,412	971
Women	127,170	84,849	6,374	34,572	1,375
Women, black	109,171	70,582	4,644	32,589	1,356
Total enrollment, fall 1990	257,152	171,969	15,077	68,528	1,578
Men	105,157	70,220	6,321	28,054	562
Men, black	82,897	54,041	3,214	25,198	444
Women	151,995	101,749	8,756	40,474	1,016
Women, black	125,785	80,883	6,066	38,115	721
Total enrollment, fall 1997	269,167	175,297	19,377	73,563	930
Men	106,865	69,338	7,921	29,286	320
Men, black	86,641	55,817	3,789	26,755	280
Women	162,302	105,959	11,456	44,277	610
Women, black	135,690	86,509	6,924	41,660	597
Full-time enrollment, fall 1997	209,301	132,231	10,205	66,196	669
Men	85,217	54,426	4,112	26,409	270
Women	124,084	77,805	6,093	39,787	399
Part-time enrollment, fall 1997	59,866	43,066	9,172	7,367	261
Men	21,648	14,912	3,809	2,877	50
Women	38,218	28,154	5,363	4,490	211
Earned degrees conferred, 1996–97					
Associate	3,222	1,275	1,751	96	100
Men	1,079	409	609	21	40
Men, black	511	159	299	16	37
Women	2,143	866	1,142	75	60
Women, black	1,267	370	768	69	60
Bachelor's	29,450	20,221	—	9,229	—
Men	10,713	7,506	—	3,207	—
Men, black	8,928	5,975	—	2,953	—
Women	18,737	12,715	—	6,022	—
Women, black	16,240	10,513	—	5,727	—
Master's	6,421	5,300	—	1,121	—
Men	1,946	1,637	—	309	—
Men, black	1,162	939	—	223	—
Women	4,475	3,663	—	812	—
Women, black	3,043	2,377	—	666	—
Doctor's	239	103	—	136	—
Men	111	39	—	72	—
Men, black	69	21	—	48	—
Women	128	64	—	64	—
Women, black	86	33	—	53	—
First-professional	1,336	504	—	832	—
Men	613	252	—	361	—
Men, black	368	116	—	252	—
Women	723	252	—	471	—
Women, black	517	170	—	347	—
Financial statistics, 1995–96, in thousands of dollars					
Current-fund revenues	$3,855,794	$2,037,292	$96,108	$1,712,458	$9,936
Tuition and fees	942,423	419,116	18,198	501,837	3,272
Federal government[2]	816,612	322,323	16,992	474,154	3,142
State governments[2]	942,577	844,659	49,045	48,406	466
Local governments[2]	96,157	80,093	6,793	9,064	207
Private gifts, grants, and contracts	240,160	36,703	170	202,049	1,237
Endowment income	37,014	2,616	3	34,385	10
Sales and services	688,975	284,649	3,651	399,285	1,391
Other sources	91,876	47,134	1,255	43,276	211

Michigan, because the stories are supposed to be told in the winter months when snow is on the ground.

A survey by AIHEC found that 42 percent of the students who earned two-year degrees before transferring to a mainstream institution were graduated, with 90 percent of them receiving bachelor's degrees. (Only 30 percent of American Indians who enter mainstream institutions as freshmen are graduated.)

Most Tribal College enrollees are the first generation in their family to attend college. One-half are part-time students and over half are single parents. In fall 1996 nearly two-thirds (64 percent) of Tribal College enrollees

TABLE 7.18

Selected Statistics on Historically Black Colleges and Universities, 1980, 1990, 1996, and 1997 [CONTINUED]

Item		Total	Public		Private	
			4-year	2-year	4-year	2-year
1	2		3	4	5	6
Current-fund expenditures		3,744,816	2,003,637	95,818	1,634,808	10,554
Educational and general expenditures		3,112,805	1,738,574	92,034	1,271,960	10,238
Auxiliar y enterprises		388,753	265,063	3,785	119,590	316
Hospitals		233,460	0	0	233,460	0
Independent operations		9,798	0	0	9,798	0

[1] Historically black colleges and universities are accredited institutions of higher education established prior to 1964 with the principal mission of educating black Americans. Federal regulations, 20 U.S. Code, Section 1061 (2), allow for certain exceptions to the founding date. Most institutions are in the southern and border states and were established prior to 1954.

[2] Includes appropriations, grants, contracts, and independent operations.

— Not applicable.

NOTE—Because of rounding, details may not add to totals.

SOURCE: *Digest of Education Statistics 1999*. National Center for Education Statistics

were females, compared to 56 percent of public-college female undergraduates. In 1997 the average age of American Indian students was 31.5 years.

Tribal Colleges are under-funded, as they are not actually given all of the government funding that they have been authorized to have. In 1999, at $2,964 per Native American student, federal funding was well below the authorized amount of $6,000. Tribal Colleges get no federal money for non-Native American students, who make up about 10 percent of the enrollment.

In 1994 Tribal Colleges earned land-grant status, giving them access to U.S. Department of Agriculture resources, as well as equity grants of $50,000 per college. They will also share, with 55 state universities and 17 historically Black colleges and universities, the interest from an annual $4.6 million endowment fund.

Black Colleges and Universities

There are more than 100 historically Black colleges and universities in the United States. In 1997, 41 Black public colleges and universities were four-year institutions, and 10 were two-year colleges. There were 47 Black private four-year schools and three private two-year colleges. The state with the largest number of historically Black colleges (14) is Alabama. North Carolina is home to 11 Black institutions, while 11 are located in Georgia and 9 in Texas.

In the fall of 1997 over 269,000 Black students were enrolled in these institutions of higher learning. Most of them (175,297) attended four-year Black public colleges or universities, while 73,563 attended four-year Black private schools.

In 1996–97, 511 Black men and 1,267 Black women earned associate's degrees at historically Black colleges and universities. Another 8,928 Black men and 16,240 Black women were awarded bachelor's degrees. At the graduate level, 1,162 Black men and 3,043 Black women earned master's degrees. Doctorate degrees were awarded to 69 Black men and 86 Black women, while first-professional degrees went to 368 Black men and 517 Black women. (See Table 7.18.)

COURT-ORDERED DESEGREGATION

On May 17, 1954, in *Brown v. Board of Education of Topeka, Kansas* (347 U.S. 483), the Supreme Court declared that separate schools for Black children were inherently unequal and that the schools had to be desegregated. More than 45 years later, more and more school districts are questioning whether the federal courts need to continue supervising desegregation. Despite regulations and busing, many inner-city schools are still not integrated, and academic achievement for Blacks is still lagging. Many White students have moved out to the suburbs or transferred to private schools to avoid inner-city schools. Typically, half the White students assigned to new schools under desegregation orders never attend those schools.

CHAPTER 8

CRIME

VICTIMIZATION OF MINORITIES

In 1998 the Bureau of Justice Statistics polled about 94,000 people 12 years and older about their experiences of criminal victimizations over the previous six months. The survey (*Criminal Victimization in the United States, 1998,* Washington, DC, 2000) found that certain population groups—the poor, younger persons, males, Blacks, Hispanics, and residents of inner cities—are more likely to be victimized and are more vulnerable to violence than other groups. As discussed in other sections of this book,

Blacks and Hispanics are more likely to be poor, to live in central cities, and to be unemployed than are Whites. These factors put minorities at an especially high risk of being victimized.

Violent Crimes

Blacks are more likely than Whites or persons of any other races, such as Asians or Native Americans, to be victims of violent crimes. In 1998 there were 5.9 robberies for every 1,000 Black persons, compared to 3.7 for every

TABLE 8.1

Rates of Violent Crime and Personal Theft, by Gender, Age, Race, and Hispanic Origin, 1998

		Victimizations per 1,000 persons age 12 or older						
		Violent crimes						
					Assault			Per-
Characteristic of victim	Population	All crimes of violence*	Rape/ Sexual assault	Robbery	Total	Aggra- vated	Simple	sonal theft
Gender								
Male	107,595,530	43.1	0.2	4.6	38.3	10.5	27.8	1.2
Female	114,285,430	30.4	2.7	3.5	24.3	4.7	19.5	1.5
Age								
12-15	15,781,590	82.4	3.5	7.7	71.2	12.2	58.9	2.0
16-19	15,620,290	91.1	5.0	11.4	74.7	19.0	55.7	2.3
20-24	17,663,220	67.3	4.6	7.9	54.8	16.0	38.8	1.8
25-34	39,263,480	41.5	1.7	4.2	35.6	8.4	27.3	1.0
35-49	63,428,180	29.9	0.7	3.2	26.1	6.8	19.3	1.2
50-64	37,939,800	15.4	0.2	1.7	13.5	3.3	10.2	1.6
65 or older	32,184,400	2.8	0.0	0.5	2.3	0.5	1.8	0.8
Race								
White	185,831,440	36.3	1.5	3.7	31.1	7.0	24.2	1.2
Black	27,020,600	41.7	2.0	5.9	33.7	11.9	21.8	2.1
Other	9,028,930	27.6	0.7	4.4	22.5	6.6	15.9	1.4
Hispanic origin								
Hispanic	21,699,490	32.8	0.8	6.3	25.6	6.1	19.5	1.7
Non-Hispanic	197,506,660	36.8	1.6	3.7	31.5	7.6	23.9	1.3

*The National Crime Victimization Survey includes as violent crime rape/sexual assault, robbery, and assault, but not murder and manslaughter.

SOURCE: Callie Marie Rennison. *Criminal Victimization 1998: Changes 1997–98 with trends 1993–98.* Bureau of Justice Statistics: Washington, D.C., July 1999

FIGURE 8.1

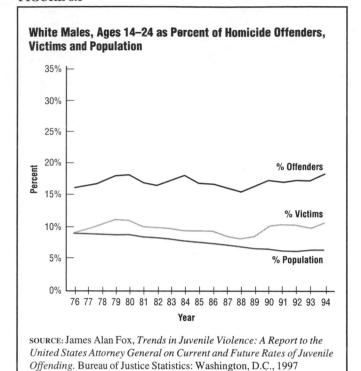

White Males, Ages 14–24 as Percent of Homicide Offenders, Victims and Population

SOURCE: James Alan Fox, *Trends in Juvenile Violence: A Report to the United States Attorney General on Current and Future Rates of Juvenile Offending.* Bureau of Justice Statistics: Washington, D.C., 1997

FIGURE 8.2

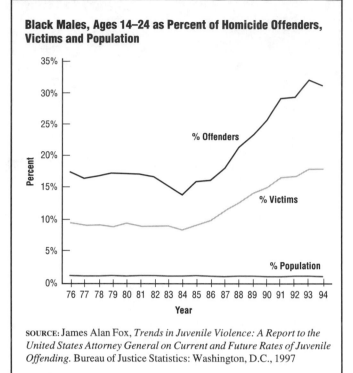

Black Males, Ages 14–24 as Percent of Homicide Offenders, Victims and Population

SOURCE: James Alan Fox, *Trends in Juvenile Violence: A Report to the United States Attorney General on Current and Future Rates of Juvenile Offending.* Bureau of Justice Statistics: Washington, D.C., 1997

TABLE 8.2

Percentage of Population, Homicide Victims, and Homicide Offenders by Age, Sex and Race

| | 14-17 | | | | 18-24 | | | | 25+ | | | |
| | Male | | Female | | Male | | Female | | Male | | Female | |
	White	Black	White	Black	White	Black	White	Black	White	Black	White	Black
1976-78												
Population	3.4%	.5%	3.2%	.5%	5.4%	.7%	5.6%	.9%	23.9%	2.4%	26.6%	3.1%
Victims	1.6%	1.3%	.8%	.4%	8.0%	7.9%	2.8%	2.4%	27.7%	25.9%	9.5%	6.0%
Offenders	3.6%	3.5%	.4%	.5%	12.9%	13.3%	1.6%	2.6%	24.2%	24.6%	4.3%	6.8%
1979-82												
Population	3.0%	.5%	2.9%	.5%	5.4%	.8%	5.5%	.9%	24.5%	2.6%	27.3%	3.3%
Victims	1.5%	1.3%	.7%	.4%	9.0%	7.9%	3.0%	2.0%	28.8%	25.1%	9.5%	5.6%
Offenders	3.4%	3.3%	.3%	.4%	13.9%	13.7%	1.5%	2.3%	25.7%	23.8%	4.1%	5.6%
1983-86												
Population	2.6%	.5%	2.5%	.5%	5.0%	.8%	5.1%	.9%	25.3%	2.8%	27.9%	3.5%
Victims	1.2%	1.3%	.7%	.4%	8.1%	7.8%	2.8%	2.0%	28.8%	23.7%	10.9%	5.8%
Offenders	3.2%	3.1%	.4%	.4%	14.0%	12.3%	1.5%	2.0%	28.0%	23.4%	4.1%	5.3%
1987-90												
Population	2.4%	.4%	2.2%	.4%	4.4%	.7%	4.4%	.8%	26.0%	3.0%	28.4%	3.7%
Victims	1.4%	2.5%	.6%	.4%	7.4%	10.9%	2.3%	1.9%	25.5%	24.5%	10.0%	6.3%
Offenders	3.8%	5.5%	.3%	.3%	12.5%	16.7%	1.4%	1.7%	25.5%	21.9%	3.6%	4.5%
1991-94												
Population	2.2%	.4%	2.1%	.4%	4.1%	.7%	4.0%	.7%	26.2%	3.1%	28.4%	3.8%
Victims	2.1%	3.3%	.5%	.5%	8.0%	13.9%	1.9%	1.8%	23.3%	23.1%	8.7%	6.0%
Offenders	4.7%	8.3%	.3%	.4%	12.7%	21.9%	I.0%	1.5%	21.4%	18.4%	3.0%	3.5%

SOURCE: James Alan Fox, *Trends in Juvenile Violence: A Report to the United States Attorney General on Current and Future Rates of Juvenile Offending.* Bureau of Justice Statistics: Washington, D.C., 1997

1,000 White persons, and 4.4 robberies for every 1,000 persons in other racial categories. Blacks were also more likely to suffer aggravated assault (11.9 per 1,000) than Whites (7 per 1,000) and people of other races (6.6 per 1,000). The victimization rates for rape/sexual assault var-

ied from 2 per 1,000 for Blacks, 1.5 per 1,000 for Whites, and .7 per 1,000 for other racial groups. (See Table 8.1.)

The Hispanic rate of violent crime victimization (32.8 per 1,000 persons) was slightly lower than the non-

TABLE 8.3

Murder Victims by Age, Sex, and Race, 1998

Age	Total	Sex			Race			
		Male	Female	Unknown	White	Black	Other	Unknown
Total	14,088	10,606	3,419	63	6,931	6,619	325	213
Percent distribution[1]	100.0	75.3	24.3	.4	49.2	47.0	2.3	1.5
Under 18[2]	1,598	1,083	515	–	842	696	44	16
Under 22[2]	3,763	2,933	829	1	1,710	1,941	86	26
18 and over[2]	12,194	9,344	2,846	4	5,983	5,829	277	105
Infant (under 1)	220	133	87	–	129	79	5	7
1 to 4	323	178	145	–	174	138	7	4
5 to 8	107	49	58	–	62	40	5	–
9 to 12	101	46	55	–	68	26	7	–
13 to 16	480	355	125	–	239	227	12	2
17 to 19	1,460	1,255	204	1	629	784	38	9
20 to 24	2,516	2,163	352	1	1,031	1,434	36	15
25 to 29	2,011	1,618	392	1	818	1,127	47	19
30 to 34	1,529	1,121	408	–	781	709	28	11
35 to 39	1,454	1,013	441	–	742	666	30	16
40 to 44	1,168	821	347	–	628	491	36	13
45 to 49	762	546	215	1	422	303	26	11
50 to 54	489	371	118	–	297	176	12	4
55 to 59	317	236	81	–	209	98	7	3
60 to 64	227	168	59	–	147	70	8	2
65 to 69	176	128	48	–	119	48	7	2
70 to 74	157	92	65	–	118	33	4	2
75 and over	295	134	161	–	212	76	6	1
Unknown	296	179	58	59	106	94	4	92

[1] Because of rounding, percentages may not add to total.
[2] Does not include unknown ages.

SOURCE: *Crime in the United States, 1998,* Federal Bureau of Investigation

Hispanic rate (36.8 per 1,000 persons). (See Table 8.1.) In 1998 Hispanics were much more likely to be robbed than non-Hispanics (6.3 per 1,000 persons versus 3.7 per 1,000 persons), but somewhat less likely to be victims of an aggravated assault (6.1 versus 7.6 per 1,000).

In 1998, according to the Federal Bureau of Investigation (FBI), in its publication *Crime in the United States, 1998* (Washington, DC, 1999), youths, Blacks, and males were most vulnerable to violent crime:

• 1 in 12 persons age 12 to 15, compared to 1 in 357 persons age 65 or over

• 1 in 24 Blacks, compared to 1 in 28 Whites

• 1 in 23 males, compared to 1 in 33 females

The ages between 16 and 19 are the most violent for victims. In 1998, according to the U.S. Bureau of Justice Statistics (BJS), the rate for assault victims ages 16 to 19 was 91 per 1,000 persons, compared to 2.8 per 1,000 persons for those age 65 and older.

Trends in Juvenile Violence: A Report to the United States Attorney General on Current and Future Rates of Juvenile Offending (1996), prepared for the BJS by Dr. James A. Fox, dean of the College of Criminal Justice of Northeastern University, found that between 1976 and 1994, rates of homicide victimization increased among White and Black males but not females. While males between the ages of 14 and 24 made up less than 8 percent of the population, they accounted for 27 percent of the victims of homicide. Young White males ages 14 to 24 made up 7 percent of the population in 1994, but were 10 percent of the homicide victims. Black males 14 to 24 years of age accounted for just over 1 percent of the population, but comprised 17 percent of the victims in 1994. (See Figures 8.1 and 8.2 and Table 8.2.)

MURDER. The FBI, in *Crime in the United States, 1998,* reported a total of 6,931 White murder victims and 6,619 Black murder victims in the United States in 1998. More than 300 victims were of other races, and the races of 213 victims were unknown. Most victims were young males—65 percent of male victims were under the age of 35. About 10 percent were under the age of 18. (See Table 8.3.) Black offenders killed nearly all Black victims (94 percent), and White offenders killed 87 percent of White murder victims. In 1998, 29.7 percent of those arrested for murder were Black and 68 percent were White.

REPORTING TO THE POLICE. According to the Bureau of Justice Statistics, Blacks are more likely to report a violent crime to the police than Whites or Hispanics. In 1998, 52.3 percent of Black victims of violent crimes reported those crimes, while 44.4 percent of Whites, and 45.7 percent each of Hispanics and non-Hispanics reported violent crimes.

Property Crimes

In 1998 there were big differences in property crime rates for Black and White households. Burglaries affected 54.8 per 1,000 Black households, compared to 36.3 per 1,000 White households. Motor vehicles were stolen from 20.1 of 1,000 Black households and 9.4 of 1,000 White households. Thefts occurred at 173.1 per 1,000 Black households and 166.9 per 1,000 White households. (See Table 8.4.)

Hispanic households were more vulnerable to property crime than non-Hispanic households. In 1998 the rate for burglaries for Hispanic households was 44.9 per 1,000 households, compared to 37.7 per 1,000 for non-Hispanic households. Motor vehicles were stolen from Hispanic households at twice the rate (22 per 1,000) that they were stolen from non-Hispanic households (9.7 per 1,000). Thefts took place at the rate of 200.7 per 1,000 Hispanic households, while 165 per 1,000 non-Hispanic households were robbed. (See Table 8.4.)

MINORITIES AS OFFENDERS

The volume of crime allegedly perpetrated by Blacks and Hispanics, as measured by the FBI in the *Crime in the United States, 1998,* is disproportionately large, compared to their percentage of the general population. Note that *Crime in the United States,* prepared annually by the FBI using its Uniform Crime Reports collected from state law enforcement agencies, counts arrests, not convictions. The person arrested for a crime may not be guilty. In 1998 nearly 13 percent of the population were Black, and 11 percent were Hispanic.

In 1998 Whites were arrested for about seven out of 10 (68 percent) crimes and Blacks for three out of 10 (29.7 percent) crimes. Blacks were arrested for 40.2 percent of all violent crimes—most notably 53.4 percent of murders and 55.3 percent of robberies. Whites were arrested on alcohol-related violations much more often than Blacks—86.9 percent of driving under the influence, 85.4 percent of liquor law violations, and 82.1 percent of drunkenness violations. (See Table 8.5.)

In 1998 American Indians/Alaskan Natives and Asians/Pacific Islanders both accounted for about 1 percent of arrests. American Indians and Alaskan Natives were arrested most often for driving under the influence, violations of liquor laws, and drunkenness, than for other crimes. On the other hand, Asian Americans had an unusually high proportion of arrests for gambling violations. (See Table 8.5.)

MINORITIES IN PRISONS AND JAILS

In midyear 1999, relative to the number of U.S. residents, the number of Black males incarcerated in prisons and jails (4,617 per 100,000 Black U.S. residents) was

TABLE 8.4

Household Property Crime Victimization, by Race, Hispanic Origin, Household Income, Region, and Home Ownership of Households Victimized, 1998

Characteristic of household or head of household	Number of households, 1998	Victimizations per 1,000 households			
		Total	Burglary	Motor vehicle theft	Theft
Race					
White	88,616,850	212.6	36.3	9.4	166.9
Black	12,992,210	248.0	54.8	20.1	173.1
Other	3,713,860	224.5	33.2	12.5	178.9
Hispanic origin					
Hispanic	8,497,710	267.6	44.9	22.0	200.7
Non-Hispanic	96,037,610	212.5	37.7	9.7	165.0
Household income					
Less than $7,500	7,427,400	209.0	55.4	11.1	142.5
$7,500 - $14,999	11,641,910	229.8	57.8	9.0	162.9
$15,000 - $24,999	14,878,040	211.0	42.6	12.0	156.5
$25,000 - $34,999	13,249,500	233.8	38.2	12.3	183.2
$35,000 - $49,999	14,903,750	221.7	32.7	10.8	178.3
$50,000 - $74,999	13,490,230	248.6	30.1	10.6	208.0
$75,000 or more	11,843,870	248.6	28.0	11.2	209.4
Region					
Northeast	20,186,010	159.3	26.0	8.4	124.8
Midwest	25,481,910	214.0	39.3	9.9	164.7
South	37,990,330	213.5	41.1	9.9	162.5
West	21,664,680	282.3	44.6	15.6	222.1
Residence					
Urban	31,153,220	274.2	49.3	17.8	207.0
Suburban	47,853,910	204.5	32.5	10.2	161.8
Rural	26,315,800	173.5	36.6	3.5	133.4
Home ownership					
Owned	69,145,000	189.6	31.7	8.5	149.3
Rented	36,177,920	270.6	51.5	15.1	204.0

SOURCE: Callie Marie Rennison. *Criminal Victimization 1998: Changes 1997—1998 with Trends 1993—1998,* Bureau of Justice Statistics: Washington, D.C., July 1999

more than seven times the number of White male inmates (630 per 100,000 White residents) and two and one-half times the incarceration rate of Hispanic males (1,802 per 100,000 Hispanic residents). (See Table 8.6.)

Like their male counterparts, Black females (375 per 100,000 Black U.S. residents) were more than seven times as likely as White females (53 per 100,000 White residents) and two and one-half times as likely as Hispanic females (142 per 100,000 Hispanic residents) to be in prison or jail. (See Table 8.6.)

At the end of June 1999 over 1.8 million persons were behind bars in the nation's prisons and jails—682 persons per 100,000 U.S. adult residents. Approximately 605,900 of these offenders were held in the nation's local jails—222 per 100,000 residents. (See Table 8.7.) The number of jailed inmates increased 5.8 percent annually from year-end 1990 to midyear 1999. (See Figure 8.3.) By June 1999, one in every 147 American residents was behind bars.

Among local jail inmates at midyear 1999, Blacks had the highest incarceration rate (730 per 100,000 Black

TABLE 8.5

Total Arrests, Distribution by Race, 1998
[9,500 agencies; 1998 estimated population 185,845,000]

	Total arrests					Percent distribution				
Offense charged	Total	White	Black	American Indian or Alaskan Native	Asian or Pacific Islander	Total	White	Black	American Indian or Alaskan Native	Asian or Pacific Islander
TOTAL	10,225,920	6,957,337	3,033,710	122,879	111,994	100.0	68.0	29.7	1.2	1.1
Murder and nonnegligent manslaughter	12,318	5,478	6,580	139	121	100.0	44.5	53.4	1.1	1.0
Forcible rape	21,646	13,022	8,112	241	271	100.0	60.2	37.5	1.1	1.3
Robbery	86,926	37,370	48,086	550	920	100.0	43.0	55.3	.6	1.1
Aggravated assault	358,506	220,777	130,018	3,645	4,066	100.0	61.6	36.3	1.0	1.1
Burglary	232,545	158,925	68,508	2,355	2,757	100.0	68.3	29.5	1.0	1.2
Larceny-theft	933,285	609,326	296,886	11,317	15,756	100.0	65.3	31.8	1.2	1.7
Motor vehicle theft	106,607	61,827	41,808	1,162	1,810	100.0	58.0	39.2	1.1	1.7
Arson	12,045	8,881	2,916	109	139	100.0	73.7	24.2	.9	1.2
Violent crime	479,396	276,647	192,796	4,575	5,378	100.0	57.7	40.2	1.0	1.1
Property crime	1,284,482	838,959	410,118	14,943	20,462	100.0	65.3	31.9	1.2	1.6
Crime Index total	1,763,878	1,115,606	602,914	19,518	25,840	100.0	63.2	34.2	1.1	1.5
Other assaults	943,293	604,058	317,905	11,697	9,633	100.0	64.0	33.7	1.2	1.0
Forgery and counterfeiting	80,979	53,801	25,717	484	977	100.0	66.4	31.8	.6	1.2
Fraud	267,447	179,870	84,266	1,306	2,005	100.0	67.3	31.5	.5	.7
Embezzlement	12,199	7,698	4,275	77	149	100.0	63.1	35.0	.6	1.2
Stolen property; buying, receiving, possessing	98,144	56,216	40,112	812	1,004	100.0	57.3	40.9	.8	1.0
Vandalism	212,136	156,150	51,298	2,638	2,050	100.0	73.6	24.2	1.2	1.0
Weapons; carrying, possessing, etc.	135,485	80,311	52,911	891	1,372	100.0	59.3	39.1	.7	1.0
Prostitution and commercialized vice	68,425	41,344	25,698	414	969	100.0	60.4	37.6	.6	1.4
Sex offenses (except forcible rape and prostitution)	65,841	49,224	15,050	754	813	100.0	74.8	22.9	1.1	1.2
Drug abuse violations	1,104,934	680,069	411,854	5,989	7,022	100.0	61.5	37.3	.5	.6
Gambling	9,213	2,753	5,985	36	439	100.0	29.9	65.0	.4	4.8
Offenses against the family and children	99,097	67,547	28,903	922	1,725	100.0	68.2	29.2	.9	1.7
Driving under the influence	950,938	826,117	99,794	13,611	11,416	100.0	86.9	10.5	1.4	1.2
Liquor laws	443,185	378,472	49,427	11,456	3,830	100.0	85.4	11.2	2.6	.9
Drunkenness	509,257	418,308	77,052	11,917	1,980	100.0	82.1	15.1	2.3	.4
Disorderly conduct	499,434	322,046	167,682	6,120	3,586	100.0	64.5	33.6	1.2	.7
Vagrancy	21,940	11,620	9,648	552	120	100.0	53.0	44.0	2.5	.5
All other offenses (except traffic)	2,683,508	1,715,532	905,171	31,170	31,635	100.0	63.9	33.7	1.2	1.2
Suspicion	3,792	2,752	965	50	25	100.0	72.6	25.4	1.3	.7
Curfew and loitering law violations	135,983	97,006	36,217	1,305	1,455	100.0	71.3	26.6	1.0	1.1
Runaways	116,812	90,837	20,866	1,160	3,949	100.0	77.8	17.9	1.0	3.4

SOURCE: *Crime in the United States, 1998: Uniform Crime Reports,* Federal Bureau of Investigation: Clarksburg, WV, 1997

residents), followed by Hispanics (288 per 100,000 Hispanic residents) and American Indians (247 per 100,000 American Indian residents). Whites and Asian Americans had lower incarceration rates, 127 per 100,000 White residents and 46 per 100,000 Asian American residents, respectively. (See Table 8.7.)

In 1997 Blacks accounted for approximately 49 percent and Whites for about 48 percent of the sentenced prisoners under state or federal jurisdiction. (See Table 8.8.) By 1998, about 57.8 percent of those in the custody of the federal Bureau of Prisons were White, 38.9 percent were Black, and fewer than 2 percent each were Asian (1.7 percent) and American Indian (1.6 percent). Nearly one-third (31.8 percent) were of Hispanic origin. (See Table 8.9.)

Between 1990 and 1997 the number of prisoners with sentences of more than one year increased by 455,518, or 61.6 percent. The number of White male inmates grew by 54.4 percent and the number of Black male inmates by 61.3 percent. While males far outnumbered females in the nation's prisons, the rate of increase for females was significantly higher than for males. The number of White females and Black females increased by approximately 80 percent each. (See Table 8.8.)

At year-end 1997, 3.2 percent of all Black males were in prison, compared to .4 percent of all White males. While the incarceration rates of both White and Black males have risen since 1985, the rate for Black males has grown somewhat more rapidly. In 1997 Black males were

TABLE 8.6

Number of Inmates in State or Federal Prisons and Local Jails per 100,000 Residents, by Gender, Race, Hispanic Origin, and Age, June 1999

| | Number of inmates per 100,000 residents of each group | | | | | | | |
| | Male | | | | Female | | | |
Age	Totalª	Whiteᵇ	Blackᵇ	Hispanic	Totalª	Whiteᵇ	Blackᵇ	Hispanic
Total	1,261	630	4,617	1,802	106	53	375	142
18-19	1,868	885	5,787	2,524	92	63	224	94
20-24	3,130	1,462	10,407	4,141	205	121	524	284
25-29	3,363	1,535	12,334	4,220	303	154	956	357
30-34	3,193	1,674	11,225	3,844	370	185	1,362	372
35-39	2,474	1,302	9,548	2,898	257	128	940	308
40-44	1,699	897	6,224	2,746	144	73	512	203
45-54	896	522	3,399	1,521	63	33	214	133
55 or older	193	129	611	460	8	5	27	11

Note: Based on estimates of the U.S. resident population on July 1, 1999, and adjusted for the 1990 census undercount.

ªIncludes American Indians, Alaska Natives, Asians, Native Hawaiians, and other Pacific Islanders.

ᵇExcludes Hispanics.

SOURCE: Allen J. Beck. *Prison and Jail Inmates at Midyear 1999.* Bureau of Justice Statistics: Washington, D.C., April 2000

TABLE 8.7

Number of Jail Inmates by Race, June 1999

	Estimated count	Per 100,000 residents in each group
Total	605,943	222
Whiteª	249,900	127
Blackª	251,800	730
Hispanic	93,800	288
American Indianᵇ	5,200	247
Asianᶜ	5,200	46

Note: Inmate counts were estimated and rounded to the nearest 100.

ªNon-Hispanic only.

ᵇIncludes Alaska Natives.

ᶜIncludes Native Hawaiians and other Pacific Islanders.

SOURCE: *Prison and Jail Inmates at Midyear 1998.* Bureau of Justice statistics: Washington, D.C., March 1999

FIGURE 8.3

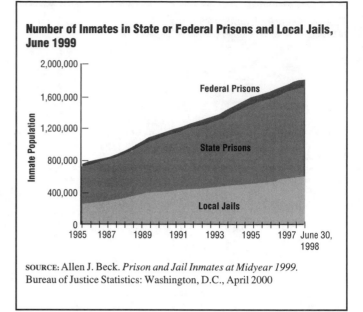

Number of Inmates in State or Federal Prisons and Local Jails, June 1999

SOURCE: Allen J. Beck. *Prison and Jail Inmates at Midyear 1999.* Bureau of Justice Statistics: Washington, D.C., April 2000

about six times more likely than White males to be in state or federal prison, similar to 1990 figures. (See Table 8.10.)

Hispanics, who may be of any race, represent the fastest-growing minority group being imprisoned, the number of which increased by 64 percent between 1990 and 1997. The Hispanic female incarceration rate rose 55 percent, from 56 to 87 sentenced prisoners per 100,000 Hispanic residents. The number of Hispanic male inmates increased by 25 percent, from 1,016 to 1,272 sentenced prisoners per 100,000 Hispanic residents. (See Table 8.11.)

Black Men Arrested Disproportionately

The Sentencing Project, an organization that seeks alternatives to incarceration, has published several reports

showing racial disparities in state imprisonment. The most recent report, *Intended and Unintended Consequences: State Racial Disparities in Imprisonment* (Marc Mauer, Washington, DC, 1997) found that between 1988 and 1994, the incarceration rate of Blacks in state prisons rose from seven to eight times the White rate. In 1988, 922 Blacks per 100,000 Black U.S. residents were incarcerated, while 134 Whites were in prison per 100,000 White U.S. residents. By 1994 the incarceration rates were 1,433 Black inmates per 100,000 Black residents and 187 White inmates per 100,000 White residents. (See Figure 8.4 for 1984 to 1993 rates.)

Most of the increase was due to drug convictions. From 1988 to 1992 there was a 33 percent increase in the number of Blacks sent to state prison for violent offenses, compared to a 27 percent increase in the number of Whites. A similar increase in both incarcerated Blacks (15 percent) and Whites (17 percent) occurred for property crimes. For drug crimes, however, 94 percent more Blacks were sent to prison from 1988 to 1992, while only 35 percent more Whites were incarcerated. (See Table 8.12.)

The percentage increase in the number of Blacks in state prisons for violent crimes (26 percent) was not as great as the percentage of Whites (38 percent). The percentage increase in the number of Blacks for drug offenses (465.5 percent), however, was four times greater than the percentage increase of Whites (111 percent). (See Table 8.13.) The report quoted "high-profile commentators" who predicted current prison expansion would result in one in seven of all adult Black males and one in four Black males ages 19 to 29 being in prison on any given day.

Mauer concluded that these high rates of incarceration will hurt the political influence of the Black commu-

TABLE 8.8

Number of Sentenced Prisoners Under State or Federal Jurisdiction, by Sex and Race, 1990, 1995–1997

Year	Total	Male			Female		
		All[a]	White[b]	Black[b]	All[a]	White[b]	Black[b]
1990	739,980	699,416	350,700	340,300	40,564	20,200	19,700
1995	1,085,022	1,021,059	487,400	509,800	63,963	30,500	31,900
1996	1,137,722	1,068,123	511,300	528,600	69,599	33,800	34,000
1997	1,195,498	1,121,663	541,700	548,900	73,835	36,300	35,500

Note: Previous estimates for 1996 by gender and race have been revised. Sentenced prisoners are those with a sentence of more than 1 year.
[a]Includes Asians, Pacific Islanders, American Indians, Alaska Natives, and other racial groups.
[b]The numbers for gender and race were estimated and rounded to the nearest 100.

SOURCE: *Prisoners in 1998.* Bureau of Justice Statistics: Washington, D.C., August 1999

nity. An estimated 1.4 million Black males, or 14 percent of the Black male population, are disenfranchised (not able to vote) because of a felony conviction. Approximately 4.2 million persons of all races are disenfranchised as a result of felony convictions.

In 1996 the Center on Juvenile and Criminal Justice in San Francisco conducted a study of California's prisons. The study found that, while Black men made up only 7 percent of the state's population, they accounted for 32 percent of its prison population. Vincent Schiraldi, director of the center and author of the study, believed that the high number of Black prisoners was due to tougher punishment for use of crack cocaine than for other drugs. He further cited stricter sentencing laws, California's prison construction boom, poverty, the lack of good jobs, and poor education in inner cities as additional causes. Alfred Blumstein, a criminologist at Carnegie Mellon University (in Pittsburgh, Pennsylvania), attributed the disproportionate figures to the war on drugs, in which police had focused their efforts in the inner cities because the drug trade was often conducted openly by Black men.

Schiraldi predicted that California's "three strikes" law (automatic life sentence for criminals convicted of three felonies and double the usual sentences for those convicted of a second serious offense) would likely further increase the disproportionate number of young Black men in the state's prisons. He also stated that Blacks are charged at 17 times the rate of Whites under the three strikes law.

Minorities on Death Row

The Bureau of Justice Statistics (*Capital Punishment 1998,* Washington, DC, December 1999) reported a total of 3,452 state and federal prisoners under sentence of death as of December 31, 1998. Whites made up 55.2 percent and Blacks comprised 43 percent of all prisoners under sentence of death. Fewer than 2 percent were of other races, including 29 Native Americans, 18 Asians, and 13 self-identified Hispanics. Of those whose ethnicity was known, 10 percent were Hispanic. (See Table 8.14.)

In 1976 a 10-year moratorium on executions ended as a result of U.S. Supreme Court decisions. The first execution occurred in 1977. Between 1977 and 1998, 6,089 persons in state and federal prisons were under death sentences. Of these, 45.5 percent were White, 41.5 percent were Black, 7.6 percent were Hispanic, and 1.3 percent were of other races. Figure 8.5 shows the increase in numbers of prisoners awaiting death, by race, between 1968 and 1998.

From 1977 to 1998, 500 prisoners were executed. Fifty-six percent were White; 35.6 percent were Black; 6.8 percent were Hispanic; and 1.4 percent were of other races. During 1998, 68 men and 2 women were executed. Thirty-five were non-Hispanic White, 18 were non-Hispanic Black, 8 were Hispanic White, 5 were White of unknown Hispanic descent; and 1 each were Native American and Asian.

GANGS

Law enforcement agencies define a street gang as a "group of people that form an allegiance based on various social needs and engage in acts injurious to public health and safety." Although gangs have been involved with the drug trade for many years, gang-related deadly violence is more likely to come from territorial conflicts.

Gangs are often (but not always) racially or ethnically based. As a rule, ethnic gangs require that all members belong to a particular race or ethnic group. Criminal activity by ethnic gangs has been increasing during the last few years. Among ethnic gangs, Jamaican and Asian gangs are considered by many law enforcement officials to pose a growing threat.

The most frightening of gang crimes is murder. A study conducted by the Illinois Criminal Justice Information Authority focused on intragang (within the gang), intergang (between or among gangs), and nongang member victimization. The study investigated 956 street gang-related homicides in Chicago between 1987 and 1994. Of

TABLE 8.9

Federal Bureau of Prisons Fact Card, April 2000

Number of Institutions:	96	
Total Inmate Population:	140,019	
In BOP facilities:	122,126	
In contract facilities:	17,893	
Inmates By Security Level		
Minimum:	29,653	(24.3%)
Low:	42,177	(34.5%)
Medium:	28,786	(23.6%)
High:	12,844	(10.5%)
(Additional inmates have not been assigned a security level)		
Inmates By Gender		
Male:	129,571	(92.5%)
Female:	10,448	(7.5%)
Inmates By Race		
White:	80,856	(57.8%)
Black:	54,515	(38.9%)
Asian:	2,367	(1.7%)
Native American:	2,281	(1.6%)
Ethnicity		
Hispanic:	44,575	(31.8%)
Citizenship		
United States:	97,491	(69.6%)
Mexico:	21,330	(15.2%)
Colombia:	4,266	(3.1%)
Cuba:	2,919	(2.1%)
Other/Unknown:	14,013	(10.0%)
Average Inmate Age: 37		
Sentence Imposed (calculated for those with sentencing information available)		
Less than 1 year:	1,838	(1.7%)
1-3 years:	14,490	(13.4%)
3-5 years:	15,438	(14.3%)
5-10 years:	31,998	(29.6%)
10-15 years:	20,855	(19.3%)
15-20 years:	9,748	(9.0%)
More than 20 years:	10,475	(9.7%)
Life:	3,187	(3.0%)
Type Of Offense (calculated for those with offense-specific information available)		
Drug Offenses:	61,547	(58.1%)
Robbery:	8,320	(7.9%)
Firearms, Explosives, Arson:	9,827	(9.3%)
Extortion, Fraud, Bribery:	5,397	(5.1%)
Property Offenses:	6,132	(5.8%)
Homicide, Aggravated Assault, and Kidnapping Offenses:	2,472	(2.3%)
Immigration:	6,941	(6.6%)
Continuing Criminal Enterprise:	645	(0.6%)
White Collar:	780	(0.7%)
Courts or Corrections: (e.g., Obstructing Justice)	618	(0.6%)
National Security:	70	(0.1%)
D.C. Offenses:	1,310	(1.2%)
Sex Offenses:	848	(0.8%)
Miscellaneous:	997	(0.9%)

SOURCE: *Quick Facts*. Federal Bureau of Prisons, April 2000

TABLE 8.10

Number of Sentenced Prisoners Under State or Federal Jurisdiction, per 100,000 Residents, by Gender and Race, 1990, 1995–97

Year	Total	Male			Female		
		All*	White	Black	All*	White	Black
1990	297	564	338	2,234	31	19	117
1995	411	781	449	3,095	47	27	176
1996	427	810	468	3,164	51	30	185
1997	445	841	491	3,253	53	32	192

Note: Based on estimates of the U.S. resident population on July 1 of each year and adjusted for the census undercount.

*Includes Asians, Pacific Islanders, American Indians, Alaska Natives, and other racial groups.

SOURCE: *Prisoners in 1998*. Bureau of Justice Statistics: Washington, D.C., August 1999

TABLE 8.11

Number of Sentenced Hispanic Prisoners Under State or Federal Jurisdiction, by Gender, 1990, 1995–97

Year	Number of sentenced Hispanic prisoners			Sentenced prisoners per 100,000 Hispanic residents		
	Total	Male	Female	Total	Male	Female
1990	130,000	123,500	6,500	548	1,016	56
1995	190,100	181,300	8,800	675	1,264	64
1996	200,400	189,300	11,100	688	1,279	78
1997	213,100	200,300	12,800	698	1,272	87

Note: Sentenced prisoners are those with a sentence of more than 1 year. The total number of Hispanic inmates was estimated in each year by multiplying the percent identifying as Hispanic in the 1991 and 1997 surveys by the NPS sentenced inmate counts. Estimates have been rounded to the nearest 100.

SOURCE: *Prisoners in 1998*. Bureau of Justice Statistics: Washington, D.C., August 1999

data from municipal and county law enforcement agencies throughout the United States. Approximately 300 law enforcement agencies participated. The study revealed the level at which nationally recognized street gangs have particularly established themselves in new communities. The NDIC noted the following trends:

- Gang activity was reported in 88 percent of the more than 300 jurisdictions responding to the survey and in 98 percent of the 120 jurisdictions with populations over 100,000.

- Gang activity was not confined to major metropolitan areas and was reported in 68 percent of the 59 responding jurisdictions with populations under 25,000 and in 78 percent of the 120 responding jurisdictions with populations under 50,000.

- Over 7,400 individual gang sets were identified.

- Hispanic gangs were reported in 167 jurisdictions in 41 states and made up 20 percent of all gangs reported.

those, 11 percent were intragang murders, 75 percent were intergang homicides, and 14 percent were murders of nongang victims by a gang member. Both male and female gang members committed crimes far more often than nongang members, and more than half of all gang members were repeat offenders.

In 1996 the National Drug Intelligence Center (NDIC) released a National Street Gang Report based on

FIGURE 8.4

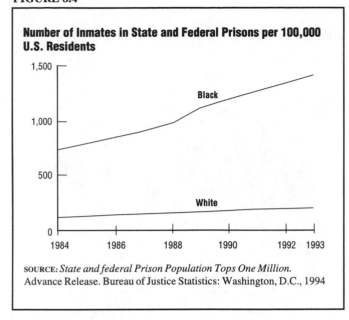

Number of Inmates in State and Federal Prisons per 100,000 U.S. Residents

SOURCE: *State and federal Prison Population Tops One Million.* Advance Release. Bureau of Justice Statistics: Washington, D.C., 1994

TABLE 8.13

State Prison Inmates by Offense and Race, 1986–1991

Offense	1986		1991		Increase	
	White	Black	White	Black	White	Black
Violent	88,591	119,694	121,865	150,972	37.6%	26.1%
Property	63,785	58,833	74,612	70,668	17.0%	20.1%
Drug	14,174	14,201	29,845	80,304	110.6%	465.5%

SOURCE: Marc Mauer. *Intended and Unintended Consequences: State Racial Disparities in Imprisonment.* The Sentencing Project: Washington, D.C., 1997

- White gangs were reported in 157 jurisdictions in 44 states.

- Asian gangs were reported in 104 jurisdictions in 41 states.

- Black gangs claiming affiliation with the Blood and/or Crip sets were reported in 180 responding jurisdictions in 42 states. Chicago-based Black gangs, such as the Black Gangster Disciples and Vice Lords, and the Hispanic gang, Almighty Latin Kings, were reported in 110 of the responding jurisdictions in 35 states.

Violent street gangs have also become a problem among American Indians. There are approximately 55 street gangs on the Navajo reservation in Arizona. These gangs have been responsible for a dramatic increase in violent crimes in the Navajo nation.

HATE CRIMES

The 1990 Hate Crime Statistics Act (PL 101-275) calls for the U.S. attorney general to "acquire data about

TABLE 8.12

Court Commitments to State Prison, 1988–1992

Offense	1988		1992		Increase	
	White	Black	White	Black	White	Black
Violent	26,299	30,677	33,376	40,803	26.9%	33.0%
Property	37,978	33,901	44,344	39,085	16.8%	15.3%
Drug	18,851	26,769	25,474	51,970	35.1%	94.1%

SOURCE: Marc Mauer. *Intended and Unintended Consequences: State Racial Disparities in Imprisonment.* The Sentencing Project: Washington, D.C., 1997

TABLE 8.14

Demographic Characteristics of Prisoners Under Sentence of Death, 1998

Characteristic	Prisoners under sentence of death, 1998		
	Yearend	Admissions	Removals
Total number under sentence of death	3,452	285	161
Gender			
Male	98.6%	97.2%	97.5%
Female	1.4	2.8	2.5
Race			
White	55.2%	50.9%	64.0%
Black	43.0	46.3	33.5
Other˙	1.7	2.8	2.5
Hispanic origin			
Hispanic	10.0%	15.4%	10.2%
Non-Hispanic	90.0	84.6	89.8
Education			
8th grade or less	14.3%	15.1%	17.1%
9th-11th grade	37.6	39.3	37.1
High school graduate/GED	38.0	36.8	37.1
Any college	10.1	8.8	8.6
Median	11th	11th	11th
Marital status			
Married	24.0%	17.1%	23.6%
Divorced/separated	20.8	16.0	22.3
Widowed	2.7	4.7	4.1
Never married	52.5	62.3	50.0

Note: Calculations are based on those cases for which data were reported. Missing data by category were as follows:

	Yearend	Admissions	Removals
Hispanic origin	299	38	14
Education	501	46	21
Marital status	327	28	13

*At yearend 1997, "other" consisted of 28 American Indians, 17 Asians, and 11 self-identified Hispanics. During 1998, 3 American Indians, 2 Asians, and 3 self-identified Hispanics were admitted; 2 American Indians, 1 Asian, and 1 self-identified Hispanic were removed.

SOURCE: *Capital Punishment, 1998.* Bureau of Justice Statistics: Washington, D.C., December 1998

crimes that manifest evidence of prejudice based on race, religion, sexual orientation, or ethnicity [and] publish an annual summary of the data acquired under this section." In 1994 the Violent Crime and Law Enforcement Act (PL 103-322) amended the Hate Crime Statistics Act to include crimes motivated by discrimination against people with physical and/or mental disabilities.

TABLE 8.5

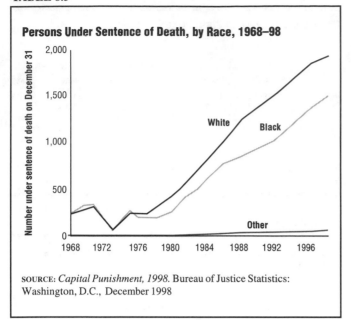

Persons Under Sentence of Death, by Race, 1968–98

SOURCE: *Capital Punishment, 1998.* Bureau of Justice Statistics: Washington, D.C., December 1998

FIGURE 8.6

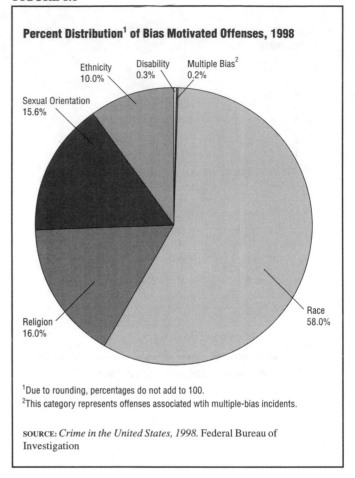

Percent Distribution[1] of Bias Motivated Offenses, 1998

[1]Due to rounding, percentages do not add to 100.
[2]This category represents offenses associated wtih multiple-bias incidents.

SOURCE: *Crime in the United States, 1998.* Federal Bureau of Investigation

In 1998, 9,235 bias-motivated offenses were reported to the FBI. Of that number, state and local law enforcement agencies reported 7,755 hate crime incidents, down from 7,947 in 1995. Racial bias (58 percent) represented the largest proportion of bias-motivated offenses, followed by religious (16 percent), sexual orientation (15.6 percent), and ethnicity bias. (See Figure 8.6.)

The Intelligence Project of the Southern Poverty Law Center in Montgomery, Alabama, a private organization which monitors hate groups and paramilitary groups, reported a 15 percent decline in the number of hate groups in the United States in 1999—from 537 to 457. The Intelligence Project ascribed this decrease in its hate-group count to its methodology—it counts only those groups that have participated in racist behavior, including crimes, marches, rallies, speeches, leafleting, or distributing literature. For example, although the Intelligence Project noted a 20 percent increase (from 254 to 305) in Internet hate sites in early 2000, it counted as hate groups only those engaging in racist behavior beyond the Internet.

Intelligence Project director, Joe Roy, observed that many smaller, less-active groups have joined larger organizations, some of which espouse political violence. In 1997, 16 percent of skinhead groups had joined large organizations. In 1999, four in five of these small groups were part of large groups. According to the Intelligence Project, some groups in the extreme right are aligning themselves with the ideologies of the left-wingers. Persons involved in issues of homosexuality, abortion, and immigration in the past are changing the "shape of hate" by taking up the causes of the liberals, including the so-called specter of growing economic globalism.

CHAPTER 9

POLITICAL PARTICIPATION

VOTER REGISTRATION

In 1998 the total voting-age population in the United States reached nearly 201 million persons. (See Figure 9.1.) The Census Bureau's voting-age population estimates includes those who are eligible to vote as well as those who are not eligible to, such as non-citizens, convicted felons, and prison inmates. Americans living overseas who are of voting age are not included. To be eligible to vote, a person must be a citizen of the United States and at least 18 years of age. The Bureau of the Census reported that in 1996, 65.9 percent of the voting-age population were registered. A higher percentage of Whites (67.7 percent) than Blacks (63.5 percent) or Hispanics (35.7 percent) were registered. (See Table 9.1.)

In 1966 only 44 percent of minorities who lived in the South (the Census Bureau did not keep separate statistics for Blacks until 1968) were registered, but by 1992, 65 percent of southern Blacks were registered. This dramatic increase was due, in large part, to the passage of the Civil Rights Act of 1964 (PL 88-362) and the Voting Rights Act of 1965 (PL 89-110). These laws removed voting restrictions and led to often volatile and dangerous voter registration campaigns conducted during the 1960s and 1970s. Before these changes, many southern states enforced poll taxes, charging citizens for the right to vote, knowing that many poor Blacks could not afford to pay. Some had "grandfather clauses" that permitted voting rights only to those whose grandfathers had been able to vote. Many elderly Blacks were the grandchildren of slaves who had not been able to vote, so these clauses restricted their rights as well. Furthermore, since they did not have the right to vote, their own children and grandchildren were also prevented from voting under the grandfather clauses. It took more than laws to open voting booths to southern Blacks—it took marches, demonstrations, and the loss of a number of lives.

VOTER TURNOUT

While Black Americans are somewhat less likely to vote than White Americans, both groups are much more likely to vote than Hispanic Americans. In the 1996 presidential election, 54.2 percent of the voting-age population voted. (Presidential elections receive more voter participation than almost all other types of elections.) White Americans (56 percent) voted in higher proportions than either Blacks (50.6 percent) or Hispanics (26.7 percent). (See Table 9.2.) The low Hispanic voting turnout is partly explained by the fact that about 40 percent of Hispanics of voting age are not U.S. citizens. (The Bureau of the Census counts people, not citizens.) Excluding non-citizens from the population base would have raised Hispanic turnout in the 1992 presidential election to about 48 percent. (See Hispanic Political Participation below for a more detailed discussion of Hispanic citizenship.)

In the 1996 presidential election, turnout was down for all three groups, compared to the 1992 and the 1988 presidential elections. The presidential election of 1992 (61.3 percent total) had the most participation of all three of these presidential elections. (See Table 9.2.)

Younger Voters

About one-third (32 percent) of young adults ages 18 to 24 reported voting in the 1996 election. Young Whites were as likely to vote (33.3 percent) as young Blacks (32.4 percent), but Hispanic youth (15.1 percent) were far less apt to vote. The percentages of White and Hispanic young voters were far smaller than the percentages of White and Hispanic youth who voted in 1972. The percentages of young Black voters who voted in 1972 and in 1996 were about the same. In 1994, a congressional election year, the percentages of students who voted were smaller than in 1996 or 1992 (both presidential election years). (See Table 9.3.)

FIGURE 9.1

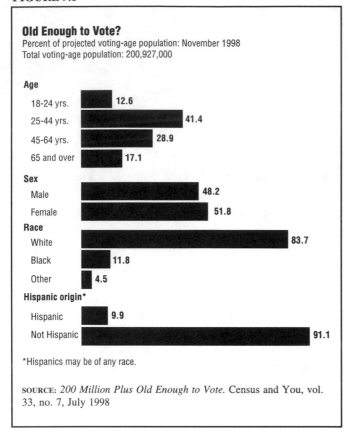

Old Enough to Vote?
Percent of projected voting-age population: November 1998
Total voting-age population: 200,927,000

Age
18-24 yrs. — 12.6
25-44 yrs. — 41.4
45-64 yrs. — 28.9
65 and over — 17.1

Sex
Male — 48.2
Female — 51.8

Race
White — 83.7
Black — 11.8
Other — 4.5

Hispanic origin*
Hispanic — 9.9
Not Hispanic — 91.1

*Hispanics may be of any race.

SOURCE: *200 Million Plus Old Enough to Vote.* Census and You, vol. 33, no. 7, July 1998

Those enrolled in school were far more likely to vote than those not in school. In 1996, among White youth, 43.9 percent of those 18 to 24 years old who were enrolled in school had voted, while only 25.6 percent of White youth not in school voted in the congressional election. Among Black youth, 36.6 percent of those in school reported voting, while 30.1 percent of those not in school voted. Nearly 30 percent of Hispanic students voted, compared to just 9 percent of those not in school. (See Table 9.4.)

Elderly Voters

Elderly Americans are more likely to vote than younger persons, and elderly minorities are more likely to vote than younger minorities. In 1996, 67 percent of persons 65 years and over voted in the presidential election. (See Table 9.1.) Senior citizens had the largest voter turnouts in the presidential elections of 1988 and 1992 and in the congressional elections of 1986, 1990, and 1994. In 1994 elderly White persons were the most active voters (62 percent), followed by 51 percent of the Black elderly and 36 percent of Hispanic persons over 65 years old.

Asian American Voters

The presidential election of 1992 was the first year that the Bureau of the Census collected data on

TABLE 9.1

Voting and Registration, November 1996
(Numbers in thousands)

Characteristics	Voting-age population	Registered Number	Registered Percent	Voted Number	Voted Percent
Gender and Age					
Both sexes	193,651	127,661	65.9	105,017	54.2
18 - 20 yrs	10,785	4,919	45.6	3,366	31.2
21 - 24 yrs	13,865	7,099	51.2	4,630	33.4
25 - 44 yrs	83,393	51,606	61.9	41,050	49.2
45 - 64 yrs	53,721	39,489	73.5	34,615	64.4
65 yrs and over	31,888	24,547	77.0	21,356	67.0
Male	92,632	59,672	64.4	48,909	52.8
18 - 20 yrs	5,372	2,294	42.7	1,521	28.3
21 - 24 yrs	6,901	3,417	49.5	2,140	31.0
25 - 44 yrs	41,005	24,453	59.6	19,211	46.8
45 - 64 yrs	25,945	18,829	72.6	16,530	63.7
65 yrs and over	13,408	10,680	79.7	9,507	70.9
Female	101,020	67,989	67.3	56,108	55.5
18 - 20 yrs	5,413	2,625	48.5	1,845	34.1
21 - 24 yrs	6,964	3,681	52.9	2,490	35.8
25 - 44 yrs	42,388	27,153	64.1	21,840	51.5
45 - 64 yrs	27,776	20,662	74.4	18,085	65.1
65 yrs and over	18,480	13,867	75.0	11,849	64.1
Race and Hispanic Origin					
White	162,779	110,259	67.7	91,208	56.0
Black	22,483	14,267	63.5	11,386	50.6
Hispanic[1]	18,426	6,573	35.7	4,928	26.7
Region					
Northeast	38,263	24,772	64.7	20,852	54.5
Midwest	45,177	32,364	71.6	26,798	59.3
South	68,080	44,891	65.9	35,550	52.2
West	42,131	25,634	60.8	21,816	51.8
Education					
Less than high school	13,986	5,697	40.7	4,188	29.9
Some high school	21,002	10,059	47.9	7,099	33.8
High school graduate	65,208	40,542	62.2	32,019	49.1
Some college, including Associate degree	50,939	37,160	72.9	30,835	60.5
Bachelor's degree or higher	42,517	34,203	80.4	30,877	72.6
Labor Force					
In labor force	132,043	87,532	66.3	71,682	54.3
Employed	125,634	84,166	67.0	69,300	55.2
Unemployed	6,409	3,365	52.5	2,383	37.2
Not in labor force	61,608	40,129	65.1	33,335	54.1

[1]Persons of Hispanic origin may be of any race.

SOURCE: U.S. Bureau of the Census, 1998

Asian/Pacific Islander (API) voters. APIs followed many of the same voting patterns as other minorities. In 1992 only 27.3 percent of APIs over age 18 voted. Approximately 45 percent of the total adult population of APIs were not U.S. citizens and were, therefore, ineligible to vote. Older Asians, those with a college education, and those who had higher incomes were more likely to vote. (See Table 9.5.)

BLACK POLITICAL PARTICIPATION

Elected Officials

The number of Blacks elected to public offices at all levels of U.S. government has increased significantly since the 1980s. The largest gain has been in city and county offices, which include county commission-

TABLE 9.2

Percent Distribution Voted and Registered by Race, Hispanic Origin, and Gender, November 1964 to 1996

Year	Total	White	Black	Hispanic[1]	Male	Female
Voted						
1996	54.2	56.0	50.6	26.7	52.8	55.5
1994	45.0	47.3	37.1	20.2	44.7	45.3
1992	61.3	63.6	54.0	28.9	60.2	62.3
1990	45.0	46.7	39.2	21.0	44.6	45.4
1988	57.4	59.1	51.5	28.8	56.4	58.3
1986	46.0	47.0	43.2	24.2	45.8	46.1
1984	59.9	61.4	55.8	32.6	59.0	60.8
1982	48.5	49.9	43.0	25.3	48.7	48.4
1980	59.2	60.9	50.5	29.9	59.1	59.4
1978	45.9	47.3	37.2	23.5	46.6	45.3
1976	59.2	60.9	48.7	31.8	59.6	58.8
1974	44.7	46.3	33.8	22.9	46.2	43.4
1972	63.0	64.5	52.1	37.5	64.1	62.0
1970	54.6	56.0	43.5	NA	56.8	52.7
1968	67.8	69.1	57.6	NA	69.8	66.0
1966	55.4	57.0	41.7	NA	58.2	53.0
1964	69.3	70.7	58.5	NA	71.9	67.0
Registered						
1996	65.9	67.7	63.5	35.7	64.4	67.3
1994	62.5	64.6	58.5	31.3	61.2	63.7
1992	68.2	70.1	63.9	35.0	66.9	69.3
1990	62.2	63.8	58.8	32.3	61.2	63.1
1988	66.6	67.9	64.5	35.5	65.2	67.8
1986	64.3	65.3	64.0	35.9	63.4	65.0
1984	68.3	69.6	66.3	40.1	67.3	69.3
1982	64.1	65.6	59.1	35.3	63.7	64.4
1980	66.9	68.4	60.0	36.3	66.6	67.1
1978	62.6	63.8	57.1	32.9	62.6	62.5
1976	66.7	68.3	58.5	37.8	67.1	66.4
1974	62.2	63.5	54.9	34.9	62.8	61.7
1972	72.3	73.4	65.5	44.4	73.1	71.6
1970	68.1	69.1	60.8	NA	69.6	66.8
1968	74.3	75.4	66.2	NA	76.0	72.8
1966	70.3	71.6	60.2	NA	72.2	68.6
1964	NA	NA	NA	NA	NA	NA

Note: Prior to 1972, data are for persons of voting age, 21 years old and over, in most states. Registration data were not collected in the 1964 Current Population Survey.

[1]Persons of Hispanic origin may be of any race.

NA Not available.

SOURCE: U.S. Bureau of the Census, 1998

TABLE 9.3

Percent of Persons 18 to 24 Years Reported Voted, by Race and Hispanic Origin, November 1964 to 1996
(Numbers in thousands)

Year	White Number	White Percent voted	Black Number	Black Percent voted	Hispanic[1] Number	Hispanic[1] Percent voted
1996	19,669	33.3	3,613	32.4	3,452	15.1
1994	20,151	21.1	3,638	17.4	3,512	10.1
1992	19,682	45.4	3,543	36.6	2,795	17.6
1990	20,357	20.8	3,525	20.2	2,711	8.7
1988	21,092	37.0	3,567	35.0	2,661	16.8
1986	21,957	21.6	3,651	25.1	2,543	11.6
1984	23,227	41.6	3,875	40.6	2,064	21.9
1982	24,133	25.0	3,850	25.5	2,019	14.2
1980	23,976	41.8	3,559	30.1	2,047	15.9
1978	23,669	24.2	3,462	20.1	1,606	11.5
1976	23,141	44.7	3,323	27.9	1,559	21.8
1974	22,187	25.2	3,113	16.1	1,481	13.3
1972	21,339	51.9	2,994	34.7	1,338	30.9
1970	11,345	31.5	1,542	22.4	NA	NA
1968	9,820	52.8	1,255	38.9	NA	NA
1966	9,405	32.6	1,208	21.9	NA	NA
1964	8,715	52.1	1,115	44.2	NA	NA

Note: Data are for persons of voting age, 21 years old and over, in most States prior to 1972.

[1]Persons of Hispanic origin may be of any race.

NA Not available.

SOURCE: U.S. Bureau of the Census, 1998

ers, city council members, mayors, vice mayors, and aldermen.

CONGRESS. In 2000, 39 Blacks served the in U.S. Congress, all in the House of Representatives. In addition, Eleanor Holmes Norton (D-DC), a nonvoting delegate, represented Washington, DC. Until the 1990 election of Gary Franks (R-CT), all Black congressional delegates in recent times had been Democrats. Representative Franks (who lost his bid for reelection in 1996) was the first Black Republican in the House since Oscar DePriest (R-IL) retired in 1935.

Of the 65 women in the 106th Congress (1999–2000), 13 were Black women. They were Representatives Barbara Lee (D-CA), Juanita Millender-McDonald (D-CA), Maxine Waters (D-CA), Corrine Brown (D-FL), Carrie Meek (D-FL), Cynthia McKinney (D-GA), Julia M.

Carson (D-IN), Carolyn Cheeks Kilpatrick (D-MI), Eva Clayton (D-NC), Stephanie Tubbs Jones (D-OH), Eddie Bernice Johnson (D-TX), Sheila Jackson-Lee (D-TX), and Delegate Eleanor Holmes Norton (D-DC).

STATE LEGISLATORS. According to the National Conference of State Legislatures and the National Black Caucus of State Legislators, in 1999, 8 percent of state legislators were Blacks—7 percent were state senators and 8 percent were members of state houses of representatives. Alaska, Hawaii, Idaho, Maine, Montana, North Dakota, Utah, and Wyoming had no Blacks serving in state legislatures. (See Table 9.6.)

MAYORS. According to the National Conference of Black Mayors, Houston, Texas; Dallas, Texas; and Detroit, Michigan, were the largest cities (with populations of more than 1 million) to be represented by a Black mayor in 2000. Although 35 Black mayors served in cities with populations of 50,000 or more, most Black mayors were in smaller communities. (See Table 9.7.) Sharon Pratt Kelly was elected in 1990 in Washington, DC, to become the second Black female to head a major U.S. city. (The first was Carrie Perry, mayor of Hartford, Connecticut.) Kelly lost her bid for reelection against Black former mayor Marion Barry, who won the November 1994 election despite having served a prison sentence for possession of cocaine. Barry's term ended on January 1, 1999; Anthony A. Williams, also Black, succeeded him.

TABLE 9.4

Percent of Persons 18 to 24 Years Old Reported Having Registered or Voted, by Enrollment Status, Race, Hispanic Origin, and Gender, November 1996
(November 1996. Numbers in thousands.)

Race, Hispanic origin, sex, age, and enrollment status	All persons	Reported registered		Reported voted		Reported that they did not vote[1]				
		Number	Percent	Number	Percent	Total	Registered	Not registered		
								Total[2]	Not a U.S. citizen	Do not know and not reported on registration
ALL RACES										
Both Sexes										
Total, 18 to 24 years old	**24,650**	**12,018**	**48.8**	**7,996**	**32.4**	**16,654**	**4,022**	**12,632**	**2,176**	**2,176**
Enrolled in school	10,258	5,877	57.3	4,232	41.3	6,026	1,645	4,381	716	1,002
18 to 20 years old	6,225	3,328	53.5	2,420	38.9	3,805	908	2,897	403	613
21 to 24 years old	4,033	2,549	63.2	1,812	44.9	2,221	737	1,484	313	389
In high school	1,722	622	36.1	457	26.5	1,265	165	1,100	143	154
In college	8,536	5,255	61.6	3,775	44.2	4,761	1,480	3,281	572	848
Full-time	7,145	4,469	62.5	3,209	44.9	3,936	1,260	2,676	444	720
Part-time	1,390	785	56.5	566	40.7	825	220	605	128	128
Not enrolled in school	14,392	6,141	42.7	3,764	26.2	10,628	2,377	8,251	1,461	1,174
18 to 20 years old	4,560	1,591	34.9	946	20.7	3,614	646	2,969	380	384
21 to 24 years old	9,832	4,550	46.3	2,819	28.7	7,014	1,731	5,283	1,081	790
Male										
Total, 18 to 24 years old	**12,273**	**5,711**	**46.5**	**3,661**	**29.8**	**8,612**	**2,050**	**6,562**	**1,189**	**1,177**
Enrolled in school	5,180	2,898	56.0	1,982	38.3	3,197	916	2,282	390	512
18 to 20 years old	3,154	1,586	50.3	1,100	34.9	2,054	485	1,569	241	304
21 to 24 years old	2,026	1,313	64.8	882	43.5	1,144	430	713	149	208
In high school	1,028	365	35.5	265	25.8	763	100	662	88	74
In college	4,152	2,533	61.0	1,718	41.4	2,435	815	1,619	302	438
Full-time	3,537	2,176	61.5	1,467	41.5	2,071	709	1,362	238	388
Part-time	615	357	58.1	251	40.8	364	106	258	64	50
Not enrolled in school	7,093	2,813	39.7	1,679	23.7	5,414	1,134	4,280	799	665
18 to 20 years old	2,217	708	31.9	421	19.0	1,797	288	1,509	200	214
21 to 24 years old	4,876	2,105	43.2	1,258	25.8	3,617	847	2,771	598	452
Female										
Total, 18 to 24 years old	**12,377**	**6,307**	**51.0**	**4,335**	**35.0**	**8,043**	**1,972**	**6,071**	**988**	**999**
Enrolled in school	5,078	2,979	58.7	2,249	44.3	2,829	729	2,099	326	490
18 to 20 years old	3,071	1,742	56.7	1,320	43.0	1,751	422	1,329	162	309
21 to 24 years old	2,007	1,236	61.6	929	46.3	1,078	307	771	163	182
In high school	695	257	37.0	192	27.6	503	65	438	55	80
In college	4,383	2,722	62.1	2,057	46.9	2,326	664	1,662	271	410
Full-time	3,608	2,294	63.6	1,743	48.3	1,865	551	1,314	206	332
Part-time	775	428	55.2	315	40.6	461	113	347	65	78
Not enrolled in school	7,299	3,328	45.6	2,085	28.6	5,214	1,243	3,971	662	509
18 to 20 years old	2,343	883	37.7	525	22.4	1,818	358	1,459	179	170
21 to 24 years old	4,957	2,445	49.3	1,560	31.5	3,396	885	2,512	483	339
WHITE										
Both Sexes										
Total, 18 to 24 years old	**19,669**	**9,800**	**49.8**	**6,556**	**33.3**	**13,113**	**3,245**	**9,869**	**1,548**	**1,652**
Enrolled in school	8,295	5,023	60.5	3,639	43.9	4,656	1,384	3,272	380	763
18 to 20 years old	5,084	2,879	56.6	2,106	41.4	2,978	773	2,205	226	472
21 to 24 years old	3,211	2,144	66.8	1,532	47.7	1,678	611	1,067	154	291
In high school	1,253	478	38.2	363	28.9	891	116	775	84	108
In college	7,042	4,544	64.5	3,276	46.5	3,766	1,268	2,497	296	655
Full-time	5,909	3,882	65.7	2,791	47.2	3,118	1,091	2,027	214	561
Part-time	1,133	662	58.5	485	42.8	648	177	470	82	94
Not enrolled in school	11,374	4,778	42.0	2,917	25.6	8,457	1,861	6,596	1,168	889
18 to 20 years old	3,557	1,199	33.7	701	19.7	2,855	498	2,358	299	286
21 to 24 years old	7,817	3,579	45.8	2,216	28.3	5,602	1,363	4,239	869	603

See footnotes at end of table.

Blacks and Political Parties

In 1994 a majority of Blacks considered themselves Democrats, some more enthusiastic than others. According to data from the Center for Political Studies at the University of Michigan (Ann Arbor), 38 percent were strong Democrats, while 23 percent were weak Democrats and 20 percent were independent Democrats. Only a small proportion (9 percent) of Blacks identified themselves as strong, weak, or independent Republicans, while 8 percent reported being independent of either party.

While the Democratic Party has, for the past several decades, been considered the party of Black Americans, the number of Black Republicans is growing among

TABLE 9.4

Percent of Persons 18 to 24 Years Old Reported Having Registered or Voted, by Enrollment Status, Race, Hispanic Origin, and Gender, November 1996 [CONTINUED]

(November 1996. Numbers in thousands.)

Race, Hispanic origin, sex, age, and enrollment status	All persons	Reported registered		Reported voted		Reported that they did not vote[1]		Not registered		
		Number	Percent	Number	Percent	Total	Registered	Total[2]	Not a U.S. citizen	Do not know and not reported on registration
Male										
Total, 18 to 24 years old	**9,895**	**4,753**	**48.0**	**3,109**	**31.4**	**6,786**	**1,644**	**5,142**	**843**	**903**
Enrolled in school	4,177	2,503	59.9	1,740	41.6	2,437	764	1,674	192	389
18 to 20 years old	2,558	1,381	54.0	978	38.2	1,580	403	1,177	126	240
21 to 24 years old	1,619	1,122	69.3	761	47.0	858	361	497	65	149
In high school	757	287	38.0	216	28.6	540	71	469	61	51
In college	3,420	2,216	64.8	1,523	44.5	1,897	693	1,204	131	338
Full-time	2,934	1,922	65.5	1,312	44.7	1,622	610	1,012	96	307
Part-time	486	294	60.4	211	43.4	275	83	193	35	31
Not enrolled in school	5,718	2,250	39.4	1,369	24.0	4,349	881	3,468	651	515
18 to 20 years old	1,764	563	31.9	337	19.1	1,427	226	1,201	149	158
21 to 24 years old	3,954	1,687	42.7	1,032	26.1	2,922	655	2,267	502	357
Female										
Total, 18 to 24 years old	**9,774**	**5,047**	**51.6**	**3,447**	**35.3**	**6,328**	**1,601**	**4,727**	**704**	**748**
Enrolled in school	4,118	2,519	61.2	1,899	46.1	2,219	620	1,599	188	374
18 to 20 years old	2,527	1,498	59.3	1,128	44.6	1,399	370	1,029	100	232
21 to 24 years old	1,592	1,022	64.2	771	48.4	821	251	570	88	142
In high school	497	191	38.4	146	29.4	350	45	306	23	57
In college	3,622	2,329	64.3	1,753	48.4	1,869	576	1,293	165	317
Full-time	2,975	1,960	65.9	1,478	49.7	1,497	481	1,015	118	254
Part-time	647	369	57.0	275	42.5	372	94	278	48	63
Not enrolled in school	5,656	2,528	44.7	1,547	27.4	4,108	980	3,128	516	374
18 to 20 years old	1,792	636	35.5	364	20.3	1,429	272	1,157	149	128
21 to 24 years old	3,863	1,892	49.0	1,183	30.6	2,680	708	1,972	367	247
BLACK										
Both Sexes										
Total, 18 to 24 years old	**3,613**	**1,783**	**49.3**	**1,170**	**32.4**	**2,444**	**613**	**1,831**	**152**	**414**
Enrolled in school	1,244	632	50.8	455	36.6	788	176	612	65	179
18 to 20 years old	776	340	43.8	239	30.8	537	101	437	49	107
21 to 24 years old	467	292	62.4	216	46.2	251	76	176	16	72
In high school	384	125	32.5	81	21.1	303	44	260	31	42
In college	860	507	59.0	374	43.5	485	133	353	34	137
Full-time	711	414	58.3	313	44.0	398	102	297	30	115
Part-time	149	93	62.3	62	41.5	87	31	56	5	22
Not enrolled in school	2,369	1,151	48.6	714	30.1	1,655	437	1,218	87	235
18 to 20 years old	845	349	41.3	221	26.2	624	128	496	22	86
21 to 24 years old	1,524	802	52.6	493	32.3	1,032	309	722	65	150
Male										
Total, 18 to 24 years old	**1,662**	**753**	**45.3**	**423**	**25.5**	**1,239**	**330**	**909**	**73**	**210**
Enrolled in school	621	285	45.9	179	28.8	442	106	336	41	92
18 to 20 years old	401	164	40.8	96	23.9	305	68	237	29	49
21 to 24 years old	220	121	55.1	83	37.8	137	38	99	11	43
In high school	221	68	30.7	44	19.7	177	24	153	14	20
In college	400	217	54.3	135	33.8	265	82	183	27	72
Full-time	327	172	52.8	106	32.6	220	66	154	22	59
Part-time	74	45	(B)	29	(B)	45	16	29	5	13
Not enrolled in school	1,041	469	45.0	244	23.5	797	224	573	33	118
18 to 20 years old	371	133	35.9	75	20.2	296	58	238	10	44
21 to 24 years old	670	336	50.1	169	25.3	501	166	335	23	73

See footnotes at end of table.

younger and more economically successful Blacks. In the past, the Republican Party had done little to encourage more than a minimal Black Republican vote. Today some Blacks feel that they have an opportunity to be heard in the Republican Party. Many feel the Democratic Party has taken the Black voter for granted and there is room for them to grow within the Republican Party. The overwhelming majority of Blacks, however, remain Democrats.

The traditional Black political goals, as presented by the 13 original members of the Congressional Black Caucus (founded in 1970), are "developing, introducing and passing progressive legislation to meet the needs of millions of neglected citizens." Government participation has not only been welcomed, but also actively sought to correct the ills of the disadvantaged, many of whom are minorities. A growing number of Blacks are feeling uncomfortable

TABLE 9.4

Percent of Persons 18 to 24 Years Old Reported Having Registered or Voted, by Enrollment Status, Race, Hispanic Origin, and Gender, November 1996 [CONTINUED]

(November 1996. Numbers in thousands.)

Race, Hispanic origin, sex, age, and enrollment status	All persons	Reported registered		Reported voted		Reported that they did not vote[1]				
						Total	Registered	Not registered		
		Number	Percent	Number	Percent			Total[2]	Not a U.S. citizen	Do not know and not reported on registration
Female										
Total, 18 to 24 years old	**1,951**	**1,029**	**52.8**	**746**	**38.3**	**1,205**	**283**	**922**	**79**	**205**
Enrolled in school	623	347	55.7	277	44.4	346	70	276	25	87
18 to 20 years old	375	176	46.9	143	38.2	232	33	199	19	57
21 to 24 years old	248	171	68.9	133	53.7	115	38	77	5	30
In high school	163	57	34.9	38	23.0	126	19	106	17	22
In college	459	290	63.1	239	52.0	221	51	170	8	65
Full-time	384	242	62.9	206	53.6	178	36	143	8	56
Part-time	75	48	63.7	33	43.6	42	15	27	–	9
Not enrolled in school	1,328	682	51.4	470	35.4	858	213	646	54	118
18 to 20 years old	474	216	45.5	147	30.9	327	69	258	12	41
21 to 24 years old	854	467	54.6	323	37.9	531	143	387	43	76
HISPANIC ORIGIN[3]										
Both Sexes										
Total, 18 to 24 years old	**3,452**	**953**	**27.6**	**523**	**15.1**	**2,929**	**430**	**2,499**	**1,277**	**234**
Enrolled in school	1,032	453	43.9	304	29.5	728	149	579	241	82
18 to 20 years old	637	244	38.3	166	26.1	471	78	393	164	55
21 to 24 years old	396	209	52.9	138	35.0	257	71	186	77	27
In high school	281	84	29.8	45	16.1	236	39	197	70	17
In college	751	369	49.2	259	34.5	492	110	382	171	65
Full-time	508	287	56.5	203	40.0	304	84	221	102	46
Part-time	244	82	33.8	56	23.1	187	26	161	69	20
Not enrolled in school	2,420	500	20.6	218	9.0	2,201	281	1,920	1,036	152
18 to 20 years old	785	142	18.1	62	7.9	723	80	643	290	39
21 to 24 years old	1,635	358	21.9	156	9.5	1,479	202	1,277	746	113
Male										
Total, 18 to 24 years old	**1,809**	**449**	**24.8**	**217**	**12.0**	**1,591**	**232**	**1,359**	**712**	**155**
Enrolled in school	522	222	42.5	128	24.6	394	93	300	120	51
18 to 20 years old	341	111	32.5	62	18.2	279	49	230	93	34
21 to 24 years old	181	111	61.3	66	36.6	115	45	70	27	17
In high school	179	61	33.8	29	16.4	150	31	119	55	7
In college	342	161	47.0	99	28.9	244	62	181	65	44
Full-time	235	122	51.9	73	31.1	162	49	113	38	33
Part-time	108	39	36.5	26	24.0	82	13	68	27	11
Not enrolled in school	1,287	228	17.7	89	6.9	1,198	139	1,059	591	104
18 to 20 years old	405	68	16.8	31	7.6	374	37	337	149	30
21 to 24 years old	882	160	18.1	59	6.6	823	101	722	443	75
Female										
Total, 18 to 24 years old	**1,643**	**503**	**30.6**	**305**	**18.6**	**1,338**	**198**	**1,140**	**566**	**79**
Enrolled in school	510	232	45.4	176	34.5	334	55	279	121	31
18 to 20 years old	295	133	45.0	104	35.1	191	29	162	71	22
21 to 24 years old	215	99	45.8	72	33.7	143	26	117	50	9
In high school	102	23	22.8	16	15.5	86	7	78	15	9
In college	409	208	51.0	160	39.2	248	48	200	106	22
Full-time	273	165	60.5	130	47.7	143	35	108	64	13
Part-time	136	43	31.8	30	22.3	106	13	93	42	9
Not enrolled in school	1,133	272	24.0	129	11.4	1,004	143	861	445	48
18 to 20 years old	380	74	19.4	32	8.3	348	42	306	141	10
21 to 24 years old	753	198	26.3	97	12.9	656	101	555	304	38

[1]Includes persons reported as "did not vote," "do not know," and "not reported" on voting.

[2]In addition to those reported as "not registered," total includes those "not a U.S. citizen," and "do not know" and "not reported" on registration.

[3]Persons of Hispanic origin may be any race.

SOURCE: *Voting and Registration in the Election of November 1996*. U.S. Bureau of the Census

with this position and are turning to the Republican Party, which believes in less government involvement.

As the Black middle class continues to grow and many of the differences among people become more a matter of economics than race, Black party loyalties may change. Some younger professional Blacks who may not have experienced poverty or the deprivation of the inner cities may be attracted to the Republican Party platform of less government and lower taxes. Many Blacks once

TABLE 9.5

Reported Voting and Registration, for Asian or Pacific Islanders, by Selected Characteristics

| Characteristic | All persons | Reported registered | | Reported voted | | Reported that they did not vote[1] | | Not registered | | |
		Number	Percent	Number	Percent	Total	Registered	Total[2]	Not a U.S. citizen	Do not know and not reported on registration[3]
Total, 18 years and over	5,129	1,602	31.2	1,402	27.3	3,727	200	3,526	2,319	338
SEX										
Male	2,387	764	32.0	670	28.1	1,717	95	1,623	1,074	170
Female	2,742	838	30.6	732	26.7	2,009	106	1,904	1,244	169
AGE										
Under 45 years	3,278	854	26.1	724	22.1	2,554	130	2,423	1,622	210
45 years and over	1,851	748	40.4	678	36.6	1,173	70	1,103	697	128
REGION										
Northeast	880	202	23.0	176	20.0	704	26	678	476	58
Midwest	484	171	35.3	151	31.1	333	20	313	224	33
South	851	250	29.3	209	24.5	643	41	601	381	57
West	2,913	979	33.6	866	29.7	2,047	113	1,934	1,236	190
RESIDENCE										
Metropolitan	4,865	1,447	29.7	1,253	25.7	3,612	194	3,418	2,265	334
In central cities	2,346	635	27.1	571	24.4	1,775	64	1,711	1,218	139
Outside central cities	2,519	812	32.2	681	27.0	1,838	131	1,707	1,047	195
Nonmetropolitan	263	155	58.9	149	56.6	114	6	108	54	4
EDUCATION										
Not a high school graduate	902	122	13.5	95	10.6	806	27	780	559	60
High school graduate	1,275	388	30.4	335	26.3	940	52	887	529	77
Some college or associate degree	1,172	396	33.8	338	28.8	834	58	776	459	84
Bachelor's degree or higher	1,780	697	39.1	633	35.6	1,147	64	1,083	772	118
LABOR FORCE										
In labor force	3,472	1,229	35.4	1,101	31.7	2,371	128	2,243	1,397	211
Employed	3,256	1,172	36.0	1,054	32.4	2,202	117	2,084	1,285	203
Unemployed	216	57	26.6	47	21.7	169	11	158	112	8
Not in labor force	1,657	373	22.5	301	18.1	1,356	72	1,284	921	128
FAMILY INCOME[4]										
Under $25,000	1,345	224	16.6	183	13.6	1,162	41	1,122	858	68
$25,000 to $49,999	1,280	419	32.8	368	28.7	912	52	860	531	80
$50,000 and over	1,420	635	44.7	577	40.6	843	58	785	418	109
Not reported	349	103	29.5	91	26.0	258	12	246	174	27
TENURE										
Owner occupied	2,886	1,229	42.6	1,093	37.9	1,792	135	1,657	872	227
Renter occupied	2,243	373	16.7	308	13.8	1,934	65	1,869	1,446	111

[1]Includes persons reported as "did not vote," "do not know," and "not reported" on voting.

[2]In addition to those reported as "not registered," total includes those "not a U.S. citizen," and "do not know" and "not reported" on registration.

[3]Includes "do not know" and "not reported" on citizenship.

[4]Limited to members of families.

SOURCE: Jerry T. Jennings. *Voting and Registration in the Election of 1992.* U.S. Bureau of the Census: Washington, D.C., 1993

embraced the programs of former President Lyndon Johnson's Great Society and his War on Poverty. Today many believe that reliance on government has caused many Blacks and other underprivileged persons to lose their initiative and rely too heavily on the government to help better their situation.

HISPANIC POLITICAL PARTICIPATION

Elected Officials

CONGRESS. In 2000, 20 Hispanics served in the U.S. House of Representatives. The five female Hispanic House members were Representatives Grace Napolitano (D-CA), Lucille Roybal-Allard (D-CA), Loretta Sanchez (D-CA), Ileana Ros-Lehtinen (R-FL), and Nydia Velazquez (D-NY).

Although Hispanics have served in Congress for many years, they did not develop an organization of their own within that body until 1976. In that year the Congressional Hispanic Caucus (CHC) was formed, with the goal of improving the condition of Hispanics and other Americans by monitoring legislative, executive, and judicial policies. During the 106th Congress (1999–2000), the CHC was

TABLE 9.6

African American State Legislators, 1999

State	Total Legislative Seats	Total African American State Legislators	% of Total Seats	Total Senate Seats	African American Senators	% of Senate Seats	Total House Seats	African American House Members	% of House Seats
Alabama	140	35	25%	35	8	23%	105	27	26%
Alaska	60	0	0%	20	0	0%	40	0	0%
Arizona	90	2	2%	30	0	0%	60	2	3%
Arkansas	135	14	10%	35	3	9%	100	11	11%
California	120	6	5%	40	2	5%	80	4	5%
Colorado	100	3	3%	35	1	3%	65	2	3%
Connecticut	187	14	7%	36	3	8%	151	11	7%
Delaware	62	4	6%	21	1	5%	41	3	7%
Florida	160	20	13%	40	5	13%	120	15	13%
Georgia	236	44	19%	56	11	20%	180	33	18%
Hawaii	76	0	0%	25	0	0%	51	0	0%
Idaho	105	0	0%	35	0	0%	70	0	0%
Illinois	177	26	15%	59	9	15%	118	17	14%
Indiana	150	13	9%	50	6	12%	100	7	7%
Iowa	150	1	1%	50	0	0%	100	1	1%
Kansas	165	7	4%	40	2	5%	125	5	4%
Kentucky	138	5	4%	38	1	3%	100	4	4%
Louisiana	144	30	21%	39	9	23%	105	21	20%
Maine	186	0	0%	35	0	0%	151	0	0%
Maryland	188	37	20%	47	9	19%	141	28	20%
Massachusetts	200	6	3%	40	1	3%	160	5	3%
Michigan	148	20	14%	38	5	13%	110	15	14%
Minnesota	201	1	0%	67	0	0%	134	1	1%
Mississippi	174	44	25%	52	9	17%	122	35	29%
Missouri	197	16	8%	34	3	9%	163	13	8%
Montana	150	0	0%	50	0	0%	100	0	0%
Nebraska	49	1	2%	49	1	2%	Unicameral Legislature		
Nevada	63	5	8%	21	3	14%	42	2	5%
New Hampshire	424	1	0%	24	0	0%	400	1	0%
New Jersey	120	12	10%	40	2	5%	80	10	13%
New Mexico	112	1	1%	42	0	0%	70	1	1%
New York	211	30	14%	61	6	10%	150	24	16%
North Carolina	170	24	14%	50	7	14%	120	17	14%
North Dakota	147	0	0%	49	0	0%	98	0	0%
Ohio	132	18	14%	33	4	12%	99	14	14%
Oklahoma	149	5	3%	48	2	4%	101	3	3%
Oregon	90	4	4%	30	2	7%	60	2	3%
Pennsylvania	253	18	7%	50	3	6%	203	15	7%
Rhode Island	150	9	6%	50	1	2%	100	8	8%
South Carolina	170	32	19%	46	7	15%	124	25	20%
South Dakota	105	3	3%	35	1	3%	70	2	3%
Tennessee	132	16	12%	33	3	9%	99	13	13%
Texas	181	16	9%	31	2	6%	150	14	9%
Utah	104	0	0%	29	0	0%	75	0	0%
Vermont	180	1	1%	30	0	0%	150	1	1%
Virginia	140	14	10%	40	5	13%	100	9	9%
Washington	147	2	1%	49	1	2%	98	1	1%
West Virginia	134	2	1%	34	0	0%	100	2	2%
Wisconsin	132	8	6%	33	2	6%	99	6	6%
Wyoming	90	0	0%	30	0	0%	60	0	0%
Total	**7424**	**570**	**8%**	**1984**	**140**	**7%**	**5440**	**430**	**8%**

SOURCE: National Conference of State Legislatures and National Black Caucus of State Legislators

chaired by Representative Lucille Roybal-Allard (D-CA) and had 17 Hispanic legislators for members.

STATE LEGISLATORS. In 1999, according to the National Conference of State Legislatures and the National Association of Latino Elected and Appointed Officials, 186 Hispanics served in state legislatures, accounting for 3 percent of all legislative seats. Fifty-one, or less than 1 percent, were state senators, and 135, or about 2 percent, served as representatives in state houses. (See Table 9.8.)

Factors Contributing to Low Political Participation

There was a tremendous increase in the Hispanic population during the 1970s (more than 60 percent) and the 1980s (53 percent), resulting in a population of 32 million persons in 2000. The Hispanic community, however, according to some observers, has not attained the

TABLE 9.7

Black Mayors Representing Cities with Populations Over 50,000

NAME	TERM EXPIRES	CITY	POPULATION	% BLACK
1). Lee Brown	01/2002	Houston, TX	1,660,533	26.91
2). Ron Kirk	05/99	Dallas, TX	1,053,292	28.20
3). Dennis Archer	11/2002	Detroit, MI	1,027,974	63.10
4). Kurt Schmoke	12/99	Baltimore, MD	736,014	54.80
5). Willie Brown	01/2000	San Francisco, CA	723,959	10.92
6). W.W. Herenton	11/99	Memphis, TN	610,337	54.84
7). Marion Barry	01/99	Washington, DC	606,900	70.30
8). Michael R. White	01/2002	Cleveland, OH	505,616	43.80
9). Marc Morial	01/2002	New Orleans, LA	496,938	55.30
10). Wellington E. Webb	6/99	Denver, CO	467,610	12.84
11). Emanuel Cleaver, II	01/99	Kansas City, MO	435,146	29.59
12). Clarence Harmon	4/2001	St. Louis, MO	396,685	47.50
13). Bill Campbell	01/2002	Atlanta, GA	394,017	66.60
14). Sharon Belton	12/2001	Minneapolis, MN	368,383	13.02
15). Sharpe James	06/2002	Newark, NJ	316,000	58.20
16). Richard Arrington	11/99	Birmingham, AL	265,968	55.60
17). Elzie Odom	5/99	Arlington, TX	261,721	8.41
18). W. Johnson	12/2001	Rochester, NY	231,636	31.53
19). Larry Chavis	07/98	Richmond, VA	203,056	55.22
20). Harvey Johnson	6/2001	Jackson, MS	196,637	55.74
21). Floyd Adams	12/2000	Savannah, GA	150,000	51.31
22). Martin G. Barnes	01/2000	Patterson, NJ	148,394	36.01
23). Woodrow Stanley	11/99	Flint, MI	140,761	47.94
24). David Moore	05/2000	Beaumont, TX	114,323	41.00
25). Roosevelt F. Dorn	04/2000	Inglewood, CA	109,602	51.88
26). Omar Bradley	06/2001	Compton, CA	90,454	54.83
27). Douglas Palmer	06/2002	Trenton, NJ	88,000	49.27
28). Robert L. Bowser	12/2001	East Orange, NJ	77,690	89.95
29). Lorraine Morton	04/2001	Evanston, IL	74,000	22.87
30). Walter Moore	01/2002	Pontiac, MI	71,166	37.20
31). James Sills, Jr.	12/2000	Wilmington, DE	71,000	52.35
32). Gary Loster	11/2001	Saginaw, MI	70,000	40.35
33). Ernest D. Davis	01/99	Mt. Vernon, NY	67,000	48.70
34). Sara Bost	07/2002	Irvington, NJ	61,018	55.30
35). Abe Pierce	01/2000	Monroe, LA	54,909	55.55

SOURCE: National Conference of Black Mayors, Inc., 1999

political power equal to its proportion of the population. Two characteristics of the Hispanic demography help to account for this. First, although the Hispanic voting-age population grew by more than 50 percent, 20 percent of voting-age Hispanics, compared to 14 percent of the population as a whole, are in the 18- to 24-year old category—the age group least likely to vote. In addition, only 19 percent of Hispanics, compared to 30 percent of the population as a whole, are in the 55 and older category—the age group most likely to vote. Second, and perhaps more important, is U.S. citizenship. About 40 percent of adult Hispanics are not U.S. citizens, thus eliminating more than 5 million potential Hispanic voters.

Political Gains

Civil rights gains of the 1960s, such as the Twenty-Fourth Amendment eliminating the poll tax, the extension of the Voting Rights Act of 1965 to the Southwest, and the elimination of the English literacy requirement, helped a number of Hispanics achieve political office. During the 1970s both major political parties started "wooing" Hispanic voters and drafting Hispanic candidates. Advocacy groups, such as the Mexican American Legal Defense and Educational Fund, the Southwest Voter Registration Project, and the Puerto Rican Legal Defense and Educational Fund, were formed. All these helped develop the political clout of the Hispanic community.

Political Concerns

The National Association of Latino Elected and Appointed Officials (NALEO) interviewed more than 800 Hispanic elected officials to determine the issues they considered most urgent for the Hispanic community. They identified the high dropout rate of Latino youth, unemployment in the Hispanic community, and access to higher education for Latinos as the three most important issues facing their communities.

Hispanic Republicans

The Republican Party has not only courted Blacks but has also turned its attention to Hispanic voters, who are an increasing proportion of the voting public. The party is appealing to traditional family values that are very important to Hispanic families. Cuban Americans, spurred by anticommunist sentiment against Fidel Castro,

TABLE 9.8

Latino State Legislators, 1999

State	Total Legislative Seats	Total Latino State Legislators	% of Total Seats	Total Senate Seats	Latino Senators	% of Senate Seats	Total House Seats	Latino House Members	% of House Seats
Alabama	140	0	0%	35	0	0%	105	0	0%
Alaska	60	0	0%	20	0	0%	40	0	0%
Arizona	90	11	12%	30	4	13%	60	7	12%
Arkansas	135	0	0%	35	0	0%	100	0	0%
California	120	24	20%	40	7	18%	80	17	21%
Colorado	100	9	9%	35	2	6%	65	7	11%
Connecticut	187	6	3%	36	1	3%	151	5	3%
Delaware	62	1	2%	21	0	0%	41	1	2%
Florida	160	14	9%	40	3	8%	120	11	9%
Georgia	236	0	0%	56	0	0%	180	0	0%
Hawaii	76	1	1%	25	0	0%	51	1	2%
Idaho	105	0	0%	35	0	0%	70	0	0%
Illinois	177	6	3%	59	2	3%	118	4	3%
Indiana	150	1	1%	50	0	0%	100	1	1%
Iowa	150	0	0%	50	0	0%	100	0	0%
Kansas	165	2	1%	40	1	3%	125	1	1%
Kentucky	138	0	0%	38	0	0%	100	0	0%
Louisiana	144	1	1%	39	1	3%	105	0	0%
Maine	186	0	0%	35	0	0%	151	0	0%
Maryland	188	0	0%	47	0	0%	141	0	0%
Massachusetts	200	3	2%	40	0	0%	160	3	2%
Michigan	148	2	1%	38	0	0%	110	2	2%
Minnesota	201	1	0%	67	0	0%	134	1	1%
Mississippi	174	0	0%	52	0	0%	122	0	0%
Missouri	197	0	0%	34	0	0%	163	0	0%
Montana	150	0	0%	50	0	0%	100	0	0%
Nebraska	49	0	0%	49	0	0%	Unicameral Legislature		
Nevada	63	1	2%	21	1	5%	42	0	0%
New Hampshire	424	0	0%	24	0	0%	400	0	0%
New Jersey	120	4	3%	40	0	0%	80	4	5%
New Mexico	112	41	37%	42	15	36%	70	26	37%
New York	211	12	6%	61	4	7%	150	8	5%
North Carolina	170	0	0%	50	0	0%	120	0	0%
North Dakota	147	0	0%	49	0	0%	98	0	0%
Ohio	132	0	0%	33	0	0%	99	0	0%
Oklahoma	149	0	0%	48	0	0%	101	0	0%
Oregon	90	1	1%	30	1	3%	60	0	0%
Pennsylvania	253	1	0%	50	0	0%	203	1	0%
Rhode Island	150	1	1%	50	0	0%	100	1	1%
South Carolina	170	0	0%	46	0	0%	124	0	0%
South Dakota	105	0	0%	35	0	0%	70	0	0%
Tennessee	132	1	1%	33	0	0%	99	1	1%
Texas	181	35	19%	31	7	23%	150	28	19%
Utah	104	2	2%	29	1	3%	75	1	1%
Vermont	180	0	0%	30	0	0%	150	0	0%
Virginia	140	0	0%	40	0	0%	100	0	0%
Washington	147	3	2%	49	1	2%	98	2	2%
West Virginia	134	0	0%	34	0	0%	100	0	0%
Wisconsin	132	1	1%	33	0	0%	99	1	1%
Wyoming	90	1	1%	30	0	0%	60	1	2%
Total	**7,424**	**186**	**3%**	**1,984**	**51**	**3%**	**5,440**	**135**	**2%**

SOURCE: National Conference of State Legislatures and National Black Caucus of State Legislators

have long tended to be Republicans. Now other Hispanic voters have also begun to show more interest in the Republican Party. In the 1993 Los Angeles election of Republican Mayor Richard Riordan, Riordan received a surprising 43 percent of the Hispanic vote, compared to his Democratic opponent, Michael Woo, who received 57 percent. Based on past elections, experts had predicted that the Democratic candidate would receive 70 percent of the Hispanic vote. Mayor Riordan is serving his second term of office, which will end in 2001.

RACE, ETHNICITY, AND ELECTORAL DISTRICTS

The design of electoral districts can have tremendous impact on the political power of minorities. It is possible either to draw the boundaries of an electoral district so that it has a large concentration of minorities, enhancing their political power, or to split minority populations up between many electoral districts, weakening their political influence.

Designing electoral districts to favor one group over another is known as gerrymandering, and has a long history in the United States. In the first half of the twentieth century, gerrymandering was widely used in an attempt to prevent Blacks and other minorities from gaining true political representation. Another practice was to create at-large districts, in which the entire population of a large area would elect several representatives. The alternative, having several smaller districts that would each elect only one representative, would have allowed concentrated populations of minorities to elect their own representative.

Under the requirements of the Voting Rights Act of 1965, jurisdictions with a history of systematic discrimination (such as a poll tax or literacy test) must create districts with majorities of Blacks or Hispanics wherever the demographics warrant it. At the same time, they must avoid weakening existing "minority-majority" districts (districts "in which a majority of the population is a member of a specific minority group"). This law helped to eliminate some districts that had been designed to favor Whites. At the same time, however, it superseded the traditional criterion of compact districts, and encouraged the creation of some very bizarre-looking districts in the name of creating Black or Hispanic majority districts.

Challenges to Electoral Districting

The last 20 years of the twentieth century saw many challenges to the way electoral districting was being handled, and the issue remains controversial today. Some challenges have come from people that felt that long established practices, such as at-large districts, were infringing on the rights of minorities. Other challenges have come in response to newer systems of districting, in which districts were designed specifically to enhance minority representation. Some people feel that these districts are just as unfair as those that were designed to decrease minority representation. Most of these issues have ended up in court, and both sides of this debate have won some victories, leaving questions about exactly how much influence race and ethnicity can and should have on districting.

In 1986 the U.S. Supreme Court, in *Thornburg v. Gingles* (478 U.S. 30), ruled in favor of a group of Black voters in North Carolina who challenged at-large voting in multimember and gerrymandered (district lines drawn so as to deliberately favor a particular candidate, party, or group) state legislative districts. The plaintiffs claimed that the state policy prevented Black voters from electing candidates of their choice. The Court ruled that at-large election systems are illegal if:

- The minority population is geographically compact enough that a single-member district can be created where minorities are in the majority.

- Minority voters tend to vote for the same candidates (i.e., bloc vote), indicating that they are "politically cohesive."

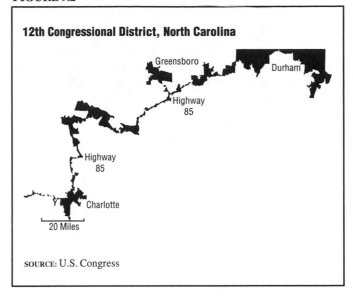

12th Congressional District, North Carolina

SOURCE: U.S. Congress

- Except for special circumstances (such as minority candidates running unopposed), the candidates preferred by minority voters usually are defeated by White bloc voting.

North Carolina's twelfth congressional district was a controversial example of a district created to follow the *Thornburg v. Gingles* guidelines. One observer cynically described it as a district in which "a politician could drive on highway I-85 with the car doors open and hit every voter in the district." (See Figure 9.2.) It snaked 160 miles from Raleigh to Greensboro to Charlotte. Similarly, Louisiana's fourth congressional district was shaped like the letter Z from Shreveport to Baton Rouge. Three redrawn districts in Texas, although not oddly shaped, were created specifically to assure that the majority of voters within them were Black or Hispanic.

The purpose of these new districts was to enable minority voters, who in the past had often been in districts that minimized their political clout, to exert their political will. Lawsuits were filed against the creation of some of these new districts, claiming that they represented "racial gerrymandering" that isolated Black voters in an artificial entity whose only justification was race.

On June 28, 1993, in *Shaw v. Reno* (509 U.S. 630), the Supreme Court did not throw out the creation of North Carolina's twelfth district, but ruled that the state's district court had to review the claim made by the White voters that it was unfair. The state, defending the district's shape, said the twelfth district had an urban identity that went beyond race. Moreover, it had complied with federal guidelines to enhance Black representation in a state that, until 1992, had not had a Black member of Congress for nearly a century.

In June 1994 the Supreme Court, in *Johnson v. DeGrandy* (512 U.S. 997), overturned a lower court's ruling to redistrict Dade County (Florida), which would have raised the number of minority districts from nine to 11. Justice David Souter, in the majority opinion, pointed out that, once a group has achieved representation in rough proportion to its population, there is ordinarily no reason to go further and that Hispanics were already adequately represented.

In June 1996 the U.S. Supreme Court, in *Shaw v. Hunt* (64 L.W. 4437), invalidated the twelfth congressional district in North Carolina. On the same day, the Court, in *Bush v. Vera* (64 L.W. 4452), invalidated similar congressional districts in the state of Texas. The justices ruled that districts could not be created solely on the basis of race.

In 1993 the Louisiana legislature created two majority-minority districts to remedy the loss of one of its districts as a result of the 1990 census. Appellees sued the state of Louisiana, claiming the creation of District 4 was a racial gerrymander that violated the Equal Protection Clause of the Fourteenth Amendment. The state legislature redrew the plan for District 4 but the appellees brought a similar suit. Relying on the Supreme Court's decision in *Shaw v. Reno,* a three-judge federal panel in Shreveport rejected Louisiana's fourth district. Louisiana and the federal government appealed the case before the U.S. Supreme Court.

On June 29, 1995, the Supreme Court, in *United States v. Hays et al.* (Docket 94-58), rejected the appellees' claim that every Louisiana voter could challenge the redistricting law as racial discrimination. Moreover, those who initiated the lawsuit failed to show the Court that the redistricting had caused them personal injury that demanded equal protection under the law. The Supreme Court subsequently annulled the lower court's judgment and remanded the case with instructions to dismiss the suit.

Race is not the only issue in the creation of these districts. Some claim that they represent partisan politics because they concentrate Black, mainly Democratic voters into single districts, leaving the rest of the districts to become greater concentrations of White, mainly Republican voters. In addition, some critics of the new districts charge that it is dangerous to have an electoral system in which Whites and Blacks are increasingly segregated, a consequence of which, they claim, will be increased racial polarization. Finally, some are concerned that while these districts may allow for easy congressional wins, they may also fail to generate broader support necessary to carry Black officials to higher offices.

Furthermore, redrawing majority-minority districts will likely bring substantial numbers of minority voters into districts that have had White majorities. Either way, the Supreme Court's ruling may likely lead to many lawsuits concerning race-based districts at all levels of government throughout the country.

Indications for Hispanics

It is unclear how the 1996 ruling will affect congressional districts other than the ones specifically invalidated. Most congressional districts with Hispanic representatives have grown in population, perhaps making them unlikely targets for merger or elimination. Redistricting and the 1990 census had resulted in gains in the number of districts with large Hispanic populations. NALEO reported that, based on 1990 census data:

• More than 50 percent of the Hispanic population in California resided in 13 of the state's 45 congressional districts.

• More than 50 percent of the Hispanic population in Florida resided in three of the state's 19 congressional districts.

• About 54 percent of the Hispanic population in Texas resided in five of the state's 29 congressional districts.

The Impact of Population Growth on Electoral Districting

Electoral districts for the national office of U.S. Representative is distributed across the country based on population. Each state is allowed to draw its own districts, but the number of districts it has is based on its population. This means that as some states' populations rise faster than others, the number of electoral districts that they have increases. Generally, most states reassign their districts about every 10 years, after each national census.

In the later years of the twentieth century, the population of the United States has steadily shifted to the Sunbelt. Many of these states also have high minority populations. So when the 1990 census was tabulated, several states with high minority populations gained additional electoral districts. California, with a population that was 7 percent Black, almost 10 percent Asian, and 26 percent Hispanic, gained seven seats. Florida (14 percent Black and 12 percent Hispanic) gained four seats, and Texas (12 percent Black and 25 percent Hispanic) gained three seats. This has the effect of increasing the influence of minorities in national politics. It is very likely that the 2000 census will add even more electoral districts to these states.

CHAPTER 10

PUBLIC OPINION

The Gallup Organization has taken numerous polls in over the years to determine the feelings of the American public concerning discrimination, affirmative action, civil rights legislation, and the progress that has been made by minorities. Polls taken in the mid- to late 1990s reveal a persistent and notable difference between the opinions of Blacks and Whites on many issues.

DISCRIMINATION

In July 1996 the Gallup Poll asked poll participants about racial discrimination on a local and a national level. When asked how serious racial discrimination against Blacks was in the area in which a respondent lived, only 10 percent thought that discrimination was a serious problem, while nearly one-fourth (23 percent) felt that it was somewhat serious. Four in 10 persons said racial discrimination was not too serious, and another quarter saw no problem at all. (See Table 10.1.) When asked how serious they thought racial discrimination against Blacks was in the United States as a whole, one-fourth (25 percent) replied that it was very serious, and about half (47 percent) thought it was somewhat serious. Nearly another fourth (22 percent) believed that racial discrimination was not too serious, and 4 percent thought it was not at all serious. (See Table 10.2.)

Personal Feelings

During the spring of 1998 the Gallup Organization asked respondents how Americans thought about persons of other races. One question asked whether few White persons dislike Blacks, many Whites dislike Blacks, or almost all White people dislike Blacks. The question was asked a number of times between May 1992 and April 1998. In the last poll, taken in April 1998, over half (56 percent) of respondents thought that only a few Whites dislike Blacks. Over one-third (37 percent) felt that many Whites dislike Blacks, while a slightly smaller proportion

TABLE 10.1

How Serious a Problem Do You Think Racial Discrimination Against Blacks is Where You Live . . .

	Discrimination in Your Area-Trend				
	Very serious	Somewhat	Not too	Not at all	No opinion
1996 Jul 18-21	10%	23	40	26	1
1996 Jun 27-30	12%	23	40	24	1
1995 Oct 5-7	8%	23	42	24	3
1993 Feb 8-9	10%	24	37	23	16

SOURCE: The Gallup Poll Monthly, July 1996

TABLE 10.2

How Serious a Problem Do You Think Racial Discrimination Against Blacks is in This Country . . .

	Discrimination in U.S.-Trend				
	Very serious	Somewhat	Not too	Not at all	No opinion
1996 Jul 18-21	25%	47	22	4	2
1996 Jun 27-30	26%	48	20	3	3
1995 Oct 5-7	23%	52	17	4	4

SOURCE: The Gallup Poll Monthly, July 1996

(35 percent) believed so in 1992. In 1998, 3 percent of Americans believed that almost all White people dislike Black people, unchanged from 1992. (See Table 10.3.)

In April 1998, when the question was reversed and the respondents were asked whether Black people dislike Whites, the ratios changed. Nearly half (47 percent) of respondents thought that only a few Black people dislike Whites. Four in 10 respondents thought that many Black persons dislike Whites, and 8 percent believed that almost all Black people dislike Whites. Since 1992 the percentage thinking only a few Blacks dislike Whites has

TABLE 10.3

Do You Think Only a Few White People Dislike Blacks, Many White People Dislike Blacks, or Almost all White People Dislike Blacks?

	Only a few %	Many %	Almost all %	None (vol.) %	No opinion %
1998 Apr 17-19	56	37	3	1	3
1996 Aug 5-7	61	32	2	—	5
1996 Jul 25-28	52	40	4	—	4
1996 Jul 18-21	52	40	4	—	4
1996 Jun 27-30	51	43	3	—	3
1995 Oct 5-7	58	33	3	—	6
1992 May 7-10	58	35	3	—	4

SOURCE: The Gallup Poll Monthly, November 1999

TABLE 10.4

Do You Think Only a Few Black People Dislike Whites, Many Black People Dislike Whites, or Almost all Black People Dislike Whites?

	Only a few %	Many %	Almost all %	None (vol.) %	No opinion %
1998 Apr 17-19	47	40	8	1	4
1996 Aug 5-7	46	43	6	—	5
1996 Jul 25-28	47	40	7	—	6
1996 Jul 18-21	47	40	6	—	7
1996 Jun 27-30	46	43	6	—	5
1995 Oct 5-7	39	44	10	—	7
1992 May 7-10	39	46	10	—	5

SOURCE: The Gallup Poll Monthly, November 1999

increased. The proportion believing almost all Blacks dislike Whites dropped from 10 percent in 1992 to 6 and 7 percent in different polls in 1996, rising to 8 percent in 1998. (See Table 10.4.)

Black Church Arson Fires

From June to August 1996 poll participants were questioned about the Black church fires that officials believed were likely to have been started on purpose. Most (58 to 62 percent) felt that they were isolated incidents, while 28 to 31 percent thought they were racist acts. (See Table 10.5.)

Teenagers' Opinions

In *YOUTHviews* (George H. Gallup International Institute, vol. 4, no. 5, 1997), a newsletter of Gallup Youth Surveys for teenagers, Gallup researchers asked about the state of race relations in the United States. Only 10 percent of all teenage respondents (17 percent Blacks and 9 percent Whites) indicated that they were very satisfied with race relations in the United States, while one-fourth (24 percent—16 percent Blacks and 27 percent Whites) felt somewhat satisfied with race relations. More than half (56 percent) were somewhat or very dissatisfied. When asked about the future, 42 percent of Black teens thought that race relations would worsen over the next 10 years, while 34 percent thought things would improve. Most White youths (48 percent) believed that race relations would improve, while 28 percent disagreed. (See Table 10.6.)

Interracial Marriages

Interracial marriages are more commonplace than they used to be. Researchers at the National Opinion Research Center at the University of Chicago asked White people if they would favor a law against interracial marriage. Seventy percent of Whites living in the South said that they would not, 26 percent would, and 4 percent did not reply. In the Midwest, 80 percent said they would not, while 17 percent indicated that they would, and 3 percent had no reply. Eighty-seven percent of northeastern residents said they would not favor such a law, while 12 percent would, and 1 percent did not reply. Of western residents, 90 percent did not favor such a law, 7 percent did, and 3 percent did not reply. (See Figure 10.1.)

AFFIRMATIVE ACTION

Affirmative-action programs were created to promote equal opportunities for minorities in housing, employment, and education. While some people believe that affirmative action is needed to correct the effects of past and current discrimination, others feel that it gives minorities an unfair advantage over Whites, or that it is no longer needed. In 1997 a *New York Times*/CBS News Poll found that most Americans supported racial diversity in schools and offices, but they did not approve of some of the methods used to achieve it.

Poll participants opposed preferences based on gender (51 percent) and race (52 percent), but favored affirmative action to help poor people (53 percent). More than half (55 percent) felt special efforts should be made to help minorities succeed, while 39 percent disagreed and 6 percent

TABLE 10.5

As You May Have Heard, a Number of Black Churches Have Been Destroyed by Fire in the United States Over the Past Year – and Authorities Have Attributed Most of These to Arson. Do You Think These Incidents Reflect the Fact that American Society is Basically Racist, or, do You Think These are Isolated Incidents that do not Reflect on Society as a Whole?

Import of Black Church Arson – Trend

	Jun 27-30	Jul 18-21	Jul 25-28	Aug 5-7
Basically racist	31%	29%	30%	28%
Isolated incidents	58	59	62	62
Neither/other (vol.)	5	7	3	5
No opinion	6	5	5	5
	100%	100%	100%	100%

SOURCE: The Gallup Poll Monthly, August 1996

TABLE 10.6

Teen Views of Race Relations

	Total	Black	White
Satisfaction with race relations in the United States			
Very satisfied	10%	17%	9%
Somewhat satisfied	24	16	27
Neither satisfied nor dissatisfied	10	8	10
Somewhat dissatisfied	27	28	26
Very dissatisfied	29	31	28
Ten years from now race relations will be			
Better	44%	34 %	48 %
The same	25	24	24
Worse	30	42	28
What kind of job are we doing to support the rights of blacks and Hispanics in the U.S.?			
Excellent	10%	14%	9%
Good	31	20	34
Fair	38	37	39
Poor	20	29	17

"No opinion" is not shown for some groups

SOURCE: *Youth Views.* vol. 4, no. 5, January 1997

FIGURE 10.1

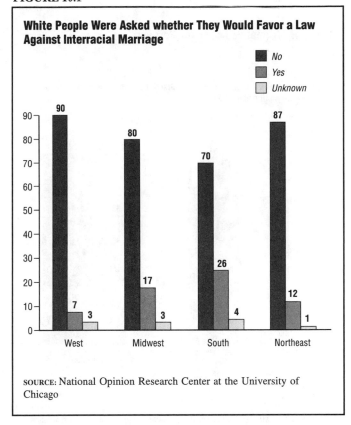

White People Were Asked whether They Would Favor a Law Against Interracial Marriage

SOURCE: National Opinion Research Center at the University of Chicago

didn't have an opinion. An even greater majority (60 percent) favored the use of outreach programs to recruit minority students and employees. (See Figure 10.2.)

Whites and Blacks Agree

Whites and Blacks agree on many basic affirmative-action principles. In 1997 more than three-fourths (82 percent) of Blacks and over half (59 percent) of Whites believed in special education programs to help minorities gain admission to college. (See Figure 10.3.)

Nearly all Blacks (95 percent) and about two-thirds (64 percent) of Whites favored government financing of job training to assist minorities in getting ahead in businesses where they are underrepresented. The vast majority (88 percent) of Blacks and two-thirds (65 percent) of Whites felt there should be laws to protect minorities

against hiring and promotion discrimination. (See Figure 10.3.)

Two-thirds of Blacks (65 percent) and half of Whites (53 percent) felt that, if all job candidates were equally qualified, the employer should hire a person from a poor family over a person from a middle-class family. More Whites (81 percent) than Blacks (67 percent) felt that less-qualified people are hired, promoted, and admitted to college as a result of affirmative action. (See Figure 10.3.)

Blacks and Whites Disagree

Whites and Blacks disagree on many affirmative-action issues. Eighty percent of Blacks felt that affirmative-action programs were necessary to ensure racially diverse workforces, while only 38 percent of Whites felt that way. Most Whites (57 percent) thought that affirmative-action programs were not necessary, compared to only 17 percent of Blacks. Two-thirds of Blacks (62 percent) but only one-third of Whites (31 percent) agreed that Blacks should get preferential treatment in hiring and promotion to make up for past discrimination, while 23 percent of Blacks and 57 percent of Whites thought Blacks should not get preference. (See Figure 10.4.)

While most Blacks (80 percent) felt that affirmative-action programs should be continued, only 35 percent of Whites did. More than half (52 percent) of Whites but

FIGURE 10.2

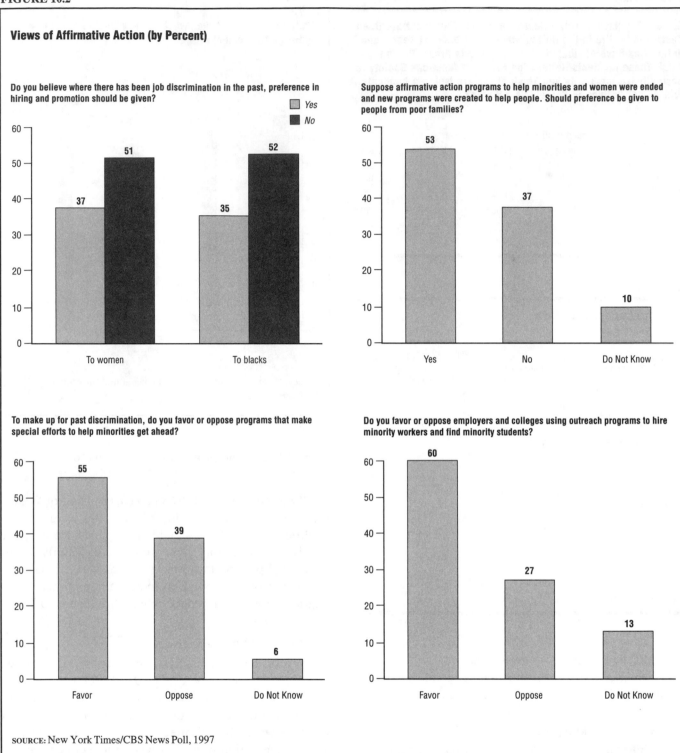

Views of Affirmative Action (by Percent)

Do you believe where there has been job discrimination in the past, preference in hiring and promotion should be given?

Suppose affirmative action programs to help minorities and women were ended and new programs were created to help people. Should preference be given to people from poor families?

To make up for past discrimination, do you favor or oppose programs that make special efforts to help minorities get ahead?

Do you favor or oppose employers and colleges using outreach programs to hire minority workers and find minority students?

SOURCE: New York Times/CBS News Poll, 1997

only 14 percent of Blacks felt affirmative action should be repealed. As to when affirmative-action programs should end, 1 percent of Blacks and 13 percent of Whites thought they should end now. Seventeen percent of Blacks and 45 percent of Whites thought they should be phased out in the next few years, and 80 percent of Blacks and 35 percent of Whites thought the programs should continue indefinitely. (See Figure 10.4.)

Blacks on Corporate America

In June 1998 *Fortune* magazine published the results of a survey of Blacks who worked for corporations. A large majority (81 percent) thought that discrimination was still a common problem in the workplace, while 13 percent said that it was rare, and 6 percent did not know. Sixty-four percent encouraged young people to become entrepreneurs, while 24 per-

FIGURE 10.3

Affirmative Action Whites and Blacks Agree (by Percent)

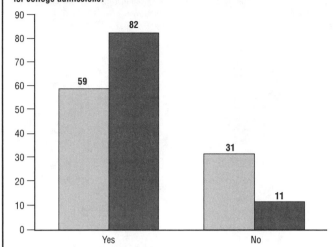

Should there be special educational programs to assist minorities in competing for college admissions?

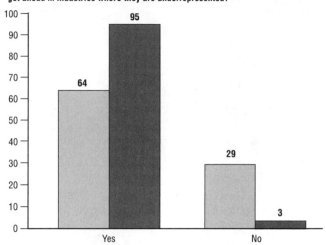

Should there be government financing for job training for minorities to help them get ahead in industries where they are underrepresented?

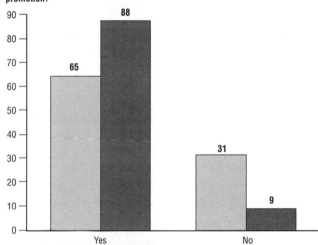

Should there be laws to protect minorities against discrimination in hiring and promotion?

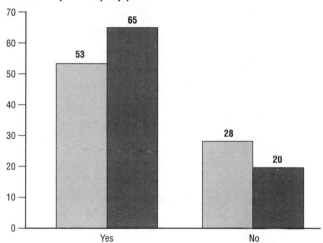

Should a person from a poor family over one from a middle-class family be selected if they are all equally qualified?

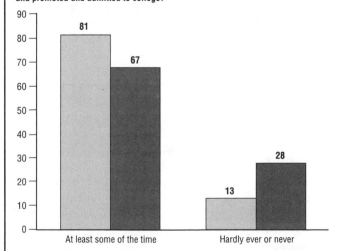

Do you think that as a result of affirmative action, less qualified people are hired and promoted and admitted to college?

SOURCE: New York Times/CBS News Poll, 1997

FIGURE 10.4

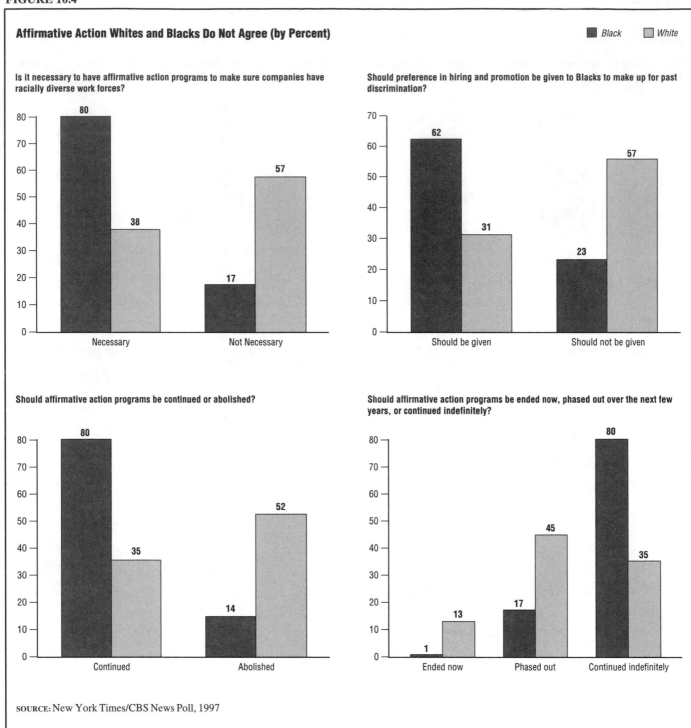

Affirmative Action Whites and Blacks Do Not Agree (by Percent)

■ Black   □ White

SOURCE: New York Times/CBS News Poll, 1997

cent recommended that young Blacks enter the corporate world. Most Black corporate workers (68 percent) were optimistic about their own professional futures; more than half (54 percent) of respondents expected to receive promotions within the next five years. Three-fourths (76 percent) of respondents said that White and Black workers with the same training and experience were not paid the same, while 17 percent said they were. The survey was conducted by the Joint Center for Political and Economic Studies in Washington, D.C.

JUSTICE SYSTEM

In 1999 the Gallup Organization asked the American people how much confidence they had in the criminal justice system. More Black respondents (28 percent) than Whites (22 percent) or non-Whites (26 percent) indicated they had a great deal or quite a lot of confidence in the criminal justice system. On the other hand, more White respondents (75 percent) than Blacks (70 percent) and non-Whites (72 percent) reported some or very little confidence. (See Table 10.7.)

TABLE 10.7

Reported Confidence in the Criminal Justice System, United States, 1999

By demographic characteristics, United States, 1999

Question: "I am going to read you a list of institutions in American society. Please tell me how much confidence you, yourself, have in each one—a great deal, quite a lot, some, or very little: the criminal justice system?"

	Great deal/quite a lot	Some	Very little	None[a]
National	23%	40%	34%	3%
Sex				
Male	23	38	36	3
Female	22	43	32	2
Race				
White	22	42	33	3
Black	28	31	39	2
Nonwhite[b]	26	31	41	2
Age				
18 to 29 years	34	32	33	1
30 to 49 years	21	43	32	4
50 to 64 years	16	46	35	3
50 years and older	17	44	36	2
65 years and older	17	41	38	2
Education				
College post graduate	23	54	22	1
College graduate	23	39	36	2
Some college	22	40	35	3
No college	22	37	37	3
Income				
$75,000 and over	23	40	35	2
$50,000 and over[c]	21	42	34	3
$30,000 to $49,999	25	43	29	3
$20,000 to $29,999	20	42	36	1
Under $20,000	26	33	38	3
Community				
Urban area	21	44	33	2
Suburban area	23	39	34	4
Rural area	23	38	36	2
Region				
East	22	45	29	3
Midwest	21	38	38	2
South	24	38	36	2
West	20	42	34	4
Politics				
Republican	25	41	30	3
Democrat	22	45	30	3
Independent	21	37	40	2

Note: The "don't know/refused" category has been omitted; therefore percents may not sum to 100.
[a]Response volunteered.
[b]Includes black respondents.
[c]Includes $75,000 and over category.

SOURCE: Gallup Organization, Inc.

TABLE 10.8

Reported Confidence in the Police, United States, 1999

By demographic characteristics, United States, 1999

Question: "I am going to read you a list of institutions in American society. Please tell me how much confidence you, yourself, have in each one—a great deal, quite a lot, some, or very little: the police?"

	Great deal/quite a lot	Some	Very little	None[a]
National	57%	33%	10%	(b)
Sex				
Male	56	33	11	(b)
Female	57	33	10	(b)
Race				
White	59	33	8	(b)
Black	40	34	26	0%
Nonwhite[c]	43	32	24	1
Age				
18 to 29 years	55	29	16	0
30 to 49 years	51	38	10	1
50 to 64 years	59	33	8	0
50 years and older	62	32	6	(b)
65 years and older	56	30	4	(b)
Education				
College post graduate	57	39	4	0
College graduate	50	38	11	1
Some college	58	31	11	(b)
No college	57	32	11	0
Income				
$75,000 and over	59	32	9	0
$50,000 and over[d]	58	33	8	1
$30,000 to $49,999	57	33	10	0
$20,000 to $29,999	53	41	6	0
Under $20,000	54	32	14	(b)
Community				
Urban area	52	34	14	(b)
Suburban area	60	32	8	(b)
Rural area	57	33	10	(b)
Region				
East	54	34	12	0
Midwest	64	27	9	0
South	56	35	9	(b)
West	52	37	10	1
Politics				
Republican	67	27	6	0
Democrat	50	38	12	(b)
Independent	54	33	12	1

Note: The "don't know/refused" category has been omitted; therefore percents may not sum to 100.
[a]Response volunteered.
[b]Less than 0.5%.
[c]Includes black respondents.
[d]Includes $75,000 and over category.

SOURCE: The Gallup Organization Inc.

When the Gallup Organization asked the same question about the police that same year, more Whites (59 percent) than either non-Whites (43 percent) or Blacks (40 percent) said that they had a great deal or quite a lot of confidence in the police. About one-third of each group reported they had some confidence in the police. One-fourth of Blacks (26 percent) and non-Whites (24 percent) said they had very little confidence in the police, while only 8 percent of Whites had very little confidence in the police. (See Table 10.8.)

Spending Tax Dollars

In a survey conducted by the Gallup Organization for the Office of National Drug Control Policy, participants were asked where tax dollars should be spent and how important spending the money in various areas was. Most survey respondents (91 percent of Blacks and 83 percent of Whites) said reducing violent crime was extremely important. Almost as many (87 percent of Blacks and 81 percent of Whites) thought reducing illegal drug use among children and adolescents was extremely impor-

TABLE 10.9

Attitudes Toward Problems on Which Tax Dollars Should Be Spent, United States, 1996

By sex, race, age, and education, United States, 1996

Question: "I am going to read you a list of concerns that people sometimes name as problems in the United States. After I read each one, please tell me if you think it is extremely important, somewhat important, not very important, or not at all important in terms of where tax dollars should be spent."

(Percent responding "extremely important")

	Reducing violent crime	Reducing illegal drug use among children and adolescents	Educational opportunities for children	Health insurance or low cost health care	Reducing drunk driving	Reducing unemploy-ment	Reducing illegal drug use among adults	Gun control
Total	**84%**	**82%**	**82%**	**66%**	**63%**	**57%**	**55%**	**36%**
Sex								
Male	80	79	79	59	56	49	51	23
Female	87	85	85	72	69	61	62	46
Race								
White	83	81	81	64	62	52	54	32
Black	91	87	92	82	74	74	76	60
Other	86	86	86	74	56	71	59	50
Age								
18 to 25 years	84	75	88	55	59	49	47	35
26 to 34 years	83	83	85	63	61	51	49	34
35 to 54 years	82	81	82	66	59	56	57	32
55 years and older	87	86	78	73	73	60	67	41
Education								
College graduate	76	72	44	54	44	44	40	29
Some college	84	84	55	66	64	55	56	31
High school graduate	88	89	63	74	72	63	69	40
Less than high school graduate	90	83	63	75	83	63	72	51

Note: These data are from a nationwide telephone survey of 2,016 noninstitutionalized adults aged 18 or older living in telephone households in the contiguous United States conducted by The Gallup Organization, Inc. for the Office of National Drug Control Policy.

SOURCE: *Consult with America: A Look at How Americans View the Country's Drug Problem.* Office of National Drug Control Policy

---

tant. Ninety-two percent of Blacks and 81 percent of Whites felt that educational opportunities for children were extremely important. (See Table 10.9.)

The two groups, however, sharply disagreed in other areas. Far more Blacks (82 percent) considered health insurance or low-cost health care to be extremely important than did Whites (64 percent). Nearly three-fourths of Blacks (74 percent) but only one-half of Whites (52 percent) thought that reducing unemployment was extremely important. More Blacks (76 percent) than Whites (54 percent) felt that it was extremely important to reduce illegal drug use among adults. Six of 10 Blacks considered the issue of gun control to be of extreme importance, while only three of 10 Whites felt that way. (See Table 10.9.)

Death Penalty

In 1999 a Harris Poll asked Americans if they believed in capital punishment (the death penalty). Overall, seven in 10 (71 percent) people favored capital punishment, while two in 10 (21 percent) opposed it. More Whites (77 percent) than Hispanics (65 percent) or Blacks (39 percent) believed in capital punishment. Over half (51 percent) of Blacks opposed the death penalty, a far higher percentage than Hispanics (32 percent) and Whites (15 percent). (See Table 10.10.)

In 1998, according to a poll conducted by the National Opinion Research Center, 72 percent of Whites and 49 percent of Blacks and other races and ethnic groups said they favored the death penalty for persons convicted of murder. Blacks and other races and ethnic groups (42 percent) were twice as likely as Whites (20 percent) to oppose capital punishment. (See Table 10.11.)

IMMIGRANTS

In January 1997 the Gallup Poll asked participants about dealing with businesses or stores in the United States that employed workers who did not speak English well. The Gallup Organization wanted to know if, during the past year, respondents could not get the desired goods because of an employee's inability to speak English well enough to understand the request. Fewer than one-fourth (23 percent) of the respondents said yes, while about three-fourths (77 percent) said no. (See Table 10.12.)

When asked if businesses should be required to provide English-language training to immigrants not fluent in English, more than half (56 percent) said yes, 40 percent said no, and 4 percent had no opinion. (See Table

TABLE 10.10

Attitutes Toward the Death Penalty, United States, 1999

By demographic characteristics, United States, 1999[a]

Question: "Do you believe in capital punishment, that is, the death penalty, or are you opposed to it?"

	Believe in it	Opposed to it	Not sure/ refused
National	**71%**	**21%**	**8%**
Sex			
Male	75	20	5
Female	66	23	11
Race, ethnicity			
White	77	15	8
Black	39	51	10
Hispanic	65	32	3
Age			
18 to 24 years	59	33	9
25 to 29 years	69	22	10
30 to 39 years	71	21	8
40 to 49 years	73	17	9
50 to 64 years	78	18	4
65 years and older	71	22	7
Education			
College post graduate	59	34	6
College graduate	74	20	5
Some college	71	23	6
Less than college	72	19	9
Income			
Over $75,000	75	18	7
$50,001 to $75,000	72	21	7
$35,001 to $50,000	74	21	5
$25,001 to $35,000	72	21	7
$15,001 to $25,000	68	25	7
$15,000 or less	68	20	13
Region			
East	67	28	5
Midwest	70	20	9
South	74	17	9
West	71	23	7
Politics			
Republican	81	12	8
Democrat	64	28	8
Independent	75	19	6

[a]Percents may not add to 100 because of rounding.

SOURCE: Louis Harris and Associates, Inc

10.13.) Respondents were evenly divided as to whether the federal government should require people to speak English fluently before immigrating to the United States. Forty-seven percent thought the federal government should have such a requirement, and 49 percent believed the government should not require immigrants to speak fluent English. (See Table 10.14.)

TABLE 10.11

Attitudes Toward the Death Penalty for Persons Convicted of Murder, United States, 1998

By demographic characteristics, United States, selected years 1977-98
Question: "Do you favor or oppose the death penalty for persons convicted of murder?"

	1977 Favor	1977 Oppose	1978 Favor	1978 Oppose	1980 Favor	1980 Oppose	1982 Favor	1982 Oppose	1983 Favor	1983 Oppose	1984 Favor	1984 Oppose	1985 Favor	1985 Oppose	1986 Favor	1986 Oppose
National	67%	26%	66%	28%	67%	27%	74%	20%	73%	22%	70%	24%	76%	19%	71%	23%
Sex																
Male	75	22	74	24	75	21	80	16	80	16	77	19	80	17	79	17
Female	61	30	61	31	61	32	69	24	68	27	66	27	72	22	66	28
Race																
White	70	24	69	25	70	24	77	18	76	19	75	20	79	17	75	20
Black/other	46	47	44	48	40	51	51	42	49	44	46	46	53	35	49	43
Age																
18 to 20 years	69	30	63	33	70	27	68	26	64	29	68	27	69	29	68	24
21 to 29 years	62	31	64	31	66	31	74	20	74	22	76	19	75	20	72	23
30 to 49 years	67	27	67	28	69	26	74	21	76	19	70	24	76	18	70	27
50 years and older	70	23	68	25	66	25	74	20	71	25	67	26	76	20	74	20
Education[a]																
College	66	29	66	29	67	30	71	21	75	22	73	22	73	22	72	23
High school graduate	69	24	68	26	71	23	78	17	75	20	71	23	78	17	73	23
Less than high school graduate	65	29	60	31	56	33	64	26	61	29	59	33	72	21	64	26
Income																
$50,000 and over	NA	NA	NA	NA	NA	NA	NA	NA	NA	NA	NA	NA	NA	NA	NA	NA
$30,000 to $49,999	NA	NA	NA	NA	NA	NA	NA	NA	NA	NA	NA	NA	NA	NA	NA	NA
$20,000 to $29,999	NA	NA	NA	NA	NA	NA	NA	NA	NA	NA	NA	NA	NA	NA	NA	NA
Under $20,000	NA	NA	NA	NA	NA	NA	NA	NA	NA	NA	NA	NA	NA	NA	NA	NA
Occupation																
Professional/business	64	28	68	28	68	28	72	23	73	23	75	20	76	19	76	21
Clerical	64	26	72	23	69	26	79	17	78	18	71	23	76	19	70	25
Manual	71	25	65	28	68	26	73	21	71	23	69	25	76	19	69	25
Farmer	74	20	76	20	71	15	77	15	85	10	61	39	76	22	83	17
Region																
Northeast	64	31	67	28	68	26	74	22	70	25	74	20	74	21	70	26
Midwest	68	25	69	24	66	26	72	21	75	21	65	28	73	20	69	26
South	64	28	64	30	66	28	74	21	70	25	68	27	76	19	67	26
West	77	20	64	31	70	25	76	18	79	16	78	16	79	17	83	13
Religion																
Protestant	67	26	67	27	67	26	73	21	74	22	70	24	76	19	72	23
Catholic	70	25	68	27	71	23	76	20	72	22	72	23	78	19	69	26
Jewish	66	26	79	21	75	22	73	19	67	26	85	4	62	31	79	16
None	64	34	58	38	54	39	73	16	72	26	68	26	75	20	73	24
Politics																
Republican	74	21	73	23	77	18	79	16	85	13	80	16	83	13	80	15
Democrat	67	27	63	31	63	31	71	24	67	28	64	30	70	24	66	30
Independent	64	29	66	27	66	28	73	20	72	22	70	23	75	19	72	23

TABLE 10.11

Attitudes Toward the Death Penalty for Persons Convicted of Murder, United States, 1998 [CONTINUED]

By demographic characteristics, United States, selected years 1977-98

Question: "Do you favor or oppose the death penalty for persons convicted of murder?"

	1987 Favor	1987 Oppose	1988 Favor	1988 Oppose	1989 Favor	1989 Oppose	1990 Favor	1990 Oppose	1991 Favor	1991 Oppose	1993 Favor	1993 Oppose	1994 Favor	1994 Oppose	1996 Favor	1996 Oppose	1998 Favor	1998 Oppose
National	70%	24%	71%	22%	74%	20%	74%	19%	72%	22%	72%	21%	74%	20%	71%	22%	68%	25%
Sex																		
Male	73	22	77	18	81	16	79	18	77	19	78	16	79	17	79	17	74	20
Female	67	26	66	26	69	24	71	21	67	25	67	24	71	22	65	25	63	28
Race																		
White	74	21	76	18	77	18	78	16	75	19	75	18	78	16	75	18	72	20
Black/Other	46	43	46	44	57	36	58	36	53	37	54	38	56	34	54	35	49	42
Age																		
18 to 20 years	64	36	61	35	69	25	66	34	60	33	70	23	73	21	70	22	60	37
21 to 29 years	69	27	73	24	71	24	79	16	74	23	69	26	72	21	72	22	69	25
30 to 49 years	74	21	72	21	76	20	74	21	71	22	73	20	75	20	71	22	69	24
50 years and older	66	26	70	22	74	19	74	18	71	21	73	20	75	18	71	21	66	25
Education[a]																		
College	70	26	71	23	72	22	73	21	69	25	69	24	73	21	69	24	67	26
High school graduate	73	20	73	20	77	18	77	18	74	20	75	18	77	17	76	17	71	21
Less than high school graduate	54	38	59	27	69	24	70	21	72	21	71	18	67	25	68	23	63	27
Income																		
$50,000 and over	NA	NA	NA	NA	NA	NA	NA	NA	NA	NA	73	22	77	18	75	20	72	21
$30,000 to $49,999	NA	NA	NA	NA	NA	NA	NA	NA	NA	NA	74	18	76	18	74	18	70	22
$20,000 to $29,999	NA	NA	NA	NA	NA	NA	NA	NA	NA	NA	81	14	75	19	72	24	68	24
Under $20,000	NA	NA	NA	NA	NA	NA	NA	NA	NA	NA	67	25	71	22	64	25	60	31
Occupation																		
Professional/business	72	25	72	21	75	19	72	20	67	25	70	23	75	20	70	22	68	25
Clerical	74	19	72	21	73	21	81	14	73	22	72	21	74	19	73	20	68	24
Manual	68	24	71	24	74	21	74	22	75	20	74	19	75	19	72	21	68	24
Farmer	65	28	67	29	91	4	78	7	81	11	74	21	74	18	72	20	71	20
Region																		
Northeast	72	23	66	26	72	19	75	20	71	23	65	26	70	24	66	26	62	28
Midwest	67	26	70	24	72	22	76	20	70	24	72	18	72	20	72	22	70	24
South	67	26	72	21	75	21	72	20	71	22	75	19	76	19	72	20	69	23
West	76	19	76	17	76	19	70	16	76	20	72	24	78	16	74	19	68	24
Religion																		
Protestant	70	24	72	22	75	20	75	19	72	22	74	20	75	18	72	20	68	24
Catholic	70	24	73	21	73	20	76	18	75	21	68	22	75	19	70	23	68	25
Jewish	80	10	63	23	87	13	74	15	53	34	70	21	72	26	63	28	72	20
None	65	28	67	26	71	24	72	24	65	28	72	23	73	20	69	22	64	26
Politics																		
Republican	83	14	81	12	82	14	83	12	84	13	81	13	84	12	85	12	77	17
Democrat	61	32	62	32	68	26	68	24	63	29	64	30	65	28	61	30	62	31
Independent	69	24	72	20	73	21	74	21	69	23	71	20	76	17	70	21	67	23

Note: The "don't know" category has been omitted; therefore percents may not sum to 100.

[a]Beginning in 1996, education categories were revised slightly and therefore are not directly comparable to data presented for prior years.

SOURCE: Louis Harris and Associates, Inc.

TABLE 10.12

Have You Personally Been in a Situation Where You Couldn't Get What You Wanted Because an Employee Who Was an Immigrant From a Foreign Country Didn't Speak English Well Enough to Understand You, or Haven't You Been in that Situation in the Past Year?

Yes	23%
No	77
No opinion	a
	100%

ᵃLess than 0.5%

SOURCE: The Gallup Poll Monthly, July 1996

TABLE 10.14

Do You Think the Federal Government Should—or Should Not—Require People From Foreign Countries to Speak English Fluently Before Allowing Them to Immigrate to the United States?

Should	47%
Should not	49
No opinion	4
	100%

SOURCE: The Gallup Poll Monthly, July 1996

TABLE 10.13

Do You Think That Businesses Should—or Should Not—be Required to Provide English Language Training to Immigrants They Employ Who Are Not Fluent in English?

Should	56%
Should not	40
No opinion	4
	100%

SOURCE: The Gallup Poll Monthly, July 1996

RESOURCES

The U.S. Bureau of the Census collects and distributes the nation's statistics. Demographic data from the bureau include *Current Population Survey, March 1999* (2000), *Resident Population Estimates of the United States by Age, Sex, Race, and Hispanic Origin: April 1, 1990 to July 1, 1999*, with *Short-Term Projection to March 1, 2000* (2000), *Population Projections of the United States by Age, Sex, Race, and Hispanic Origin: 1995–2050* (1996), *Population Profile of the United States 1995* (1995), and *1990 Census Profile: Race and Hispanic Origin* (1991). The Bureau also produces studies on the different racial/ethnic origins, including *The Black Population in the United States: March 1999 (Update)* (2000), *The Hispanic Population in the United States: 1999 (Update)* (2000), *The Asian and Pacific Islander Population in the United States—1999 (Update)* (2000), *We the... First Americans*, and *We the Americans... Blacks/Hispanics/Asians/Pacific Islanders* (1993).

The Bureau published financial and family statistics in *Money Income in the United States: 1998* (1999), *Poverty in the United States: 1998* (1999), *Who Could Afford to Buy a House in 1995?* (1999), *Asset Ownership of Households: 1993* (1995), *Marital Status and Living Arrangements: March 1998 (Update)* (1998), *Household and Family Characteristics: March 1998 (Update)* (1999), and *Fertility of American Women: June 1995 (Update)* (1997). The Census Bureau periodically publishes a *Survey of Minority-Owned Business Enterprises: Blacks/Hispanics* (1996). Voting information came from *Voting and Registration in the Election of November 1992/1994/1996* (1993, 1998) and "200 Million Plus Old Enough to Vote," *Census and You* (1998).

The Bureau of Labor Statistics provides labor force data. The monthly periodical *Employment and Earnings* and the frequently released *News* bulletins were used in this publication.

The U.S. Equal Employment Opportunity Commission published *Job Patterns for Minorities and Women in Private Industry, 1998* (2000). The Department of Commerce released the third in a series, *Falling through the Net: Defining the Digital Divide* (1999). The Department of Health and Human Services provided information from *Characteristics and Financial Circumstances of AFDC Recipients: Fiscal Year 1996—Aid to Families with Dependent Children* (1996).

The National Center for Health Statistics produced the annual *Health, United States, 1999* (2000), which gives the most complete, detailed statistics of American health. The Centers for Disease Control and Prevention publishes the *Monthly Vital Statistics Report, Morbidity and Mortality Weekly Report*, and *HIV/AIDS Surveillance Report*. The Substance Abuse and Mental Health Services Administration published the annual *National Household Survey on Drug Abuse* (1999). The National Cancer Institute published *SEER Cancer Statistics Review, 1973–1997* (2000).

The U.S. Department of Education's National Center for Educational Statistics published the annual *Digest of Education Statistics 1999* (1999) and the *Condition of Education 1999* (1999). The Gale Group thanks Phi Delta Kappa, a national teachers' organization, which published *Growing Up Is Risky Business, and Schools Are Not to Blame* (Bloomington, IN, 1992). The College Board kindly granted permission to use data from *1999 Profile of College-Bound Seniors* (Princeton, New Jersey, 1999). The Gale Group also thanks the American College Testing for permission to reproduce materials from the *1999 ACT National Score Report* (Iowa City, Iowa, 1999).

The Bureau of Justice Statistics (BJS) produced *Criminal Victimization in the United States, 1998* (2000), as well as numerous reports. BJS reports used in this publication include *Prison and Jail Inmates at Midyear 1999* (2000), *Prisoners in 1998* (1999), *Capital Punishment 1998* (1999), and *Federal Law Enforcement Officers,*

1998 (2000). The Federal Bureau of Investigation published its annual *Crime in the United States, 1998* (1999). *Trends in Juvenile Violence: A Report to the United States Attorney General on Current and Future Rates of Juvenile Offending* (James A. Fox, 1996) offered valuable information on juvenile crime trends.

The Gale Group would like to thank the National Foundation for Women Business Owners for use of its graphics and data. The Sentencing Project very kindly granted permission to use material from its report *Intended and Unintended Consequences: State Racial Disparities in Imprisonment* (Marc Mauer, 1997). The Na-tional Conference of Black Mayors, Inc., graciously provided its list of Black mayors of large American cities. Special thanks go to the National Conference of State Legislature (NCSL) and the National Black Caucus of State Legislators for permission to use the chart on African American state legislators for 1999 and to the NCSL and the National Association of Latino Elected and Appointed Officials for its chart on the Latino state legislators for 1999. The Gale Group is particularly grateful to the Gallup Organization and to Louis Harris & Associates, Inc., for their continued kindness.

IMPORTANT NAMES
AND ADDRESSES

Bureau of Indian Affairs
U.S. Department of the Interior Office of
Public Affairs
1849 C St. NW Washington, DC 20240
(202) 208-3711
FAX (202) 501-1516
URL: http://www.doi.gov/bureau-indian-
affairs.html/

Bureau of Justice Statistics
U.S. Department of Justice
810 7th St. NW, 2nd Floor
Washington, DC 20001
(202) 307-0765
FAX (202) 307-5846
E-mail: askbjs@ojp.usdoj.gov
URL: http://www.ojp.usdoj.gov/bjs/

Bureau of Labor Statistics
U.S. Department of Labor
2 Massachusetts Ave. NE
Washington, DC 20212
(202) 606-7800
FAX (202) 606-7797
E-mail: blsdata-staff@bls.gov
URL: http://www.bls.gov/

Bureau of the Census
U.S. Department of Commerce
Washington, DC 20233
(301) 457-4100
FAX (301)457-4714
URL: http://www.census.gov/

Children's Defense Fund
25 E St. NW
Washington, DC 20001
(202) 628-8787
FAX (202) 662-3520
E-mail: cdinfo@childrensdefense.org
URL: http://www.childrensdefense.org/

Congressional Black Caucus Foundation
1004 Pennsylvania Ave. SE
Washington, DC20003
(202) 675-6730

FAX (202) 547-3806
URL: http://www.cbcfnet.org/

Congressional Hispanic Caucus Institute
504 C St. NE
Washington, DC20002
(202) 543-1771
FAX (202) 546-2143
URL: http://www.chci.org/

Japanese American Citizens League
1765 Sutter St.
San Francisco, CA 94115
(415) 921-5225
FAX (415) 931-4671
E-mail. jacl@jacl.org
URL: http://www.jacl.org/

League of United Latin American Citizens
2000 L St.
Washington, DC 20036
(202) 833-6130
URL: http://www.lulac.org/

**National Association for the Advancement
of Colored People**
1025 Vermont Ave. NW, #1120
Washington, DC 20005
(202) 638-2269
FAX (202) 638-5936
URL: http://www.naacp.org/

**National Black Child Development
Institute**
1023 15th St. NW, #600
Washington, DC 20005
(202) 387-1281
FAX (202) 234-1738
E-mail: moreinfo@nbcdi
URL: http://www.nbcdi.org/

**National Caucus and Center on Black
Aged**
1424 K St. NW
Washington, DC 20005
(202) 637-8400

FAX (202) 347-0895
E-mail: ncba@aol.com
URL: http://www.ncba-blackaged.org/

**National Center for Neighborhood
Enterprise**
1424 16th St. NW, #300
Washington, DC 20036
(202) 518-6500
FAX (202) 588-0314
E-mail: info@ncne.com
URL: http://www.ncne.com/

National Hispanic Council on Aging
2713 Ontario Rd. NW
Washington, DC 20009
(202) 265-1288
FAX (202) 745-2522
E-mail: nhcoa@worldnep.att.net
URL: http://www.nhcoa.org/

National Urban League
120 Wall St.
New York, NY 10005
(212) 558-5300
FAX (212) 558-5332
E-mail: info@nul.org
URL: http://www.nul.org/

Navajo Nation
1101 17th St. NW, #250
Washington, DC 20036
(202) 775-0393
FAX (202) 775-8075
URL: http://www.navajo.org/

Organization of Chinese Americans
1001 Connecticut Ave. NW, #707
Washington, DC 20036
(202) 223-5500
FAX (202) 296-0540
E-mail: oca@ocanatl.org
URL: http://www.ocanatl.org/

Population Reference Bureau
1875 Connecticut Ave. NW Rm. 520

Washington, DC 20009-5728
(202) 483-1100
FAX (202) 328-3937
E-mail: popref@prb.org
URL: http://www.prb.org/

Poverty and Race Research Action Council
3000 Connecticut Ave. NW, #200
Washington, DC 20009
(202) 387-9887

FAX (202) 387-0764
E-mail: info@prrac.org
URL: http://www.prrac.org/

U.S. Department of Labor Office of Public Affairs
200 Constitution Ave. NW Rm. S-1032
Washington, DC 20210
(202) 693-4650
URL: http://www.dol.gov/

U.S. Equal Employment Opportunity Commission
1801 L St. NW Rm. 10006
Washington, DC 20507
(202) 663-4900
FAX (202) 663-4912
(800) 669-4000
URL: http://www.eeoc.gov/

INDEX